"WE WILL NEVER YIELD"

GERMAN JEWISH CULTURES

Editorial Board:

Matthew Handelman, Michigan State University
Iris Idelson-Shein, Ben-Gurion University of the Negev
Samuel Spinner, Johns Hopkins University
Joshua Teplitsky, University of Pennsylvania
Kerry Wallach, Gettysburg College

Sponsored by the Leo Baeck Institute London

"WE WILL NEVER YIELD"

Jews, the German Press, and the Fight for Inclusion in the 1840s

DAVID A. MEOLA

INDIANA UNIVERSITY PRESS

This book is a publication of

Indiana University Press
Office of Scholarly Publishing
Herman B Wells Library 350
1320 East 10th Street
Bloomington, Indiana 47405 USA

iupress.org

© 2023 by Indiana University Press

All rights reserved
No part of this book may be reproduced or utilized in any form or by any means, electronic or mechanical, including photocopying and recording, or by any information storage and retrieval system, without permission in writing from the publisher.

First printing 2023

Cataloging information is available from the Library of Congress.

ISBN 978-0-253-06521-6 (hardcover)
ISBN 978-0-253-06522-3 (paperback)
ISBN 978-0-253-06523-0 (e-book)

*To my father, Anthony J. Meola z"l,
whose time on this planet was far too short, and
who brought so much joy and laughter to everyone around him.
There is not a day in which I don't see his gregarious personality and
influence supporting me, my sisters, our children, and our mother.*

*And to Jason Young, fellow academic traveler and an
amazing friend, you will be remembered and
missed dearly by all.*

CONTENTS

Acknowledgments ix

Note on Translations xi

List of Abbreviations xiii

Introduction 1

1. The Development of Jewish Life and the German Newspaper during the Early Nineteenth Century 14
2. Jewish Emancipation in the Badenese and German Press 43
3. Jewish Religious Reform in the German and Badenese Press 82
4. The Fight for Jewish Admission to Constance in the Bodensee Press, 1846 127

   Conclusion: Fighting for Inclusion in Vormärz German Society 149

Appendix A: Badenese Synagogue Ordinance (1824) 159

Appendix B: Published Will and Testament of Salomon Heine 163

Notes 167

Bibliography 213

Index 241

ACKNOWLEDGMENTS

THROUGHOUT THE CREATION OF THIS book, there have been numerous individuals and institutions that have gone out of their way to help me. But more than those in the field, I owe the most gratitude to my wife, Veronica, and my four children. Having a partner who shows unflinching support and who has sacrificed her own career for mine is just the beginning of what has been an almost two-decade-long relationship. Our four children joined us at various stages throughout this process—from the beginnings of my doctoral program to the present day. They have brought so much joy and much-needed time away from professional matters. All of the work and hours away from home have been worth the effort, albeit at a price. In addition to those closest to me, I want to thank my mother and sisters and my in-laws for all of their support throughout our various moves and difficult times. Finally, I am indebted to my other "families"—my German family, my work families, and my friends—all of whom made this process not just bearable but also often enjoyable beyond belief.

In addition, I am personally indebted to the varied institutions that have supported this project from its inception through its wide-ranging changes and growth over the past ten years. Foremost, I need to thank the Department of History at the University of British Columbia and especially my advisor, Dr. Chris Friedrichs, and my committee, Drs. Richard Menkis and Michel Ducharme, who were steady hands and courteous, sage advisors. I need to thank the Leibniz-Institute for European History and the Mitteleuropa-Zentrum at the Technisches Universität Dresden for the fellowship and research opportunities that provided the basis for some of this material. I would like to thank the Deutscher Akademischer Austausch Dienst and the Leo Baeck Institute New York for their research support and Sewanee: The University of the South for providing opportunities to teach and continue researching this project. Last, but certainly not least, I would like to thank the generous support from the Department of History at the University of South Alabama as well as the College of Arts & Sciences for taking a chance on me, providing me with a great opportunity, and helping support my research in myriad ways. From small grants to travel funds, and, most importantly, the counsel and support of wonderful colleagues, I could not have completed this project without them, especially David Messenger, Mara Kozelsky, Rebecca Williams, and Michele Strong. To Rebecca Young and Debbie Cobb, our Interlibrary Loan savants, I owe a special debt of gratitude for going out of their way to get items from around North America and Germany to help me finish. To Katie Pfeiffer, you were an invaluable asset in the History Department Office, and I hope you have a long, successful career in public health. One last *Todah rabah* ("thank-you" in Hebrew) to everyone in the Mobile (Alabama) Jewish community whom I have had the fortune of befriending. You have provided endless hours of conversation, comradery, support, and friendship throughout my time in Mobile.

I would like to thank a few more individuals who have supported this project more directly in its final stages. First, to Rachel Reynolds for her help in editing this text and getting it ready for submission and publication. With her help, this project moved significantly forward, and for her efforts, I cannot but be effusive in my praise. To Jason Young, Adam Blackler, Alex Ruble, Catherine Soussloff, and the British Columbia Jewish Studies reading group, I appreciate all your efforts in looking over various chapters and providing feedback. To Kerry Wallach, I thank you for supporting this project when I needed a hand and helping make publishing this book with Indiana University Press a reality. To the several anonymous readers, I offer a thank-you for your help and suggestions and for pushing me to improve the manuscript. And to Dr. Gary Dunham and the staff at Indiana University Press, thank you for supporting this project and bringing it to fruition and doing so during as stressful a time as the pandemic.

NOTE ON TRANSLATIONS

THE RESPONSIBILITY FOR ALL TRANSLATIONS from German are my own, unless otherwise noted. I did receive help from others to smooth out translations at various stages, including from Rachel Reynolds, who helped edit this material. In a few instances, I have left the text in the original German with an English translation. I have kept the German quotes as written during the nineteenth century and have not updated the spelling to modern German.

ABBREVIATIONS

AAZ	*Augsburger Allgemeine Zeitung*
AZdJ	*Allgemeine Zeitung des Judenthums*
DAZ	*Deutsche Allgemeine Zeitung* (formerly, the *Leipziger Allgemeine Zeitung*)
DT	*Deutsche Tribüne*
FJ	*Frankfurter Journal*
FZ	*Freiburger Zeitung*
GLAK	Generallandesarchiv Karlsruhe
HC	*Hamburgische unpartheyische Correspondent*
Heid Jour	*Heidelberger Journal*
IEG	Leibniz-Institute for European History, Mainz
KZ	*Karlsruher Zeitung*
KölZtg	*Kölnische Zeitung*
KonZtg	*Konstanzer Zeitung*
LBIYB	*Leo Baeck Institute Yearbook*
LTZ	*Landtagszeitung*
MAbZ	*Mannheimer Abendzeitung*
MJ	*Mannheimer Journal*
MM	*Mannheimer Morgenblatt*
ObRhZtg	*Oberrheinische Zeitung*

RF	Frankfurt Reformfreunde
RG	Berlin Reformgenossenschaft
TZW	*Der treue Zions-Wächter*
VZ	*Vossische Zeitung* (officially known as the *Königlich priviligierte Berlinische Zeitung*)

"WE WILL NEVER YIELD"

INTRODUCTION

IN MAY 1845, ADOLPH ZIMMERN, the head of the Jewish community in Heidelberg, one of the leading towns of the Grand Duchy of Baden, used the pages of an influential regional newspaper to comment on an important gathering of reform-minded German rabbis and preachers that had taken place almost ten months earlier:

> The Rabbinical conference, which met together last year in Brunswick, put the first hand on this [reform] work, true and heartfelt, but still hesitant as befits the beginning, and all like-minded people took hold of its beginning with confidence.... This attempt at unity gave us satisfaction because it emerged from deeply felt needs without worldly influence, without hierarchical compulsion, without any other concern other than the awareness of the good cause. The most enlightened and scientific rabbis and preachers in Germany were united; the deliberations were held in an open meeting accessible to everyone, and the humble beginnings lie open before the eyes of every examiner.[1]

The group of twenty-five men gathered in the city of Brunswick to debate and discuss a future for Jewish reform, as Zimmern noted. Their meeting, whether intended or not, was inherently political, as one of their first decisions taken was to affirm the responses given by French Jewish leaders in 1806, to whom Napoleon had posed a set of questions to determine whether Jewish rules and practices were compatible with French social norms.[2] The rabbis had deftly defended Judaism and Jews' allegiance to France and their compatriots and pushed back on the emperor's assimilatory impulses.[3] In endorsing the stand taken by the French Jewish leaders in 1806, the rabbis and preachers meeting in

Brunswick confirmed German Jewish reformers' allegiances to their own states while addressing the need for reforms in Jewish life and practice.

Zimmern's article exuded confidence in the conference for its ambition and humility as well as its ability to be a self-directed movement internal to Judaism without compulsion from the state. Zimmern also lauded the conference's transparency, a move that was certain to bring peering and critical eyes on its work. It was, according to Zimmern, a necessary step to bring Judaism and all Jews into modern times. Zimmern's advocacy for reform and against those who stood in the way of progress—addressed later in this contribution—was in line with his advocacy for Jewish emancipation. He also made clear his conviction that "age-appropriate reforms" (*zeitgemäße Verbesserungen*) in Judaism were intrinsic to the emancipation effort "in the entire Fatherland, as far as the German tongue reaches and until the borders where German civilization is felt and recognized."[4] This open letter in the Mannheim press showed that Jewish reform was no longer an internal debate for German Jewry but a political debate to be brought before and judged by the entire German public.

The politicization of the Brunswick rabbinical conference (in addition to those in Frankfurt [1845] and Breslau [1846]) did not end there. These religious leaders, who represented a small but growing and active minority of German Jews, understood that their actions—and their decisions—would likely find reverberation in both the Jewish and non-Jewish world. To ensure that both communities knew of the conference's proceedings, Rabbi Ludwig Philippson of Magdeburg—the conference's convener and organizer—published the protocols of the conference in his journal, the *Allgemeine Zeitung des Judenthums* (*AZdJ*, general newspaper of Jewry). Philippson knew that bringing such information to the public had the potential for stirring up controversy, as the Orthodox could potentially see such public declarations as having a modicum of legitimacy and authority.[5] But this publication—intended or not—also served a different purpose: to inform the broader German-speaking, non-Jewish public of the direction in which modern Jewry was moving and of the changes that had been expected of Jews in modernizing their religion as part of what David Sorkin has called "the quid pro quo of rights for regeneration."[6] Just like the French Jewish leaders, the rabbis at this conference—though not having any official authority—made an emphatic political statement: German Jews were Germans, yet they were going to be so on their own terms.[7]

All of these conferences were public events and were widely covered in both the German Jewish and non-Jewish press. During 1845 and 1846, press coverage of the conferences was significantly greater than had been the case for the 1844 one, especially in pan-German newspapers that had national and more liberal readerships. Yet pan-German newsprint was not the only location in which these discussions appeared: in smaller regions, such as the Grand Duchy of Baden—a bastion of German liberalism where Jewish emancipation was believed to have its best prospects—such ideas about Jewish reform and the fallout from the rabbinical conferences found important resonance in local and regional newsprint, as seen in Adolph Zimmern's previously cited panegyric. So long as Jews remained unequal citizens or *Schutzbürger* (protected residents) in their states and the accepted paradigm for inclusion was predicated on the modernization of their religion, any discussion about Judaism in newsprint was inherently a political one that affected Jews' fortunes.

The discussions about Jewish reform and Jewish emancipation in local and pan-German newsprint were not casual and happenstance encounters but ideological and orchestrated interventions that discussed Jewish inclusion in a society that was itself under redefinition and change. Contributions within these discussions came from both Jews and Christians (Protestants and Catholics), and many of the statements made by Jews and their supporters were not just ideological responses to anti-Jewish or religious sentiments but were assertions and claims to participation within the German public sphere, which German Jews increasingly saw as a more inclusive space where they could assert both their German- and Jewishness.

This study interrogates Jewish agency during the fights for emancipation and over religious reform, with a focus on how German Jews conveyed their ideas, concerns, and arguments through local and pan-German newsprint. By presenting their ideas to the local German populace, German Jews not only publicized their positions but also made broader claims on German society and the German public sphere—that newsprint was not just a hegemonic space for German Christians but one that incorporated German Jews, too. As such, German newspapers became more inclusive locations to challenge orthodoxies—political, social, religious, and otherwise.

German Jewish comfort within German newsprint, signified by an increase in Jewish contributions, appeared alongside and complemented the intellectual and political work of those Jews who wrote larger treatises, petitioned German governments, and created the German Jewish press. Within their contributions, German Jews argued for their rights and about their religion by demonstrating their acculturation to German norms and by maintaining that they, therefore, were already German. Participation in the German newspapers and their use of numerous genres within these pages demonstrated Jews' acquisition of *Bildung* (formation) and adherence to bourgeois values—two of the most important categories by which Jews were judged as part of the quid pro quo. The publication of Jews' own voices and even of their actions alongside that of "other Germans" signifies that German Jews believed that the efforts of German liberals and their supporters were not sufficient, in and of themselves, to achieve equality.[8] Moreover, Jews felt compelled to demonstrate in these discussions and debates their acquisition of cultural and social capital, which they hoped would convince enough German Christians that Jews were just like them and were worthy civic, social, and political equals. Even as German Jews repeatedly demonstrated the vicissitudes necessary for equality and inclusion, they still needed sympathetic ears that would hear and act on their message. The German newspaper was the platform most likely to facilitate that message and get it to those whose power and clout were on the rise—the liberal bourgeoisie.

Nonetheless, Jews' participation in debates about their own lives testifies to the importance of local and pan-German newspapers as a medium of communication that documented how Jews were portrayed by non-Jews and how they depicted themselves to the general public. However, and more importantly, the usage of newspapers by Jews demonstrates that they understood the importance of newspapers in achieving individual and communal success—whether that meant winning the battle for public opinion in defending an individual's or community's honor, pressing local communities to accept their Jewish neighbors as compatriots with equal rights and obligations, and even putting pressure on Jews who had yet to become sufficiently "modern." With the ascendancy of liberal thought throughout the German states and the increasing acceptance of public opinion in determining the viability of public policy, members of the Jewish community and their allies saw newspapers as an important pillar in their attempt to not only transform the narrative about Jewish lives, but to change the hearts and minds of "other Germans" who could then put public pressure on the decision-makers.[9] The hope was that the repeated failures of Jewish emancipation in political chambers—the procedural status quo—could potentially be affected by a more sympathetic public, which was not only reading more Jewish-friendly news but also hearing directly from Jews about their own lives. The newspapers amplified Jews' voices through the reprinting of news from more distant regions and through news discussions in coffeehouses and taverns. Where possible, this new, and hopefully Jewish-friendly (or at least not anti-Jewish), sentiment could then be turned into direct political action and legislative votes.

Participation in the German press by Jews signified their accumulation and development of Bildung, which is a "never-ending" development of the fully formed bourgeois subject devoted to the "self-cultivation of one's intellectual and moral faculties." German Jews, as part of the quid pro quo, were expected to embrace this ideal and change their culture, education, morals, occupations, patriotism, religion, and values to resemble the class through which they would enter German society—in other words, it was their "gateway to bourgeois respectability."[10] Attaining Bildung meant that Jews were acquiring what the sociologist Pierre Bourdieu calls cultural and social capital. In order to acquire cultural capital, German Jews needed to devote time and resources (typically economic capital) to doing so, and one of the easiest methods of acquisition was through private tutors (for the wealthy) or the creation of free schools (for indigent Jewish students). In states that supported Jewish education, of which Baden was one, Jews created state-regulated schools when there were enough students. These students could then acquire more cultural capital by attending and graduating from a German university. Many German Jewish communities and individuals also worked tirelessly to modernize their other communal institutions as well as create a German Jewish public sphere.[11]

Bourdieu defines social capital as the "actual and potential resources" within a "durable ... membership in a group." The actual value of such social capital is thus dependent on "the volume of the capital (economic, cultural, or symbolic)" possessed by each member of that network as well as the size of the network.[12] In these ways both cultural and social capital are interrelated. For German Jews, education (the acquisition of cultural capital) could lead to membership and participation in both economic and educated (*gebildete*) networks, leading to more social capital. German Jews acquired Bildung by doing the following: building their careers and earning degrees; participating in German society; reshaping their religious, cultural, and social institutions to mimic those in the society around them; and partaking in local bourgeois institutions (joining fraternal and economic associations, participating in philanthropy, etc.). German Jews' achievements and participation in these areas has led Simone Lässig to claim that they acquired Bildung more so than any other group during the first half of the nineteenth century. To evaluate that claim, Lässig uses Bourdieu's conception of cultural capital to argue that Jewish emancipation was more of an educative and cultural project than a political one.[13] Despite the central importance of Bildung as part of Jews' embourgeoisement and the evolution of Jewish reform, this trend was nonetheless motivated by political ends. Rights and social integration mattered, and the acquisition of cultural capital through the demonstration of Bildung (and the potential building of social capital as a result) was the means by which to attain these. As such, I build on Lässig's use of Bourdieu to show that in the case of the German press, German Jews demonstrated, through their participation therein, the acquisition of cultural capital while using that capital in order to sway their fellow Germans to support their full social and political equality.

In addition to the demonstration of Bildung, Jews' participation in German newspapers in such a wholehearted and engaged fashion demonstrated that local and national German newspapers were not external and ancillary locations for Jewish lives. In fact, these German, non-Jewish newspapers were intrinsic parts of Jews' daily lives and their fight for emancipation. As such, German newspapers, which before the 1840s were locations that witnessed few Jewish voices, not only became sites that had a multiplicity of Jewish voices but also became *the* platforms through which to influence public opinion in their fight for emancipation, though the voices there—like the rest of the German public sphere at that time—were generally men's voices.[14] With the rise of liberalism in the 1840s and Jews' increasing local commitment to engage and influence public opinion, two processes occurred concurrently: Jews sought to use their accumulated capital to acquire political rights, and they actively demonstrated that the local and pan-German newspapers were places of publication in which, borrowing an idea from spatial theory, they increasingly felt comfortable and secure—despite those spaces' continuous evolution—when addressing issues of importance to their lives.[15]

This comfort was evident in the manifold ways in which German Jews argued and positioned themselves for emancipation within the pages of the local and pan-German press. Whether it was participating directly in debates about emancipation—countering anti-Jewish stereotypes and calumnies—or having their positive contributions broadcast throughout the German press (and then pointing to those achievements as part of their arguments), German Jews did not wait for their liberal friends in society and the state legislatures to try to convince others of their adherence to German cultural norms, of the value of a more inclusive society, or of German Jews' and Judaism's modernity. In debates about internal Jewish religious reform, German Jews participated in defense of both Orthodox and traditional Judaism as well as advocating for wide-ranging and more conservative reforms, though it was the voices of reformers that were heard most often and most vociferously. Nonetheless, those who participated in these discussions did so on their own terms, demonstrating to the broader public that German Jews were similar to "Other Germans."[16] In many instances, the political and religious discussions overlapped, as they were intrinsically linked in the broader discussions about emancipation, yet they are important to view separately and as having different attributes.

This project builds on prior scholarship that insufficiently addresses local Jewish agency in the fight for Jewish emancipation in the German states. While there have been more general calls to look more closely at Jewish agency in this fight, including Robert Liberles's influential article in the *Leo Baeck Institute Yearbook*, if one were to examine most of the more general studies about German history—even recent ones—there would be sparse information about Jewish life, and even less about Jewish individuals or groups who sought change in their political status or in their religion.[17] In fact, Jewish agency during the ascent of the liberal and democratic movements during the Vormärz has often been overlooked, and the fight for Jewish rights is generally postulated as a Christian endeavor.[18] Even in works that are more sympathetic to Jewish voices and reactions to political events, such as Dagmar Herzog's *Intimacy and Exclusion*, the focus is on the broader Jewish response in the German Jewish press and not, as this project tackles, the voices of local Jews in local papers about issues that affected them in their communities.[19] Moreover, Herzog's work concentrates more on the responses to "exclusion" (as seen in the title) and how those individuals, affected by the state's policies, fought back; in contrast to Herzog's approach, though by no means eschewing the important ways that German Jews countered anti-Jewish polemics, this study integrates "inclusionary" actions that pointed to Jewish societal contributions within the local and pan-German environments.

More recently, scholars have called for a more thorough interrogation of Jewish lives through the utilization of source materials that have traditionally been excluded or underused. Scholars have reengaged newspapers as important sources in the analysis of Jewish life, something that was common in studies of German Jews decades ago.[20] In her recent study of the Ladino and Yiddish press in the Ottoman and Russian empires, Sarah Abrevaya Stein views newspapers not only as an invaluable contribution to the history of Jewish cultural engagement but also as important sources to uncover the history of an understudied community within Jewish studies. As she states about the importance of newspapers in the study of Jewish life: "Yet it is precisely in newspapers, with the plurality of subject matter and authors, their immediate reactions to cultural and political events, their need to appeal to many kinds of readers, and—not least—the responses provided by their readerships, that emerging Jewish modernities may be read more vividly."[21]

However, Stein's work—like many other studies that have delved into Jews' participation in national press landscapes—is limited to Jews' contributions to their own public sphere.[22] One important exception to this trend is Jonathan Frankel's *The Damascus Affair*.[23] Frankel deftly uses publications from around Europe, including the Jewish press, to reveal how events in the Ottoman Empire became public knowledge, how the public reacted to the developments at each stage, and how German Jews specifically negotiated their own hopes and desires for emancipation within the much broader intellectual debate. In many ways, Frankel's methods follow that of Moshe Zimmermann, who also used a combination of local and German Jewish newspapers to detail the fight for the emancipation of Hamburg Jewry. Similar to Zimmermann, Shulamit Magnus utilizes local papers in Cologne (especially the *Kölnische Zeitung*) to track local Christian support of Jewish emancipation in that city, although she only uses writings by non-Jews and does not evaluate Jews' contributions to these discussions or even articles related to Jewish religious reform—in either the main news section or the feuilleton.[24] This book follows these aforementioned three scholars' use of German newspapers in order to look more closely at Jewish life during the 1840s. I also follow the recommendations of Robert Weltsch and Jonathan Hess, who advocate using non-Jewish newspapers as a lens to examine German Jewish life.[25] As Eleanor Lappin and Michael Nagel rightly argue, "for many events the contemporary press is the most important, if not the only source."[26] For any discussion about Jewish emancipation and Jewish religious reform, the German press provides us with access to events and considerations often unseen in the German Jewish public sphere.

Another important way to think about German Jewish participation in the press is through the process of dissimilation. As Jonathan Skolnik writes, "dissimilation is the crystallization of a new form of Jewish identity and distinctiveness that occurs as part of the dynamic of acculturation and alongside the phenomenon of assimilation."[27] More than just a creation of a "German Jewish subculture," dissimilation was a response to the time and place in which these specific German Jews lived.[28] Yet how German Jews participated in the local and pan-German newspapers during the 1840s both incorporates and argues against this notion. While Jews were developing their own unique identity as German citizens of the Jewish faith and working toward Germanness through their participation therein, they were simultaneously creating their own, unique Jewish identity that clearly differentiated themselves from the dominant ideas surrounding the Christian state. Often, these Jewish identities dovetailed with more liberal political sentiments, while they also appeared very similar to the Christian reform movements of the era. As such, developments within Jewish life reflect a hybridization that "could be accumulative (German and Jewish), combative (German versus Jewish), or binary (German or Jewish)."[29] The local and pan-German press are ideal locations to see the process of dissimilation and hybridization at work, as Jews presented themselves as worthy citizens for full emancipation—united as Germans, differentiated and unique by religion.

Jewish participation in the local and pan-German press can be analyzed by looking at Jewish intercessions in both the main news and classified (*Anzeiger*) sections. In these sections, we can observe many important methods by which Jews and Christians opined on Jewish emancipation and internal Jewish religious reform. For this project, I chose newspapers that had either significant regional or pan-German appeal, which could be determined by their subscription bases and national cachet. In some cases, newspapers with relatively small subscription bases were consulted due to their local political importance.

The papers chosen for this study reflect the criteria mentioned previously. For the Grand Duchy of Baden, papers from four cities were chosen: Mannheim, the economic engine of the state; Karlsruhe, the political capital; Heidelberg, a university center and a hub for German liberalism; and Constance, a city steeped in Catholic tradition, which became a hotbed for Vormärz liberal and revolutionary activity. With the exception of Heidelberg, more than one paper was selected for each city, and those selected represented a spectrum of views. Heidelberg stands as the exception because only one paper existed through most of the 1840s, and because Heidelberg was an extension of the Mannheim public sphere due to the cities' proximity to each other. As becomes apparent, Heidelbergers freely read and published in the Mannheim papers as well as the *Heidelberger Journal*.

The pan-German newspapers selected also reflect a range of viewpoints—though most tended to be more liberal than conservative—as result of the rise of liberalism (and the liberal bourgeoisie) and the development of the German press. All of the national papers researched as part of this project—the *Augsburger Allgemeine Zeitung (AAZ)*, *Kölnische Zeitung (KölZtg)*, *Frankfurter Journal (FJ)*, *Vossische Zeitung (VZ*, officially called *Königlich priviligierte Berlinische Zeitung)*, and *Deutsche Allgemeine Zeitung (DAZ)*—were in the top eight in terms of readership during the middle of the 1840s, with a combined circulation of approximately 40,200 copies (or about 402,000 readers).[30] The *AAZ* and *DAZ* were especially well known as "their voices stretched out across Germany."[31] The papers selected also represent a wide geographical footprint and were scattered across different states: Bavaria (one), Prussia (two), Saxony (one), and the Free City of Frankfurt (one; Frankfurt was also the seat of the German Bund [Confederation]).

In order to determine whether an item could be considered "Jewish," I follow Leora Auslander's argument that "Jews are not only Jews when they say they are, or when they feel they are. . . . Judaism is a set of cultural practices and, like all other cultural practices, it is transmitted, reproduced and transformed even when the people doing so are not consciously acting as Jews."[32]

I sought out any mention of Jews, Judaism, or Israelites within each paper and evaluated their content. I also searched for familiar and common names from local Jewish communities, many of which can be located in local histories. By looking at all Jewish intercessions in the newspapers, we can then evaluate Jews' motives for publishing and determine if they were similar to non-Jews' intercessions, which they often were.[33] Another important guide for viewing Jewish engagement is Jews' responses to important events, such as pan-German causes like recuperation from the Hamburg fire of 1842, anti-Jewish incidents like the rioting that occurred during the Haber Affair (1843), or the rabbinical conferences of 1844–46.

It is through the pages of the newspapers that this project evaluates German Jewish claims to membership in the local and pan-German communities. Certainly, the picture provided by local newspapers of German Jewish lives and Jews' participation in German newspapers is not a complete one, just as using traditional archival sources could not achieve such an aim. These sources need to be integrated into a narrative that conceives of German Jewish appearances in the press as signifying more than just confirmation of events that happened or of ideas that were published in the press. German Jews' participation in the press must be analyzed through their contributions to newspapers, and as such newspapers are important locations of German Jewish life. Newspapers reflected the ongoing changes within German Jewish culture, the desire of those who sought change, and the resistance of those who wanted life to stay the same. Nonetheless, Jewish participation in the German press was a unique engagement that showed the power of the press, how comfortable Jews felt in making their contributions, and ultimately, how integrated German Jewish lives had become within German society.

The rest of this book focuses on various vignettes from the Grand Duchy of Baden and across the German states that functioned as important markers of Jewish participation in local and pan-German newspapers, foremost regarding disputes about Jewish emancipation and internal Jewish religious reform. This project moves beyond the insularity that is typically found in studies of the German or German Jewish press and examines more comprehensively the discussions about emancipation and religious reform that played out in the pan-German press. In order to understand the context in which such public debates were held and operated, chapter 1 presents the history of Jewish life in Baden and the German states, the developments of the press throughout those areas, and Jews' engagement more generally within the German public sphere. By interrogating each of these topics, we can understand more about the foundations and terms of existence under which Jews lived in the grand duchy and the German states as well as the conditions that would facilitate their participation in the print media throughout the first decades of the nineteenth century.

Chapter 2 provides an analysis of how Jews participated in public debates about Jewish emancipation and how they presented and argued for themselves in both the regional and pan-German public spheres. Discussions within Baden (especially its legislature) often acted as a barometer of German liberals' appetite for emancipation across Central Europe. Yet a better indication for support of Jewish rights in the grand duchy can be seen in the local newspapers in its most liberal region—that which included Mannheim and Heidelberg. In the first part of this chapter, we explore how local Jews argued with non-Jews about interpretations of state law and presented their case to the public at large. Those who participated in this fight did not let their adversaries dominate the press, and there was a clear challenge to the dominant anti-Jewish and misanthropic narrative of those who continued to deny Jewish equality. The intercessions in this debate generally appeared in a common form familiar to newspaper readers—articles, opinion pieces, and responses. The second part of the chapter, in contrast to the first part, analyzes a couple of nontraditional frameworks for arguments related to emancipation and demonstrations of public virtue—donations (*Spenden*) and obituaries (*Nekrologe*). Studying these more common forms of German publicity, albeit novel contexts for debates about emancipation, expands our knowledge of how Jews presented their lives through a "complex and ambiguous lens" instead of one that focuses solely on "success and failure."[34] The section on philanthropy builds more intensely on Bourdieu's concept of cultural capital, proposing that not only should studies of philanthropy focus on earlier periods (they generally concentrate on postemancipatory efforts) but also that looking at Jewish philanthropy in the context of national catastrophes supplies evidence of German Jews acting as Jewish Germans. The uncovering of several news reports and Nekrologe shows that while cherishing the dead was a common practice in the public sphere, Jews also used obituaries to bolster their chances for integration and emancipation. Just like the details about Jewish philanthropy, the obituary essays add to the richness of materials in which to view and evaluate the methods by which German Jews tried to persuade German Christians that they were worthy of *Gleichstellung* (equalization).[35]

In chapter 3, I deconstruct arguments about Jewish religious reform during the mid-1840s. While one could certainly keep abreast of reforms in the German Jewish press through the three established journals of the time—*Allgemeine Zeitung des Judenthums, Der Orient*, and *Der Israelite des Neunzehnten Jahrhunderts*—these papers discussed events through a narrow, particularistic lens for a nearly completely Jewish audience. In fact, how would the general public know what was going on in the world of German Judaism if that information had stayed confined therein? To the contrary, what I propose is that the fight over Jewish reform was never limited to one specific niche sphere, and on the local and pan-German level, debates about religious reform were important vehicles by which Jews were able to inform the broader public about acculturation and, ultimately, emancipation. This chapter, unlike the others, reverses the focal lens—instead of viewing emancipation through Badenese Jews' experience and then incorporating the pan-German experience alongside it, the debates among German Jewry take primacy. The debates in Baden about Jewish reform in the 1840s were not as public as elsewhere in the German states, especially those in Frankfurt and Berlin pertaining to radical reform. Debates about reform in Baden—while certainly intense and part of the state's program for Jewish "regeneration"—followed the heated discussions that occurred elsewhere, especially given that the first real discussion in the Badenese press about Jewish reform took place in the wake of the Brunswick rabbinical conference in 1844 and the Orthodox protest in early 1845.

Thus, before covering the debate about religious reform in the Mannheim and Heidelberg press in 1845, I present the history of the movement for reform in the German states up to 1840 and then shift focus to how these debates about German Jewish reform manifested themselves during the mid-1840s in the pan-German press. The sheer volume of articles discovered in those papers demonstrates the importance of these discussions, which encompassed the following: debates about the importance of circumcision for Jewish identity and community membership; the installation of a second, reform-leaning rabbi in Frankfurt; and the creation of reform societies that resembled a "German-Jewish Church"—the short-lived Frankfurt Reformfreunde (Association of the Friends of Reform) and the much more successful Berlin Reformgenossenschaft (Reform Society).[36] These debates in some of the largest German Jewish communities set the stage for the heated discussion about Jewish reform in Mannheim and Heidelberg during 1845. In the wake of the Haber Affair (1843–45) and the subsequent renewed effort for emancipation, as well as the public acrimony stemming from the Brunswick rabbinical conference (1844), tensions ran high in northwestern Baden as community members aired their grievances—even about their rabbi—in front of the entire local public.

Chapter 4 concentrates on a case study in the German press from southern Baden that highlights the intersecting nature of Jewish emancipation and Jewish religious reform. This chapter looks at Jewish contributions within the local Constance newspapers during the 1840s but especially during 1846. This year is significant for Jews in Baden due to the passage of Jewish emancipation in the Lower Assembly. Even though the measure ultimately failed to become law, the ground on which Jewish rights had hitherto stood was shaken by the important discussion about the rights of other discriminated-against religious minorities (in this case, the *Deutschkatholiken* [German Catholics]). For many liberals in Baden, the potential rescinding of Christians' rights (though not of the three official confessions) led to a reevaluation of their views on Jewish emancipation. While German Jews may not have been officially emancipated in 1846, there were local attempts to redress long-standing discriminatory policies—in this case, the continued permanent exclusion of Jews from residing in the city of Constance, from which Jews had been expelled in 1448 in the wake of the Council of Constance. It was the newspapers of the city, especially moderate liberal and radical liberal newspapers, that provided venues for local Jews from the Hegau region (west of the city) to present their case for admission and the building of an official Jewish community. In this discussion, various groups within the Jewish community—associations, individuals, and a rabbi—went to great lengths to discredit their opponents' outdated and misanthropic views about Jews and Judaism while presenting themselves as having fulfilled their part of the quid pro quo and, thus, being worthy of admission to the city.

ONE

THE DEVELOPMENT OF JEWISH LIFE AND THE GERMAN NEWSPAPER DURING THE EARLY NINETEENTH CENTURY

JEWS' PARTICIPATION IN THE GERMAN press is a direct reflection of changes in the political situation in the German states, Jews' status within those states, Jews' adherence and acculturation toward German cultural norms (including *Bildung*), and intrinsic developments in the German press. Beginning with new ideas about humanity and citizenship developed during the Enlightenment and the Revolutionary Era, the German states redefined their relationship to all of the outstanding medieval and early modern corporations (their subjects), including their Jewish communities. All of the changes in German Jewish life throughout the early nineteenth century can be seen very clearly in the Grand Duchy of Baden, a state known for its enlightened and reforming tendencies. Baden's centrality to developments within Jewish life, including emancipation and religious reform, are not a result of having either the largest (Prussia) or most concentrated (Hamburg) Jewish populations (table 1.1).[1] Rather, Baden's importance lies in the state's development as the *Musterländle* (model small state) for German liberalism—especially since German liberals are typically viewed by scholars as the Jews' "best friends."[2] It was in Baden that German liberalism became intellectualized, "Liberals" were first elected (1831), and democratic liberals (the so-called radicals) were first elected (1845). This state functioned as a litmus test of liberal ideology on several issues, including how liberals (big *L* and small *l*) treated Jews and the question of Jewish emancipation and the way in which liberals were responsible for the growth and dynamism of the Badenese press during the late 1830s and 1840s. Baden was also among the first German states where Jews were to receive permanent citizenship (1807) and where debates and votes on Jewish emancipation happened with regularity (during every legislative session, once liberals were elected en masse in 1831).

Table 1.1. Jewish Population in the German States

	1816–17			1848		
State	Jews	General Population	% of Population	Jews	General Population	% of Population
Baden	17,600	1,100,000	1.6	23,500	1,382,353	1.7
Bavaria	53,200	3,800,000	1.4	61,000	4,357,143	1.4
Hesse-Darmstadt	20,000	666,667	3.0	29,000	852,941	3.4
Hesse-Kassel	14,400	654,545	2.2	18,500	740,000	2.5
Hannover	6,400	1,280,000	0.5	11,600	1,933,333	0.6
Prussia	123,800	10,316,667	1.2	218,750	16,826,923	1.3
Saxony	1,000	1,250,000	0.08	1,300	1,857,143	0.07
Wuerttemberg	83,000	1,383,333	0.6	12,000	1,714,286	0.7
Total (All German states, not including Austria	257,000	23,577,982	1.09	394,650	34,021,552	1.16
Habsburg Empire	71,000	5,916,667	1.2	112,300	8,197,080	1.37

However, even before liberalism took root in Baden and became the ruling party, developments during the Napoleonic period helped secure Baden's status and importance among the German states.[3] It was the French emperor who granted Margrave Karl Friedrich of Baden-Baden and Baden-Durlach the title of Grand Duke in 1806 while expanding and making contiguous the new grand duke's territory bordering imperial France, including areas in Vorderösterreich (Anterior Austria) in the south and the Electoral Palatinate in the north. Karl Friedrich and his administration then went about reforming life in the new state in a manner consistent with the principles of enlightened absolutism in financial, policing, and educational areas.[4] Even though Baden allied with France through much of this period—it was part of the Confederation of the Rhine—the state was not penalized during the Congress of Vienna (like Saxony), and its gains and stability remained intact. The changes brought forth by Karl Friedrich proved to be a fertile ground for liberal ideas throughout the early nineteenth century, though they did not always make a deep impact, as Baden still had its roots in pre-Napoleonic times: it kept a closed guild structure and devolved power from the centralized absolutist state to the towns. As Mack Walker wrote, this "hometown" atmosphere present in southern Germany was exclusivist and fearful of the promise of liberalism and individualism.[5] This dual nature of Baden—the spirit of change and Enlightenment versus conservatism, chauvinism, and exclusivity—made Jewish life at times particularly difficult.

For the Jews of Baden, their history within the ducal lands during the eighteenth century set the stage for the Janus-faced nature of Badenese politics vis-à-vis Jewish rights during the Vormärz (1830–1848). Jews were first invited to Karlsruhe at the personal behest of Margrave Karl Wilhelm III of Baden-Durlach after he had the city built in 1715 to mimic Louis XIV's Versailles.[6] Jews in Karlsruhe—as in other princely cities—were involved in the financial business of the Margrave and had the status of Schutzbürger (protected residents); several prominent families joined the ranks of a new class of Jewish courtiers, collectively known as "Court Jews," though most Jews in the Margrave's lands (and the eventual territories in the grand duchy) lived a marginal existence.

Jews' fortunes in Baden changed as Karl Friedrich ascended to a position of political prominence during the revolutionary and Napoleonic eras, and as Enlightenment ideas influenced thinkers and politicians alike. All of the changes in Jewish life in Baden over the course of the late eighteenth and first half of the nineteenth century—in citizenship, education, and religion (among others)—had their germination in ideas developed during the Enlightenment. Thinkers, cultural creators, and politicians—inspired by the Enlightenment ideals of religious toleration and individualism—began seeing Jewish residents as potential contributors to the modern states. These ideas about religious toleration have a much longer history that stemmed from John Locke's famous *Second Treatise on Government* (1689), which explicitly calls on governments to practice the concept, and in fact, the concept had already been used in the process of peacemaking (Peace of Westphalia, 1648), if not in parlance and in practice. While toleration during the seventeenth and early eighteenth centuries was not extended to Jews, as there was no perceived need to do so, the Enlightenment and its focus on rationality and individuality, along with the Age of Revolutions, changed that relationship.

In 1781, ideas about incorporating toleration of Jews into state policy throughout the German-speaking areas were the legacy of a Prussian bureaucrat, Christian Wilhelm von Dohm, who wrote *Über die bürgerliche Verbesserung der Juden* (On the civic improvement of the Jews) to defend the Jews of Alsace. Dohm proposed what David Sorkin calls the "quid pro quo of rights for regeneration." Dohm saw Jews in a tutelary state, as valuable assets for the state and as capable of "improvement" (*Verbesserung*). However, the exact measures Jews had to achieve *as a group* were neither clearly defined nor set in stone, leaving evaluation of Jews' fitness for full equality on shaky and (often) moveable ground.[7]

At the heart of the Dohmian paradigm of "improvement" or "regeneration" was the concept of Bildung—the formation of the mind, body, and soul in a harmonious way. This ideal became a (if not *the*) core value of the rising liberal middle class.[8] In addition to pursuing education, Jews were also expected to reform their occupational structure: that is, switch from traditional occupations in trading, peddling, and business activities (originally imposed by Christian princes) to more "German" (read: respectable) occupations, such as artisan crafts, trades, and agriculture.[9] As part of this process, German Jews were also expected to speak High German (*Hochdeutsch*) and discard Yiddish as their primary language. And ultimately, Judaism itself was expected to modernize, as many Christians—Johann David Michaelis, Jacob Friedrich Fries, and Immanuel Kant—believed Judaism was in torpor and/or had been superseded by Christianity. The process of formation and integration could, as Stefan-Ludwig Hoffmann writes, be seen not only as a positive path for change within Judaism but also as a way to emancipate individuals *from* Judaism.[10]

Alongside this Dohmian paradigm, one of Europe's most influential leaders also made significant changes to Jewish life in his dominions. Habsburg Emperor Joseph II, in 1782 and 1783, issued *Toleranzpatenten* (Patents of toleration) for Jews in Austria and Bohemia. To the Jews of Vienna, Emperor Joseph granted freedom of education (*Bildungsfreiheit*), freedom of occupation

(*Gewerbefreiheit*), admittance (*Zugang*) to state universities, and where possible, permission to purchase real estate of every kind.[11]

Following the lead of the Habsburg emperor, Karl Friedrich began changing Jewish lives in 1783 with his decision to have a minister investigate how the Habsburg Toleranzpatenten could be applied to the Jews of Baden-Baden and Baden-Durlach, even though the regent had already begun looking into German schooling for Jews a decade earlier. As such, emancipation politics through "enlightened governmental maxims" were already part of the "daily business of Badenese politics."[12] However, even in light of these ideas to change the status and lives of Jewish subjects, one of the commissioners in Karlsruhe expressed a commonly held belief about the uphill battle that Badenese Jews faced: "The Jew [even if he were to reform and change his ways] will always just be a Jew."[13] Almost two decades later, when the Margrave was elevated by Napoleon to grand duke, he permanently improved Jews' fortunes in the expanded state along Dohmian lines. As part of the incorporation of more territory into the new grand duchy, the Jewish population under the grand duke's rule sextupled from 2,265 in 1802 to 14,200 in 1808. Mannheim supplanted Karlsruhe as the city in Baden with the largest Jewish population, and Heidelberg became the fifth-largest Jewish community (map 1.1).[14] Karl Friedrich then followed the Napoleonic model of an interventionist government that sought to control and reshape Jewish life by issuing two foundational constitutional edicts (1807 and 1809)—the first of their kind among the German states. Karl Friedrich's government—and those of his successors—was far more active in Jewish education and occupational and religious life than other German states, especially when compared to the absence of such an intervention in Prussia, which was opposed to full emancipation even though the government may have ameliorated some degrading features of Jewish life.[15] While the enlightened absolutist policies of Karl Friedrich were an improvement over their prior corporative status, these constitutional edicts granted all Jews in Baden hereditary citizenship (*erbfreie Staatsbürgerschaft*)—Jews were now citizens subject to state laws, and they could likewise make demands on the state. Moreover, the state officially recognized the Jewish religion.[16]

However, such an advancement in Jews' status did not mean they were equal—the principles of toleration still held sway. Those same constitutional edicts legislated Jews as second-class citizens, whereby they were put into a state of tutelage and had to *earn* the remaining rights—for which Badenese Jews had to wait until 1862. As such, the good intentions of "improving" the lives of Jewish citizens were paradoxical: such toleration, in fact, occasionally resulted in a crystallization of Jewish difference, anti-Jewish attitudes, and anti-Jewish

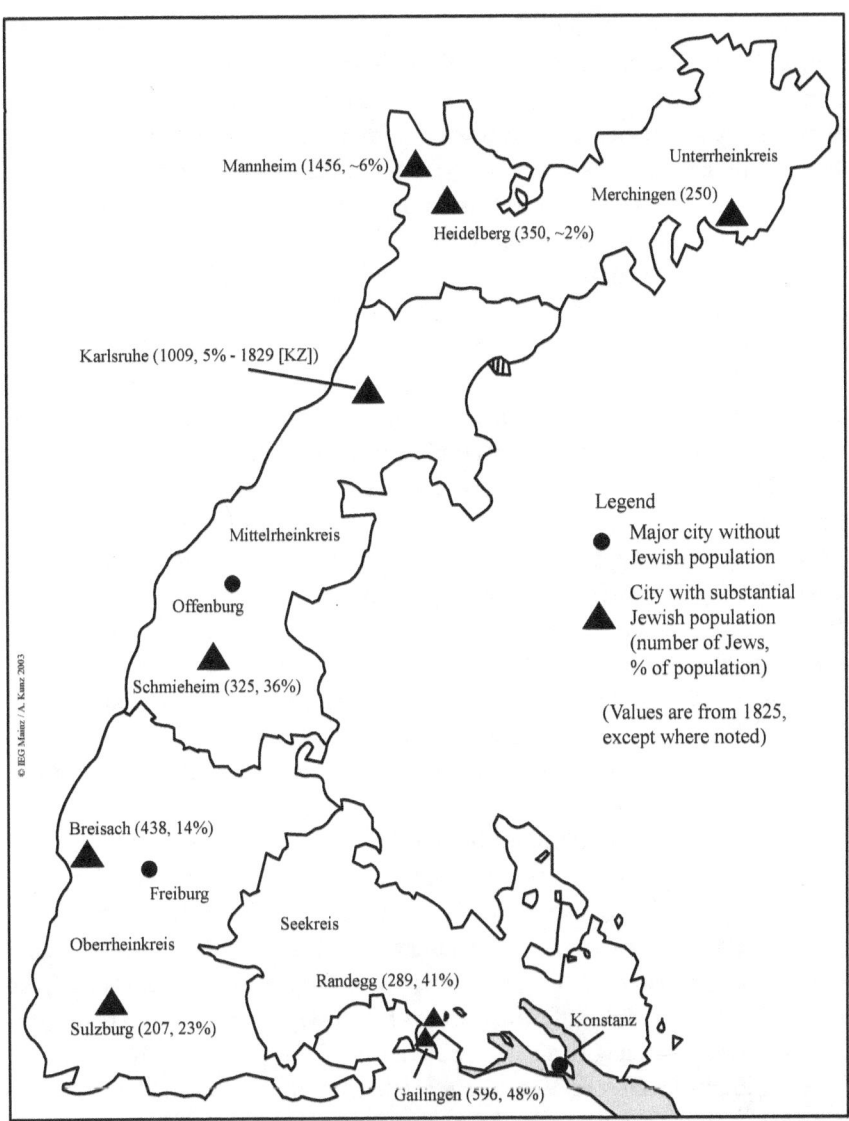

Map 1.1. Jewish Communities in the Grand Duchy of Baden.

violence.[17] Rights withheld from Jewish Badeners included the ability to be elected to public office at the state and communal level (passive rights), the ability to be appointed to public and military office, and the freedom of mobility—that is, to be able to move to any town they desired.[18] Jews in Baden could only live in 11 percent of Badenese towns and could only move to towns where Jews already had permission to live; this law prevented Jews from moving to cities like Constance, which restricted Jewish settlement. Jews could also not serve in the Badenese military, a situation that hampered Jews' claim to citizenship: martial masculinity became a defining feature of German citizenship, and this specific form of citizenship also became paramount within German liberals' ideology.[19] Local rights were of particular importance in "hometown" Baden as it was at the municipal level that many of these rights had their efficacy. While some Jews could earn (or be granted) local citizenship, most Jews (and Christians, for that matter) were protected persons in the communes. In 1831, Jewish disabilities were reconfirmed by the *Gemeindeordnung* (communal ordinance), which kept Jews as the only protected residents in the state while emancipating all Christians. It would be these remaining rights, along with the (in)formal exclusion that plagued German society, that Jews would fight for throughout the nineteenth century and that would be a prominent part of Vormärz public discussions about Jewish emancipation and religious reform. For Jewish Badeners, the full package of rights was contingent on a reformation in German Jewish life that was judged acceptable by Christian legislators, ministers, and monarch.[20]

In order to bring about these religious changes, the Badenese government in 1809 established the Oberrat der Israeliten Badens (Consistory of the Israelites of Baden) in Karlsruhe, which had government-appointed Jewish members and an appointed Christian leader/observer. Such a body devoted to changing Jewish life signaled the state's intentions toward its Jewish citizens. At first, the government divided the administration of Jewish religious life into three provincial districts, each with a head rabbi. In 1827, these districts were split apart, creating fourteen independent rabbinical districts that reported directly to the Oberrat.[21] These districts—and the three state conferences (administrative, religious, and educational)—helped fulfill the Oberrat's and the government's aims of successfully promoting a modern Jewish lifestyle, with a particular emphasis on promoting bourgeois religiosity through proper behavior and decorum during synagogue services as well as education through Bildung (see appendix A). The education of Jewish children, which generally took place in Jewish schools provided by the community, was—like the German Jewish journal *Ha-Me'assef*—"out of the control of the rabbis," as rabbis typically did not involve themselves in the schools. Education was thus the location in which reformers could most effectively challenge traditional and Orthodox Judaism and train a new generation with reformist and more secular ideas. The structure of the Oberrat—and its power to appoint educators (and rabbis)—ensured that the reformist policies of the government were generally reflected in the schools, and eventually the rabbinate, as openings occurred. The reformist leanings of that regulatory body had the ability to affect Jewish life for decades to come.[22]

Governmental intervention in education ensured that this topic would become important in debates about Jewish integration and emancipation, and this situation was reflected in both the German Jewish and non-Jewish German press. As seen in the Kingdom of Hannover, education was front and center in debates about a new law regulating Jews' lives in the kingdom during the 1830s. Local Jews argued vigorously about teacher credentials, the language of instruction, and the importance of these matters in terms of favorable legislation. Education also became an occasional flashpoint for violence, as seen in the murder of the Immendorf (near Cologne) teacher Jacob Schatz by a Jewish youth who was furious about the modernization of Judaism—though such an incident was rare. In Baden, education functioned as an important part of Jews' public presentation of their attainment of Bildung and the fulfillment of the quid pro quo. One example of education's importance for Jews in the grand duchy was the placement of an advertisement in the *Karlsruher Zeitung* for a new Jewish school to be built in Mannheim. This advertisement was one of a kind, and the creators placed it in this paper with the intention of showing the local public and lawmakers that Jews were fulfilling their obligations. The advertisement demonstrated how Jewish education mimicked the curriculum in local *Gymnasia* and prepared Jewish students to be full participatory members of Badenese society.[23] These examples suggest that German Jews recognized the importance and power of newspapers both for getting the message out to Jews in outlying communities and for winning over public opinion. Moreover, these examples show an understanding of how Jews used the newspapers to help shape religious reform by subjecting internal Jewish reform to the pressure of external, societal conformity.

As a comparison to the situation in Baden, the Jews in Prussia received their citizenship in March 1812 in alignment with French ideas regarding Jewish citizenship. Jews were granted more individual freedoms, such as the toleration of Judaism as a religion, the ability to purchase property and land, and permission to work in occupations that had been previously off-limits to them (such as civil service and university positions). However, Jews were also placed under obligations by the state. In return for these individual freedoms, Jewish families had to take on a permanent family name (this was a common feature among German states' Jewish legislation), Jewish men were expected to serve in the military, and German became the official language for communal record keeping. Yet, just like in Baden, Jews were not given full rights, and even though Jews were henceforth officially permitted to work in civil service positions, many Jews still found it necessary to convert to Christianity to be able to obtain positions and advance their careers. Moreover, these laws only applied to the core Prussian lands as of 1812 (Brandenburg, Saxony, Pomerania, and East and West Prussia); those areas acquired after Napoleon's defeat and the Congress of Vienna (Posen, Westphalia, and the Rhine province) had different laws in effect for their Jewish residents. This edict, thus, applied to only 70,000 Jews (out of 124,000 Jews in all of Prussia). Overall, and as Deborah Hertz maintains, "the spirit of the new law [the 1812 edict] was that if Jews became modern and served the state loyally, eventually a wider equality *might* be granted."[24] But Prussian Jews had neither a centralized organization (like the Badenese Oberrat) to help direct Jewish life nor a government invested in helping Jews throughout the kingdom to improve their station; in fact, Jews in each region of Prussia were left to their own devices, and as a result, Jewish life in the three regions of Prussia (Rhineland, core Prussia, and Posen) progressed at varying speeds, though as will be shown later, religious reform was still able to find a fruitful home in Berlin despite governmental antipathy to change (chap. 3).

Jews' plights and fights for rights stem from a tradition of Christian anti-Judaism throughout the German states. Even with the seemingly more enlightened policies of some German governments, Jews were not welcome in many corners of society. As seen in Baden and Prussia, even the toleration patents and constitutional edicts were implicitly anti-Jewish, since they promulgated ideas to "regenerate" Jews and their religion and to force Jews to show allegiance and cultural development before being granted more rights; Jews were seen more generally by many German Christians as inherently corrupt and misanthropic. Such laws and directives by German states easily functioned on occasion as "a substitute ... to formal liberal equality or liberty."[25] These challenges entailed renewal and reinvigoration for some, including the adherents to Judaism and their allies who would create a modern Jewry. For others, the same paradigm was simply the most recent attempt to accomplish what others had failed to do—that is, to convert all of the Jews to Christianity and make Judaism disappear.

The fundamental changes in Jewish life in Baden, Prussia, and the German states were, thus, a result of both intellectual developments during the Enlightenment and the events of the Revolutionary and Napoleonic Eras across

Europe. Jews were incorporated into French society (by the French National Assembly in 1790–91), the Napoleonic satellite states of the Batavian Republic (1796; later, Kingdom of the Netherlands), Italy (1797–99), and lastly, the Kingdom of Westphalia (1808). Jews were given rights *as individuals* in these places and were incorporated into the national body politic.[26] As Jews accepted the responsibilities of citizenship—including military service—being forced back into or being kept under an early modern existence (i.e., living inside a real or imagined ghetto) was for many Jews no longer palatable or acceptable.

In essence, the specific German states that had emancipated the Jews generally accepted Judaism as a religion that *individuals* could believe and follow; it is clear that French policies vis-à-vis the Jews had an influence on German legislation. However, Jews still had to defend their religion as a *collective* before the public. Despite Napoleon's attempted annulling and "repudiation of unconditional [Jewish] emancipation" in Alsace (the Infamous Decree [1808] limited Jewish settlement in Alsace, forced Jews to get certificates of good conduct, and absolved non-Jews of supposedly "illegitimate" debts) and its applicability in German areas west of the Rhine, many Jews began changing their identity: Frenchness (or other national identities) became a primary form of self-definition, while Jewishness became secondary.[27] The legacy of emancipation in Napoleonic-controlled areas had significant reverberations across the continent for decades to come. These effects, especially the inclusion of Jews as citizens, were felt acutely in the German states—both in those areas under direct French domination (primarily Rhenish Prussia, Hamburg, and Hesse-Kassel) and in those that remained independent (like Baden and Prussia). It was after the Napoleonic period ended that earnest discussions of Jewish lives throughout the entirety of the German states (and not just individual states) became a significant political topic.

After the upheaval of the Napoleonic era, European governments that were charged with putting Europe back into a workable political order wanted to restore prior systems of rule and ensure that such a catastrophic war would be unlikely to occur in the future. In that process, governments made difficult decisions, including how to organize a system that recognized the changes over the previous twenty years would not simply disappear, including those dealing with Jewish rights. The Congress of Vienna—convened by Austrian count Clemens von Metternich—met to restructure Europe after Napoleon's defeat based on Metternich's ideas of stability. One of the most important tasks was creating a successor to the defunct Holy Roman Empire, which Napoleon dissolved in 1806. The German Confederation (*Deutscher Bund*) arose to regulate supranational issues throughout the German states, though it often dictated policy to its members. The Bund also addressed the issue of Jewish emancipation, resolving in article 16 of the Bund Constitution that Jews should be given rights. Traditionally, the "infamous preposition"—the change of "*in* the individual states" to "*from* the individual states"—has been seen as the difference between full Jewish rights and the Jews' reversion back to being Schutzbürger, but Brian Vick has recently suggested that the strict and misanthropic interpretation of the phrase "rights already granted" in the same sentence as the preposition had more efficacy. For the Hanseatic cities (Bremen, Hamburg, and Lübeck), in which the French military was not considered a legitimate government, this negative interpretation allowed the local governments to legally strip away Jewish rights.[28] In Baden, however, these changes would have little import, as the grand duke had already issued legislation in 1807 and 1809 that affected Jewish rights more positively.

Once the Napoleonic era gave way to the Biedermeier and Vormärz eras that followed, Baden became a breeding ground for liberal ideas, like other areas along the Rhine and bordering France. These new ideas were especially prevalent in the newly incorporated Palatinate region of Baden, which included Mannheim and Heidelberg—the new financial and intellectual capitals of the state—and these ideas were also quite popular among the local Jewish populations. The intellectual and political climate in the grand duchy was conducive to both emancipation and religious reform. However, not all Jews in the liberal areas were supportive of emancipation or religious reform, just as many Jews who lived in more rural and conservative areas (generally known as *Landgemeinden*) did not support a separate Jewish existence or traditional Judaism.[29] In Baden, reform blossomed in rural communities like Randegg (near Constance), while orthodoxy flourished in cities like Mannheim. This disunity among Baden's Jews would eventually spill over onto the pages of the local papers, where their disagreements were laid bare for all to see.

Throughout the German states, the individual histories of the various Jewish communities were affected by the histories of those locales and whether Jews faced a sympathetic or antagonistic general public. Furthermore, with more Jews entering the *Bildungsbürgertum* (educated middle class) and the *Wirtschaftsbürgertum* (economic middle class), there were certainly many Jews who saw themselves as a new, modern generation that had innovative visions of the future, varying ideas on how to get to the same religious goal as prior generations, or different goals altogether. German Jews' relationship to the developing press industry and the individual societies that contained these spheres—especially over the course of the eighteenth and nineteenth centuries, when Jews participated in increasing numbers—was an important process of their embourgeoisement; so much so, in fact, that Simone Lässig argues that the project of the public sphere was also a Jewish project, not just a Christian or even a bourgeois one.[30]

This communal project of defining and redefining the public sphere can be seen in the history of the newspaper as a media platform both before and during the early nineteenth century. As a transconfessional project, the newspaper allowed its participants to explain themselves in myriad ways and forms. Even those on the social periphery, like German Jews, were an integral part of newspapers' evolution, and they played a significant role in developing the press as an organ for mass consumption. For many scholars, discussions of Jewish participation in the press has entailed the excavation and detailing of the German Jewish press and sermons and the examination of how these vehicles helped German Jews in their quest for integration, acculturation, acceptance, and foremost, equality. Yet while the German Jewish press was perhaps the most significant avenue for the expression of Jewish political and religious developments, it can only reveal part of the German Jewish experience. Local German newspapers provide us insight into Jewish lives and how they negotiated their local circumstances. Through study of the local and pan-German newspapers, a fuller picture will emerge of how Jews presented themselves to the public and argued on behalf of their ideas and for their future as Germans.

THE DEVELOPMENT OF THE GERMAN AND BADENESE PRESS

The increase in Jewish voices in the press during the 1830s and 1840s in Baden and the German states was not only a result of their status as second-class (or not full) citizens and their acculturation to German values and accumulation of cultural capital. It was also a result of intrinsic developments within the German public sphere and the world of German publishing, which "coincided" with the intellectualization of the press and push for Jewish rights.[31] By the onset of the post-Napoleonic period, the publishing industry (especially the world of newsprint) had changed dramatically. No longer did newspapers serve only the interests of the crown and the elite; they also began to more regularly serve the interests of commoners and those on the periphery of society. This transition to a more inclusive position was not an overnight phenomenon, though it was also not a gradual, long-term change.

By 1800, the German press was widespread (there were *Intelligenzblättern* [Intelligencers] in 220 cities and over two hundred newspapers)—but it still had only "contingent autonomy," as governments and churches attempted to prevent subversive news through censorship. But states did not just restrict the press. Some princes also adhered to an active press politics, supporting papers financially and participating in their production. The expansion of the press during the early modern era was facilitated by war—the Thirty Years' War accelerated and created a market for news. It is no coincidence that a daily newspaper, the *Einkommende Zeitung* (Leipzig), provided services in that war's wake, despite limits to its offerings: only foreign news appeared before the literate public, and neither critical commentary nor local coverage were presented.[32]

In the German states, the rise of the press also went hand-in-hand with a change in reading habits. Whether or not one agrees with Rolf Engelsing's theory of the change from intensive to extensive reading—that is, reading more broadly while often reading texts only once instead of reading few texts multiple times—scholars generally concur that changes in reading practices evolved beyond private consumption and affected public communication. The ground had been laid for "the possibility of bourgeois political enlightenment in the following eighteenth century." And this reading revolution also affected German Jews in an intense and important way—during the late Enlightenment, they also joined and created reading societies and participated in developing the salon culture.[33] This change in reading among German Jews was a factor in their increased societal participation, including the production of newsprint.

However, newspapers were only part of the panoply of platforms and locations that facilitated such public engagement. Other locations that symbolized the ideals of the "enlightened/bourgeois" (Habermasian) public sphere—critical debate, rationality, inclusivity, and problematization—were coffeehouses, freemason lodges, and salons. In those contexts, published material, including regularly produced scholarly journals, or *gelehrte Zeitungen*, provided the substance for sustained discussion.[34] The journal was also a means for those in the educated classes to transmit knowledge to other elites; the state—as the employer of university professors (and journal editors)—also took an interest in these journals.

Thus, the journal, through its function of communicating knowledge to the upper class and rising bourgeoisie, prepared the way for one of its most important later functions—as educator of the public, and specifically those who were in or aspired to the *gebildeter Stand*, like German Jews. This can be seen through the use of the term *gelehrte* (learned) for the genre. The educational function came directly from the journal's conceptual predecessor, the *moralische Wochenschrift* (moral weekly). In terms of its importance for the beginnings of the bourgeois public sphere, the educator function of journals helped "project the bourgeois inner-world as the obverse of the noble façade."[35]

One newspaper that reached a successful halfway point between the newspaper and the journal was the *Hamburgische unpartheyische Correspondent* (*HC*). This paper was similar to contemporaneous newspapers in that it typically only printed foreign news and eschewed printing news about local matters. The *HC*, as its official name suggests, prided itself on its *unpartheyisch* (impartial) nature, as it sought to present as much firsthand material from various sides of political issues. The *HC* was also limited by the Hamburg Senate's desire to stay on the good side of the courts in both Berlin and Vienna. However, the *HC*'s claim to fame and success was its role as a transmitter of Enlightenment values through the *gelehrter Artikel* (learned article). The *HC* took this newspaper convention from a neighboring journal—the *Holsteinischen Correspondenten*—and incorporated it into its format starting in 1731. The *HC*'s success can be measured by its subscriptions: in an era where six hundred to one thousand subscriptions was average and eighteen thousand was excellent, the *HC* had thirty thousand with the occasional increase to fifty-six thousand—making it the largest newspaper in all of Europe during the late eighteenth century. The paper had regular contributions that expounded on all sorts of topics, especially original articles covering a diverse array of disciplines: "theology, law, medicine, natural science, philology, literature, philosophy, history, etc."[36] Yet the *HC* could not stay successful through the Revolutionary Era and had a precipitous fall in subscriptions, while other papers—most notably the *Augsburger Allgemeine Zeitung*—surpassed it in importance, subscriptions, and reach.

All of these steps in the development of the newspaper would, however, be important once the platform became an increasingly popular instrument at the end of the eighteenth century. At that time, the newspaper was "for quite an extensive public the most important reading material and already a trusted everyday object, hardly requiring any reflection."[37] Another evolution that helped establish a precedent for the modern newspaper was the Intelligenzblätter, which Astrid Blome calls "the first periodicals that appeared in and for a defined region with external—territorial state—borders, and which could and should have promoted the internal process of regional education."[38] Three elements of the Intelligenzblätter were important for the evolution of the modern German newspaper: the official announcements (i.e., the absolute state showing its centralized and dominant character), the classified marketplace, and what one could classify as a culture section (articles, puzzles, political news, and literary reviews)—a predecessor of the *Feuilleton*. The official announcements and the classifieds provided an important future source of income for editors and printers, which had mostly operated as one-man operations. The classifieds also demonstrated the financial strength of those who placed (and could afford) advertisements. Furthermore, as Ian McNeely has pointed out, the Intelligenzblätter made the public sphere more accessible to rural communities.[39] This transformation would be important during the hyper-political decade of the 1840s, in which liberals claimed to be speaking for the people.

Another important element of the journals that developed over time was their increased frequency. The *Einkommende Zeitung* was the first daily paper in Europe, though most papers appeared as weeklies until the Vormärz, due to the immense financial burdens of running a paper. Having advertisements helped keep papers solvent. Even though the advertisements were quite banal, the inclusion of such items increased participation, provided a different way for readers to view their local (and supra-local) environment, and shaped both newspapers and society. In fact, the inclusion of advertisements expanded readership and gave people a sense of the everyday needs in their locales, since many individuals had limited interest in world affairs.[40]

Until the early nineteenth century, free opinion and commentary in the German press were not permitted. As Heinz-Dietrich Fischer has discussed, "the newspaper was permitted to spread new news, so long as it was truthful (*wahrhaftig*) and acceptable to the earthly governance (*irdischen Gewalt*). It was fundamentally not allowed to opine (*räsonnieren*), and that counts in politics as a sign of a supporter of unrest."[41] It was not until the Napoleonic period that opinion articles became effective tools that could support the state's aims. The first German newspaper to print critical evaluations of society—and not just enlightened ideals like the *HC* (which often took the form of reformist ideas which were supported by the states)—was the *Rheinische Merkur* (hereafter, *Merkur*). The German nationalist Joseph Görres, who founded the *Merkur* in 1814, used his platform primarily to agitate against the French occupation. The *Merkur*'s success, even though the paper only lasted about two years before it ran afoul of Prussian censors, was so well known that it became a road map for future editors and publishers trying to arouse public sentiment. Görres saw himself as an "interlocutor between the people and the state," and he used "public opinion" to help guide his views. However, the *Merkur* was a victim of its own success—its sharply critical style was acceptable when aimed at France, but when used to criticize the Prussian state, it was seen as an obstacle to stability. Despite the short tenure of the *Merkur*, Görres planted the seeds of the newspaper not only as an educational or opinion-sharing medium, but as one that was meant to shape public opinion and form a national consciousness. Such an intentional form of argumentation would find its way back into the press in the form of the "leading article," a mainstay of late Vormärz publishing.[42]

While the *Merkur* was a one-man enterprise whose editor sought to challenge governments and empires on his own, another man sought a different path to newspaper success. Johann Friedrich Cotta became the first person in Germany to develop a modern press company. His most successful paper was the *Augsburger Allgemeine Zeitung* (*AAZ*), which he founded in 1798. It became the most read paper throughout the German states during the Napoleonic era and the Vormärz; the paper was also the basis of Cotta's political and societal power.[43] The *AAZ*'s success came from Cotta's decisions to align his paper with Count Metternich and the Austrian government, to professionalize the job of editor, and to employ university-educated men as journalists. The decision to align with Metternich allowed the *AAZ* to receive privileged treatment, including reduced censorship and expanded access to privileged information. Professionalizing the editor's job allowed the *AAZ* to be printed more often, which meant more news and income. The hiring of professional correspondents allowed the *AAZ* to have more dependable news providers, and it allowed individuals to earn an income doing so—Heinrich Heine (a German Jewish convert to Christianity) did so from Paris. This last development helped shape the Restoration and Vormärz as more liberally inclined men, Jewish and non-Jewish, reported on events and influenced public perception; in fact, as Jacob Toury writes, a "not inconsequential number" of Jews partook in the publishing industry as contributors and editors.[44] All of these innovations were very costly, and the price of the *AAZ* reflected that—it was one of the most expensive papers in Europe—yet it survived and thrived. When Johann Cotta died in 1832, his son Georg took over the *AAZ*, and the younger Cotta changed the paper into a conduit for ideas associated with ascending German liberals in the wake of the 1830 revolutions. These innovations during the early nineteenth century—in both the *Merkur* and the *AAZ*—were important to the germination of liberal ideas and the demand for a free press, which furthered liberals' aims to increase their political power.[45]

As seen in the story of the *AAZ*, the state played an important role in its success, facilitating Johann Cotta's goal to make the *AAZ* indispensable for the Austrian public; this dependency served Cotta by at least temporarily limiting state intervention and action against the *Deutsche Tribüne* (*DT*) in 1831. Owned by Cotta and edited by Johann Georg August Wirth, the *DT* ran afoul of Bavarian and Bund authorities in its first issues. Eventually, the *DT* moved from Munich to the Bavarian Palatinate—where censorship was less strict—yet the Bavarian state forced the *DT* to fold within one year. The short history of the *DT*—much like that of other early 1830s newspapers in Baden, such as *Der Wächter am Rhein* (The sentry on the Rhine, Mannheim) and *Der Freisinnige*

(The progressive, Freiburg)—pertains directly to censorship in the German states, which Robin Lenman has argued, was "never more intricately so than in the century following the Napoleonic wars."[46]

However, the omnipresence of censorship during the post-1815 period does not mean that censors were always repressing liberty. As Robert Darnton has argued, censors in prerevolutionary France did not just "purge heresies. It [censorship] was *positive*—a royal endorsement of the book and an official invitation to read it." Thus, censors and authors were not necessarily antagonistic but potentially collaborative. In an enlightened society where one of the goals of the state was to facilitate (at least in part) a "free and open republic of letters," this collaboration was possible.[47] After the Revolutionary Era, however, the German states worked to make sure that "openness" that they believed had facilitated the revolution was repressed.

After 1815, authorities were more conscientious of publicly reported news, and they created systems to control the spread of information and, therefore, also public opinion. States' desire to control the spread of ideas received an unexpected jolt from the assassination of August von Kotzebue—a Russian emissary in Mannheim—in 1819. The assassination, perpetrated by a member of a nationalist fraternity, catalyzed states to create the Carlsbad Decrees, which were particularly heavy-handed toward the publishing industry. In addition to these decrees, Bund members also restricted states from making drastic changes to their constitutions ("Final Act of Vienna," 1820), and reinforced censorship and monitoring of the press (Six Articles from June 1832). The Bund also established an institution to deal with potential circumventions of the law, and its second iteration—the *Mainzer Informationsbüro* (Mainz Information Office, 1833–48)—investigated over two thousand suspects during a nine-year period.[48]

However, it was the state level at which hostile and limiting environments for the press appeared. Nearly all of the German states complied with the Bund requirements, but Prussia went above and beyond the twenty-sheet (320-page) standard and censored all material published and sold in the state. For example, the *Leipziger Allgemeine Zeitung* (from Saxony) was banned by the Prussian government in 1843, but was allowed to reestablish itself under a new name (*Deutsche Allgemeine Zeitung*) and a less-threatening tone. States could also lodge complaints with other governments about newspapers that published classified material—this was one of the *DT*'s early transgressions—and it could enact a more active press politics by supporting papers financially through direct subsidies or by paying favorable newspapers to print official announcements (*Insertionsprivileg* [insertion privilege]). Two other methods by which states could affect the press were by pressuring printers to drop a suspect paper and by convincing other journals to print negative and critical articles about their competitors.[49]

Many of the tactics mentioned here were soft-power techniques, and the state, when it needed to, could be more direct. States could summarily ban papers, and as an added effect (and in conformity with Bund dictates), editors of those journals could receive a five-year employment ban. States—through their censors—also could prevent papers from printing controversial material. Items could be stricken from pages, and the papers were required to make it appear as if there were no *Zensorlücken* (censor holes). Decisions about struck material could be appealed, and if overturned, the material could be included in a newly reprinted edition.[50] However, some editors printed the material or the "holes" anyway to make a political point (such as happened with Gustav Struve and the *Mannheimer Journal*), or the material was smuggled out of the German states to more friendly press environments in France or Denmark, printed anew, and then smuggled back into the German states. Before complete prohibition, states could also fine and jail editors for violations. Another tactic that states had at their disposal was the use of the postal service. The development of the postal networks in the German states was one of the most important reasons for the successful development of the press in Central Europe. Yet the success of an individual paper could be halted and stunted by using postal pricing as a tool to make a papers unaffordable for target audiences, which is one way that Prussia dealt with the *DT*.[51] One final method of control was through the printing concessions—if an editor was unwilling to change course, the state could pressure his printer by withholding a concession, which allowed a state to prevent a publication from becoming public without having to "expressly forbid" it.[52] All of these methods that the states had at their disposal were in effect after 1819, and as Frederik Ohles argues, "policing in the individual German states began to smother literary liberty in the way envisioned in the Metternichean decrees [of 1819]."[53]

Despite the potential for heavy-handed application of censorship by German authorities, the newspaper still became an effective means of communication for spreading news to the general public, and one in which more of the public could participate as readers and as contributors. Newspapers over the first half of the nineteenth century took the most effective practices from previously printed media and melded them into an effective medium that supplanted "the static libraries, bibles, calendars, and books."[54] The importance of the press' development into a wide-ranging informational medium stemmed from the ability of publishers and editors to reach a wider audience through greater geographical and social (class) reach, which also coincided with an increasing literacy rate. For example, in the Grand Duchy of Baden during the early nineteenth century, nearly 90 percent of men and 45 percent of women were literate, whereas estimates for the rest of the German states suggest about 25 percent literacy. Programmatically, the newspapers stopped serving up information about the ruling families and the nobility and started presenting events and details to support bourgeois interests. Through the combination of these two developments, journals could more effectively communicate and "educate" larger numbers of people in more areas; this trend was furthered by the communal reading practices of the eighteenth and early nineteenth centuries.[55] Nonetheless, such changes in the press were not uniform throughout the Bund, despite the sometimes-dictatorial nature of censorship. In Baden, the newspaper evolved throughout the period to reflect the state's unique history as well as the society's engagement, acceptance, and rejection of liberal and bourgeois ideology.

In the Grand Duchy of Baden, the history of the press had analogs to the histories in other German states, as the state was one of the core bastions of German liberalism. Demands for *Pressefreiheit* (freedom of the press) were discussed frequently throughout the Restoration and Vormärz, albeit without much success.[56] Baden took many ideas and governing concepts from its western neighbor (France), such as the consistorial system (mentioned previously), but it also imported some negative laws, including Napoleon's draconian censors. "The suppression of the Badenese press," declared Günter Stegmaier, "was the gravest intervention of Napoleon in German press matters."[57] As a result of this policy, the government in 1810 only permitted one newspaper to report political news in the entire country, the *Karlsruher Zeitung*. All other papers during the Napoleonic period and for a few years thereafter were local informational papers with local items, notices, and advertisements, very similar to Intelligenzblätter in the Kingdom of Württemberg. The grand duke worried about controlling not only the press but also the information and the messages therein, much in the way that Abigail Green identified for later periods.[58]

The grand duchy gradually permitted other newspapers to print political news. In November 1821, the state gave permission to the *Mannheimer Nachrichten*, *Freiburger Zeitung*, and *Konstanzer Zeitung* to operate as providers of political news. However, a breakthrough in Badenese press politics was not possible without a change in the leading spirit of the *Landtag* (parliament), as well as a change in leadership, which occurred when the more liberal Grand Duke Leopold ascended to the throne in 1831. His ascension heralded a new era in which liberals could set the agenda, be elected to the Landtag "without interference," and see much of their program on the legislative agenda. Foremost among their aims was securing Pressefreiheit. The speed with which Liberals and the grand duke in 1831 enacted freedom of the press democratically should not be overshadowed by its equally quick and unilateral revocation by the grand duke, who was under pressure from Prussia, Austria, and the Bund.[59] However, during this important five-month period, progressive journals sprang up throughout the grand duchy, including *Der Freisinnige* and *Der Wächter am Rhein*. Like non-Badenese papers (such as the *Deutsche Tribüne*), both of these Badenese papers promoted liberal values, critiqued monarchical power, and fomented a movement that culminated in the nationalist Hambach Festival of 1832 (in the neighboring Bavarian Palatinate). Karl Mathy, one of the leaders of the Badenese liberals throughout the 1840s and the leader of their parliamentary faction later in the decade, contributed to *Der Wächter* and believed that "people must be taught about their situation," which could sum up the paper's *Weltanschauung* (worldview). It is no wonder that the Bund was so worried about popular political enlightenment, and that Metternich moved so quickly both to ban these papers throughout the German states and to pressure the Badenese governments to revoke its Pressefreiheit. Yet as Rainer Schimpf rightly points out, "the law could be eliminated again, but the memory of it stayed intact."[60]

As the Vormärz moved closer to the 1848 revolutions, it became necessary for the Badenese government to allow liberal newspapers to exist, if only to help alleviate some of the social tensions caused by the continual suppression of dissenting opinion. Fearful of increasing unrest, the Badenese government allowed dissenting views in a controlled manner and with censorial oversight. Such oversight was made easier due to three factors: available printing technology, which limited printers to being able to print only two newspapers at a time; the concentration of printers in the big cities (Karlsruhe, Mannheim, Constance, Freiburg, and Heidelberg); and a locally based censorship system. The government also counteracted the influence of oppositional opinion by flexing its monetary power through the *Insertionsprivileg*. As Hanno Tauschwitz wrote, "by 1832, they [the Badenese government] realized how valuable the press could be not only for a bourgeois public life, but also for the state."[61] The Badenese government's reaction to the liberal press was similar to that in neighboring Württemberg, where control over the press promoted and benefited at least some of the citizens under constant state tutelage. Another alternative for states was providing a direct subvention to government-friendly newspapers, as happened in Mannheim (*Mannheimer Morgenblatt*, MM).[62] Yet despite the Badenese state's greatest efforts, the press increasingly became more oppositional.

During most of the 1830s, the Badenese press and state interests were closely aligned: few papers were allowed to print the news, and all news printed was strictly regulated. This meant that the bourgeois interests that controlled most of the printing houses and production facilities could not print news promoting their own class or national interests. The late 1830s and '40s were a different story, however, and it was during this period that the interaction between individual papers and the local censors became a "daily fight."[63] The *Seeblätter*, which grew into one of the most radical papers during the 1848 revolutions, waged an ongoing battle with the Constance censor that dated back to its inception in 1837. A similar phenomenon occurred in Mannheim after the establishment in 1842 of the *Mannheimer Abendzeitung (MAbZ)*, which was the most important paper in Baden during the Vormärz and the intellectual heir to the more radical *Rheinische Zeitung*, published by Karl Marx and Arnold Rüge. These were just two of the numerous examples of liberal Badenese newspapers that sought to influence society.[64]

Both papers led the left-liberal push to have their opinions included (they were joined in 1843 by the *Oberrheinische Zeitung* [*ObRhZtg*] from Freiburg), and in effect, they provided venues for dissenting views and news. These organs were also instrumental in fomenting left-liberal ideas throughout society, including their advocacy for Jewish emancipation. However, these papers did more than just advocate for Gleichstellung, they also became important platforms for German Jewish participation in the local press. These papers evolved into preeminent locations for Badenese Jews to regularly present themselves, their coreligionists, and their religion.

In the middle of the ideological spectrum were the newspapers of more moderate (*gemäßigte*) liberals, all of whom were involved in the fight for Pressefreiheit. The papers created in this political orientation reflected the liberal belief that this group of men was the "carriers of political publicness" and the "mouthpiece of public opinion."[65] The most notable personality that ties these papers together was Karl Mathy. The papers in this middle grouping often did not last very long, primarily spanning a year or two with the *Landtagszeitung (LTZ)* and the *ObRhZtg* lasting longer. Whether for financial or political reasons, these papers did not generally maintain public support as effectively as their more radical competitors. The *LTZ* and *ObRhZtg* had longer success because they were reasonably priced and were able to present a moderate liberal position that eschewed lengthy and boring intellectual essays while presenting difficult material in summarized articles. The *ObRhZtg* also had the advantage of being the only liberal paper between Karlsruhe and Constance. However, the *ObRhZtg* did not achieve its greatest success as a moderate liberal paper;

it only became successful once it became more radically liberal in 1847. The owner of the *ObRhZtg*, Adolph Emmerling, attributed that success to a more practical vision and not being tied to the liberals in the *Landtag*, unlike other liberal journals (the *LTZ, Die Rundschau,* and the *Deutsche Zeitung*).[66] The radical and moderate liberal press in Baden never saw eye-to-eye, just as their political representatives did not, as shown in the very public rupture in the liberal faction during 1845–46.

Opposing the left-liberal newspapers, there was also an increase in conservative newsprint. The most notable of these papers was the *Mannheimer Morgenblatt*; it was first printed in 1840 and became the "antipode" to the *MAbZ*. The *MM* was "easily the most unpopular paper in Mannheim" and, as a result, had a much smaller subscribership. In order to survive, the paper turned to and received direct monetary support from the central Badenese government. Another conservative paper that appeared during this time was the *Süddeutsches katholisches Kirchenblatt* (later called the *Süddeutsche Zeitung für Kirche und Staat*; hereafter, *Süddeutsche Zeitung*). Produced in Freiburg, the *Süddeutsche Zeitung* focused on Catholic issues, followed an archconservative and ultramontane ideology (even more so than the *Mannheimer Morgenblatt*), and directly reflected the views of the archbishops of Freiburg. This paper was diametrically opposed to the Freiburg-based and Protestant-run *Oberrheinische Zeitung*, which reflected the views of the Freiburg liberals, whose influence at the university and in city politics waned after the purging of anti-Catholic sentiments. The significance of the *Süddeutsche Zeitung* undoubtedly lies in providing a voice for Catholics in Baden, as they represented the majority of citizens in the grand duchy (and a supermajority in the southern rural areas). Both of these papers, however, were not very popular and struggled to keep up with the more liberal papers from the liberal enclaves. As Hildegard Müller has detailed, the *ObRhZtg* catapulted ahead of the *Freiburger Zeitung* (*FZ*) in subscriptions by 1847, with the more liberal paper jumping to 2,000 subscriptions while the *FZ* languished around 950.[67] These conservative papers were also expressly anti-Jewish, although the *Mannheimer Morgenblatt* became an important outlet during the 1845 debate on Jewish emancipation and Jewish reform, showing that it could still be a paper of publication for a group it officially opposed.

What the previous exposition about newspapers in the Grand Duchy of Baden reveals is the transition from the pre-1830 political newspapers with advertisements and official announcements (like the *Karlsruhe Zeitung*) to organs that had not only "leading articles" (*leitende Artikeln*) but also spaces on the back pages for individuals to present their own issues. This development was additionally a reflection of the newspapers' transition into the party papers of the 1848 revolution and the 1850s, where different papers contained only certain viewpoints rather than supplying diverse opinions within one location. Badenese newspapers continued to evolve, and they became more open, thus providing venues in which people from all over the ideological spectrum could find their niche. But this project has not used those papers, like the *Freisinnige*, *Der Wächter am Rhein*, and the other short-lived liberal papers of the 1840s, as they had minimal impact on German Jewish lives. However, these papers did serve an important function: they were directed in an oppositional manner and generally supported the idea of Jewish emancipation, much like the *Deutsche Zuschauer* and Karl Mathy's *Rundschau* (Heidelberg).[68] Instead, this project has concentrated on long-standing major newspapers published in the bigger cities and within which Jewish voices were more present.

THE DEVELOPMENT OF JEWS' PARTICIPATION IN THE GERMAN PRESS

The development of the German press landscape from the Enlightenment through the Vormärz affected the ways in which Jews were able to participate in the discussions about Jewish emancipation and religious reform during the 1840s. The Enlightenment's incorporation of toleration and individualism brought attention to Jewish lives as individuals and as a group, and Jews were required to respond to others' assertions in ways they never previously had to.

Within the German public sphere, the first German Jew to have a sustained presence was Moses Mendelssohn (1729–86). Mendelssohn wrote on more than just Judaism, covering matters of import to a broad readership, such as defining the scope and limits of the Enlightenment. Mendelssohn was active as a journal editor—coediting *Der Chamäleon* (The chameleon), a moral weekly, and publishing *Kohelet Mussar* (The teacher of morals), the first Hebrew-language journal. Both journals were a result of Mendelssohn's engagement with the Berlin Enlightenment, though the former was also linked to his association with other scholars at the *Gelehrtes Kaffeehaus* (learned coffeehouse) in Berlin.[69]

Mendelssohn's stature towers above others of his generation and of most individuals in the history of German Jewry. His engagement, erudition, and publishing success during the Berlin Enlightenment earned him the respect of his Jewish and non-Jewish peers, yet also the scorn of those who believed he provided the basis for Judaism and Jewry's destruction.[70] His most important intercessions—among the many—were securing Dohm's services to write

Über die bürgerliche Verbesserung der Juden and publication of his magnum opus *Jerusalem; or, On Religious Power and Judaism* (1783), which argued directly about Judaism's modernity and about the need for the state to allow religious freedom.[71] His publications often combatted the anti-Jewish sentiments of important scholars and also dealt with conversion challenges from those who believed Judaism was an unenlightened religion.[72]

Mendelssohn's *Kohelet Mussar*, published during the 1750s, only lasted for two issues and encompassed eight pages in total, though its importance went far beyond its limited print run. The journal devoted itself to spreading Enlightenment values and also promoted Hebrew as a scholarly language—a venture that proved untenable at that time. However, *Kohelet Mussar* was the beginning point for the "intellectual writer" to become "one of the spokesmen in the Jewish public sphere."[73] Mendelssohn did not, however, live to see the results of his efforts.

Mendelssohn's role in bridging the Christian-Jewish divide and in creating a sustained presence in the publishing world is well known. However, a few years before *Kohelet Mussar* came to fruition, Benjamin Croneburg from Neuwied (in the Rhineland) published two periodicals in Judeo-German: *Der Grosse Schauplatz* and the *Kuriöser Antiquarius*. However, as Jacob Toury suggests, Croneburg made a limited impact in educating Jews in High German, due to the journal's low journalistic and intellectual quality and the author's own poor grasp of German.[74]

The Emden-Eibeschütz controversy, which began in 1752, shows another early instance of Jewish participation in the German press. The controversy involved two prominent rabbis (Jacob Emden and Jonathan Eibeschütz) and their respective supporters. The controversy started when Eibeschütz's opponents claimed that he was promulgating discredited Sabbatean messianic beliefs among his congregants. In terms of this debate's relevance for Jews' participation in the press, focus needs to be on the medium and locations of the arguments instead of their content. While many Jews expressed themselves in print by using Jacob Emden's Hebrew-language printing press, important contributions by and about Jews also appeared in gebildete German-language journals, including the *Göttingische Zeitung von gelehrten Sachen* (known later as the *Göttingische Gelehrte Anzeigen*) and the *Mecklenburgische Gelehrte Nachrichten*, among others. By the end of this controversy, it was apparent that Jews needed to participate and defend themselves before the general public, due to the amount of writings in German publications that were not controlled by the rabbis.[75]

While the Emden-Eibeschütz controversy was a marker with regard to the participation of Jews in the general press, it does not signify the beginning of a concerted effort by German Jews to publish more regularly about Jewish issues within the German press. Significant numbers of German Jews participating freely and repeatedly in the general press for specifically Jewish purposes would not occur until the nineteenth century. Moreover, what Mendelssohn's writings and the Emden-Eibeschütz controversy reveal is that participation in the German world of letters at that time was geared toward one specific *Schicht* (stratum) of German society—the decision-makers who were responsible for the Jews' political and social situation. In both examples, the presence of individual Hebrew- and German-language newspapers indicates that there were indeed two mostly, though not completely, separate publics in German society around 1750.

Later during the German Enlightenment, Isaac Euchel—a student of Kant's, an admirer of Mendelssohn's, and a member of a new, educated Jewish elite (the *Maskilim* [educators])—created *Ha-Me'assef* (*The Gatherer*, 1783–1812). Euchel modeled *Ha-Me'assef* after popular Enlightenment journals, like the *Berlinische Monatsschrift*—one of the most successful periodicals of its era—and some scholars consider this journal the "beginning of a modern Jewish press."[76] Part of *Ha-Me'assef*'s success came from its support network, including those in the *Gesellschaft der Förderer der hebräischen Sprache* (Society of the promoters of the Hebrew language), though it was limited by the choice of Hebrew as its print language. This journal intended to close the gap between German Jews and German Christians by inculcating other Jews with the values and knowledge that the Maskilim had adopted themselves, and moving German Jewry closer to the rest of society, "out of the control of the rabbis."[77] In fact, the Maskilim needed to be the interlocutors for this engagement, since rabbis—through translation, concealment, and Judaizing—had controlled and "heavily monitored" secular knowledge and its dissemination to central European Jewry throughout the early modern era.[78]

At the beginning of the nineteenth century, there was a dramatic change in German Jewish print culture. New German Jewish journals made the switch to German, as seen in the journal *Sulamith* (first printed in 1806) by David Fränkel and Joseph Wolf. The first advantage of this switch was an expanded readership, including both princes and state officials. Second, and perhaps more importantly, the journal educated the masses of German Jews in the German language, especially those not attending educational institutions. As Lässig writes, Fränkel and Wolf, like other forward thinkers, had anticipated the necessity of the change to German and its importance in the German states. The periodical's most lasting achievements, however, were that *Sulamith* became the "Sprechsaal der Israeliten" (conference room of the Israelites): it reported news items from around the German Jewish community, participated in the struggle for Gleichstellung, and promoted the reform of German Jewry, including changing religious practices and women's position in Jewish society.[79] As the first German Jewish paper to be so involved in the lives of its constituents, it provided an invaluable organ in which German Jewry could participate in discussions about their lives on a more regular basis. However, by the late 1830s, when German Jewish newspapers started resembling the local German newspapers, *Sulamith* had been supplanted by both a new generation of German Jewish publications and by written articles and other contributions in the broader German press.

These new German Jewish publications appeared in two distinct waves. The first wave, which appeared during the 1820s and '30s, included journals that were based on and promoted the new *Wissenschaft des Judentums* (science of Judaism), including Leopold Zunz's *Zeitschrift für die Wissenschaft des Judentums* (Journal for the science of Judaism) and Abraham Geiger's *Wissenschaftliche Zeitschrift für jüdische Theologie* (Scholarly journal for Jewish theology). Both journals devoted themselves to the scholarly practice of history, which the creators acquired at German universities, and the men behind these journals used these new methods to interpret modern Judaism. Another journal among the first wave was *Der Jude* (The Jew), a political journal written by Gabriel Riesser. Riesser's focus on Gleichstellung was unique, and no other German Jewish journal was ambitious enough to emulate Riesser's endeavor.[80] This first wave of journals, thus, set the stage for later journals, like Zacharias Frankels's *Zeitschrift für religiöse Interessen des Judenthums* (Journal for the religious interests of Jewry), which began publication in the mid-1840s. A second wave of German Jewish journals included those that established themselves as news- and opinion-oriented newspapers similar to local German periodicals. This tradition began in May 1837 with the appearance of the *Allgemeine Zeitung des Judenthums* (*AZdJ*), edited by Rabbi Ludwig Philippson in Magdeburg. The *AZdJ* was "the first 'Jewish' one [newspaper] in the full sense," and it ran until 1922.[81]

Both types of publications were undeniably important. Scholarly journals brought a critical analysis of Judaism to the German Jewish public, and they provided a platform for modern Jewish scholars to present their views on Judaism and its future. However, these journals were by German Jewish elites for other German Jewish elites; they were not meant for the masses. On the other hand, the German Jewish newspapers started to resemble bourgeois German printing sensibilities in how they integrated debating and educational functions; they also adopted similar printing conventions, such as more regular printings and printing rubrics, including the leitende Artikeln. The German

Jewish newspapers were thus able to market themselves to a broader audience, and their success can be seen in their larger readerships—*Sulamith* had a readership of 2,800, while the *AZdJ* had a readership of approximately 16,000. German Jewish newspapers became, as Judith Bleich surmises, an "ideal media" for religious discussions within German Jewry, though the German press was also well-suited for this task.[82]

German Jewish newspapers flourished not only due to internal dynamics within German and German Jewish society but also as the result of external events. In particular, the Damascus Affair of 1840 and the rabbinical conferences of 1844–46 helped shape the German Jewish press in important ways. The Damascus Affair, which involved an accusation of blood libel against Damascus Jews who had been falsely accused of murdering a Franciscan monk, mobilized German Jews to create journals to report on and defend Jews around the world. The journals *Der Orient* (The Orient, founded 1840), *Der Israelit des neunzehnten Jahrhunderts* (The Israelite of the nineteenth century, founded 1839), and the *Israelitische Annalen* (founded 1839) all joined the *AZdJ* in printing news about the affair. Collectively, these journals became important information sources for German Jews, as they also combatted many biased reports from leading "liberal" German newspapers.[83]

However, none of these new journals—led by reformers—represented the interests of the majority of Jews living in Germany at that time: the traditional and the Orthodox. Orthodox Jews, as a whole, did not engage much in the publishing industry at that time, especially when compared to their reformist counterparts. A notable exception was Rabbi Samson Raphael Hirsch, who published both books and pamphlets, such as *Horeb* (1837) and *The Nineteen Letters* (1836). Hirsch and other modern Orthodox voices made limited use of the existent German Jewish press, as it was the only available platform to write opinions and advertise vacant positions to the mass of German Jewry.[84] For example, Rabbi Jakob Löwenstein from Gailingen (Baden) used the *AZdJ* to ask the Brunswick conference attendees to clarify what they meant by "Fortbildung des Judenthums" (advancement of Jewry); he also published his full response to the answer in the *AZdJ*. Despite confidently printing their ideas and arguments within the German Jewish press, Orthodox contributions to the pre-1845 German Jewish press were subjected to the perspectives and control of reformist editors, who not only framed these articles for the audience but also criticized the articles through introductory remarks.[85] Although not the ideal situation for the Orthodox, it was a beginning.

This situation in the regular German Jewish press made it incumbent on Orthodox Jews to form a journal of their own, to have a place where their views could be expounded on and spread within the German Jewish public sphere. In 1845, in response to the Brunswick rabbinical conference of 1844 and its publication in the pages of the *AZdJ*, Jacob Ettlinger (chief rabbi in Altona [Schleswig-Holstein]) and Samuel Enoch (director of the Altona Talmud Torah school) began publishing *Der treue Zions-Wächter* (The loyal guardians of Zion, *TZW*) and *Shomer Tsion ha-Ne'eman* (The loyal guardians of Zion, a Hebrew supplement to *TZW*). As its name implies, the German-language *TZW* counterbalanced Jewish religious reform, and as a result of its editors' efforts, it gave Orthodox Jews a sense of public pride. Furthermore, the *TZW* "convinced the Orthodox of the crucial role played by communications media in the modern world." Such developments laid the foundation for later, more successful Orthodox journals, most notably *Jeschrun* (founded 1854), *Der Israelit* (founded 1860), and *Die jüdische Presse* (founded 1870).[86]

As a whole, the German Jewish press helped transform Jewish life in the first half of the nineteenth century: it served as an educational medium, acted as important forums of informational exchange and opinion, and functioned as a motor of language change from Yiddish to High German. All of these processes facilitated the embourgeoisement and integration of German Jews. Yet there is one often-overlooked aspect of the German Jewish press—the interactions between the German Jewish and the local German newspapers. These publications did not exist in mutually exclusive universes, and the German Jewish newspapers were not a "ghetto press." As seen throughout the *Allgemeine Zeitung des Judenthums*, the German Jewish press depended on the local presses for local news items, and in some cases, Jewish editors allowed non-Jews to publish items on their pages.[87] But it was not just a one-way relationship. The German Jewish newspapers were also suppliers of news to the local papers, as seen in the *Mannheimer Abendzeitung*. More importantly, however, the interactions between the two presses show that the German Jewish one was not just "for Jews, by Jews"; the platform was more open, and while incorporating the aforementioned sentiment, reflected the broader goals of societal integration and dissimilation. The German Jewish press became an important platform where Jews could communicate with each other, regardless of where they lived, and in which their voices stood "side-by-side with those of non-Jews."[88]

Yet for all of the ink spilled about the German Jewish press, that is but one facet of the experience for German Jews within the broad spectrum of German newsprint. The German Jewish press actually reveals little about the local debates and issues that concerned Jews in the public realm and which were read by their non-Jewish neighbors. In light of this reality, this study moves forward with an analysis of how Jews participated in the German-language press to detail the public sentiments of this minority and to explore how these much larger issues facing German Jewry were interpreted, formulated, implemented, and argued within these local and pan-German press contexts. Moreover, as newspapers became more popular and accessible, Jews' statements and lives increased in visibility, and their incorporation into the press demonstrated that they used newspapers in ways analogous to their neighbors. Participation in the local and pan-German press was a performance to demonstrate to Christians that Jews had fulfilled their part of the quid pro quo. Moreover, many of the contributions of Jews to the press had a profound effect within German society. By inserting themselves into discussions at various junctures, Jews were in a position to potentially influence readers' and lawmakers' perception about Jewish rights and Judaism while hopefully steering discussions toward emancipation.

TWO

JEWISH EMANCIPATION IN THE BADENESE AND GERMAN PRESS

> The emancipation of the Jews here is progressing slowly, but is definitely moving forward.
>
> —Correspondent from the Duchy of Nassau, *Frankfurter Journal*, May 13, 1844, Nr. 133 (B)

The development of Jews' participation in the Badenese and German press during the 1840s was a direct result of the confluence of several important histories—that of the development of the Grand Duchy of Baden itself, the evolution of Jewish rights and religion as a function of the major political changes in German and Badenese society, and progression within German public sphere, including the evolution of newsprint and the means by which individuals—including Jews and non-Jews—were able to contribute to local and pan-German news outlets. By far the two most important topics for German Jews—regardless of state—were Jewish emancipation and internal Jewish religious reform. Regardless of the discussion, the two topics—which were part of the framework in the evolution of Jewish rights—were inextricably linked: one could not discuss emancipation without delving into religious issues. This was a function of the "hardwired" religious society in which Jews found themselves throughout much of the nineteenth century. The concept of a secularized society—which would need to be created (or would de facto be created) in order for Jews to be included as full members of German society—was supported only by a minority of individuals, as German princes and legislators throughout most of this period implicitly or explicitly believed in the idea of the "Christian state."[1]

Such notions about the nature of society provided the foundation for beliefs about practically everything, even officials' responses to anti-Jewish violence. These beliefs and the responses to these beliefs became more public as the Badenese and pan-German newspapers developed along ideological lines and started presenting more news to the public, including correspondent reports and above-the-line feuilleton pieces that blurred the boundary between fact and opinion.[2] One of the major ways that we can observe Jewish participation in the local and pan-German press is by interrogating how Jews responded to issues that were existential in nature and affected them daily. The Haber Affair of 1843 to 1845, which directly impacted the lives of the Jews of Karlsruhe (and more broadly the Jews of Baden), shows the importance of local and pan-German newspapers to Jews' constant and overall struggle for emancipation, including the continuities of anti-Jewish tropes and beliefs. Yet this affair also reflects the struggle within German society itself, as the forces of liberalism and democracy expanded and clashed with the conservative and monarchical state.

Toward the end of the affair, in late February 1844, seventeen Badenese noblemen published the following in the *Kölnische Zeitung* (*KölZtg*): "We hereby repudiate the unfounded and erroneous opinions that we earlier made of an honorable judgement in the dispute in question, and likewise do so for all derived consequences. And we will (in this) relevant case not refuse further satisfaction from Herr von Haber."[3] With this statement, hidden in the classified section of the *KölZtg*, these noblemen conferred *Satisfaktion* (societal respectability and acceptability within an honor situation) on Moritz von Haber—a Jewish convert to Christianity and the eldest son of Salomon von Haber, who had been the Grand Duchy of Baden's most important court banker during its aggrandizement and centralization during the Napoleonic and Restoration eras. The Haber Affair had begun almost six years earlier (1838) as the byproduct of international politics during the Carlist Wars in Spain, and had resulted in Haber's refusal to duel an English officer (Haber was the suspected informant leading to the Englishman's arrest), which earned the enmity of a particular Badenese noble, Julius von Göler. Even after the Englishman's death, the affair continued to cause ripples, as indicated by the fact that Haber had a ball invitation rescinded in 1843 by an associate of Göler's. In response to this slight, Haber challenged Göler to a duel. As a sign of disrespect, Göler avoided Haber by convening a makeshift "honor court"—the seventeen noblemen mentioned previously—to reject the challenge. Instead of dropping the challenge, Haber enlisted a friend, Michael von Werefkin (a Russian noble), to help him arrange the duel. However, Göler continued his evasiveness and directly challenged Werefkin instead; these two men dueled and killed each other on September 2, 1843.

Yet as the recantation in February 1844 shows, the affair did not stop with the death of one of the principals. In the six months prior to the nobles' mea culpa, news about the Haber Affair spread far and wide across the German states because of Haber's centrality in this honor transgression that transcended class, national, religious, and ethnic lines—it was as newsworthy an event as they come. This series of events also brought the grand duchy into conflict with its own image as the most liberal of the German states. The state's transgressions were numerous during the affair's investigations: the state denied Haber his right to a lawyer, it did not follow protocol in allowing a letter from Haber's adversary to be given to him in prison, state authorities illegally searched papers in the Haber home, and—after Haber was done serving his two-week sentence for being the "Anstifter" (inciter) of the duel—the state unceremoniously escorted him (a Badenese citizen) out of the grand duchy into exile, as if he were a "tramp (*Landstreicher*) from a guest-friendly bathing resort."[4] And while there were liberals in Baden who came to Haber's defense, such as his lawyer and assemblyman, August Sander, there was a clear indication made during the Haber Affair—in the form of anti-Jewish violence and rhetoric—that many in society did not welcome Jewish emancipation. For an average reader of the German and Badenese press, it would have been difficult to remain unaware of this affair.

For the Jews of Karlsruhe, the nobles' apology was of little solace; as a result of the general animus against Haber among the citizens and the elite, combined with the extant anti-Jewish sentiment in the city, a pogrom broke out following Göler's funeral procession on the evening of September 5, 1843. The tumult that followed caused significant physical damage to the Haber home, but it extended far beyond there as the 150-person mob also attacked nearby Jews and Jewish businesses—a scene reminiscent of the 1819 Hep-Hep riots.[5] The mob was given a free hand by authorities, who, either because of malicious intent or ineptitude, did not adequately prepare for the event despite the fact that rumors about it had circulated freely in the capital. The grand duchy, which many people considered a beacon of liberalism among the German states, descended briefly into chaos and showed again how Janus-faced Badenese society was.

The events of the Haber Affair were transmitted to Germans via the emerging newspapers in all of the German states. Local and pan-German newspapers covered these events extensively—a far cry from the traditional news coverage of duels. One reason for the generous coverage of the affair was the centrality of a German of Jewish descent—Haber, whose father and brothers were the court bankers in Karlsruhe—and the ongoing public preoccupation with Jewish emancipation. However, another reason that an event like this was such a popular media event was because Haber and the Badenese state "transgress[ed] . . . legal and moral norms."⁶ Such an interest in Jewish rights was punctuated by concurrent public debates in 1843 over Bruno Bauer's "Die Judenfrage," in which the Left Hegelian argued against Jewish emancipation and particularistic religion as a whole, and by the passage of Jewish emancipation by the Rhenish provincial assembly in June.⁷

Despite the negative public reaction in Karlsruhe to Haber and Jews in the Badenese press, newspaper coverage throughout many of the German states was generally on Haber's side and sympathetic to the Jews of Karlsruhe, who had just endured a pogrom. As a result of these events, the Jewish community petitioned once again for Jewish emancipation in early 1844—with the petition by the Karlsruhe community being reported in both Jewish and non-Jewish newspapers.⁸ Shortly thereafter, the Mannheim Jewish community also submitted a supplication to the Lower Assembly in support of emancipation. Such intercessions became more commonplace during the 1840s, as liberals throughout the German states, but especially in Baden, won elections to the Lower Assembly. Such support had made it seem as though Jewish emancipation—despite the occasional negative societal outburst—was "a demand of the period."⁹ In terms of the German Jewish community, involvement in the press was not merely rooted in the fact that the Haber Affair was a popular media event, considering that the issues surrounding this event had significant reverberations in their lives, which, like the Emden-Eibeschütz Affair a century earlier (chap. 1), they could not ignore.

German Jewish participation in the German newspapers in the 1840s was, thus, a reflection of the necessity to be involved in issues of existential importance. The Jews' participation throughout debates on Jewish emancipation and internal Jewish religious reform demonstrated that they were willing to take the initiative, and did not let others define them and their aspirations. Along the way, they redressed the inconsistencies and falsehoods attributed to them and their religion by their antagonists. In addition, Jews staked out positions on many issues that promoted a specifically Jewish interaction and voice in the conversations. Jewish participation throughout different newspapers showed a certain integration into the general society, as Jews appropriated the tools that others had used. This more broadly "showed how deeply print culture had infiltrated German-Jewish culture."¹⁰ However, through most of the 1830s, Jews did not have an appreciable role in the news production industry, with a few notable exceptions.¹¹

One major paper that included Jewish voices as a regular part of its correspondence network during the Vormärz was the *Augsburger Allgemeine Zeitung*. In the early decades of the *AAZ*, Jewish voices were nonexistent, but once Georg Cotta took over the firm upon his father's death in 1832, there was a significant increase in Jews' participation as correspondents. Georg, whose sympathies were more aligned with the liberals of his day (and not necessarily the more moderate liberalism of his father), paid several Jews (and Jewish converts) to write correspondence for the *AAZ*. For instance, Heinrich Heine and Gustav Weil both contributed regularly from outside the German states, the former from Paris and the latter from Egypt. Neither man contributed significantly to discussions on Jewish emancipation in the *AAZ*, although as you see in what follows, Heine used the *AAZ* as a forum to criticize the German states on this topic through an obituary for his friend, Ludwig Marcus. In terms of articles written specifically about Jewish emancipation, Salomon von Haber (Moritz's father) provided information about the Badenese Landtag's deliberations in 1833, and Rabbi Samuel Meyer (chief rabbi for the Kingdom of Württemberg) wrote an essay on the topic in 1845 ("Das auserwählte Volk" [The chosen people]). Meyer's essay directly refuted the arguments of Friedrich Ghillany—a Protestant theologian in Nuremberg who had similar ideas to that of Bruno Bauer—who wrote an essay in the *AAZ* on August 12, 1845.[12] Ghillany, who also published anti-Jewish tracts during the Damascus Affair and throughout the 1840s, used his article to summarize the arguments from his book, *Das Judenthum und die Kritik* (A critique of Jewry), including that Jews only supported themselves through trade and financial transactions, Judaism was antihumanist, circumcision was a sign of separateness, and emancipation was conditional on changes within the Jewish religious community.[13] Another very important intercession on behalf of Jewish emancipation by the *AAZ* was its solicitation of pro- and antiemancipation essays in 1833. Due to the overwhelming response from the public, the *AAZ* only printed one representative essay for each side (for or against) in issues 123 through 125 (May 3 through May 5, 1833). Six years later, in 1839, the *AAZ* again printed articles that represented both sides of the emancipation argument.[14]

Papers other than the *AAZ* also promoted Jewish voices, with a significant increase in appearances in the 1840s in both the Badenese and the pan-German presses. Most of these contributions discussed specifically Jewish issues (emancipation and religious reform) among a very interconfessional audience. Even though these two topics often overlapped—as religious reform was generally considered by Christians to be a precondition for emancipation—it is important to separate them out and see how these arguments developed and evolved separately. Through analyzing how emancipation became a topic for general discussion in the Heidelberg and Mannheim presses, we can observe how comfortable Jews felt in participating in these discussions in a local setting—regardless of how contentious they became.

However, direct participation and argumentation in the German press was not the only method by which arguments about emancipation were furthered. By scouring the newspapers, one can find plentiful examples of publicity that surround charity and philanthropy within society. Individuals published pleas to support their friends, neighbors, and communities; as seen in the collection lists in these newspapers, many individuals were very generous to these causes. But if we take a closer look at those lists, we see that many Jews contributed to numerous causes. The broadcasting of philanthropy and charity—though it may not have been intended to highlight a specifically Jewish predilection to do so—showed that German Jews participated in the institution of bourgeois giving in a similar fashion to their neighbors. This similarity in ideas and values would become an important facet in Jews' arguments in the press for emancipation.

Another interesting way that we can observe arguments for emancipation—through a less direct appeal—was from the remembrance of those who passed away. While in most newspapers the *Todes-Anzeigen* (death announcements) were a standard practice, they were not generally effective at communicating more than a brief expression of sorrow for a family at their loss. In some locations, like in Baden, people were notified through the *Kirchenbücherauszüge* (church book extracts), which listed deaths alongside births and marriages. This format provided mere perfunctory data about the individuals who died. In the pages of the press, a writer would occasionally give the public a carefully crafted yet opinionated essay of an individual they deemed worthy of public recognition and remembrance. While there were few of these *Nekrologe* (obituaries), their appearance was all the more striking when they did appear, and that included two obituaries about prominent Jewish individuals, Ludwig Marcus (one of the founding members of the Society for the Scientific Study of Judaism) and David Zimmern (one of the original appointees to the *Oberrat der Israeliten Badens*). These Nekrologe, the former in the *AAZ* and the latter in the *MAbZ*, while presenting stories from the lives of these individuals, argued for more than remembrance: by presenting the lives of these men to the public as exemplars of the quid pro quo, they implicitly (if not explicitly at points) argued on behalf of all Jews in the German states and Baden for emancipation and societal inclusion.

THE 1845 PETITION FOR JEWISH EMANCIPATION AND THE NORTHERN BADENESE PRESS

In Baden during the 1830s, newspapers lacked the sort of freedom seen in other parts of the German states, either in Prussia or in generally archconservative Hannover.[15] It was not until the 1840s that an observable shift in publishing practices in the grand duchy facilitated a lifting of restrictions within which Jews could express themselves. It was no coincidence that the increase in periodicals throughout Baden was a product of the increased liberal sentiment in society and the ability of liberals to influence society through legislation. The increasing liberalism—though by no means a torrent—allowed for more favorable discussions about Jewish emancipation, often despite many liberals' personal opposition to Jewish rights throughout much of the Vormärz. Jewish emancipation functioned as a barometer of German liberalism's commitment to its purported embrace of equality, and the constant and consistent debate about Jewish rights in the Badenese Lower Assembly reinforced the notion that German liberals were both the "best friends" of the Jews and their biggest obstacle—it was Baden's Janus-faced relationship with its Jewish population writ small. The fight for Jewish emancipation in Baden reflected the broader struggle throughout the German states, yet Baden—which saw the quickest liberal ascendancy, combined with a rapid evolution/explosion of newsprint—was perhaps the best place to see these debates within public view. The Mannheim/Heidelberg public sphere—the largest and most influential region in the grand duchy—was the most important and dynamic location in which this struggle for emancipation played out with a panoply of Jewish voices.

Much like other efforts for emancipation, an 1845 petition for Jewish emancipation put forth by the Badenese Jews was unsuccessful, but unlike the other debates (with minor exceptions), this effort was front and center in public view. Mannheim and Heidelberg were the grand duchy's respective financial and intellectual capitals, and both had significant Jewish populations. These cities were relatively liberal in their treatment of Jews politically, despite the occasional tension and flare-ups of violence against Jews by those lined up against the political and financial elites.[16] In both cities, numerous Jews participated in local and state politics, as the intellectual and economic German Jewish elites had already been granted the status of *Orts/Gemeindebürger* (local citizen). This designation conferred on these individual Jews active voting rights, which allowed them to both vote and be elected as *Wahlmänner* (electors)—the men responsible for electing the state *Abgeordneten* (assemblymen). Their political struggle centered on the ability to be voted into public office, something that had been denied to all Jews regardless of their importance to crown and country. However, this fight was not just for those Jews who constituted the elites within German Jewish society; rather, it involved all Jews, including those at the bottom of the socioeconomic scale. Many poor Jews in Baden were not yet local citizens (they were still Schutzbürger), and Jews as a whole, of all wealth levels, strove to acquire the right to free movement, since at that time they could only legally live in 11 percent of Badenese towns. Indeed, throughout all the German states, the fight for equality often focused on poor Jews as well as those who were the most traditional in terms of religiosity. The struggle for pan-Jewish rights was a novelty in the nineteenth century, as states often targeted poor Jews and treated them more harshly than wealthier Jews.[17] Even though political, social, and economic rights took center stage in the fight for Gleichstellung, the debates about these rights were ultimately about the Jewish religion and customs, cultural modernity, and Jews' ability to be modern Germans worthy of respect, honor, and inclusion.

In order to properly analyze the debates about Jews during the 1840s in the Badenese press, it is necessary to understand how Jewish emancipation functioned legislatively on a governmental level. Starting in 1831 with the rise of the liberals to power in the Lower Assembly of the Badenese Landtag, Jews were able to petition the Lower Assembly for emancipation. Once received, petitions were entered into the parliamentary record (sometimes they were even read aloud), and then a commission composed of Abgeordneten from the Lower Assembly convened to research, discuss, and produce a report about the topic. The commission reporter (*Berichterstatter*) then read the report to the assembly, a debate ensued, and, finally, a vote occurred. This process could be followed by locals and other interested parties in many newspapers' correspondent reports from the Landtag, and sometimes these reports included the texts of the debates themselves, instead of just summaries (though this privilege of printing the official protocols was granted only to government-friendly newspapers).

Throughout the Vormärz, Jews petitioned every Landtag that gathered in Karlsruhe. In each attempt for Gleichstellung by Jews up to 1846, the commission returned an unfavorable opinion. Even though Liberals regularly claimed the majority of seats in the Badenese Landtag after 1831, no more than 30 percent of the delegates viewed Jewish Gleichstellung favorably.[18] And the opposing side (greater than 70 percent) was composed of many who identified as members of the Liberal faction, including anti-Jewish delegates such as Karl von Rotteck (who argued that Jewish inclusion was not an important issue when compared to the plight of Christians or even other liberal and societal concerns) and Adolf Sander (who in 1837 was the Berichterstatter for the Lower Assembly's commission that dealt with Jewish emancipation). Sander based his position on his belief in the "Christian state," and he held that Jewish emancipation would be the first step of society toward becoming atheist or secular—a view shared by many politicians and thinkers across the liberal and conservative ideological divide in the German states. Along with Rotteck and many other liberals, Sander believed Jews to be particularistic, antiquated, and antagonistic toward Christians as well as out of step with modernity. Such antipathetic views about Jews and Judaism by Badenese Liberals in the Landtag were prevalent until the "radical," or more democratic, wing came to power in the elections of 1845 and 1846. It was no coincidence that a change in attitudes vis-à-vis Jewish rights coincided with the rise of the Free Religion movement, which sought to "erase divisions between Protestants, Catholics, and Jews and prepare the way for a spiritual union of free German citizens," as well as the challenge that such a movement posed to biconfessional states (Catholic/Protestant [including Reformed]).[19] Despite the dominance of anti-Jewish views in the Landtag, these views did not go uncontested.

The debates in Mannheim and Heidelberg about Jewish emancipation during 1845 came on the heels of two very important events within the history of the grand duchy—the *Verfassungsfeier* (constitutional celebration) of August 1843 and the Haber Affair shortly thereafter. The juxtaposition of these events provides an important lens through which to view Jews' struggles for emancipation. The Verfassungsfeier was a euphoric celebration across the grand duchy that celebrated twenty-five years of constitutional order and the state's progression toward a more liberal, rights-based society. As a remembrance of the state's move away from absolutism, celebrations became public displays; the (liberal) press recorded the events, and Karl Mathy collected and published the accounts. Mathy believed this pamphlet "[gave] a true representation of the real disposition of the *Volk*."[20] Throughout the pamphlet, Mathy reproduced speeches that tied the past to the future, thanked Grand Duke Karl for the constitution, expressed national German sentiment, and advanced liberals' aims, including their most important issue, freedom of the press.

Notable in the front of Mathy's pamphlet was a description of the celebration in Mannheim, the most important "liberal" city in the grand duchy and the location where the largest festivities occurred. During the Mannheim celebration—and curiously included in the middle of the text—the lawyer Dr. Elias Eller, an influential member of the Mannheim Jewish community and also one of the most dedicated democrats in the city, gave a rousing speech. He spoke before the crowd and trumpeted the belief that the Badenese constitution was moving the people away from the "capriciousness" (*Willkühr*) of absolutist rule toward "rights and the constitution." After extolling the virtues of the bourgeoisie (*Bürgerthum*) to which he and other acculturated German Jews belonged, Eller mentioned the *Volkswohl* (popular prosperity) as one of the main causes to be furthered. He ended his speech with a rhetorical flourish that was indicative of the bourgeoisie's view of itself: "ihm (das Bürgerthum) gehört die Gegenwart, ihm die Zukunft ... Das Bürgerthum lebe hoch!" (to it [the bourgeoisie] belongs the present, to it the future ... Long live the bourgeoisie!).[21] That Eller could participate in such a celebration and say such sentiments, despite not being an official first-class citizen of the state, suggests that many liberals in Baden in 1843, as well as a broader swath of society, had no problem with Eller's role and comments. Alternatively, Eller's participation was an opportunity for liberals in Baden to promote Jewish equality and contributions to constitutional life.

The Haber Affair, in comparison to the Verfassungsfeier (which took place mere weeks before this event), was a brief societal descent back into absolutist and antisemitic anarchy. Spurred on by conservative, elitist, and anti-Jewish elements in Karlsruhe, a mob attacked the Haber home after the mutually fatal duel between Göler and Werefkin. The mob then attacked several Jewish businesses while the state (through its prior knowledge of the planned unrest and the gendarmes who encouraged more violence) sat by and did little to protect *its* citizens—a seemingly deliberate abrogation of its role as guarantor of the rights that it had just celebrated. The state's abandonment of liberal and constitutional norms through its treatment of Haber and other officials during the affair, in juxtaposition with the Verfassungsfeier, revealed a society struggling to come to grips with those democratic and liberal norms as a daily, widespread practice to be applied to *all* citizens. In the end, Haber's adversaries and those deemed responsible by the state for the anti-Jewish violence were punished with fines and/or jail time, but the state did not accept *any* responsibility for the environment it had fomented. By the time the Haber Affair concluded in 1845, there was a full-scale societal debate about Jewish rights; however, this time there were many Jews who also participated in this public discussion.

The public debate in 1845 took on a more public nature when Jews from Mannheim responded in the press to the commission report by Assemblyman Franz Burkardt Fauth to the Lower Assembly, a report that the *Mannheimer Morgenblatt* printed over the course of six days in late February and early March 1845.[22] The report, which returned a negative assessment of the Jews' petition for immediate and unequivocal emancipation, was similar to prior commission reports. Throughout the report, Fauth repeated many untruths about Judaism and even misstated some facts about Jewish existence in the grand duchy, basing many of his statements on Ghillany's *Das Judenthum und die Kritik*. Fauth's core argument was that Jews could not become full citizens without giving up specific perceived aspects of Judaism, including Jewish national aspirations (that is, claiming Jewish separateness within another state) as well as what was perceived to be hateful and anti-Christian dogmas. Fauth argued that Jews, if they were emancipated, would not give up their national prejudices. However, Fauth also believed changes to Judaism and Jewish practices could potentially be given up in exchange for their emancipation. Fauth then claimed that the decision of the commission had nothing to do with religion and beliefs; rather, it was Jewish morals and the ways in which Jews lived (foremost, their antisociality) that was the cause of yet another negative evaluation.

Yet throughout his report, Fauth referenced Jewish holidays and religious texts to base his claim that Jews were different and that the "Christian state" could not lift the four remaining political disabilities off the Jews. Overall, Fauth refused to give credit to any changes that Jews had already made to satisfy the quid pro quo and, furthermore, argued that the petitioners did not have "the mandate [*Vollmacht*] of the greater portion of their people," whom he believed had not separated "from their nationality, their Talmudic statutes, their dietary laws, their sabbath celebrations, their language, their understanding of pure and impure, their separate customs, and their haggling." However, Fauth contradicted himself in this report. As he offered Jews the possibility of fulfilling the quid pro quo, he slammed that door shut by equating full citizenship with Christian mores: "our states touch upon the elements of *Christianity*, and the predominant nationality of the Jews in this separates us." To close his commission report, Fauth relied on the words of Heidelberg professor Heinrich Eberhard Gottlob Paulus's 1831 report to the Badenese Landtag about Jewish emancipation and reiterated the tropes that were common to both this work and Ghillany's, most notably that Jews were a "state within a state" and that they were applying under "false pretenses" (*falschen Prätensionen*) of supposed "truthful improvement" (*wahres Besserwerden*).[23] Throughout his commission report, Fauth combined the older argument of Jews' separateness with the more modern "theologico-political arguments" that would later appear in Friedrich Julius Stahl's 1847 essay, *Der christliche Staat und sein Verhältniss zu Deismus und Judenthum* (The Christian state and its relationship to deism and Jewry), in which Stahl (a Jewish convert to Protestantism) proposed that Judaism's transformation into a state-accepted (and not just tolerated, in which Jews would have limited rights) religion would secularize and negatively affect the state.[24]

There were several responses to Fauth, observable in all three of the major regional papers. The first reaction was a direct response to the report in the

Heidelberger Journal from March 3, 1845, which in turn started a debate among Christian contributors in the *Heidelberger Journal* spanning five articles and two months.[25] The next response, by two members of the *Synagogenrat* (synagogue council)—Joseph Hohenemser (the community *Vorsteher* [head]) and another council member, Eller—appeared in the *Mannheimer Morgenblatt* on March 7, 1845 (dated March 3).[26] Adolph Zimmern, head of the Heidelberg Jewish community, published a response on March 8 (in the *MM*) and on March 10 (in the *MAbZ*) that also directly attacked Fauth's report. Fauth then responded to all of these Jewish responses on March 12, 1845, while an anonymous article attacking Fauth's report appeared on March 13. After Fauth's response to the heads of the Jewish community, two other pieces by Mannheim Jews appeared in the *MAbZ*: one by Mannheim's first Jewish *Obergerichtshofadvokat* (higher regional court lawyer) Dr. Leopold Ladenburg and another by *Klausrabbiner* (seminary rabbi) Hayum Wagner.[27] This public discussion about Jews' rights was quite different than those from prior years, as exemplified by the muted public response in 1842 when Heinrich Bernhard Oppenheim, the first Jewish *Privatdozent* (lecturer) at the University of Heidelberg, wrote two pieces supporting Jewish emancipation for the *Mannheimer Abendzeitung*.[28] A month lapsed before anyone responded to Oppenheim's piece in the *MAbZ*—one article highlighted the business dealings of one Jew and extrapolated his behavior to all Jews, one article denounced this generalization, and another presented documents from the Netherlands in support of emancipation—though none of these articles dealt directly with the earlier commission report.[29] Another big difference between the 1842 and 1845 discussions was that Fauth responded directly to the community, which might have been a sign that he felt compelled to respond in order to reassert anti-Jewish sentiment in the face of the increasingly Jewish-friendly Mannheim public.

The debate in the *Heidelberger Journal* is particularly noteworthy, as the first two respondents were Christians who gave their opinions about emancipation. In general, these two articles were hostile to traditional rabbinical Judaism but were not anti-Jewish overall; that is, the respondents held not all Jews to be outside the German nation but only those who stood fast to what they perceived were outdated traditions. Both openly called for the incorporation of those Jews who had accepted the radical platform of the Frankfurt-based Reformfreunde (RF), a society whose members advocated religious reform along the lines of three principles:

1. We recognize in Mosaism the possibility of unlimited further development.

2. The collection called the Talmud, as well as all the rabbinic writings and statutes that rest on it, possess no binding force for either us in dogma or in practice.
3. We neither expect nor desire a messiah who is to lead the Israelites back to the land of Palestine; we recognize no fatherland other than that to which we belong by birth or civil status.[30]

As the second respondent wrote, "in any case, the whole world will give their approval, and will then grant these reformed Jews equality, and if they appear to us as *such* [reformed] Jews, then we will willingly reach out our hands in brotherhood."[31] In other words, until Judaism was reformed enough for Christians, Jews should be kept in a different legal status (see chap. 3 for more on the RF). The next three articles in this series, while related to the first two, almost constituted a separate discussion, as they more directly engaged with each other, although all of them stemmed from what is called the "cardinal question" (*Kardinalfrage*) in the *Heidelberger Journal* discussion—whether or not Jews in Baden should be politically and socially equalized. Christians wrote these three articles, and each of them looked at emancipation through juridical-occupational lenses, as they considered the laws governing Jewish work and participation in "German" occupations as the "only real emancipation."[32]

Badenese Jews would not just let others dictate the public debate. One response, from March 7, 1845, was conspicuous not because of what it did include but because of what it did not. The entire *Berichtigung* (corrective) from the Synagogue Council was directed at one falsehood written by Fauth, which described the Talmud as the basis of teaching at one general religious school for German Jewish children in Mannheim.[33] The Synagogue Council countered that the described situation had not been true for some time, and in fact, for the past thirty years (as seen in advertisements from 1816), the only school in town was the Israelitische Volksschule (Israelite elementary school), which used the same educational model as other German schools. As the council argued, teaching the Talmud could not be part of the education program, since the school's board of directors consisted of both Jews and Christians.[34] In Fauth's response to the Synagogenrat, instead of engaging with the arguments presented by his Jewish opponents, he attacked the timing of their responses, victim-blaming Jews for the commission's misunderstanding, saying "you [were] a bit late" and asking "where were the Jews" when the original report from which this information came—the 1837 commission report by Adolf Sander—was published in the Landtag's protocols.[35]

Adolph Zimmern first responded on March 8, 1845, in the *Mannheimer Morgenblatt*, and then republished his response on March 10 in the *Mannheimer Abendzeitung*. Zimmern did not engage Fauth on the contents of his letter but decried that such comments were given in front of the Badenese *Ständeversammlung* (Landtag). Zimmern wrote that "we [the Jewish community] reject the picture of us presented in front of the country with indignation" and that "thankful memories of our greatest benefactor, the wise Carl Friedrich, assuage our grief; but all of the deep wounds of the past centuries . . . bloom anew if a man of your stature disturbs with injustice the soul of that most honorable prince."[36] Fauth dismissed this argumentation by Zimmern (who wrote on behalf of the Heidelberg Jewish community), and he pushed back against Zimmern's criticism of the information in the report—he passed that responsibility onto the commission as a whole. Fauth also pressed Zimmern to respond directly to him only on the form of his report, which he admitted was his responsibility. In one short article, Fauth dismissed the claims by both the Synagogenrat and Zimmern, who publicly aired their problems with the commission's report.[37] Fauth also implied in his response that the Jews could have appealed such inaccuracies made by prior Landtag commissions regarding Gleichstellung.

Both the Synagogenrat and Adolph Zimmern tried to discredit the commission's historical reports, including drawing attention (in Zimmern's case) to the knowingly scandalous and inaccurate nature of them. Zimmern appealed to Fauth's indiscriminately publicly presented, printed, and distributed report as awakening hatred against the Jews, who were just a small proportion of the population. Zimmern further wrote that his own actions should be understood as "an attestation of our indignation, [which] we owe . . . to our [the Jewish community's] honor," since Fauth had spoken in such a high-profile location (the Badenese Landtag) and was himself the commission reporter.[38] Despite Fauth's assertion to the contrary, such an opportunity for rebuttal was not available to Jews back in 1837 when the Sander report was first published—neither the *Mannheimer Morgenblatt* nor the *Mannheimer Abendzeitung* existed at that time. In actuality, Fauth, by deflecting these two comments, demonstrated directly the bad faith with which Zimmern had accused him, and indirectly the bad faith with which the commission had proceeded since the Liberals' ascension in the Landtag in 1831. Moreover, given the recent violence in Karlsruhe during the Haber Affair, Zimmern (and the rest of the Jewish community) surely knew such official expressions of hatred could sow the seeds of violence should another high-profile incident occur.

The last writing in this series was published in the *MM* by an anonymous writer on March 13, 1845. In a very methodical counterstatement, the writer dismissed all of Fauth's claims. Coming on the heels of Fauth's counterargument to Zimmern and the Synagogenrat, this article was an effective rebuttal to the commission's report, and made even clearer the bad faith with which the commission had consistently acted. Foremost among the points were the questions about Jewish observance of the Sabbath and the fulfillment of both important human and patriotic duties: "He [the Jew] thus understands his main obligations." As an anonymous article this was a very effective piece in a conservative and anti-Jewish newspaper. The author wrote in a pro-Jewish tone, and yet he kept himself distant from the subject, referring often to "the Jews" in the third person. However, the article was not completely anonymous; one clue points to the author as having been an engaged member of the Heidelberg Jewish community. Early on in the contribution, the writer used the pronoun *wir* (we) in a passage that he took from Fauth's article, although the original contribution by Fauth never utilized the pronoun *we*.[39] Nonetheless, the article was effective in refuting the negative statements about the Jews and the Jewish religion, and presented an affirmative view of Jewish patriotism and faithfulness as Badenese citizens worthy of emancipation.

The lengthiest and perhaps most effective responses, not surprisingly, were found in the pages of the *MAbZ*, one of the most important "republican" and "radical" papers during the 1848 revolutions.[40] As Baden's most favorable paper on the topic of Jewish emancipation (even more so than either the *Seeblätter* from Constance or the *Oberrheinische Zeitung* from Freiburg) and also the most welcoming to Jewish contributors, the *MAbZ* was not just a paper where one could see favorable sentiments in news reports or in editorials by the editor, Friedrich Moriz Hähner—a committed democrat. It was also a paper where German Jews could contribute items that were important to them. These contributions to the *MAbZ* were distinct from the contributions to the *MM*, most notably because they were longer and not anonymous. Dr. Leopold Ladenburg, an important contributor to Jews' rights in Baden, wrote the first response, while Rabbi Hayum Wagner wrote the second. The fact that two high-profile Jews in the city took the time to confront the commission report is not necessarily noteworthy, especially in the case of Ladenburg, whose occupation and education were in law. Wagner, on the other hand, was the only rabbi in the city to write such a piece. Given Wagner's political views, education, involvement in the Reform movement, and his associations with Ladenburg, his engagement is not surprising.[41]

What was notable about the two pieces in the *MAbZ* attacking Fauth's report was the length of Ladenburg's and Wagner's responses. These were not short comments, but well-argued pieces that cut to the heart of Fauth's motives and methods. Ladenburg started by calling into question Fauth's method of reporting, saying "altogether the truth in relation to facts and unaffiliated judgment should be the first and holiest responsibility of a report-giver." Additionally, Ladenburg called into question the Badenese constitution and argued that all Badeners in section 7 are equal in rights "except where there is an exception." Ladenburg then questioned Fauth's interpretation of section 9, where the Berichterstatter claimed that Jews in Baden existed in an exceptional state, and he responded by arguing that there was no such exception. Ladenburg restated the law as follows: "All citizens of the three Christian confessions have the same claim to all civil and military positions." He also argued that in this formulation, there were no exceptions. As Ladenburg wrote, Jews were not mentioned *specifically* by name as being denied such rights, and therefore, they should be made equal. He went on to show that Fauth completely disregarded the beneficial documents submitted to the chamber and published in the local papers.[42] Ladenburg also lambasted Fauth for ignoring the Dutch government's attestation of the Jews' faithful military service in the Netherlands over the past fifty years. Ladenburg further noted that Dutch Jews' military service was in a country whose capital, Amsterdam, had more Jews than all of Baden.

Ladenburg then took issue with Fauth's description of Badenese Judaism. Ladenburg's strongest arguments both combated the fears that Fauth presented in his report and showed the Berichterstatter's hypocrisy. In the second half of the article, Ladenburg excoriated Fauth's use of Ghillany's *Das Judenthum und die Kritik*, which Ladenburg characterized as a reprisal of Eisenmenger's discredited *Entdecktes Judenthum* from the early eighteenth century. Additionally, he challenged the common accusation (and Christians' fears) that Jews would flock to opened professions, which had yet to happen in the field of law to which Ladenburg belonged. Perhaps most damningly, Ladenburg showed Fauth's (and by extension the commission's) hypocrisy by demonstrating his reliance on "public opinion" (*öffentliche Meinung*) for his general unwillingness to recommend equality, especially when "public opinion" was clamoring for freedom of the press, ministerial accountability, and other new laws. As Ladenburg wrote with some sarcasm, "it would make us very happy, if he [Fauth] would convert himself [to other liberal causes which have public opinion behind them]." That Ladenburg was so "tenacious" (*beharrlich*) is not unique in this instance—he was, according to Dieter Hein, part of a circle of up-and-coming "radical liberals," who, unlike their parents, "fought the fight with all tenacity and severity."[43]

The second article, by Klausrabbiner Wagner, was as informative and biting in its critique of Fauth's report as Ladenburg's, although as the author mentioned, it dealt solely with religion. Wagner's most caustic statement was the following passage about so-called Jewish difference: "The report goes on to say: you (the Jews) differentiate yourselves in the celebration of your Sabbath.... There (see Neander's *General History of the Christian Religion and Church*, Volume 2, pages 512-onwards) we learn, that opposition to Judaism was taken up by moving the Sabbath to Sundays during the 2nd century. It was then not the Jews who separated themselves in celebration of the Sabbath, but rather much more the Christians, who did not want to have anything in common with the Jews." Wagner's deft and historical argumentation left no doubt that he felt that the Jews were not the ones responsible for their situation. Wagner believed that ultimately, the entire argument came down not to the progression of German Jewry to a more bourgeois religion in the style of Protestantism but rather that Fauth, and all of the others who agreed with the commission reporter, never had any intention of looking favorably on Jewish petitions for equality. As he mentioned, the most recent deliberations in the Ständeversammlung were not going to be decided favorably for Jews. Not a single anti-Jewish Abgeordneter defended his position, as it was clear that the group's anti-Gleichstellung position needed no defense. Undoubtedly, this was due to Wagner's observation that the argument was never about the progress of Badenese Jews and the Jewish religion, which had been promised to Jewish citizens in the IX Constitutional Edict in 1809, for "the Jews could never be given equal rights with Christians, because they—are Jews."[44]

These two critiques combined, one from the legal side and the other from the religious, took a stance against the prejudices inherent in the commission's report. But the actual content of these articles, along with all of the other pieces that responded to Fauth's commission's report, are just as important for the actions that they document in terms of Jewish defense, Jewish development, and Jewish honor. Comparing these reactions to the one response in the *Karlsruher Zeitung* to the debates in the Badenese assembly in 1837 and the meager (although important) contributions in the *Mannheimer Abendzeitung* in 1842, we can observe the increasing confidence with which the Jews responded to their accusers and antagonists.[45] Looking farther back, one singular article from 1837 served as a gentle reminder to the public that in section 1 of the IX Constitutional Edict of January 13, 1809, the Badenese state declared Judaism *constitutionsfähig* (constitutionally recognized) and as a recognized religion. Its members—Jews—were thus entitled to equality, according to this author. No other articles about Jewish emancipation appeared in the newspaper at this time, including not even one response to the inaccurate report from the Lower Assembly. And while five responses in the 1845 debate hardly resemble any "breaking of a dam" on their own, these political debates and contributions were more than just theoretical writings. These discussions in the newspaper specifically addressed the political debate taking place in the grand duchy, but there was also an overarching religious aspect to them.

PHILANTHROPY AND REMEMBRANCE IN SERVICE OF EMANCIPATION

Within the Grand Duchy of Baden and in the pan-German press, the emancipation debates were the primary vehicle through which German Jews stated their cases before their fellow countrymen. However, German Jews and their supporters addressed similar issues using other types of writings in these newspapers—through the public acknowledgment of charitable contributions and the use of obituaries (*Nachrufe/Nekrologe*). The utilization of public recognition and presentation of philanthropic and charitable contributions as well as obituaries (the presentation of the life of a deceased person of note) exposed more broadly how the press could be employed as a vehicle to affect change in the long run and how such instances could help build the necessary cultural capital to barter for emancipation.

The philanthropic tradition within Judaism, as seen from today's perspective, is bound up with notions of tzedakah, which is often misinterpreted as "charity." While giving charity is certainly a part of tzedakah, the term translates directly as "righteousness" or "justice." In the Jewish communities of Central Europe, taking care of less fortunate coreligionists was an obligation, and eventually charitable organizations sprang up to meet these needs. For example, between 1745 and 1870, Jews created more than 150 charitable associations. Advocates of Jewish emancipation and their antagonists viewed these organizations differently—for the former, the philanthropic impulse was a sign of "fitting in" and making sure Jews were not a burden on the state, while for the latter, the distinct religious associational nature of many of these societies showed the obverse: that Jews kept to themselves, "maintained a Jewish identity," and only cared about Jews and not society at large.[46] As Jews pushed for integration and adhered to bourgeois norms, they, like their Christian peers, also increased acts of philanthropy, such as providing funds for the creation of art, establishing self-help organizations, distributing traditional poor relief, founding educational institutions, and creating social housing. These acts were ways for Jews to "express an aspiration to improve their economic status and raise their social status" and perhaps even to celebrate what they had already attained.[47] Philanthropic activities could be a reflection of how Jews saw themselves and where they fit within their society. In other words, engaging in acts of philanthropy indicated that German Jews acted and behaved like "other Germans" because they already saw themselves as integrated Jewish Germans, who—despite their political disabilities—"demonstrate[ed] middle-class virtue."[48]

It would, however, be cynical to interpret Jews' devotion to philanthropy as merely a tool for emancipation and integration. The Jews' philanthropy was guided by an urge to provide for all mankind, a notion known as *Menschenliebe* (love of mankind). Moreover, as Abigail Green has detailed, such philanthropic efforts were deeply concerned with the issues of Jewish persecution around the world as well as broader universal and transnational concerns, including antislavery efforts. Yet this love of mankind was perhaps one of the most important parts of the process of acculturation. As Benjamin Baader concluded, "Hamburg Jews of the era before emancipation aimed at becoming honorable and respectable citizens, claimed to be *gebildet*, and declared 'the higher love of mankind,' or Menschenliebe, to be the motive and the goal of benevolence."[49]

Aside from large, philanthropic endeavors or philanthropy-based organizations, German Jews also participated in communal charity work, specifically giving to causes that were tied to catastrophic events. These one-time charitable donations (in German, *Spenden*) do not easily fit within the notion of bourgeois patronage and communal giving, and it is difficult to fit them within traditional studies that use big gifts as evidence of converting cultural capital into political rights. However, during the 1840s, there were numerous examples of how individuals, Jewish and non-Jewish, gave money for causes that did not necessarily establish a specific charity or institution but helped repair the damage caused to a community or an individual resulting from a disaster—whether it was a disaster that engulfed an entire city (Hamburg in 1842), a smaller community (Markdorf, Baden in 1842), a Jewish synagogue (Emden in 1832 and Rethem in 1835, both in Hannover), or a Jewish individual (Leopold Stein, Baden in 1846). These acts of philanthropy revealed more than just communities coming together—they were public displays of collective identity and nationalism. These instances of kindness crossed religious boundaries and complicated the notion of the antisemitic society so often associated with Central Europe of the mid-nineteenth century. However, there is another important lesson observable in these acts: newspaper editors considered them worthy of recognition in the pages of the newspaper. The publication of individuals' identities in these papers was more than just a display of philanthropy—it showed social philanthropy, and in each case, Jewish and Christian Germans from different regions came together and helped each other, eschewed religious distinctions, and participated in nation-building exercises that helped build not only an "imagined community," but a real, tangible, and "contemporaneous" one.[50]

Driven by a desire to convert their generosity into the cultural capital that would be needed in their fight for rights on the local, state, and national levels, Jewish individuals and bourgeois social organizations that donated to "national" causes and contributed to the well-being of others made sure that their contributions became public. Furthermore, observing how non-Jewish individuals donated to Jewish institutions and individuals illuminated the reciprocity of giving and standing side-by-side with individuals and communities, thus confirming that many Jewish and Christian Germans held similar views about philanthropy.

One example of an individual who both acted and gave generously was Moritz von Haber. At the end of the Haber Affair, a Hessian tribunal sentenced Moritz to six months in prison for killing Georg von Sarachaga-Uria in a duel. During his sentence, Moritz could leave prison during the day and work at local charities in Babenhausen (Hesse), where he performed "grosse Mildthätigkeit" (great relief) for the poor. As a result of these actions, his sentence was reduced to two months. Later that summer, Haber sued both the *Karlsruher Zeitung* and Friedrich Gauner, a journalist for the *Frankfurter Journal*, for slanderous reporting during the affair. Haber won both cases, received judgments for 125 and 100 Gulden, respectively, and then promptly donated the funds to charity.[51] Haber's actions were charitable and his donations an act of goodwill—he did not need 225 Gulden. Coverage of these actions portrayed Haber and German Jews favorably, promoted a spirit of brotherhood and togetherness, and directly combatted the negative tropes spewed against Jews throughout the affair.

Another important charitable event occurred after the tragic, disastrous, and destructive fire in Hamburg during 1842, which caused 78 to 90 million Mark Banco of damage, and this disaster became a pan-German cause—regardless of state or religion.[52] August Lewald, one of the most popular and prolific writers/editors of the Vormärz period (and German Jewish apostate—he was the cousin of Fanny Lewald, a notable German Jewish writer), wrote a dedication pamphlet to the city and the tragedy in the fall of 1842. As he wrote, Hamburg held a special place in the hearts and minds of Germans, as reflected in the following sentiment, "My God! Hamburg has burned—yes! Let us all mourn!" He believed Hamburg was Germans' *Weltstadt* (world city), where persons from all nations could trade with the continent. Later in his homage to the city, Lewald praised Germans for coming together: "But the behavior of our entire fatherland is no less worthy of recognition than the mourning heard in other places. Once again, we saw an example of beautiful unification, and it became clear how such a loss was also felt by every single state, by every single city, and how everyone felt inspired to collect, to donate, to alleviate the great need of their brothers on the distant beaches of the North Sea. All petty business was silent; everyone thought only of one thing: to alleviate misfortune, not to make the calamity even more oppressive." As Lewald proclaimed, the *Bruderliebe* (brotherly love) evident across all of the various states and cities was expected; in fact, such actions in the face of destruction showed, "a strengthened devotion to Germany's collective interests." This praise was directed not just at the princes of Germany, who stood out as the largest contributors to the recuperation efforts, but also to everyone who gave money. Lewald held in the highest regard "the small contributions of the poorest," whose contributions, he felt, "have as much influence as the thousands from the rich."[53]

Lewald, who lived in Baden-Baden at the time, would likely have known of or even read the *Oberdeutsche Zeitung*, a pan-German newspaper printed in Karlsruhe that argued for secure borders, German unity, and creation of a "national" militia. This newspaper played a seminal role in publicizing the contributions of Germans from the Karlsruhe region who contributed to the Hamburg recuperation efforts. The newspaper was supported by Moritz von Haber, and the paper clearly wanted to publicize his family's efforts at supporting this cause, both in terms of their contributions and their role as collecting agents. In total, and as of July 8, 1842, the newspaper documented a total of 1,577 individual contributions with a total value of 28,542 Rhenish florins and 27 kreuzer (approximately 306,000–11,790,000 pounds sterling today).[54] As can be seen in table 2.1, the largest donations came from either members of the Badenese/Karlsruhe elite and/or institutions and businesses that did not individuate the amounts. After removing the princely amounts from the total Badenese contribution, what remains are 1,570 contributions that averaged 11 florins, 3 kreuzer. Many of these contributions were between 1 and 3 florins, though smaller amounts were donated, including 1 florin from two children who withdrew from their *Sparbuch* (savings book).[55] By looking at these amounts, we can confirm Lewald's justified celebration of the lower classes and the German sentiment that poured out from all corners of society.

The same goes for members of the Karlsruhe Jewish community, who also gave generously. In total, 100 of the 1,577 contributions came from German Jews, and the average contribution was 15 florins, 2 kreuzer (for a total of 1,503 florins, 16 kreuzer). The largest contributions came from members of the Karlsruhe Jewish elite—the Habers and the Kusels, both of which were involved as bankers with the grand ducal family. Together, members of both of these families and

Table 2.1. Largest non-Jewish donations to the Hamburg Recouperation Efforts in the Oberdeutsche Zeitung

Largest Donations	fl	kr
Grand Duke Leopold	8,000	
Grand Duchess Sophie (through the Women's Society)	1,000	
Margrave Wilhelm	600	
Margrave Maximillian	600	
Duke Karl Egon von Furstenberg	600	
General Collection in the Upper Rhine district	542	7
Women's Society (not including Grand Duchess Sophie)	540	11
Heir Apparent Karl von Fürstenberg	200	
Prince Maximilian von Fürstenberg	200	
Boatmen's Society of Wolfach	200	

their firms donated 942 florins to the Hamburg recuperation efforts. (Moritz von Haber personally donated 200 florins and his family another 500 florins, and Jakob Kusel donated 150 florins.) Outside of these large philanthropic gestures, most Jewish contributions came through individuated associational donations: either from the *Gesellschaft* (association) "Harmonie"—a Jewish society formed because Jews were not generally accepted to other associations—or through the Karlsruhe *Handelskammer* (chamber of commerce). While many associations and collections left individual contributions anonymous, these organizations—both of which had all (in the former) or substantial (in the latter) Jewish contributions—took the opposite tactic. In figure 2.1, the contributions of both regular and probationary members from Harmonie are noted. Noticeable from the outset are the occupations of the members, who were overwhelmingly businessmen. The average contribution of the regular members of the society was 10 florins, 42 kreuzer, while the average donation of the temporary members was 3 florins, 18 kreuzer. Combined, members of Harmonie gave 376 florins, 56 kreuzer. Among the Jewish members (17 individuals) of the Handelskammer, the average contribution was 4 florins, 34 kreuzer, for a total of 77 florins, 48 kreuzer. One can assume from their involvement in the Handelskammer that they were also businessmen.

However, there were others who also donated to the Hamburg efforts, and through the *Oberdeutsche Zeitung*, their names became public knowledge. Foremost were the contributions by "Mrs. Ludwig Weill," who donated 30 florins,

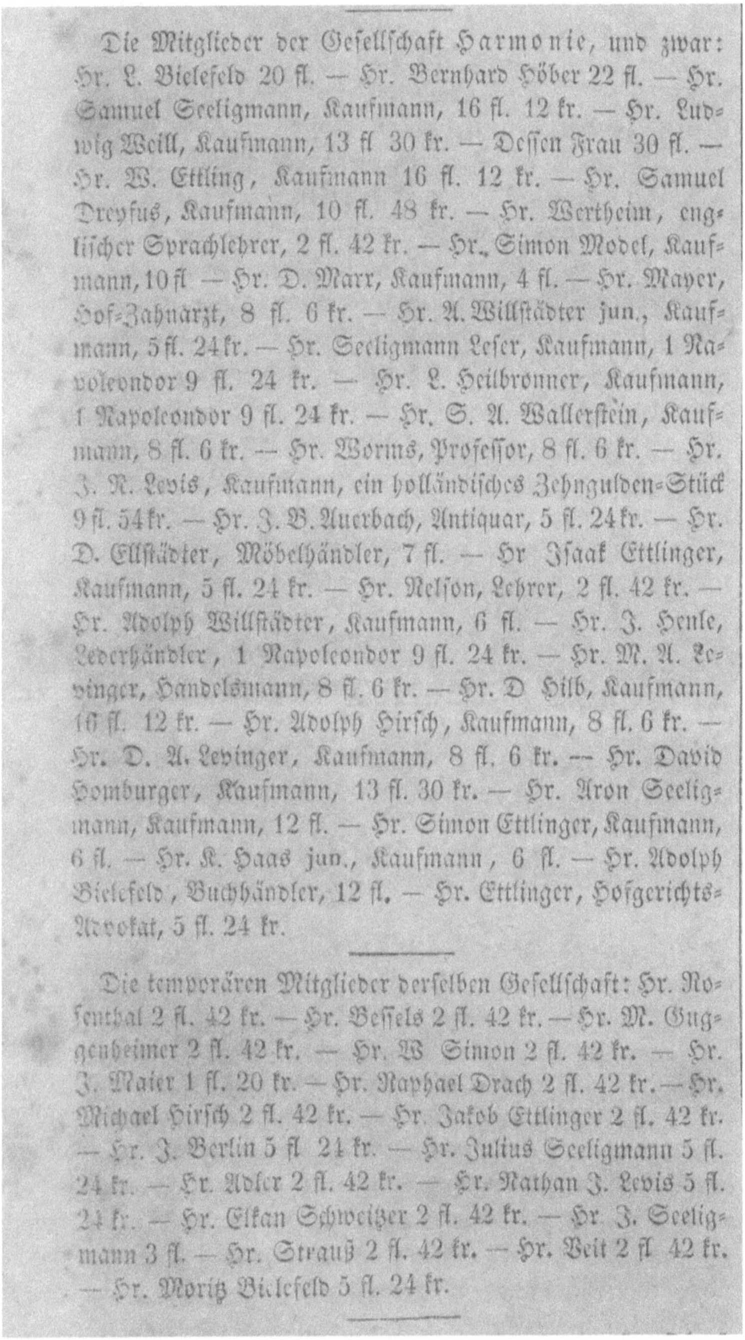

Die Mitglieder der Gesellschaft Harmonie, und zwar: Hr. L. Bielefeld 20 fl. — Hr. Bernhard Höber 22 fl. — Hr. Samuel Seeligmann, Kaufmann, 16 fl. 12 kr. — Hr. Ludwig Weill, Kaufmann, 13 fl 30 kr. — Dessen Frau 30 fl. — Hr. W. Ettling, Kaufmann 16 fl. 12 kr. — Hr. Samuel Dreyfus, Kaufmann, 10 fl. 48 kr. — Hr. Wertheim, englischer Sprachlehrer, 2 fl. 42 kr. — Hr. Simon Model, Kaufmann, 10 fl — Hr. D. Marr, Kaufmann, 4 fl. — Hr. Mayer, Hof-Zahnarzt, 8 fl. 6 kr. — Hr. A. Willstädter jun., Kaufmann, 5 fl. 24 kr. — Hr. Seeligmann Leser, Kaufmann, 1 Napoleondor 9 fl. 24 kr. — Hr. L. Heilbronner, Kaufmann, 1 Napoleondor 9 fl. 24 kr. — Hr. S. A. Wallerstein, Kaufmann, 8 fl. 6 kr. — Hr. Worms, Professor, 8 fl. 6 kr. — Hr. J. R. Levis, Kaufmann, ein holländisches Zehngulden-Stück 9 fl. 54 kr. — Hr. J. B. Auerbach, Antiquar, 5 fl. 24 kr. — Hr. D. Ellstädter, Möbelhändler, 7 fl. — Hr Isaak Ettlinger, Kaufmann, 5 fl. 24 kr. — Hr. Nelson, Lehrer, 2 fl. 42 kr. — Hr. Adolph Willstädter, Kaufmann, 6 fl. — Hr. J. Henle, Lederhändler, 1 Napoleondor 9 fl. 24 kr. — Hr. M. A. Levinger, Handelsmann, 8 fl. 6 kr. — Hr. D Hilb, Kaufmann, 16 fl. 12 kr. — Hr. Adolph Hirsch, Kaufmann, 8 fl. 6 kr. — Hr. D. A. Levinger, Kaufmann, 8 fl. 6 kr. — Hr. David Homburger, Kaufmann, 13 fl. 30 kr. — Hr. Aron Seeligmann, Kaufmann, 12 fl. — Hr. Simon Ettlinger, Kaufmann, 6 fl. — Hr. K. Haas jun., Kaufmann, 6 fl. — Hr. Adolph Bielefeld, Buchhändler, 12 fl. — Hr. Ettlinger, Hofgerichts-Advokat, 5 fl. 24 kr.

Die temporären Mitglieder derselben Gesellschaft: Hr. Rosenthal 2 fl. 42 kr. — Hr. Bessels 2 fl. 42 kr. — Hr. M. Guggenheimer 2 fl. 42 kr. — Hr. W Simon 2 fl. 42 kr. — Hr. J. Maier 1 fl. 20 kr. — Hr. Raphael Drach 2 fl. 42 kr. — Hr. Michael Hirsch 2 fl. 42 kr. — Hr. Jakob Ettlinger 2 fl. 42 kr. — Hr. J. Berlin 5 fl 24 kr. — Hr. Julius Seeligmann 5 fl. 24 kr. — Hr. Adler 2 fl. 42 kr. — Hr. Nathan J. Levis 5 fl. 24 kr. — Hr. Elkan Schweizer 2 fl. 42 kr. — Hr. J. Seeligmann 3 fl. — Hr. Strauß 2 fl. 42 kr. — Hr. Veit 2 fl 42 kr. — Hr. Moritz Bielefeld 5 fl. 24 kr.

Fig. 2.1. Donation lists from the Harmonie Society in the *Oberdeutsche Zeitung* in response to the fire in Hamburg, May 20, 1842, Nr. 118, p. 470. © Universitätsbibliothek Freiburg.

by a rabbi (Willstaetter), and by his son (Rabbinatskandidat Willstaetter). The contribution from Mrs. Weill and the recognition of *her* generosity (though not of her personal name) was one of the few contributions from women that have been documented, other than that of the grand duchess and the *Frauenverein*. The contributions of the rabbi and his son are important from an optics standpoint; by contributing to the pot, they showed their care and concern for other Germans. And overall, it is clear from German Jews' contributions that they were just as generous and felt the same camaraderie toward Hamburgers as other Badeners. As C. K.—likely a local Karlsruhe resident—stated in the motto attached to his contribution:

> There lives in the German Fatherland
> Some brotherly love, some mild hand
> Which is ready and open to help
> when a brother burns in danger:
>
> So everybody open your hand
> to the unlucky ones caught by the large fire
> And everybody give your contribution
> to show—that there is *one* Germany.[56]

By publishing their individual names in the newspaper, they (and their associations) placed their names alongside others, believing that they were not only members of a bourgeois society but also members of the German people.

The Hamburg fire was an opportunity for German Jews to make contributions to a German cause and show how German they felt. It was no coincidence that this came during the decade of the 1840s, when the fight for Jewish emancipation was in full swing. As Moshe Zimmermann noted, the Jews of Hamburg hoped that they (and their contributions) would not be forgotten. In Hamburg, as a result of Jews' generosity and patriotism, some restrictions on their lives were removed (including restrictions on purchasing property and settlement in the city). In other German states, such acts did not immediately yield fruit. However, these demonstrations of brotherhood were part and parcel of German Jews' efforts to use economic and social capital, and turn it into cultural and political capital. Jews' efforts in 1842 were not forgotten in the struggle for emancipation, as seen in 1846 when Hegauer Jews used their charitable acts as evidence of their Germanness in their fight for *Aufnahme* (acceptance) in the city of Constance (see chap. 4).[57]

But these were not the only important acts of philanthropy for a nonreligious cause publicized in the local press. The donations received during 1846 for the Jewish teacher Leopold Stein in Diersburg (a town between Lahr and

Offenburg in Baden) were an example of philanthropy that happened to be *for* a Jew and his family.[58] Stein suffered from *Rückenmarkentzündung* (inflammation of the spinal marrow), which eventually resulted in paralysis of both feet and one of his arms, meaning he could no longer work and earn enough for his family's livelihood and his medical expenses.[59] Some donations included poems or sayings intended for public consumption, such as this one:

> Fate did not ask what you are;
> If you were a Jew, Turk, or Christian,
> Everyone receives their blows.—
> And then you also make your contribution,
> And ask not, for whom it is
> When you meet misfortune on your way![60]

That this collection of money occurred to help a Jew is noteworthy—contributors treated Stein first as a person who had suffered a tragic event, while his Jewishness was a secondary concern. In total, the *Mannheimer Abendzeitung* announced that it had raised approximately 168 florins for Leopold Stein. Although modest compared to the sum for Hamburg, this amount shows that many Jews and Christians were sympathetic to his family's predicament. The request from G. Meyer on behalf of Stein appeared in the *Seeblätter* (Constance), *Oberrheinische Zeitung* (Freiburg), and *Mannheimer Abendzeitung*—reflecting how widespread in Baden the plea was distributed.[61] The newspapers chosen for this request were also important. All three of these publications were "liberal" papers, and only the *ObRhZtg* was not yet a radical paper (though it would become radical in 1847). These advertisements were intended for liberal audiences, and we can surmise that Meyer was deliberate with this placement, as those who read these papers—along with pro-Jewish emancipation editors and audiences—would be more sympathetic to this particular cause. Those who sent in contributions (in the form of money and/or personal notes) also did so with a more liberal and sympathetic audience in mind. In the grand scheme of Jewish life in the German states, philanthropy was not necessarily the most significant lever by which German Jews gave back, yet it was one important way in which they could integrate within society, build cultural capital, and argue for their social inclusion. Moreover, as with Leopold Stein, German Jews dealing with difficult life situations were not shunned because they were Jewish; to the contrary, the generosity shown to Stein proved his humanity above all, and a sense of brotherhood and camaraderie that was also existent after the Hamburg fire.

One of the most important people in the city of Hamburg, Salomon Heine, offers another example of a Jewish philanthropist who made a difference in society. Heine, the uncle of the famous poet Heinrich, was well-known throughout German society for his efforts at making the world a better place, for promoting Bildung and bourgeois morals, and for generously giving to charitable causes throughout the city.[62] He espoused Menschenliebe, and in accordance with traditional Jewish philanthropic endeavors, Heine donated large sums to educational institutions, created a microfinance institution for Jews (the Hermann Heine'sche Stiftung, created in 1837) and provided funds to build new medical facilities (the Jewish hospital, named after his deceased wife, Betty [dedicated in 1843]). In a sense, Heine lived out the pinnacle of a charitable Jewish life, according to the great Sephardic Jewish sage, Maimonides (RamBaM), by giving other Jews opportunities to earn their own livings, though his other charitable efforts also fall high on RamBaM's list.[63] Many people saw Heine as Hamburg's *Mäzen* (patron) due to his generosity and as "Hamburg's Rothschild" on account of his tremendous wealth—estimated at his death in 1845 at a minimum of 17 million Mark Banco.[64] This was quite remarkable since he had moved to Hamburg in 1783 with little money. During the Hamburg fire, Heine destroyed his own home so that the flames could not spread to the other houses on the *Jungfernstieg* (see fig. 2.2)—the wealthiest and ritziest part of town—and thereafter, he helped save Hamburg's credit and financial business by offering loans at 4 percent interest, much lower than other available rates (12 percent). Despite everything that Heine did for the city—building a state-of-the-art hospital, donating generously to Christian and Jewish causes, and destroying his own home to save the city—he never achieved the one thing that he saw as his *Hauptgesichtspunkt* (main focus): emancipation for and inclusion of Jews in the city. In fact, as Rainer Liedtke shows, Hamburg Jews perceived these efforts, and especially institutions like the hospital, "clearly ... as a means of promoting Jewish equality." Despite everything, members of the Hamburg Senate would not budge on their opposition to Jews becoming citizens of the city—no matter how "German" they felt and acted.[65]

When Salomon Heine passed away in December 1844, his death was a widely reported event.[66] However, the publicizing of his death was more than just a byline or a short column in a newspaper; detailed reports covered the last days of his life, his funeral, and the unveiling of his last will and testament (table 2.2; see also appendix B for a more detailed list). As reflected by the will and the description of Salomon Heine, he seems to have been a socially conscious individual who gave to organizations across all social and religious groups in society. In total, Heine donated 179,000 Hamburg Courant (2016 value of £6,228,000–27,730,000) to institutions, plus significant funds in Mark Banco to families and individuals (table 2.2). By giving to groups across societal

Fig. 2.2. Blowing up the Heine home on the Jungfernstieg during the Hamburg fire. Peter Suhr, *Hamburg — Der Jungfernstieg in Hamburg am 6ten May 1842. Das Sprengen der Häuser, um der Feuerbrunst Einhalt zu thun*, Kreidelithographie 1842. Nach der natur gez. Gedruckt und verlegt bei P. Suhr. © Heine-Haus e.V.

Table 2.2. Summary of Will and Testament of Salomon Heine

Organization	Amount (1845 Hamburg Courant)*	Present Value (2016 Pounds Sterling)
Christian Organizations	14,500	504,000–2,245,000
Jewish Organizations	86,200	3,000,000–13,360,000
Medical Organizations	28,000	974,400–4,338,000
Poor Organizations	34,300	1,194,000–5,315,000
Educational Organizations	16,000	557,000–2,481,000
Personal Relations	The rest, including estate to his son	
Total (not including personal)	179,000	6,228,000–27,730,000

Augsburger Allgemeine Zeitung, January 6, 1845, Nr. 6, pp. 44–45
*1 Courant = 0.8054 Mark Banco = 0.322 Reichsthaler = 0.045 Pounds Sterling

boundaries, Heine showed his (and by extension, Jews') willingness to contribute to the betterment of society, an act that reflected bourgeois values. Heine embodied the spirit of Menschenliebe, which the Jewish community celebrated years earlier at the dedication of the new Jewish hospital in Hamburg. The community commissioned a medallion for the event, and on the backside of the coin, it read: "Salomon Heine. Love of man is the crown of all virtues" (fig. 2.3). Heine, in many ways, was another example of how Jews in Europe used philanthropy not to necessarily "become part of the host community" but to show that Jews "already belong[ed] to that community."[67]

Salomon Heine's philanthropy was part of his way of negotiating with his environment and building cultural and social capital, which in his own case and for the rest of Hamburg's Jews, did not immediately turn into the capital necessary for emancipation. The Hamburg Patriotic Society (*Patriotische Gesellschaft*)—considered the most representative, enlightened, and bourgeois association in the city—refused to grant Heine full membership. Despite his demonstration of *Gemeinwohl* (communal prosperity) and *Gemeinsinn* (communal feeling), the society only gave him an *Ehrentitel* (honorary title). While Heine may not have become a full member, his efforts certainly paved the way for others to gain membership after him. Shortly after Heine's death, Gabriel Riesser—native Hamburger, associate of Salomon Heine, and the most important and public of the "fighters for Jewish emancipation"—was given full membership.[68]

Fig. 2.3. Back and front of the Hamburg Jewish Hospital commemorative coin. Hans Frederic Alsing, Medaille anlässlich der Einweihung des Krankenhauses der Deutsch-Israelitischen Gemeinde Hamburg, Hamburg, ca. 1841–50, Kupferlegierung, patiniert, T = 0,35 Dm = 4,5 cm. © Jüdisches Museum Berlin, Inv.-Nr. 2010/238/1, Foto: Roman März.

Heine's generosity and dedication to his community were certainly well known throughout Hamburg, but his death and the public celebration of this figure were not just a local affair. As reported in the *AAZ*, Heine's death took on a Germany-wide meaning. For most Jewish and Christian Germans, however, death was a private affair. Except for a communal announcement, such as was the case with the Kirchenbücherauszüge in the Mannheim papers, the formal announcement of a person's death was usually the responsibility of the family of the deceased, if they even chose to do so. For German Jews, the decision to publicize their life events was one way to notify the general community about their existence and their losses. It could also have been a means to heighten recognition of their humanity among their coresidents, to point out that Jews had held up their part of the quid pro quo, and perhaps to even instill some empathy toward them among their neighbors.[69]

However, the case of Salomon Heine was clearly privileged; much like those of other very notable and wealthy German Jews, his life and death would have resembled those of the most notable of German princes and dignitaries. As the first news article in the *AAZ* reported, the city had lost "one of its most notable men." Note that the author used not just the comparative but the superlative form of the adjective *notable*. This article details Heine's suffering: he had not left his room in six weeks due to an extended fight against "hydrothorax and other maladies." The author recognized that Heine was not just a local personality but someone who had been recognized "by the German and foreign newspapers" for his "world-famous" (*weltbekannt*) generosity.[70]

The three articles about Heine's death detailed some of his greatest achievements but focused almost exclusively on how he saved the city and its financial sector from ruin. Still, one notable line from the January 2, 1845, article in the *AAZ* asserted that the rumors about Salomon's son, Karl, moving to Paris to be with his wife's family and to have greater rights were unfounded. Such rumors had "quieted not only the local business class, but also those residents for whom *wellness of the city lies close to their hearts*." The unfounded rumors aside, the author focused on Heine's actions and then made a keen observation: "It is quite difficult to accept that the old man had to fall so severely sick after he had done so much for the Exchange, while constantly being excluded from by the Assembly [the Senate] because of his religion, despite being an honorable businessman." The author wrapped up his article by describing Heine's (lack of) reaction to the repeated denials of his applications for citizenship and how Heine continued doing what he felt was right. Heine's largesse and importance to Hamburg society was eloquently captured in a description of the funeral procession, which included among its participants "many members of the Senate and diplomatic corps"—a scene reminiscent of the dedication of the Israelite hospital in 1843.[71]

The third and fourth articles in this series were a bit more descriptive: in addition to the detailing of Heine's "Last Will and Testament" (the fourth article), the third article described the local reaction to his death. Against the wishes of the deceased, a large contingent of Jews and non-Jews followed the casket all the way to the Jewish cemetery in Ottensen, and they buried Heine according to Jewish customs next to his wife, Betty, who had preceded him in death by five years. The third article's author noted that while the overwhelming outpouring of Jews in the streets was noticeable, there was an astonishing number of Christians there as well, who also suffered through this "bitter loss" (*herben Verlust*), which would be "a *generally* deeply felt [one]."[72]

As part of these articles, a very conspicuous poem was reprinted in the footnotes on January 6, 1845, one written by none other than Salomon's nephew Heinrich. It was well known that Heinrich and his uncle did not always see eye-to-eye; in fact, they were often critical of each other. As the fourth article mentioned, Salomon often called his nephew a "dumme Junge" (dumb youth). Still, Salomon was very supportive of and generous toward Heinrich. Supposedly, when the nephew asked for 100,000 thaler, his uncle agreed. As part of the settlement of Salomon's will, Heinrich's debts were wiped out, and he was given 8,000 Mark Banco, just like all of his siblings and cousins.[73] Regardless of their strained relationship, Heinrich composed the following poem around the dedication of the Jewish hospital (named for his aunt) in 1843:

> A hospital for poor, sick Jews
> for children, who are threefold in misery
> imprisoned with the horrible three afflictions:
> Poverty, bodily pain, and Jewishness.
>
> Incurable deep pain! Against this helps
> not steam bath, showering, no surgical
> apparati, nor all the medicine,
> that this house can offer the sick guests.
>
> (The worst of the three is the last [one],
> the thousand-year family evil,
> the plague carried from the Nile valley
> the old Egyptian, unhealthy beliefs)[74]
>
> Is it now time for the eternal goddess to wipe out
> the dark pain, passed down from father
> to son, will the grandchildren finally
> Recover, and be happy and proper?
>
> I don't know! In the meantime, we
> want to bless every smart and love-filled
> heart that longs to offer solace, whatever that relief
> Can bring, timely balsam trickles into the wounds.
>
> The precious man! He built a home here
> for sufferers, who are curable through the art
> of the doctor (or also of death!), provided
> for bedding, drink, attention,[75] and care—
>
> A man of action, he did what was doable,
> for good works, he handed out a daily salary
> On the eve of his life, philanthropic,
> Through benevolence, he raised himself above his work.
>
> He gave generously with his hand
> Tears often welled in his eyes,
> the precious, beautiful tears that he shed
> For the incurable brotherly sickness.

This poem highlights one man's love for his uncle, despite their differences. More importantly, Heinrich approved of his uncle's generosity within the community. The poem also emphasized "Jewishness" as an affliction, which the removed paragraph (in parentheses) makes even clearer. Why the sender of this article/poem to the *AAZ* removed this paragraph is unclear, as this "affliction" drove home the point that discrimination against Jews was the impetus behind the creation of a Jewish hospital and for Salomon's emancipation efforts. The poet had done something about his own attachment to Judaism, having converted in 1825 to Lutheranism; perhaps that is why the sender of this article removed the third stanza, as it was clear that Heinrich held deeply critical and negative views toward Judaism. In the third stanza, Heinrich hoped that one day there would be a deity who could remove this deep affliction and, in the end, also cure the social sickness among brothers (*Brüderkrankheit*) that Salomon tried to heal through his good works.

These four articles in the *AAZ* are quite a contrast to the coverage of Heine's death in other large newspapers across the German States. Those from the *Deutsche Allgemeine Zeitung* (January 1, 1845), the *Kölnische Zeitung* (December 27, 1844), and the *Vossische Zeitung* (December 27 & 29, 1844, and January 4, 1845) were not nearly as descriptive or laudatory as those in the *AAZ*. In fact, the January 4 article in the *Vossische Zeitung* was a partial reprint of the *Weser Zeitung* article from December 30 that was printed in full in the *AAZ* two days later (January 6). Most of these articles merely detailed the economic and philanthropic aspects of Heine's life, describing the charity contained in the will, his loss to the Hamburg business community, and his son Karl's seamless transition into management of his father's business. The exception to this generality was the article in the *Kölnische Zeitung*, which supplied a more sympathetic account of Heine's philanthropy and his *Ehrenstelle* (honorable place) in Hamburg. The article emphasized that Salomon's wealth was as great as his *grossartigen Wohltätigkeitsinnes* (outstanding sense of philanthropy). The variation in coverage reflected the interests of the various editorial staffs, though it is clear that Cotta's *AAZ* allowed more coverage and promoted a more sympathetic view of Heine's life. Perhaps such coverage was due to Heinrich's long-standing service to the paper or, more generally, to the Cottas' professed support for Jewish emancipation and Heine's exemplification of Jews' acceptability as bourgeois citizens.[76]

The coverage of Heine's death also fits within a broader context of publicizing the deaths of German Jews in the press. Jewish lives and deaths appeared regularly on the local level. Mannheim, for example, published Kirchenbücherauszüge so that the general populace could stay informed about life events (birth, marriage, and death). However, there were other, more personalized ways that deaths could be publicized.

The most frequent appearance of people's deaths, outside of the church extracts, came in the form of individualized Todes-Anzeigen that could be found in the newspapers' classified sections. Most of these announcements were very basic: they introduced the deceased with the date of death, the name, and then the name of those who grieved. Occasionally, the survivors wrote a little more. As seen in the January 11, 1844, issue of the *MAbZ*, Therese Goldschmidt wrote the following after her husband Moses's death: "Those who knew his soulful patience, gentleness, faith in God, and other good characteristics will silently sympathize with my justified anguish." It is clear that the grieving widow, whose husband had passed away on January 6 and who had sent the announcement to the paper on January 9, wanted to notify the general public about his death. However, she also wrote the following: "As I mail off this advertisement, I am also taking over the flour trade that runs out of my tranquil yard."[77] This declaration reflected Therese's recognition that she needed to continue her husband's business to support herself. The fact that this advertisement was published during the traditional shiva period reveals Therese's awareness of her existential circumstances and of the audience she was trying to reach. It was no coincidence, just as we saw with the appeal on behalf of Leopold Stein earlier, that this obituary only appeared in the *MAbZ* and not in the *MM*.

More dramatic are the full-length obituaries reserved for those who were among the most important people in the community. On both the local and pan-German level, there were several noteworthy obituaries, including those of Ludwig Marcus in the *AAZ* (May 2 and 3, 1844) and David Zimmern in the *MAbZ* (June 27, 1845). These obituaries were written by Jews: the Marcus obituary by Heinrich Heine, and the Zimmern obituary by Rabbi Ephraim Willstätter. These obituaries are valuable for analyzing how Jews portrayed the lives of important community elders and how they framed these essays into political arguments for emancipation.

Obituaries, as a whole, have a long tradition within German and European writing. Dating from the sixteenth century, *Nachrufe* (obituaries; literally, "call backs") fulfilled different purposes. They originally functioned as religious texts of sorts, but with the widespread distribution and development of newsprint, they adapted to a more accessible format. Obituaries have not always been a widely used primary source, as most death-related announcements were short and did not relate much biographical information. Yet they can be very valuable sources, as Wendy Anne Stross contends, to "provide a window through which historians may view the attitudes of the groups and communities who read them." The English- and German-language discussions about obituaries could not be any more dissimilar. For the most part, English-language studies have focused on the modern, public instances through newsprint, whereas German studies have examined the various printed and performed frameworks, especially those related to important literary figures and the way they were sacralized in the public sphere.[78]

The most important and wide-ranging work on Nachrufe is Ralf Georg Bogner's *Der Autor im Nachruf* (2006). Bogner viewed these texts not as representative of the deceased but as a window through which to analyze the time periods in question as well as the writers themselves. As Bogner writes, "The deceased's life and work mutate into a suitable exemplary or contradictory projection field for the personal poetic, political, or religious interests of the Necrologist. To a certain extent, every Nachruf author thematized themselves, their era, and the utopia of the future."[79] As such, the text and the deceased function as a self-reflection and ideological slate on which obituary authors could promote their own agendas. Often these texts used a comparative (*comparatio*) framework with figures from the past, in order to present a politicized and intellectual characterization in service of a specific end.

Commentators on Jewish life also found the *Nachruf/Nekrolog* genre useful in terms of politicizing one of the most important issues of the early nineteenth century. For example, Ludwig Marcus's obituary became a vehicle for Heinrich Heine to criticize the German states and their handling of Jewish emancipation. Marcus, born in Dessau in 1798, was a founding member of the Verein für Cultur und Wissenschaft des Judenthums (Society for Culture and Scientific Study of Jewry) and then moved to France in 1825 to become a professor, where he researched the Vandals and the Abyssinians; his move to France was a direct result of the German states' policies that prohibited full-time professorships for Jews. As Heine recalled, Marcus "lived approximately five years [his last five years] with the most contented peace of mind in Paris," where he was supported by Fr. von Rothschild. In the second part of his obituary, Heine devoted the end of the first and the entire second paragraph to the subject of emancipation. He argued that the state "can buck all storms" and have "pride in its chest," but along with such pride, there is pain (*Schmerz*) "if the small toe suffers from a corn." He then wrapped up his paragraph with the following: "die Judenbeschränkungen sind solche Hühneraugen an den deutschen Staatsfüssen" (the Jewish restrictions are such corns on the pillars of the German states). Heine's Nekrolog, despite the author's own complicated relationship with Judaism, was well received by some members of the Jewish community, who in a backhanded way, saw Heine as "a not entirely reprehensible witness for the Jews" due to his prominence in the *AAZ* and "unswerving fight for freedom."[80]

Nonetheless, Heine's criticism of the handling of Jewish emancipation was not the only reason why he wrote this lengthy obituary. This skilled utilization of the comparatio format allowed him to write more broadly about his own journey and the people from Marcus's life that were also important to his. On page 980, Heine discussed the Verein für Cultur und Wissenschaft des Judenthums, of which both he and Marcus were founding members. Heine waxed fondly about Leopold Zunz's central role in the society, glowed in remembrance of "my dear [Lazarus] Bendavid," and celebrated the often-unrecognized bourgeois contributions of Moses Moser, another one of the founders. In fact, Heine wrote that he "instinctively" (*unwillkürlich*) turned from the Nekrolog of Marcus to that of the society as a whole. He juxtaposed the downfall of the Verein with that of Edward Gans, one of the society's most (in)famous members. Gans came from an important Berlin Jewish family and studied in Berlin and Heidelberg, where he became one of Hegel's students. In 1825, Gans converted to Christianity to further his career and become a regular professor (*Ordinarius*). Heine compared Marcus favorably to Gans, arguing that the latter "sav[ed] himself" while the former "towered above."[81] Without directly stating it, Heine criticized Gans for taking the easy way out—converting to Christianity while Marcus had not. Heine's statement, however, drips with hypocrisy since he criticized Gans for the very decision he himself had made. Yet perhaps this excoriation of Gans reflected Heine's personal regret. As Amos Elon wrote in *The Pity of It All*, Heine seethed about Gans's conversion and the subsequent dissolution of the Verein in the following unpublished poem "To an Apostate": "See what comes from all that reading / Schlegel, Haller, Burke and all: / Yesterday you were a hero / Look how low the mighty fall."[82] Otherwise, why else would Heine write such a wide-ranging Nekrolog about someone who was probably not that well-known within the public in order to get at his real aim—writing about the situation of Jews in the German states? Such a theme—and the tie to Marcus—can be seen even after the 1848 revolutions: "The Jews finally may have come to the realization that they cannot be truly emancipated until the emancipation of Christians is also fully fought for and secured. Their cause is identical with that of the German peoples, and they may not yearn for as Jews what is long overdue to all Germans."[83] In this postscript, Heine—referencing the 1848 revolutions—tied the future of Jewish emancipation to that of all Germans, a link very similar to the one made decades earlier by Karl von Rotteck in the Badenese legislature. Throughout Heine's texts about Ludwig Marcus, while he praised his former intellectual comrades and criticized the German states for the "failed emancipation" (*gescheiterte Emanzipation*), he was foremost writing about himself and his German Jewish past, his present, and hopefully a future where Gans's and his own choices would not need to occur.[84]

The next Nekrolog was that of David Zimmern (1766–1845), one of the most important Jews in the Grand Duchy of Baden. Zimmern's death occurred on June 8, 1845; he was seventy-nine years old. The author, "W—r," wrote the Nekrolog on June 17, 1845, though it did not appear in the *Mannheimer Abendzeitung* until June 27, 1845. Of note, this Nekrolog was printed approximately two weeks after the family published their own obituary in the *AAZ*. One of the interesting notes about this text, when compared to Heine's Nekrolog about Ludwig Marcus, is that from the beginning the author established that this remembrance was not about Zimmern being a "hero of the arts or sciences"; rather, this honoring was for a "herrvoragenden *öffentlichen* Character" (extraordinary *public* figure).[85] The author set up a very flattering and sympathetic description of Zimmern, one which, in the context of the continuing battle for Jewish emancipation in the Grand Duchy of Baden and the ongoing Reform movement within German Jewry, was much more than a paean in memoriam.

The author presented Zimmern as a man of God, who "wandered before and with [him]," and whose disposition was as honorable as his countenance, manners, and dress were respectable. However, these personal descriptions of the man paled in comparison to the atmosphere he built within his family, among his circle of friends, and in his home: "David Zimmern's house, open to every *Wohlgesitteten* [well-mannered person], had become over the past 50 years not only a convivial asylum, but also ... a school of formation [*Bildungsschule*] for manners and decency." The author made sure to press the point that Zimmern did all of this, not in spite of his Judaism, but *through* his Judaism and his Jewishness: "his virtuous negotiations grew out of the Jewish base because he found his roots and sustenance in Jewry and because his entire art of living was an application and expression of true, pure Jewry." The author continued to praise Zimmern's attachment to a "pure Jewish" life and his promotion of this lifestyle among his coreligionists. However, the author was clear to point out that Zimmern was a champion of Jews making their own decisions about religion, which echoed the discussion about Jewish acceptance in Constance (see chap. 4). The author also praised Zimmern's presentation before the Badenese Lower Assembly in 1832, when he defended not only his coreligionists but also the devotion of German Jews to their beliefs: "You may always call us a haggling people [*Schachervolk*], but we will never haggle with our religion."[86]

Throughout this piece, the author tied Zimmern's life directly to the concept of Bildung and other attributes that the German bourgeoisie held dear. In fact, this characterization of Zimmern powerfully contradicted the sentiments about Jews held by many in Badenese society, especially considering that Zimmern's death occurred around the same time as the last events in the Haber Affair. Unlike Haber, the stereotypical transgressive Jewish outsider (despite his conversion), Zimmern was portrayed as a more typical Badenese Jew who exemplified the bourgeois definition of morality. And like many others who chose the *Mannheimer Abendzeitung*, this author selected this paper—the leading left-liberal, bourgeois newspaper in the grand duchy and the German states—to reach the widest possible audience.

The author of this Nekrolog, as suggested by the moniker "W—r," was Rabbi Ephraim Willstätter, a Badenese Jew from Karlsruhe who had studied at Yeshiva in Mannheim and who served as the *Bezirksrabbiner* (district rabbi) in Bühl. What Willstätter wrote about Zimmern needs to be compared to what he wrote almost a decade earlier in his *Allgemeine Geschichte des Israelitischen Volkes: Von der Entstehung desselben bis auf unsere Zeit* (General history of the Jewish people: From their emergence to our times, 1836). In the foreword and introduction of his book, Willstätter stressed progress and Enlightenment and, more importantly, contended that religion—and in this case, also Judaism—could fulfill *bürgerliche Rechten* (bourgeois rights). Later in the introduction, Willstätter claimed that Jews were not a separate people, nation, or segregated society; as far as he was concerned, Jews in Baden were integrated and were German because Baden and Germany were their homeland. For Willstätter, the grand duke—at that time and in 1844, Leopold—was also their father, and he asked God "that the full freedom and security of Israel [the Jewish population of Baden] could be established in the full freedom and security of *our dear fatherland*."[87]

Willstätter's beliefs in the unity and equality of Jewish and Christian Germans, and his belief that David Zimmern was an exemplar of this relationship were part of his politicization of this text. Zimmern was revered, but the obituary was not necessarily about his life, but about the fact that he, his offspring, his friends and acquaintances, and Jewish Badeners writ large should be granted full emancipation and inclusion because they were equal to Christians since they had fulfilled their part of the quid pro quo. That this piece appeared in the news section of the *MAbZ* and not as a classified feature tells us something about the audience to which this was directed and reveals that the editor wanted this published in front of an overwhelmingly liberal and emancipation-supportive audience throughout the German states. As a stand-alone article, Willstätter wrote a powerful obituary as a witness to the life of an exemplary individual. Within the context of its publication and the fight for emancipation, we see a continuation of Jews' struggle and the diversification of the means by which Jews argued for political rights.

CONCLUSION

These three vignettes—the 1845 discussion in the Mannheim/Heidelberg press, the charitable donations at the time of the great Hamburg fire of 1842, and the Nekrologe in the newspapers—represent different, yet important interrelated intercessions in the German newspapers by German Jews. The first section detailed the confidence with which Jewish Badeners disputed others' claims about Jews and Judaism. And in this response, there was not only a secular reaction but also one that came from religious leaders. These responses reveal that German Jews were not willing to stand idly by while others defamed them or their religion, and these texts also show the Jews as actors in their engagement with German citizenship and rights and that such engagement would be on their terms, not forced on them by outsiders. These debates indicate that emancipation was never just a political issue; it was about how Jews fit into a society that was dealing with the pressures of secularization on the one hand, and the reactionary push to reembed and reaffirm the Christian nature of German society on the other.

In the second section, Jewish German charity and philanthropy reflected how, similarly to Moses Montefiore in England, Jews in the German states believed themselves to be part of the German bourgeoisie and the German nation, despite their real political and social disabilities. Moreover, the vignettes about Salomon Heine and Leopold Stein revealed a generosity toward all in society—Christian and Jew, men and women, and for the poor—and a benevolence beyond individual group and station. Yet this example also indicated how "egoistic" philanthropic concerns could be motivated by more than purely personal reasons and could benefit an entire group. Salomon Heine could have merely demanded emancipation for himself as an exception—a practice that was more common in pre-Confederation Prussia—but instead, he advocated and acted in a way that sought to benefit all of Hamburg's Jews.[88]

The third example focused on the various ways in which Jews eulogized the death of famous and important German Jews, and how the deceased's lives became symbols for a modern German Jewry that believed itself to be equal and worthy of rights. On the national level, Ludwig Marcus's life, and especially his relocation to Paris to fulfill his career aspirations, served as a vehicle by which Heinrich Heine promoted emancipation for his former coreligionists. This Nekrolog also allowed Heine to promote the virtues of Jewish scholarship and the Jews' adherence to Bildung. Ultimately, Heine's obituary of Marcus functioned as a meditation on his own life choices—for better and for worse. The other Nekrolog—about David Zimmern—also promoted a politicization of the deceased in the service of emancipation, by showing the virtues of German Jews. Willstätter argued that Zimmern made enormous contributions to Jews and other Badeners in the grand duchy and to the advancement of a bourgeois lifestyle in Mannheim and Heidelberg. Zimmern was cherished as a paragon of modern Jewish life—one that integrated Jewish and German identities while simultaneously embodying everything that had been asked of the Jews as part of the quid pro quo.

All of these actions were related to the notion of building both cultural and social capital and then turning that capital into political rights and full emancipation. Clearly, Salomon Heine's explicit and generous efforts were part of his self-identified quest to achieve this end. The 1845 discussion in Mannheim followed the generosity and participation of German Jews in Badenese society. The donations and charitable acts exhibited the selflessness required of them within the bourgeois concept of Menschenliebe and attempted to use that capital to build sympathy for their cause. German Jews explicitly claimed that they were already a part of the German nation, as shown by their actions and deeds. Indeed, the question of "actions" was at the heart of the discussion about citizenship. There is an irony in how these discussions functioned: liberals and many Jews (like Salomon Heine) saw Jews' individual deeds as the basis for a collective granting of rights that were of a more liberal and individual nature. Moreover, these acts tended to fit in well with the German nationalists' ideas of nationhood, where Menschenliebe was part and parcel of Bruderliebe. Their opponents not only saw these actions as individualistic but also interpreted Jews' acts and demands for equality as fundamentally altering the Christian foundation of German society. Thus, even Jews' charitable goodwill toward Christians was ultimately irrelevant, as Menschenliebe was not a basis for inclusion in the German polity; one still had to be Christian to be a full member.

Despite the importance of these displays in the German press, there were not an overwhelming number of them. Still, these unique contributions within the press (the notices of philanthropy and the Nekrologe) should be considered alongside traditional writings when discussing public discussions and debates about Jewish emancipation. Just as authors who wrote pamphlets and essays sought a broad audience, the authors of these articles in favor of Jewish emancipation (or those using other genres to argue for the same concepts)—knowing full well that certain papers had higher circulation numbers, specific audiences, and a broader geographical circulation—sought an audience with all Germans or, at least, with all *liberally inclined* Germans, in order to promote their agenda and potentially expand their support.

THREE

JEWISH RELIGIOUS REFORM IN THE GERMAN AND BADENESE PRESS

GERMAN JEWS' FIGHT FOR EMANCIPATION was never just about politics; debates were always imbricated with religious content. Politics and religion in German society were inextricably linked. Emancipation was defined as Jews entering a Christian society, so any regeneration that occurred necessarily meant Judaism appearing more like Christianity. The 1845 Badenese emancipation debate discussed in chapter 2 as broadcast in the *Mannheimer Morgenblatt, Mannheimer Abendzeitung,* and the *Heidelberger Journal* saw participants on both sides—the Landtag Commission and its spokesman, Assemblyman Fauth, and Leopold Ladenburg and Rabbi Hayum Wagner—base arguments against and for emancipation, in part, on their religious views of Judaism.

One of the core issues for Jews' opponents (such as Jacob Friedrich Fries and Friedrich Ghillany) was the belief that Jews formed a state within a state; that is, Jews did not follow the laws of the countries in which they lived but, rather, followed the Talmudic laws, which antagonists believed separated Jews not just from the Christian populace but also from the state itself. Indeed, there were many Jews who wanted to adhere to a stricter and more traditional Judaism, yet they did not generally disregard the laws of the land. Jews had always found ways to balance the strictures of secular and Jewish laws. More importantly, as the published documents from the Dutch ministers indicated during the 1844 Badenese debate about Jewish emancipation, Jews since Napoleonic times had lived and participated as integrated and invaluable members of Dutch society, having found a balance between their religious and secular obligations.[1] Judaism—contrary to opponents' characterizations—was thus not an obstacle to Jews' ability to serve the state, even in a state where both the number and percentage of Jews was considerably higher than in Baden. Despite such official support for the Jews, their opponents' prejudice prevented them from accepting Jews' contributions and the testimonies on their behalf as valid. As such, any debate for Jewish rights also involved a substantial debate about Judaism.

Yet while political debates about Jewish emancipation called attention to Judaism, not all debates about Judaism referenced the obverse—it was probably unnecessary to do so, since Germans at that time likely understood that the two discussions were intrinsically linked. While many German Jews were having these debates in the German Jewish press among a mostly German Jewish readership, there was plenty of debate about Judaism in both the local and pan-German newspapers. The importance of having these discussions in front of the general public has not received much scholarly attention, as most studies on German Jewish emancipation and German Jewish reform have focused on official debates, pamphlets, and the German Jewish press. These local and pan-German newspaper debates about Jewish reform offer us another lens through which German Jews sought to influence public opinion and perhaps apply pressure to other Jews who had yet to adapt and were seen as holding back Jewish Reformers and Jews as a whole from equality.

But where the discussions took place would not have mattered much if the content of those discussions had proved detrimental to German Jews' claims for equality. So, what exactly did adherents of the Reform movement advocate in these discussions? Foremost, the reformers tried to make Judaism appear similar to their Christian (mainly Protestant) middle-class counterparts in each of the German states.[2] At the core of Jewish reform stood a religion that was compatible with the demands and sensibilities of modern society; for most reformers (except those reformers who are now considered modern Orthodox), this meant separating Judaism from the strictures of halacha. This change was imperative for the religion, as reformers believed they needed to attract those Jews who had become more secular and had either stopped going to synagogue and/or following the dietary laws.[3] Given what reformers sought to introduce to Judaism, conflict with those who held more traditional beliefs was inevitable.

The growing differences between the various factions led both reformers and traditionalists to make claims as being the legitimate representatives of Judaism in the eyes of both Jews and Christians; the success of one or the other faction had real consequences. These differences percolated below the surface during the first several decades of the nineteenth century, and except for the few public controversies mentioned previously, the sides reached a modus vivendi whereby "intracommunity disputes over religion would diminish as the principle of mutual toleration within the larger community gained widening acceptance. Only the most radical at each end of the spectrum would find it necessary to take separatist paths."[4] Despite the coexistence and toleration of differing religious sentiments within the Jewish community, the distinctions became more pronounced over time, especially as most Jews—even if they did not attend services regularly—desired to go back to a traditional religious experience when they did attend. This dynamic was prevalent within myriad communities during the hiring of reform-leaning rabbis, preachers, and educators; alliances also shifted among community leaders, state officials, other rabbis, and others in the Jewish community. As Andreas Brämer observed, "working together could only function, if and as long as both sides [rabbis and laymen] accepted the halacha as a normative fundament and aligned their own actions with this sentiment."[5] Brämer further noted that by the time of the rabbinical conferences, unity and understanding in the Jewish community had, for all intents and purposes, fundamentally broken down.

In the public disputes discussed in this chapter, the debates about Jewish identity and the lasting authority of halacha disrupted this fragile balance. This dynamic was apparent in the public spat about the validity of circumcision as a necessary identifier of one's Jewishness in the Frankfurt press, as well as throughout the discussions about Jewish reform in the pan-German and local, Badenese press. Given that the cooperation that had characterized German Jewish life had begun to wane during the first-half of the nineteenth century, it should come as no surprise that, as debates about Jewish reform moved into the non-Jewish public sphere, these conversations reflected the intensity of an existential conflict that would also play an important role in concurrent debates about Jewish emancipation.

In these discussions, issues that appeared in the newspapers were the products of developments within German Judaism and the movement for Jewish reform as a whole, yet local and regional issues—such as education—simultaneously informed those broader topics at the rabbinical conferences and when disputes occurred in the German press. The internal Jewish debates about Jewish reform throughout the German states are important for understanding how these discussions manifested themselves within the Grand Duchy of Baden. And while reforms at the local and regional level certainly impacted and influenced discussions about Jewish reform in the abstract, it was the broader ideological debates and novelties within the larger Jewish communities—like those surrounding radical reform in Frankfurt and Berlin—that captured the public's attention and drove direct and immediate responses to those ideas, whether they were from moderate reformers, radical reformers, or Christians. It was in these Germany-wide public debates that lines were drawn by antagonists, and local Jewish communities reacted to and defined their relationships to the Reform movement and Orthodoxy in more concrete ways through public disputations, such as that which occurred in 1845 in the Mannheim and Heidelberg press in the wake of the 1844 Brunswick rabbinical conference.

A BRIEF HISTORY OF JEWISH RELIGIOUS REFORM THROUGH THE EARLY 1840S

Religious reform within the Grand Duchy of Baden closely followed developments within Judaism throughout Central Europe and stemmed from Jews' engagement with the European Enlightenment. This intellectual movement among Jews produced a cadre of individuals—the Maskilim (educators)—who overcame the limitations of traditional Jewish life and associated themselves with Christian and secular cultures. The Maskilim, who had taken their lead from Moses Mendelssohn, sought to develop ideas about Judaism compatible with the demands and decorum of the modern age. Guenther W. Plaut, Solomon Bennett Freehof, and Howard A. Berman view the Reform movement in *The Rise of Reform Judaism* as part of the revolutionary trend of that period: "it [the movement and the reformers] wanted salvation *now*."[6] There were two tasks that Maskilim and their adherents set out to accomplish, according to Philipp Lenhard: (1) "to carry over (*hinüberzuretten*) the tradition into the modern" and (2) "to subject the [Jewish] tradition to criticism using the philosophical tools of their time."[7] But what exactly did these two points mean? What did bringing "Judaism into modernity" look like? When considering Judaism in the spirit of the late Enlightenment and the Napoleonic age, one could surmise that all Judaism needed to do was align itself with the values of the state and its reorientation to citizenship instead of subjecthood. By doing that, Judaism would not stand in the way of Jews being good citizens, yet the definition of "citizen" and related responsibilities varied state by state. And if one were to follow the second point, as times changed and philosophical tools evolved, so too did the critiques of Judaism. For those who were steeped in traditions and were the purveyors of religiosity—the rabbis—such a situation would destroy the binding authority of the Talmud, which had been codified in 1542 by Joseph Caro and had been the guiding principle in rabbinical interpretation after the Sabbatean movement during the late seventeenth century. Subjecting Judaism to Kantian, Hegelian, or Rankean methods would open up Judaism and Jewish tradition to criticism from outside the religion, something that the rabbis vehemently protested and fought against. This "religionization" of Judaism ultimately became a threat to traditionalists and the Orthodox "due to the lessening of traditional collective identity."[8] The Orthodox were rightfully worried, as their idea of the Jewish collective was being fundamentally altered by reformers, who, as Plaut, Freehof, and Berman suggested, did not see the "Jewish people" as an existing collective and as the intrinsic tie among Jews; instead, reformers believed that it was the "Jewish religion" that "formed the bond across the lands and ages."⁹

One of the greatest challenges to Jewish life in Central Europe came as political exigencies changed people's relationship to the modern nation states. This was especially apparent during and after the French Revolution, as Jews became the subject of heated debates in the various legislatures. In France, discussions took place in the National Assembly, which eventually sided with proemancipation sentiments. However, this initial emancipatory impulse was threatened by the lingering suspicion of Jews as devoted citizens. When Napoleon became emperor, he caved to this suspicion and asked (demanded) the Jewish community of France to respond to twelve questions that clarified Jews' relationship to the state and their fellow citizens:

1. Is it lawful for Jews to marry more than one wife?
2. Is divorce allowed by the Jewish religion? Is divorce valid when not pronounced by courts of justice by virtue of laws in contradiction with those of the French Code?
3. Can a Jewess marry a Christian, and a Jew a Christian woman? Or does the law allow the Jews to marry only among themselves?
4. In the eyes of Jews, are Frenchmen considered as their brethren? Or are they considered as strangers?
5. In either case, what line of conduct does their law prescribe towards Frenchmen not of their religion?
6. Do Jews born in France, and treated by the laws as French citizens, consider France their country? Are they bound to defend it? Are they bound to obey the laws and to conform to the dispositions of the civil code?
7. Who names the rabbis?
8. What police jurisdiction do rabbis exercise among the Jews? What judicial power do they enjoy among them?
9. Are these forms of election, and that police-jurisdiction, regulated by law, or are they only sanctioned by custom?
10. Are there professions which the law of the Jews forbids them from exercising?
11. Does the law forbid Jews from taking usury from their brethren?
12. Does it forbid or does it allow to take usury from strangers?

These questions and their answers became the basis for many Jews' engagement with the state during the nineteenth century, and they also motivated Jews to view themselves as both Frenchmen *and* Jews rather than as Frenchmen *instead of* Jews. The answer to the second question is of particular importance, as it was in this formulation that the rabbis pronounced the concept of *dina de-malkhuta dina* (the law of the state is the law). As the Assembly of Jewish Notables wrote, "at the epoch when they were admitted to the rank of [French] citizens, the rabbis and the principal Jews appeared before the municipalities of their respective places of abode, and took an oath to conform, in every thing to the laws, and to acknowledge no other rules in all civil matters."[10] In the third answer, with regard to interfaith marriage, the rabbis again sided with the state, mentioning that Jews could marry outside the religion and still be considered Jews. However, as Ismar Schorsch contends, though Jews seemingly agreed with the state, they pushed back against the assimilatory intent of the Emperor in their disapproving of such unions (just like their Christian counterparts did among the various Christian confessions).[11] The strategy of conciliation and resistance shown here became a constant theme for German Jews throughout their emancipation struggles, as religious reform remained front and center in the minds of Christians and depicted in the pages of the German press.

The Napoleonic era was also a period of upheaval and identity construction in which Jews took concrete steps toward a reform of Judaism, even though a movement would not come to fruition for decades to come. Those who sought to reform the Jewish religion tried to bring Jews back to synagogue worship, but doing so was not an easy fix. Many Jews eschewed worship for practical reasons, such as keeping their businesses open on Saturday, and others were disinterested in change. Reforming the religion to align with bourgeois mores (aka—modernize and confessionalize the tradition) was an uphill battle for reformers and success was not guaranteed. In fact, as seen throughout the literature, the transformation of Judaism into a modern, nineteenth-century religion "did not necessarily entail the repudiation of Halakha and religious observance."[12] While reform was difficult, even the Orthodox and traditional Jews agreed to make some changes, despite insisting that even the most miniscule change was not permitted. Still, all Jewish groups saw change as an internal Jewish matter and not up for negotiation with Christians as part of the quid pro quo. Andreas Gotzmann, writing about the relationship between religion and society more generally, put it best: "everyone sought to define Judaism as a religion in a 19th century manner. . . . The goal was the definition of Judaism as a religion, more precisely said as a confession that could be integrated next to the others in the realm of the bourgeois state."[13]

The reasons for the uphill battle, aside from indifference to reform among many Jews, were twofold: the ambivalence of states and the antipathy of the older generation. From the states' perspectives, Judaism was a tolerated religion, but not one that signified membership into full citizenship. Immediately after the Napoleonic Era, few, if any German states permitted an official reform within Judaism—at best, those who sought to reform the religion had to find new and indirect avenues to change the hearts and minds of Jews. Thus, reformers sought different avenues through which to influence Jewish life, particularly through education, as the rabbis' reach rarely extended there. In the schools, reformers influenced new generations with a novel form of Judaism and the inculcation of Bildung, bourgeois values, and individuality.[14] The changes in education brought conflict within communities, such as the public discussions during the 1830s in Hannover (in the *Hannoversche Zeitung*) and the early 1840s in Heidelberg (in the German Jewish press).

The Grand Duchy of Baden, foremost among German states during the early nineteenth century, took a more active role in "regenerating" its Jewish population, including changing Jewish customs through a top-down state tutelage; in fact, they sought change in line with those instituted at the Hamburg Israelite Temple Society, including changing elements of the liturgy and modernizing the prayerbook. To achieve this end, the Badenese government instituted the Oberrat der Israeliten Baden, which was empowered to regulate Jewish life and to ensure that Judaism and Jews conformed to its demands—even in more rural areas. During the Napoleonic era, and shortly after developments in Hamburg, reform found an experimental base in Karlsruhe: the 1809 edict mandated that Jewish students had to be enrolled in local schools (without having to participate in Christian religious lessons), which prompted the creation of new Jewish religious schools in 1814, followed by the creation of Jewish elementary schools in 1817. Concurrently, reform religious services were led by two families in their homes (the Kusels and Habers). Yet this experiment would not last long, as the Badenese government forbade private services through the 1824 *Synagogenordnung* (synagogue ordinance; see appendix A).[15]

A similar shutdown of reform services occurred in Prussia in 1823. Prussian authorities had tolerated some reform services in the Beer home since 1812, but King Frederick William III—who in this instance aligned himself with traditional rabbis—opposed and eventually shut down the services (which nearly one-third the adults in the Berlin Jewish community, approximately one thousand people, attended), thus hindering the possibility for further change. The Prussian king was concerned about Jewish reform for two reasons: foremost, he preferred conversion (and he supported societies in carrying out this conversionary work), and secondly, he saw any reform as a dangerous societal precedent. The prohibition of religious reforms set the movement back decades and adherents of reform were unable to find a footing until the 1840s. Despite monarchical antipathy to reform in the early 1820s, Prussian ministers and bureaucrats were more focused on the acculturation of Jews, as seen in the Education Ministerial decree from May 1824, which modernized Jewish education—though its efficacy and enforcement were suspect.[16] Nonetheless, a demand for more reform was building in the Jewish community, as evident in 1840 when the Breslau Jewish community invited Abraham Geiger—one of the leading intellectuals of Jewish reform—to become their second rabbi. Geiger's appointment became a flashpoint for Rabbi Salomon Tiktin and his Orthodox supporters, who petitioned the government to intercede and refuse Geiger's position. This uproar became an explosive event in the German Jewish press and in published pamphlets, and this conflict's resolution showed the power of reformers—Geiger refused to accept a Hamburg-style compromise that allowed him to act as a rabbi but without holding the official title, showing times as well as the balance of power between reformers and traditionalists in the Jewish community had changed. Yet only so much change was acceptable, as Geiger's expected presence in a rabbinical gown at the new Breslau mayor's inauguration was so controversial for both the Christian community and Orthodox Jews that the invitation was rescinded; such sumptuary concerns show how much clothing mattered to notions of German- and Jewishness. The resolution to this conflict also set a tenuous existence for the community, which was divided along religious lines while administration and social welfare efforts remained unified. Nonetheless, Geiger was able to institute some reforms in the community, including girls' confirmation, though some commenters were not impressed by the late arrival of such novelties in comparison to those changes in other parts of Prussia and southwest Germany. Around the same time as the Geiger-Tiktin Affair, a new king—Frederick William IV—took the throne, and he was just as disinclined toward the Prussian Jewish community and Jewish reform as his father. In 1847, the king sought (unsuccessfully) to put Prussian Jewry back into what Moritz Veit called a "medieval corporation separated from the political community in which it resides."[17]

Such a political outcome and mendacious attitude toward its Jewish population—despite the sporadic, yet recurring violence—was not under consideration in Baden; in fact, in 1846, full emancipation passed in the Lower Assembly (though it did not pass in the Upper Assembly or the Ministry), and when that failed, local Jewish communities sought alternative ways to make gains (see chap. 4). And while the outcomes of early reform services were similar in Karlsruhe and Berlin, the intention and desired result of those actions could not be more dissimilar. Instead of restricting reform, the closing down of services allowed the Badenese state to centralize control and further reform Judaism by mandating other changes: the abolishment of rowdiness, the introduction of German-language sermons, and the introduction of choirs and organs to the service. Other changes to Jewish life, including to occupational structure, were also part of this program, which resulted in the creation of societies to promote farming, trades, general improvement of status, and religious reform. The Badenese state—despite Orthodox opposition to many of the changes—was able to impose some reform on even the most unwilling rabbis and communities. The Oberrat and the Badenese authorities were the most successful in promoting reform in the following areas: in hiring and approving rabbis who were mandated to know and give sermons in German; in promoting the hiring of qualified educators that taught in Jewish schools, which were controlled by the Oberrat and Jewish communities, not the rabbis; in permitting Jewish students to attend Christian schools if there were no Jewish schools available in their area; and in funding Jewish schools from the state treasury, similar to how Christian schools were funded, thus bringing a more equitable (though not equal) status in society.[18]

The support for reform in Baden—in comparison to the half-hearted measures and nonexistent monarchical support in Prussia—and that of Jews' allies there (including some liberal politicians and businessmen) facilitated the Jewish community's fulfillment of their obligations, which then allowed for serious consideration of emancipation by the mid-1840s. In more liberal areas of the state, Jewish leaders (including those on the Oberrat) were able to accelerate reform in defiance of Orthodox rabbis' wishes, thus shaping a more progressive generation of Badenese Jews. An example of the results of this process is the Feierlicher Act der Religionsprüfung (Celebration of religious examination) for the Karlsruhe Jewish community in 1836, in which students (two individuals at first and then all students as a choir—inclusive of boys *and* girls) recited Psalm 119:9–17 in both Hebrew and German, followed by a religious examination. Toward the end of the celebration, Rabbi Elias Willstätter gave a sermon that was—except for one small prayer—entirely in German. While such an alignment of state, rabbi, and community in Karlsruhe was a public performance to show off modern, bourgeois German Jewishness and its embodiment of Bildung, such celebrations did not occur all over the state. Resistance to these changes occurred in more peripheral and traditional communities; so much so, that as Reinhard Rürup details, "despite the improved school lessons..., [rural Jews'] educational level (*Bildungsstand*) ... was still low."[19] As will be seen in the last section of this chapter, the potential for conflict among Jews was created as a result of the Badenese state's assertion of authority in the promotion of Jewish reform and in the incorporation of reform elements such as those performed in the Karlsruhe celebration.

One critical arena that generally remained unchanged in Baden—with the exception of the services in the Kusel and Haber homes—was the liturgy and the prayer book. Changes in these areas were among the most contentious in the early stages of reform, and continued to be so throughout the first half of the nineteenth century. Changes in the liturgy and prayer book were closely aligned with the history of the Hamburg Israelite Temple Society, and provide an important backdrop to the events of the early 1840s, including the vigorous and explosive nature of the reform debates. For many Orthodox, reform—if it stayed out of the public eye—could be ignored, and there was no need to address it. However, once these changes—or, in the case of the rabbinical conferences, their discussions—became fodder for public discussion and broadcast throughout the German-speaking realm, those threatened by these changes—Orthodox rabbis and supporters—could no longer ignore what was before their eyes.

The importance of the public disputes during the early post-Napoleonic era revolved around the creation of the Hamburg Israelite Temple Society, the dedication of its synagogue in 1818, and the attempted creation of a new prayer book in 1819. This group of reformers sought a new understanding of Jewish life within the bourgeois world of the nineteenth century, and most importantly, they sought a way to bring back those who had wandered away from Judaism. Much like the changes that Israel Jacobson had fomented as head of the consistory in the Kingdom of Westphalia and those shown in the new temple in Seesen (consecrated in 1810), these changes in Hamburg made it appear as if "Jews worship as Christians do." The focal point of this new style of devotion was the edifying and more universally understandable German-language sermon; this innovation supplanted reading from the prophets (haftarah). The proof of the reformers' success was in the community's ability to build its own synagogue with nearly 250 seats (142 for men, 107 for women in a separate section), space for an organ and choir, and a noticeable lack of a partition in front of the women's seats.[20] Along with the structural changes, the prayer book also received a dramatic facelift. The new version opened from left to right (traditionally, Jewish prayer books open from right to left), and prayers appeared in both Hebrew and German. Temple leaders also instituted a triennial cycle for the reading of the Torah instead of an annual one—an innovation still in use today.

These changes led to a public split in the Jewish community, and the Temple Association became an unofficial leader of reform, as Jewish communities in Leipzig (though only during fair days) and in Karlsruhe adopted similar innovations. These developments aroused consternation among the Orthodox community, and the Hamburg Senate stepped in and forced a compromise among the factions. The Temple Association had to settle for something less than it wanted but more than its detractors wanted to permit: instead of officially recognizing the Temple Association as a separate entity, it was allowed to call itself a "place for public edification" and not a temple or a synagogue (though reformers had to pay for both communities' upkeep). The reform community's leaders (Kley and Salomon) could only be called teachers (*Lehrer*) and not rabbis. The new community was not official in any capacity—it was tolerated, however—and due to the senate's protection, it was allowed to develop without fear of being shut down (as happened to the Beer services in 1823). However, increasing antipathy to reform from governments (especially in Bavaria and Prussia) and Orthodox rabbis affected reforms from moving beyond the community's borders. Still, as Lenhard has pointed out, the opening of the Hamburg Temple could not be ignored.[21] The development of Jewish reform in Hamburg and the fight over the temple and its prayer book, along with developments in Jewish education in Baden, as well as the varying reasons for closing down reform services in Berlin and Karlsruhe, show that in order for reform to thrive, the movement needed both state support (or perhaps, at a minimum, ambivalence) and an internal Jewish drive for it to succeed. Such conditions for reform throughout the German states would not come to fruition until the 1840s, when the ground was sufficiently prepared for reformers within an increasingly more liberal and inclusive society.

"CUTTING" TIES: CIRCUMCISION, LAY LEADERSHIP, AND COMMUNAL SPLITS

One of the most important aspects within the fight for religious reform in the Jewish community during the 1840s was the appearance of radical reform groups headed by lay persons, as well as the effect that these groups had on the pace, nature, and acceptability of reform.[22] These groups appeared because decades had gone by without any substantive change in Jews' position within German society—whether that meant the lack of societal integration or the seemingly diminishing prospects of Jewish emancipation. Moreover, those who became affiliated with Jewish reform sought a complete change of direction from those who did not endorse the reform effort. As Benjamin Baader argues, reformers believed "that Judaism possessed a core and a spirit distinct from Halakha, and that this core needed to be preserved."[23] As discussed in the following paragraphs, reformers no longer viewed Joseph Caro's *Shulchan Aruch* as the ultimate textual authority guiding religious life. Instead, these reformers sought a return to reine Mosaismus (pure Mosaism)—what they called the beliefs and mores as written in the Torah.

As seen previously, the desire for change percolated and simmered below the surface for decades while reform was only able to gain minimal traction in a few communities. While the most infamous reform group, the Reformfreunde (RF) in Frankfurt, did not necessarily have a large base of support or a long-term impact on the direction of Jewish reform, its influence on the debate in the mid-1840s was unsurpassed in the German press. Not only did the members cause alarm within private circles, but their detractors also brought their complaints to the German press for all to observe. Rabbis and theologians responded to the RF's religious program, and they felt compelled to come up with their own answers to satisfy the modern, bourgeois demands imposed by German society.[24] Such conflicts between the reformers and the Orthodox became a commonplace occurrence from 1844 to 1846. Not only were there discussions about the RF and their Berlin counterpart, the Reformgenossenschaft (Reform Society, RG), but there were also complicated discussions about the rabbinical conferences over those three years. All-in-all, Jewish reform from 1843 to 1846 was *the* most discussed topic about Jewish life and Judaism in the German press.

Perhaps the most important reason for the reform associations' prominence within the pan-German newspapers was their alignment with the liberal spirit of the times, especially their demands for a "German-Jewish Church," which were similar to the Vormärz Christian reform movements—the Friends of Light (*Lichtfreunde*) and the German Catholics (*Deutschkatholiken*).[25] Indeed, there were many at that time who believed there were Jews who favored these societies and followed the teachings of Johannes Ronge, leader of the Deutschkatholiken.[26] Liberal papers supported the Christian dissidents' movement and their claims for recognition by the states and equalization of their rights with the believers of the three officially recognized Christian confessions. Many of these papers not only advocated for Christian reform, but were also at the forefront of agitating for Jewish religious reform and supporting Jewish emancipation. However, the newspapers that are a part of this study—the *Frankfurter Journal*, the *Leipziger/Deutsche Allgemeine Zeitung*, the *Augsburger Allgemeine Zeitung*, and the *Vossische Zeitung*—were not just papers in which Christians wrote about Jews, Judaism, and Jewish reform; they also became important vehicles by which Jews presented their arguments and expressed their displeasure against their adversaries.

We also need to keep in mind that editors wielded significant power in this dynamic. These men's views toward Jews, Jewish reform, and emancipation shaped the nature and tone of the newspaper coverage; they were the gatekeepers of public knowledge and influenced discussions by editing reports, reprinting carefully chosen article segments from other papers, printing competing claims, or refusing to print a submitted article. Still, many liberal editors allowed this discussion to take place, which showed their interest in—and perhaps also support of—these groups, just as they endorsed other reform groups and liberal causes.

Unsurprisingly, personal power was another factor in these struggles, specifically who had the power to represent Jews and Judaism in the public space and who had the power to modify Judaism. In each of the specific debates discussed here—the circumcision debate in Frankfurt, the debates involving the Frankfurt RF and Berlin RG, and the debates in Mannheim and Heidelberg in the wake of the rabbinical conferences of 1844 to 1846—various groups presented their own answers to these questions in front of the general public. Germans of all confessions observed these discussions, as the four newspapers used for this study had a combined readership of 30,000 printed copies, which amounted to a minimum of 300,000 readers.[27] Each of these newspapers ranked in the top seven in terms of readership in the German states (and many articles were reprinted in other papers, thus extending their reach), making them perfect platforms to view the public presentation of the Jewish struggle about reform.

Discussions about Jewish life were not peripheral during the years 1843 to 1846, and an examination of the number of newspaper items (articles and insertions [usually personal rebuttals or arguments]) that dealt specifically with Judaism confirm this. Table 3.1 shows the number of articles about the Jewish religion that appeared in each of the newspapers.[28] Both the *FJ* and the *DAZ* were leading sources for information about Jews and Judaism among these pan-German papers. One can easily make the claim, as Ludwig Philippson did in 1845, that the *FJ* was the "Staatszeitung der neue Bewegung" (state paper of the new movement) and helped the RF promote its agenda. Anti-Jewish opponents, such as Alban Stolz in Baden, had negative views of the *FJ* and denigrated it as "that Jew paper."[29] Likewise, if one considers the dramatic increase in articles in the *DAZ* about Judaism from 1844 to 1845, it is clear that this paper also became a mouthpiece not only of the RF and the RG, which it willingly promoted, but that it was the most important venue for the presentation of Jewish religious reform in the non-Jewish press.

Table 3.1. Articles about Jews, Judaism, or Jewish Reform in Pan-German Newspapers

	Circulation 1845	Circulation 1847	1843		1844		1845		1846 (through August)	
			Total	Religious	Total	Religious	Total	Religious	Total	Religious
Leipziger Allgemeine Zeitung (Deutsche Allgemeine Zeitung)	6,000*	n/a	177	39	162	33	198	100	127**	45†
Vossische Zeitung	7,000	19,850	n/a	n/a	85	14	86	31	66	12
Augsburger Allgemeine Zeitung	9,172	9,847	n/a	15††	88	14	56	17	67	4
Frankfurter Journal (in 1844–45, April through December)	8,000	10,000	178	17	92	29	105	60	124#	40##

* From Hannoversche Morgenzeitung.
** Plus 40 more through December.
† Plus 10 more through December.
†† This number reflects only articles about the Reformfreunde in Frankfurt.
# Plus 52 more through December.
Plus 13 more through December.

However, these numbers simplify what is a messy and complicated history. Historically, Jews did not necessarily desire public debates about their religion, as these often ended negatively for Jews. Any appeals to non-Jewish authorities or public debates had the potential for negative ramifications for the entire community, as seen in the Emden-Eibeschütz Affair a century earlier. However, as Robert Liberles noted, the Frankfurt reformers intentionally used the general press to "spur Jews into action" and "wanted [Christian] Germans to encourage such notions further"—regardless of the potential negative consequences of bringing their disputes before the discerning and critical public that was overwhelmingly anti-Jewish.[30] The debates in the press reflect this dual aim of the reformers. The public airing of dirty laundry in the newspapers and the impetus for dramatic change within Judaism started with debates about circumcision in 1843 and whether rabbis and communities could compel men to have the rite performed on their sons. Nonetheless, this discussion was a mere pretext for the larger debate surrounding the Reform movement driven by Jewish laymen who sought a radical break with Jewish tradition. The opening up of Judaism by lay reformers was a deliberate act designed to harm the authority and power of the rabbis, of the Orthodox, and of anyone who stood in the way of reform. As such, the lay reformers forced others to defend themselves by initiating and participating in public disputes. Those who were moderate reformers (and opposed to the lay reformers) were uniquely qualified to handle this challenge, as most of them were university educated, and many had already participated in the world of German letters by publishing pamphlets or treatises in the German Jewish press. Such qualities allowed moderate reformers to stave off the challenges of radical lay reform in the short run, and in the long run, the challenge presented by the radical reformers helped each movement create its own unique identity and voice.

The debate over Jewish circumcision was part of a wholesale attack on the nature of Jewish ritual practice. These debates became a popular topic from the 1840s through the 1850s (and for decades beyond that) precisely because they affected Jewish lives in existential ways, including the debate about Jewish emancipation and Jewish citizenship.[31] However, the debates were not just about the rite as a religious symbol of Jewish modernity but also about who had the power to decide who counted as a Jew. Above all else, the discussion about circumcision was about Jewish difference, and whether or not this rite separated Jewish Germans from Christian Germans—physically, morally, socially, and otherwise.

During the 1840s, discussions revolved around Jewish fathers who refused to have their sons circumcised yet still wanted their sons registered as full members of the Jewish community. Jewish law commands the following in Genesis 17:11: "You shall circumcise the flesh of your foreskin, and that shall be the sign of the covenant between me and you. And throughout the generations, every male among you shall be circumcised." The law was not ambiguous, and uncircumcised men were called *aral* and were not full members of the local, Jewish community.[32] However, one's Jewishness was *not* determined by circumcision but, rather, by matrilineal descent. Yet defining who was a Jew was not the sole province of the Jewish community; the state also had a say. German governments generally allowed Jewish communal authorities to exercise sole authority in internal Jewish matters, yet they cared about making sure that the community counted each individual.

The public debate about circumcision became an important flashpoint in the public presentation of Jews and Judaism before public eyes. Not only was it an important marker of Jewishness within the Jewish community, but it was also a critical signifier of Jewish difference for those looking from the outside in. As Robin Judd notes, "the mid-century discussions about circumcision gained a national audience because they lent themselves to the contemporaneous phenomena affecting Jews and the relationship to the communities among whom they lived." Regarding circumcision in the public sphere, some studies have already analyzed the numerous treatises, governmental edicts, and discussions in the German Jewish press about the topic.[33] However, none of these studies looked at how Jews presented these debates to the general public; they focus more on internal Jewish discussions and reactions.

In February 1843, the authorities in Frankfurt took up the issue of circumcision, and while confirming the rite and trying to make sure that it was done in a medically acceptable manner (fig. 3.1), they used the following phrasing as part of their ruling, "Israelite citizens and residents, so long as they desire to have their children circumcised..."[34] This minor modification, "insofern sie ihre Kinder beschneiden lassen wollen," was neither requested nor desired by the community, and in fact, this wording changed the necessity of the rite to be performed. Individuals could choose *not* to have the ceremony performed, and as a result, several fathers selected this path. The ensuing public debate, which included many medical treatises and rabbinical assessments (*Gutachten*), provided grist for the public mill. In sum, nearly every rabbi who submitted an assessment, except for the most radical ones, approved and supported Rabbi Salomon Trier's push to keep the rite and enforce the procedure. However, the Frankfurt Senate, despite officially proclaiming that it did not want to usurp Jewish law, was less than genuine in its public expression. In fact, as Robert Liberles has shown, the Frankfurt government deliberately sought to

Fig. 3.1. Postcard depicting Brit Milah (circumcision), ca. 1880. "Die Beschneidung (Bris milo)," circa 1880. © Musée d'art et d'histoire du Judaïsme (Paris, France).

sabotage Judaism and provided reformers (whom the politicians also saw as "buffoons") "with the opportunity for the blatant disintegration of Judaism." One could also argue that since the *FJ* was the "Staatszeitung" of the RF, the government—through its censors—also facilitated the reformers' agenda.[35] In the end, Trier's protestations went unheeded, and the four fathers did not have to circumcise their sons.

These discussions appeared in all of the major newspapers, and they often interacted with each other. The discussion in the *FJ* started a few months after the edict's issuance. The first article appeared in the supplemental section (*Beilage*) of the newspaper, and the reference to circumcision was embedded in a more general discussion about Jewish reform. In the middle of the passage, the correspondent wrote that circumcision had "no purpose or meaning" in the current era, and that the rite was a signal of a "foreign custom." In this article, the author also took aim at Jews' belief in the Messiah and the prominence of the Talmud. In response to this article, on July 5, 1843, a contributor countered each of the claims and also targeted the RF by arguing that their adherence to a negative program resulted in dispensing with so many Jewish customs and religious practices that one could no longer call it "reform." The respondent went further when speaking of circumcision, saying "through the non-recognition of circumcision, the Jew ceases to be a Jew; without circumcision, Judaism is not possible, and therefore, it [circumcision] is dogma and not ritual." Such a claim did not go unchallenged, and within five days, another contributor chose to enter the fray. This writer attacked the July 5 piece, claiming the author "shows great ignorance of Judaism" before providing a list of five points/questions that addressed the issues at hand. The response started by mentioning that the practice was Abrahamic, not Mosaic, and that other descendants of Israel who were Abrahamic, such as Arabs and Midianites, used the practice. The respondent then challenged the argument that the practice was, in fact, a law. The author argued that while the practice was described in Genesis 17:11, Deuteronomy—where all the laws were recapitulated—did not include the practice; however, the author failed to mention that the procedure did actually appear in Leviticus 12:3. The next line of attack drew on Moses, who did not circumcise his sons, and on the Israelites who did not circumcise children during their forty years in the desert after escaping Egypt. And finally, the author raised a question about the place of women in this formulation, as they are not circumcised; thus, the author concluded, Jews are Jews through matrilineal descent, "so long as they do not disavow a singular God and revelation."[36] This miniargument in the pages of the *FJ* reflected both the ideological arguments about the practice and the fact that it was of significant public interest.

While this discussion stalled in the *FJ*, circumcision was one of the hot-button topics that surrounded the RF. Although this group did not *officially* proclaim disdain for or rejection of the rite, it is clear that they chose to highlight less controversial positions because they wanted to win over supporters. Despite downplaying circumcision in their program, it was widely known that Gabriel Riesser, the "champion" of Jewish emancipation and one of the named leaders of the RF (though he disavowed this title), abhorred the practice and believed it to be barbaric.[37] This position, which many radical reformers held, provided intensity to this conflict, and the animosity appeared not only in discussions about this rite but also in nearly every issue for which reformers desired change.

In the *DAZ*, the discussion about circumcision lasted longer, generated increased interaction with correspondents from other leading papers (in this case the *AAZ*), and resulted in more printed articles. This topic also revealed the strategy of the reformers in their more general fight. The first article, in the *DAZ* from July 31, 1843, included a few interesting tidbits that were picked up by other papers. Foremost, this contributor focused on the alleged retaliation against one of the fathers who refused to circumcise his son. This man, who was considered a well-respected businessman, lost business from more devout individuals. As the article mentioned, the father's decision was "(brought) before the judge of public opinion" and not kept within the Jewish community. The rumor, confirmed in other papers, named the Rothschild family as the one that severed ties with this father, supposedly causing a "shivering" effect in the community. Later, in November, a correspondent in the *AAZ* alleged that Amschel Mayer Rothschild was a hypocrite, since the magnate did business with Jewish apostates and appeared to tolerate his nephew's less strict religious outlook.[38]

This report in the *AAZ*, however, was not left unchallenged. In his first correspondence in the *DAZ* on this matter, the correspondent from Frankfurt am Main (☿) challenged the positive nature of the prior report regarding reform (especially regarding its "progress" and the fact that "Männer von Ansehen" [men of status] spoke out on its behalf) and challenged the assertion that Rothschild broke off his relationship with the other Jewish banker due to his decision about his son's circumcision. The author also questioned the motive behind disparaging the religiosity of Rothschild's nephew. In response, the Δ correspondent for the *AAZ* questioned what the *DAZ* correspondent meant by "men of standing" and then listed those who supported the society: "many notable educated lawyers, doctors and writers, and also two members of the (Jewish) Board."[39] The *AAZ* correspondent then attacked the *Rabbinische Gutachten* (rabbinical testaments) submitted to the Frankfurt Senate, arguing that none of those submitted argued that an uncircumcised Jew would be "fully excluded from the Jewish community." This correspondent then tied the board and its reform leanings (and, therefore, the society) to the election of Leopold Stein as rabbi. The *DAZ* correspondent responded to the *AAZ* writer and found it "lächerlich" (laughable) that the latter used Stein in his defense, as the rabbi wrote a "full-throated testament against the *Reformverein*" in *Der Orient*. Moreover, the *DAZ* correspondent highlighted the fact that even more Gutachten had arrived (about thirty, up from sixteen) and that all of them—including those from reformers—"speak on behalf of circumcision." Still, as seen just a week after this response, the Frankfurt Jewish community board did not necessarily regard these Gutachten as a settled matter. Another Jewish father chose to not have his son circumcised, and the community still registered the son in the community records. The senate confirmed this registration, and they regarded the decision as "belong[ing] to the competence of the Jewish community board." As the article mentioned, those who "subscribe to progress" (*dem Fortschritte huldigen*) welcomed the disinterest of the senate and the decision to send the matter to the board, which at that time was controlled by reformers.[40]

This report came only days after an *AAZ* article in which a correspondent (◉) detailed some of the Gutachten from notable rabbis. It should be noted here that most of the responses to Trier's call were from German rabbis, and that during the following year (1845), the same would remain true about opposition to the reform rabbis and preachers who gathered in Brunswick for the first rabbinical conference.[41] Here are two noteworthy responses from the article: the first pointed out that three rabbis did not even bother writing a Gutachten because "they found the question so simple to answer through the words in the text of the holy scriptures," and secondly, many of the rabbis believed that members of the RF had completely exited the Jewish religious community, so much so that they should no longer be considered Jews. Additionally, many rabbis believed that both the father, who did not want his son circumcised, and the son should not be considered Jewish and that the son should not be permitted to marry a Jewish woman (in nearly all German states, Jews could only legally marry other Jews while also remaining Jewish).[42] It was clear from this interchange that the rabbis nearly unanimously opposed losing control over their communities and over their influence in *how* and *by whom* Jews should be defined.

In the middle of February, the discussion about circumcision ratcheted up a notch, when the ⊠ correspondent from Frankfurt railed against "rabbinic-talmudic Jews." Foremost, this correspondent (falsely) claimed that circumcision and the RF did not "have a connection." As shown by later correspondents (◉ and ☿) in the first publicized details about the society and its principles, and confirmed by the modern scholarship about the debate, this correspondent's claims were not accurate. The correspondent then argued that these attacks were due to Orthodox rabbis' fear of losing their "already insignificant importance" and lambasted those who made the Stern and Riesser correspondence public. The author referenced Alexander Behr's *Lehrbuch der mosaischen Religion* (Munich, 1826) to support his claim. Behr wrote this text under the supervision of Rabbi Abraham Bing (Würzburg), one of the most well-respected rabbis in the German states. It was through his guidance that the first rabbi with a doctorate was ordained, Dr. Nathan Marcus Adler of Hannover (who became chief rabbi of England in 1845). This contributor cited Behr (and Bing) to lend credence to his view that circumcision was not necessary ("In no way is circumcision a *condition* of entrance in to the Jewish collective") and then compared such nonobservance to Jews who chose to eat leavened bread during Passover.[43]

Both the ◉ and ☿ correspondents then took aim at different parts of the ⊠ correspondent's text. The ◉ correspondent in the *AAZ* countered by calling circumcision "indispensable" (*unentbehrlich*) and went further by writing that

Jewish law asserted that "a Jew who does not let his son get circumcised should be thrown out of his people and that he has broken the bond of Jehovah with the people." Despite the agreement about the "barbaric" nature of circumcision, this correspondent retorted that the observance of the rite must continue because no practice had superseded it nor had it been in disuse for an extended period. This correspondent then concluded as follows: "whoever throws away circumcision does not reform, rather they 'break the bond' with all of Jewry who has given them their existence." In a similar way, the ☿ correspondent from the *DAZ* attacked the veracity of the ☒ correspondent's claims. He first asked whether the one who questioned the "rabbinic-talmudic Jews" had actually read the Gutachten that he railed against and whether the writer was even familiar with Jewish prayers. In perhaps the most vindictive insult used during this exchange, this writer claimed the other writer—whom he believed to "clearly be a Jew"—had become an "Eisenmenger." In other words, the author argued that the other Jew had become an implacable enemy who spewed anti-Jewish invective and falsehoods, relying solely on cherry-picked evidence from the Talmud that painted Judaism negatively and Jews as incapable of being patriotic, just as Eisenmenger had in 1700. This correspondent also challenged the former's use of Behr's *Handbuch*, and correctly stated that only the first fourteen words of the quote were accurate, while "the other nineteen lines were fabrications of the correspondent." This article writer then concluded with the belief that Dr. Behr would join this discussion to counter "such a clear falsification of his book."[44]

Ultimately, the discussion about circumcision across the German states was an opening salvo in the mid-1840s fight about Jewish reform. As can be seen from Rabbi Trier's collection of rabbinical Gutachten, rabbis tried to preserve their authority against two powerful foes: a state (Frankfurt) that relished the idea that the Jewish community was cannibalizing itself, and a group of Jewish Germans who, having eschewed traditional Jewish learning and entered the world of German letters and society, challenged their authority (and their adherence to the Shulchan Aruch) in front of a German society to which most German Jews desired full and unequivocal integration.

As seen in the previous discussion, there were several individuals willing to deftly defend the rite of circumcision using multifaceted arguments. This chutzpah (audacity) was allowed to play itself out in front of the German Christian public in order to spur the rest of Jewry from its slumber. Those that became members of the Berlin and Frankfurt reform associations, much like the Hamburg Israelite Temple Society, were from the rising Jewish middle class—either through their wealth or through their university education. The first of these associations appeared in September 1842 in Frankfurt, concurrent with the circumcision debate. The society called itself the Verein der Reformfreunde (Association of the Friends of Reform), and as its name suggests, it was a movement that had similarities to other "Friends" movements of the era, most notably the Lichtfreunde—a movement dedicated to reform in the Lutheran Church—and the Deutschkatholiken. In fact, as Ari Joskowicz has contended, these Jewish reform movements cannot be understood outside of the context of broader religious dissent and protest against the Catholic Church, in particular. As noted in the German Jewish press, contributors often linked Jewish reformers and Christian dissidents directly, and while there were many who sought to deny these associations (such as Ludwig Philippson), by 1845 the links were clear not only to those within the Jewish press but also to those who contributed to the regular German press as well.[45]

The fight over reform was particularly visible in both the *Frankfurter Journal* and the *Deutsche Allgemeine Zeitung*. As mentioned earlier, Ludwig Philippson called the *FJ* the "state paper" of radical reformers, but this characterization could equally apply to the *DAZ*. As seen in table 3.1, both of these journals published stories and contributions about reform much more frequently than either the *Augsburger Allgemeine Zeitung* or the *Vossische Zeitung*. What separated these discussions in the German newspapers from those in the German Jewish press was the nature of the contributions, as many Christians provided their opinions about Jews and Judaism, which indicated how important this discussion was to people across religious and cultural boundaries. Just in the *FJ*, some Christians criticized Jews and Judaism for holding onto circumcision (June 29, 1843), while others applauded the election of Leopold Stein as second rabbi in the city (July 29, 1844).[46] Many other news reports were also probably written by Christians, though the authorship of these articles is tough to determine. Regardless of authorship, the discussion in the regular press is an important way of understanding how Jewish reform was presented to the public at large.

An examination of these reform-friendly newspapers provides additional color around the development (or lack thereof in the case of the Frankfurt RF) of the Reform movement. As Michael Meyer has written, the RF did not ultimately create their own movement that resonated throughout the German lands. In fact, the Frankfurt friends completely dissipated by 1846. As David Philipson pointed out, the Frankfurt friends were "a complete failure as an organization." This statement by Philipson echoed the sentiment that was elucidated at that time by Dr. Moritz Freistadt from Königsberg, who wrote the following: "The Frankfurt Society already carries the germs of death, and it confuses the minds, instead of enlightening them. In the history of Jewish cultural development, it will form a sad episode which attests to its own unscientific and irreligious amateurism (*Dilettantismus*)."⁴⁷ The Berlin RG, on the other hand, was able to create a lasting community within Berlin (it lasted until 1939), and it influenced other communities outside of the metropolis. In the long run, the Reformgemeinde (as it was renamed in 1850) could not survive the Nazi onslaught, and the individuals who did survive went into diaspora, where they found more traditional religious alternatives. Yet in the 1840s, the RG not only was able to make a mark in its own community—especially among women and despite nonacceptance of its separateness from the officially recognized Jewish community—but also spurred individual Jews and non-Jews to action.⁴⁸

In the *Frankfurter Journal* and the *Deutsche Allgemeine Zeitung*, the creation of the RF was discussed alongside the circumcision debate; in fact, the society was inextricably linked to its views on the matter, even if circumcision was not an officially published part of its program, which consisted of the following three points:

1. We recognize the possibility of unlimited progress in Judaism.
2. The collection of controversies, dissertations, and prescriptions commonly designated by the name Talmud possesses for us no authority either from the dogmatic or the practical standpoint.
3. A Messiah who is to lead the Israelites back to the land of Palestine is neither expected nor desired by us; we know no fatherland except that to which we belong by birth or citizenship.

There were also two other, nonpublished elements to their program which became part of the more general conversation, despite efforts to exclude them: firstly, RF members viewed ancient rituals and laws, such as kashrut (kosher) laws, as nonbinding, and secondly, they rejected circumcision as a binding act or religious symbol.⁴⁹ The latter excision, despite the society's desire not to tackle the issue (due to its extremely contentious nature) became a flashpoint in the history of the RF and the Reform movement, as seen previously.

Almost immediately, criticisms of the RF flooded both the German Jewish and regular press. The first controversy surrounded the publishing of personal letters from Moritz Abraham Stern to Gabriel Riesser, two of the named "leaders" of the group. As published on August 5, 1843, in the *FJ*, the respondent—alluding to the discussion of the society in the *Allgemeine Zeitung des Judenthums*—argued that such a publication was done in a "fiendish manner" (*perfide Weise*) in order "to place [the society] in a bad light." The author also offered a fifty-florin reward for the name of the person who had leaked the information, while Louis Simon, a member of the RF, denounced the leaking of these documents as "traitorous." An article in the *DAZ* gave even more detail as to the circumstances of the personal correspondence falling into the wrong hands (it was supposedly sent around by Theodor Creizenach—another founder of the RF—as part of the society's appeal to gain signatures). Regardless, observers were keen to mention that in Stern's correspondence, he proposed nothing less than "the destruction of the entire religion" and had offered nothing to replace it; therefore, such a reform should not be permitted by the authorities. Indeed, this lack of positive religious position was one of the reasons why the RF struggled to gain adherents—never gaining more than forty-five members and modest popularity in nearby cities (Darmstadt)—and quickly died a "natural death."[50] Still, the impact of this group—and of the interest in reform among Frankfurt's Jews in general—pushed reform in the city and led to conflicts over the election of a second rabbi (Stein), the building of a new synagogue, and the rabbinical conferences, the second of which occurred in Frankfurt.

The election of a second rabbi in Frankfurt was a topic of public interest, especially for advocates of reform. Leopold Stein, who was Rabbi in Burgkunstadt in Bavaria, was elected in December 1843 to this open position, and the community hoped that he could both woo the Rothschild family and get along with Rabbi Trier. However, as reported in the press, the existing rabbi, Salomon Trier, protested this election and sought to have the senate intervene on his behalf to prevent Stein's candidacy. Instead of supporting his claim, the senate pushed for Trier to retire, and in indignation, the aged rabbi refused his pension.[51] The end of Trier's tenure as rabbi was a topic of interest in the German press, especially his antagonistic relationship with the reformers. This episode did not end with Trier's resignation, however, as the Rothschild family—supporters of Jewish Orthodoxy—reneged on their promise to give 150,000 florins for a new synagogue in Frankfurt. The family explicitly stated in the donation contract with the community that they would not support any new rabbi who did not have Trier's approval. This action caused a slight uproar in the community, as those with additional gripes against the family took issue with the community's unfair taxation policies, which favored the family. Despite the negative coverage and the consequential split in the community, the Rothschilds did not change course. As related on August 30, 1844, in the *AAZ*, the family cared little about what the Jewish community or the general public thought of its religiosity—it stood true to its defense of "historical

Orthodoxy."[52] This episode marked the official split within the Jewish community of Frankfurt, one that would never be resolved. Though the RF was unable to establish a permanent institutional presence in the community, its efforts pushed the community toward reform and conflict.

The story of the Frankfurt RF was quite different than that of its Berlin successor, the RG. This society formed in 1845—right in the middle of the reform debates and rabbinical conferences—and its formation can be interpreted as a reaction to both the election of Michael Sachs as the assistant rabbi in Berlin and the strong, Orthodox bent of the community. Sachs was an adherent to Jewish Orthodoxy, though he was fine with making minor reforms, and he was known in the German states as being an adherent to wissenschaftliche Orthodoxie (scientific orthodoxy). Still, Sachs's election was controversial: reformers saw it as both "surprising" and "counterproductive."[53] His appointment became a flashpoint in the community—both the reformers and the Orthodox signed petitions against his appointment. As a report from August 31, 1845, mentions, "he [Sachs] spoiled it with the Reform friends from the beginning, and the Orthodox will likewise never trust him."[54] However, the newspapers did not really follow Sachs as closely as they had the activities of the RG (one could say the *DAZ* was overly preoccupied with the association and its activities), though there were a few (mostly negative) articles written about him shortly after the Frankfurt rabbinical conference.[55]

The blossoming of this organization was a public affair. From the moment the RG's "Aufruf an die deutschen Glaubensbrüder" (Call to our German coreligionists, April 1, 1845) hit the Jewish and non-Jewish presses, the society was in the spotlight. Just a week after the publication of the "Aufruf," a correspondent in the *DAZ* wrote that it was mere words, "like Hamlet," and that like the attempted reform half a century earlier, this attempt would neither find a "base" (*Boden*) nor "leave a trace" (*spurlos verschwunden*). Other correspondents supported the cause of the RG, sometimes even parroting the "Aufruf" in presenting information about the society. As one correspondent (+) described, "in any case this reforming movement within Judaism earns general attention and support. It clearly drives the Jews closer to the pulsating rhythm of our lives.... Therefore, the current Jewish reform is well advantaged." Such positive evaluation of the movement for reform tied the RG to the intellectual and religious currents of the mid-1840s. Still others saw what was going on not as a flash-in-the-pan, as Freistadt had predicted for the RF, but as a movement that was built on the past and the ideas that were presently circulating within German Jewry. Others questioned whether or not the project could even get off the ground, mentioning that not only were the Orthodox holding the RG (and reform, in general) back, but more generally, there was indifference among the populace. Overall, despite these obstacles, observers felt more positive about the RG's potential success when compared to that of the Frankfurt reformers.[56]

These initial discussions were not the only ones that appeared in the *DAZ*, and as the RG sought out a location for its services, held its first holiday services, and chose a rabbi to lead the community (eventually, Dr. Samuel Holdheim), the public was informed of all of the details.[57] Correspondents in the *DAZ* also encouraged the RG to keep implementing change. The critiques of the society, despite appearing in the press, were not of huge concern for the organization as it sought to create Judaism *on its own terms*. As stated in the "Aufruf": "We want belief. We want positive religion. We want Judaism." In fact, the frequency of the reporting about the RG in the *DAZ* makes it seem as if its members had a vested interest in ensuring that this information reached the public, and that the RG saw itself as a group that should not be defined to one locale—it needed to spread to other regions.[58] Choosing the *DAZ* as the main location for this effort was well-justified: the paper had liberal leanings and generally supported Jewish emancipation, and its readers were from groups most likely to support its cause—those from the educated classes, those who were more liberal politically, and those in Jewish communities that had similar reform sympathies.

The struggles and activities of the RG, as seen through the regular press, revealed how contentious religious life during the Vormärz had become. As society itself destabilized and contention became endemic throughout the entire system, Jewish life (and specifically Jewish religious life) was not isolated from its effects. Still, the RG throughout these tribulations had qualities that its defunct predecessor organization never had. Foremost, whereas the RF only ever had three to four dozen official supporters, the RG had hundreds. The RG also had a more positive view toward Judaism. They did not just want to tear down rabbinical Judaism; instead, they wished to replace outdated and incompatible elements with new structures and ideas that could facilitate its members in defining themselves as both German and Jewish. As Ralph Bisschops maintained, "[Sigismund] Stern [the leader of the RG and its chief intellectual] wanted a Judaism built up from scratch and not made up of re-contextualized pieces of rabbinical lore; he wanted it to be a faith and a practice designed for modernity, 'tailor-made' as one might suspect." Members of the RG realized that there must be a theological and liturgical component to their movement, for which the reformers in Frankfurt only advocated once it was too late. The RG also had a leadership that was dedicated to its survival, existence, and expansion while leading from within the community. The Frankfurt RF had leaders (or those that were called its leaders) who lived elsewhere (Riesser in

Hamburg, and M. A. Stern in Göttingen), while the leaders of the RG lived and worked in Berlin, though many of the supporters of reform in Berlin were not native Berliners and were not tied to its Orthodox community.[59] Still, as the renting of the Gropius Panorama for religious services showed, it was the members of the community who were willing to put their own money and financial security on the line for the general welfare. Additionally, the rest of the community revealed its willingness to support services and its activities through very generous donations. But perhaps the most important attribute in the RG's success in comparison to the RF was that it was constantly in the public eye as the group's publications promoted its activities and agenda. And while there certainly were negative pieces written about reform, reformers, and the RG, these pale in comparison to the good press received—coverage that intimately detailed the group's activities that could help influence reformers elsewhere.

JEWISH RELIGIOUS REFORM AND THE RABBINICAL ASSEMBLIES OF THE 1840S

The conflict between factions within German Jewry became hardened during the mid-1840s, and much of this conflict centered on the rabbinical conferences of 1844 to 1846. As Michael Meyer has noted, the conflict developed despite reformers' intentions to seek a "middle path." Furthermore, most of the reformers were moderates who sought "historical continuity while at the same time [remaining] willing to make some sharp distinctions from tradition." Those who congregated at these conferences were hardly the RF, who, as seen previously, "were ready to cast virtually every distinctive characteristic of Judaism aside."[60] The conference members were looking to change Judaism from within to conform to the religious and societal sensibilities of the Vormärz. Thus, these conferences are of interest for this study for two reasons. First of all, few scholars have dealt with the conferences in detail. Secondly, the rabbinical conferences and the local Jewish reactions to these events were prominent both in the general and local presses.

The three conferences, held in Brunswick (1844), Frankfurt am Main (1845), and Breslau (1846), were important for the official creation of the Reform, Conservative, and modern Orthodox movements, although an official split in the Jewish communities did not occur at that moment.[61] Despite the growing and ever-present antagonism between factions, the rupture did not occur until the Austritt (exit) Law passed in Baden in 1869 and in Prussia in 1876.[62] Neither reformers nor the Orthodox wanted to live under the political influence of the other group, but until the 1870s, those in the confessional minority had to coexist with the majority, whether or not they agreed with the majority about religious practices. There were few alternatives: atheism and nonaffiliation were illegal, and the only other option was conversion.

The rabbinical conferences afforded plenty of rabbis and preachers the opportunity to raise concerns and to start debates about changes and trends within German Jewry. In fact, the participants who went to Brunswick and the other cities were not required to implement any of the changes to which they had agreed; changes were only "morally binding." Yet the reformers sought public affirmation for their work so that "if the people had confidence in them their work would prove to be of a lasting character, and would receive an authoritative stamp." So the question can be raised: Why was there so much fuss over decisions that had no binding authority? Part of the answer goes to the nature of reform and how nonreformers, traditionalists, and modern Orthodox viewed these changes. According to Sylvan Schwartzman, "to the Orthodox of Europe, Reform was not only a challenge to religious authority, it was unmitigated heresy, to be extirpated at all cost; no measures were too severe to root it out." Even contemporaries saw the developing Orthodox position as a "Vernichtungskampf" (extermination fight) against reform.[63] As seen in the disputes during early reform, traditionalists did not desire any changes, even minimal ones; thus, to them, what the conferences promised in terms of solidifying a Reform movement was clearly out of bounds.

In fact, the reformers did not achieve much at first. Participants decided only two issues during the first conference: removal of Kol Nidre prayers the evening of Yom Kippur and an agreement about a new Jewish oath for legal proceedings. All the other issues were sent to committees for future consideration. Interestingly, the removal of Kol Nidre prayers had already been implemented in Oldenburg during Samson Raphael Hirsch's tenure; thus, one of the discussion items had already been accepted and used by a member of the Orthodox faction back in the 1830s (though Hirsch reversed course later).[64]

From the Orthodox and traditional perspectives, the Brunswick conference was a threat to their supporters' views about Judaism, despite the inability of those assembled to accomplish very much. The Orthodox rabbis primarily concerned themselves with how the rabbinical conferences appeared to the public. On the one hand, the Orthodox objected to the perception that the conference was a legislative body with some sort of authority. On the other hand, they also objected to the protocols appearing in the German Jewish press and being more widely distributed, especially since all of the German Jewish newspapers before 1845 were reform leaning. In response to the conferences, the Orthodox formulated two responses. The first was the widespread distribution of a petition against the Brunswick conference that was signed by 77 (and later 116) rabbis. This petition subsequently received significant coverage in both the Jewish and non-Jewish press.[65] Notable signatories included, from the Kingdom of Hannover, Samson Raphael Hirsch from Emden and Dr. Nathan Marcus Adler from Hannover and, from the Grand Duchy of Baden, Hirsch Traub from Mannheim, Salomon Fürst from Heidelberg, and Jakob Löwenstein from Gailingen. The second reaction was perhaps more important in the long run. The printing of the protocols in the German Jewish press convinced some Orthodox rabbis that they needed a newspaper to represent their voices, and as a result, Samuel Enoch and Jacob Ettlinger founded *Der treue Zions-Wächter* in July 1845.

Conflict within the German Jewish community did not just confine itself to reactions to the Brunswick conference; there was plenty of conflict surrounding the following two conferences in Frankfurt (1845) and Breslau (1846). The Frankfurt rabbinical conference, just like the one in Brunswick, did not accomplish very much. This was a direct effect of the heated debates during the conference about messianic beliefs and changes in the religious service, especially the debate surrounding a proposed shift away from using Hebrew as the language of prayer to the vernacular, in this case, German. The issue of devotional language was an important one for reformers; for many, language was believed to be the main reason why religiosity and religious attendance had decreased among German Jews. At the conference, the participants were asked to respond to a few questions regarding language use: Was Hebrew "objectively legally binding" as a prayer language? Was Hebrew subjectively necessary? And finally, was Hebrew "objectively necessary" for reasons other than legal ones? Moses Reiss from Altbreisach (Baden) believed there was a prohibition against eliminating Hebrew, yet he still voted with the committee's recommendation that the use of Hebrew was not "objectively legally necessary." Zacharias Fränkel (Dresden) believed that Hebrew was a "symbol" that reminded people of God and that Hebrew needed to dominate the service. Salomon Herxheimer and Abraham Geiger, in opposition to Fränkel, argued that the vernacular was more important, and that it helped people to understand and feel the religion. At the end of the discussions, conference participants voted nearly unanimously on the first two questions, voting no for the first question and yes for the second. However, the third question produced a deep split among the participants, with those in favor of retaining Hebrew outvoted by those who wanted to eschew it thirteen to fifteen.[66]

The fallout from this vote was swift, with two participants, Zacharias Fränkel and Leopold Schott (Randegg, Baden), leaving the Frankfurt conference. Fränkel, who was reform leaning, had originally sided with the reformers on the question about the nonlegal necessity of Hebrew, but he would not agree to change the service to the vernacular (German).⁶⁷ There was also a very public discussion that followed Fränkel's and Schott's departures from the conference. Fränkel penned an open letter to the conference explaining his exit in the Frankfurt newspaper, the *Ober-Post-Amts-Zeitung* (his letter appeared in many German newspapers), while both Fränkel and Schott published letters in the *Allgemeine Zeitung des Judenthums* (*AZdJ*) and *Der Israelit*. A further outcry and "most bitter denunciations" of the conference were featured in the more conservative reform-oriented *Der Orient*.⁶⁸ In the German Jewish press, there was much discussion in the late summer and fall of 1845 about Fränkel's decision to leave the conference, yet these discussions did not cross over to the non-Jewish press. Instead, a parallel discussion took place there among Christian observers and Jews.

The Breslau conference in 1846 was controversial from the moment the reformers decided to hold the conference in this important German Jewish city. As David Philipson wrote, choosing Breslau was "equivalent to throwing down the gauntlet to the opposition to the conferences."⁶⁹ Given the contentious nature of reform in Breslau, especially surrounding Abraham Geiger's election, the uproar was unsurprising. Despite the controversy, the conference was more productive than the first two, and the decisions made there were perhaps the biggest step forward in the transformation of German Judaism into a "bourgeois" religion. The participants agreed on the following notable changes: reducing the length of sitting shiva (mourning) from seven to three days; elevating the status of women to be the equal of men within the religion was recommended (although a vote was postponed due to time constraints); and abolishing all second days of holidays, except for Rosh Hashanah (Jewish New Year). The other issues that were decided all dealt with the Jewish Sabbath. Firstly, participants abolished the strictest Sabbath restrictions for civil servants and soldiers. Next, and most importantly, the rabbis affirmed Saturday as the Sabbath, against the wishes of the RG, which later changed its Sabbath to Sunday. As Ludwig Philippson—the original convener of the Brunswick conference and the editor of the *AZdJ*—remarked, it was Christianity and Islam that had deviated from Judaism about the Sabbath, and therefore Judaism should not change the original Sabbath date, an argument also seen in the debates about emancipation in Baden (see chap. 2). To almost all conference participants in Breslau, moving the Sabbath would have been deeply injurious to preserving Jewish honor and difference.⁷⁰

The Breslau rabbinical conference thus became a topic of public debate. Articles about the conference appeared in two Frankfurt-based papers—the

Ober-Post-Amts-Zeitung and the *Frankfurter Journal*—as well as the *Deutsche Allgemeine Zeitung* from Leipzig. Publication in these widely distributed papers meant that knowledge of the conference spread throughout the German states. Those who did not agree with the proceedings at the conference—from both the more progressive and more conservative wings—used the press to present their views. Those advocating a more conservative reform felt the changes had gone too far, while radicals on the left felt the changes did not go far enough. Those who were participants in Breslau also found it necessary to defend themselves in the press. Chief Rabbi Bernhard Wechsler of Oldenburg published an article in the *Bremer Zeitung*, while *Klausrabbiner* Hayum Wagner (Mannheim) and Abraham Adler, a preacher from Alzey, used their journal, *Die Reform des Judenthums*, to defend the reformers and their accomplishments.[71]

While the rabbinical conferences of 1844–46 are important for understanding the German roots of the Reform movement in Judaism, their significance for this study comes from the responses in both the pan-German and local Badenese presses and the conferences' ultimate effectiveness. One can discern details about the conferences from the German Jewish press, but the non-Jewish press was just as important a venue for portrayals of potential Jewish reforms. Fränkel's decision to publish his withdrawal letter from the conference in the *Ober-Post-Amts-Zeitung* was wise—the *Ober-Post-Amts-Zeitung* had a circulation in 1845 of three thousand copies.[72] However, as this letter was published in full in the *DAZ* and the *FJ*, there were approximately 14,000 more subscribers who could have read this letter. In just these three non-Jewish publications, approximately 170,000 people could have seen this letter.

An example of how those in favor of and against the rabbinical conferences used these newspapers is reflected in the rash of reports and "Danksagungen" (thank-you letters) that appeared in 1845. Regarding Fränkel's "Austritt," the *DAZ* ran one series of articles. The first article (from Breslau) discussed how one letter circulated and accumulated 180 signatures against the *Rabbinerversammlung* (rabbinical conference), but it also pointed out that those who were more reform-inclined also felt dissatisfied with the results of the conference. Within days, another response from Breslau contradicted the first article, pointing out that there were only 120 signatures (and not 180 as had been asserted) and that, more importantly, the circulated letter was not a "real ethos reflection" (*wahre Gesinnungsausdruck*) of the Orthodox members of the community. Rather, the author suggested that this protest of the Frankfurt conference was a "personal demonstration" against Rabbi Abraham Geiger's appointment in 1838. Another fascinating part of this response was the accusation that Orthodox rabbis would infiltrate and then overwhelm the reformers in Breslau the following year. The author then excitedly proclaimed that such an action would force reformers to proclaim a Berlin-style RG.[73] While this scenario did not come to pass, these articles show how important the press became in the overall fight.

If a casual reader looked at the pan-German press, the coverage about reform would have seemed overwhelmingly positive, especially in terms of the conferences. While there were reports that elucidated the arguments against the conference participants and in support of Fränkel's and Schott's departures (such as those letters from Jewish communities in Breslau, Hannover, and also Frankfurt), there were more articles that presented the conferences in a favorable light.[74] One can see from the coverage throughout this three-year period, but more pointedly on the two sides of the individual conferences, the range of emotions from all the contributors. From joy and satisfaction to revulsion and disappointment, the German press provided commentary that gave viewers great insight into changes in Judaism and opinions about the direction of those changes.

In April 1845, beginning with the well-covered Orthodox protest against the 1844 Brunswick conference, there was a swelling of articles about reform. One author, in a long contribution in the supplement to the *DAZ* on April 15, 1845, gave a very favorable evaluation of Jewish reform and encouraged the RG to move forward. The ∇ correspondent acknowledged that there were many critics of the organization that saw the organization as "künstlich" (artificial) and in violation of state law. Contrary to that sentiment, this writer believed that Jews, like Christians, should have an experience that goes "deep into the soul." As such, the author labeled current attempts at reform as half-hearted and insufficient, especially when "rotten, cracked and decomposing cornerstones remain." Another article challenged the tactics used by the Orthodox while claiming that reform was striking and destroying "deeper roots." And although it is clear that the RF in Frankfurt did not gain adherents as it desired, the claim that reform had broadened its base is evident from the increase in communities that supported parts of the RG's program.[75] Moreover, even the superficial changes that had been introduced by Orthodox rabbis like Michael Sachs demonstrate that some reform had been accepted across the spectrum of religiosity.

The coverage of the rabbinical conferences was also an important lens through which to view reform more generally. In 1845, newspaper correspondents flocked to Frankfurt to cover what was expected to be a very well-attended and fruitful discussion about Judaism. However, from the beginning of the conference, coverage of it was generally negative and reports framed the endeavor as exclusive, snobbish, and lacking enthusiasm from the community. A report from the ☉ correspondent in the *DAZ* framed the conference in a negative light, and the author blamed the poor attendance on "indifference, material needs, old Judaism, and outlooks." Another critique (from *) attacked the perceived unavailability of *Eintrittskarten* (entrance tickets) to the event, and this author believed that organizers wanted to have a "Beschränkung der Öffentlichkeit" (limitation of transparency). Another correspondent criticized the conference, assuming that the rabbis in attendance were clinging to a hierarchical structure and were disinterested in members of both the RF and RG. Yet another correspondent questioned why members of the RG even bothered going to Frankfurt to seek rabbinical legitimacy and partnership.[76]

Contrary to this negative perspective, other reports presented a more favorable view of reform and its reception among participants, those in the gallery, and within the broader community. Notable reports indicated the importance of this conference to women in the Frankfurt community, a topic well-addressed in scholarship on Jewish reform. Approximately one hundred women attended one session of the Frankfurt conference, though many of them probably attended other sessions as well. This same report also noted the attendance of Karl von Rothschild and his son, Anselm. As mentioned earlier as part of the fallout from the circumcision debates and election of Leopold Stein as Second Rabbi in 1844, it was already common knowledge that Karl and his son did not share the same religious sentiments as the family patriarch.[77] This report could have potentially embarrassed the Rothschilds, though as noted earlier, the family was unconcerned with public perception of the family's religiosity. The article also commented that Frankfurt authorities warmly received the conference; officials attended both the closing feast and a production of Gotthold Lessing's *Nathan the Wise*. The local Jewish community's choice of Lessing's play was no coincidence. The play embodied the spirit of toleration and harkened back to the relationship of Lessing with Moses Mendelssohn, functioning as a projection of what the community desired in the present.

As seen by the antagonism between supporters and detractors of Jewish reform, many people felt the need to send articles into papers to voice their opinions. A letter printed in the *DAZ* on August 20, 1845, encouraged the RG to create their own path and to not expect the rabbis' support, and the author believed that the conference had produced no positive results for the organization. A few months later, in September, upon reflection of what had happened in Frankfurt, another contributor came to a different conclusion—he believed that this gathering not only was successful but also was so successful and the Frankfurt Jewish community so important within the German states that every other conference should be held there.[78] A third response, published in the *FJ* on July 30, 1845, generalized the impression left by the moderate reformers: "However, as we may confidently hope that they take with them pleasant memories of Frankfurt, and may feel encouraged and strengthened in their striving and zeal by the universal and sincere acknowledgment that has come to them here, so on the other hand to be assured that they have left truly benevolent and enduring impressions in the hearts of all those who appreciate research and knowledge, value loyalty, and acknowledge open and decent behavior."[79]

Unfortunately, such dreams of moving forward confidently and without recriminations would be disappointed by the tone in many of the pieces about, and ultimately in denunciation of, the third rabbinical conference the following year in Breslau (1846), by both the Orthodox and those from the radical reform societies. The former railed against any concessions at all—especially regarding the adaptation of Sabbath prohibitions—while the latter believed that substantial change should be forthcoming, especially regarding moving the Sabbath to Sunday. One radical reform-leaning respondent viewed such lack of substance and change by the rabbis in Breslau as giving a "most embarrassing impression" (*peinlichste Eindruck*)—this author clearly saw Christians as the audience of his article and the conference as a public spectacle.[80] Such a view of the Breslau conference only pushed those demanding reform further from the center and led directly to the increased concretization of the RG movement in Berlin as a predominantly independent community.

It was clear by the end of the third rabbinical conference that numerous parties were vying for the future of Judaism: the Orthodox, the Conservatives, the moderate reformers (those at the conferences), and the radical reformers. While each group had their acolytes writing in the press, there was a clear proreform bias in both the *FJ* and the *DAZ*, and in most cases, such support leaned more toward radical reform. Perhaps this bias was due to the nature of those newspapers (the *DAZ* was known as a proreform paper, for both Jews and Christians) and also the audience of those papers. But debate in the press also tended toward a more reform position because reformers as a whole had the writing and rhetorical tools that could be acquired only from a German university.[81] Still, as the existence of *Der treue Zions-Wächter* showed and as some of the respondents in these discussions in the pan-German press likewise reflected, various Orthodox voices held their ground and challenged both the reform societies and the rabbinical conferences. Nonetheless, during this three-year period, if one examines this venue of publication rather than the German Jewish press (controlled predominantly by those aligned with the rabbinical conferences), a different picture emerges—one in which the forces of reform and separation, and not of moderate reform, dominated. That these forces did not ultimately carry much weight in the future direction of Judaism reveals how strong the German Jewish press was a counterweight to the regular press. It likewise reflects the resolve of the moderate reform rabbis to maintain a balance of tradition and change, and how authority and power within the Jewish community still resided within a traditional structure. Religious matters were seen mainly as the domain of the clergy and not, like both the RF and the RG wished, of the laity.

These responses in the press, some of which were reproduced in the German Jewish newspapers, were obviously intended for a broader audience, otherwise printing in the German Jewish press would have been sufficient. In the cases of these newspapers, which had larger and wider circulations, it was not only a local audience being addressed but a national one. However other reactions in the press to the developments of the rabbinical conferences of 1844–46 had more local meanings, and more directly influenced the local pursuit of integration, emancipation, and confessionalization.

THE LOCAL DEBATE ABOUT JEWISH REFORM IN NORTHERN BADEN

Debates about Jews' rights had been a common feature within Badenese society since pre-Napoleonic times. Both Karl Friedrich's *Tolerenzpatent* (Patent of toleration) and the later constitutional edicts brought Jewish rights into the world of public discussion. The 1809 edict established an Oberrat, which directed Jewish religious life and became the public face for the Jewish community. Eventually, Naphtali Epstein became its head (he was initially its secretary) and led the fight for Gleichstellung by organizing statewide petitions and supplications. Before Epstein became the head of the Oberrat, the consistory primarily concerned itself with gaining respect for Judaism within Badenese society, which meant changing many of the external forms of religious devotion. In 1824, the Badenese Oberrat became the first Jewish political organization in the post-Napoleonic German states to issue a Synagogenordnung (appendix A).[82] Included in this ordinance were important changes to Jewish religiosity, including the institution of wearing robes for rabbis and cantors, the institution of a boys' choir, a ban on the auctioning of Torah honors, the introduction of confirmation, the prohibition against wearing prayer shawls in the streets, and the prohibition against loud noises during services (especially at the mentioning of Haman during the celebration of Purim).[83]

German-wide conflict about Jewish reform also manifested itself within the individual states. The Badenese Oberrat had the support of the government and tried to spread changes throughout the state, but this was easier said than done. There were still many rabbis who opposed most, if not all, changes to devotional practice, and the government had the power to step in and nullify any change from the Oberrat if it so desired. Conflict was built into the system, as the state tried to change Jewish religious practice. Such conflict occurred where there were rabbis on opposing sides of an issue. For example, one of the most Orthodox rabbis in Baden, Jakob Löwenstein from Gailingen (one of the Orthodox petitioners), led a community that was only kilometers away from a more liberal community headed by Leopold Schott of Randegg, an attendee at two rabbinical conferences (1844 and 1845) before he exited with Fränkel. Another location of conflict between the reform and Orthodox camps was the Mannheim community, where Klausrabbiner Hayum Wagner, who attended both the 1845 and 1846 conferences, was coeditor of the reform-leaning and conference-supporting *Die Reform des Judenthums*. Wagner also participated in the 1845 discussion about Gleichstellung (chap. 2) and can be juxtaposed with the Orthodox rabbis in Mannheim—namely, Hirsch Traub, who signed the Orthodox petition, and Leib Ettlinger, who contributed articles to his brother's journal, *Der treue Zions-Wächter*.[84]

However, sometimes rabbis were not the only individuals in conflict, as entire communities often grappled over issues of reform, such as occurred in the university town of Heidelberg. As a result of the Synagogenordnung, which functioned as a compromise among competing parties, there was a belief that the movement for reform needed to be kept away from rabbinical control and handed over to the educational institutions; in Heidelberg, the reform spirit was embodied in the person of Karl Rehfuß, a reformist educator who was hired in 1823 and had a controversial past—having fled from Gailingen in 1812 for using "contraband" German books. Hans-Martin Mumm considered Rehfuß one of the "most important Jewish pedagogues and reformers of the first half of the nineteenth century." Rehfuß made an immediate impact in the community, instituting significant changes in Jewish education, such as the introduction of confirmation and the holding of German-language sermons. Those reforms, while welcomed in certain quarters of the Jewish community, were not universally accepted by the Orthodox opposition in 1824 or after Salomon Fürst became rabbi in 1825.[85]

Fürst was not, however, an orthodox rabbi in the mold of either traditional Judaism or modern Orthodoxy; he was a moderate reformer like many of the other Badenese rabbis. Fürst had a university education (he studied three years at the University of Würzburg), although he did not have a doctorate like many of the other reformers. While he may have supported some reforms in the community, he was originally not in favor of quick or substantial change—he opposed the more drastic changes in synagogue devotion, including the addition of confirmation which Rehfuß promoted. Furthermore, Fürst and Rehfuß had a fractured relationship, as noted by contributors to a discussion in January 1845; all of those who sided with Rehfuß made sure to portray Fürst's actions and words negatively. Rehfuß's son, Jakob, wrote that Fürst "never accepted my father as a colleague or as a preacher" and that Fürst was guilty of harming his father's "honor and dignity." It was clear that these two men had different visions about the direction of Jewish life, yet they coexisted in the Heidelberg community for almost two decades. Their quiet struggle became part of a public dispute in 1845 but also functioned as a reflection of the struggles in Heidelberg, Badenese, and German Jewry as a whole.[86]

Jakob Rehfuß's contribution to *Der Orient*, a moderate-reform German Jewish newspaper, as well as Fürst's defense, indicated that something was amiss in the Heidelberg Jewish community. The rabbi's negative position toward reform (and antipathy toward those associated with Rehfuß) was not universally shared nor was it quietly accepted, as former students defended Rehfuß in different German Jewish publications.[87] This discussion in the German Jewish press, however, was just the opening salvo in a more spectacular debate that occurred in April 1845; local newspapers took center stage as reformers confronted Fürst in front of the Mannheim and Heidelberg public.

As mentioned previously, Fürst was one of the seventy-seven Orthodox signatories to the petition against the 1844 Brunswick rabbinical conference. This petition appeared in the German Jewish press on March 30, 1845—more than two months after Jakob Rehfuß's article against Fürst. The discussions in the local newspapers shortly after this public rebuke were endemic of the animosity which had built up over time between the reformers and the Orthodox.[88] Throughout the German states, tensions among Jews simmered below the surface; it did not take much for the internal Jewish fight to spill over into the local press. The Brunswick rabbinical conference (1844) and the Orthodox response to the reformers provided that fuel. This debate occurred nearly simultaneously with the 1845 debates in Heidelberg and Mannheim about Gleichstellung, and this overlap certainly loomed large for this debate, even though these debates themselves were distinct.

The first broadside, written by Heidelberg Jewish community leader Adolph Zimmern, appeared in the *Mannheimer Abendzeitung* on April 26, 1845 (the *Mannheimer Morgenblatt* published the exact same polemic on May 11, 1845). Zimmern—in this full-page exposition—took aim at Fürst and his attachment to the seventy-six other orthodox petitioners.[89] Not unexpectedly, Zimmern provided an unequivocal endorsement of the rabbinical conference in

Brunswick and the upcoming conference in Frankfurt. But before attacking Fürst and extolling the new ideological movement in Judaism, Zimmern tied Jewish lives to modern society and to the local public they were trying to influence. Zimmern also recognized that this conflict within Judaism was now public; he expressed his optimism that reformers would win, saying "the most intense conflict changes natures." He tried to convince readers of the reformers' desire to bring Judaism and Jewish religious practice into harmony with the modern era, stating that "what fit well for the time and manners of our forefathers does not work anymore for the grandchildren." He further promoted what Jews had done for the "Fatherland," clearly stating that the older generations had paved the way for the current freedoms and lives of Jews. Instead of just accepting Jewish life as it had existed, Zimmern boldly stated that Jewish success might not come from "society" but, rather, from an individual, stating that "soon a good genius will also remove our last restrictions."[90] This was not an allusion to some messiah-figure but, rather, an assumption that some Christian would need to be the force behind Jewish emancipation. In essence, Zimmern was waiting for Christians to keep their part of the quid pro quo as he argued that Jews had sufficiently fulfilled their part of the bargain. As seen one year later in Baden, when "radical" liberals became the leaders of the Lower Assembly, there were indeed more Christians willing to vote in favor of Jewish rights—even if such benevolence only came about because of the Christian dissidents' (the Deutschkatholiken) own concurrent struggles in the grand duchy.

Zimmern also tried to connect Jews and Judaism to the high points of the German past, and likewise to both Christianity and the more pronounced liberal spirit in the region. He wrote that Jews believed in "die volligste Freiheit" (the fullest freedom) of the individual, and that they did not espouse any hierarchical order; that is, that there was not a single person who could direct Jewish lives.[91] Zimmern's claim thus directly challenged the authority of Orthodox rabbis to prevent local changes in religious devotion, to define what Judaism was or was not, and to sketch out the definition of what being a "modern" rabbi meant. Furthermore, Zimmern wanted to disrupt the notion that it was the rabbi's role to be the representative of and interlocutor between the Jewish community and German Christian society. In a way, Zimmern saw himself in that role, a more traditional Court Jew/*Parnass* position like his father, David Zimmern, had filled (see the discussion about his Nekrolog in chap. 2).

More spectacularly, Zimmern linked Fürst to the "Polish and Hungarian rabbis" in the same manner as was presented in a May 3 article in the *MAbZ* from Bühl, which not only disparaged the Orthodox petitioners but wholeheartedly supported the Mannheim community's endorsement of the rabbinical conferences. A side-by-side comparison of the two articles shows how they buttressed each other's arguments:

From Adolph Zimmern (*MM*):

> Mr. District Rabbi Fürst from Heidelberg has found it advisable to bind himself to the rabbis from Poland and Hungary, to count himself among the chosen defenders of Zion, and to accuse those that met in Brunswick of being unbelievers—these should nevertheless be known as *his* beliefs. We, however, gave him no such commission. He does not speak for our convictions, and we protest strongly against the implication that the fundamental beliefs and views of *this* rabbi are held by the majority of the community.[92]

From Bühl (*MAbZ*):

> It is with this intention [to brand as heretics (*Verketzern*) those who advocate Jewish reform] that 77 rabbis—mainly of *Polish and Hungarian* origins—have sought to spread a protest among their similarly minded colleagues, not only against the decisions of the conference the prior year in Brunswick, but also those which would come from the upcoming conference in Frankfurt on the Main.[93]

These passages clearly show that the reform/liberal Jewish elements in different communities were not standing idly by as the Orthodox protest rallied followers and sought to be seen as the "official" voice of German Jewry. Furthermore, it is clear that Zimmern, along with the heads of the Bühl community (religious and lay), distinguished between German and Polish/Hungarian sentiments, regarding the former as progressive and the latter as regressive. These formulations, supported by both lay and religious leaders, clearly placed Jews from the East on a lower societal rung. Similar to the debates about Jewish education, some participants in this discussion looked negatively at eastern influences as being un-German and then further associated the rabbis from these areas (as well as their German sympathizers) as hindrances to Gleichstellung and the general position of Jews in the German states. This dispute should be considered a forerunner of a more expanded *Ostjuden* discourse that occurred during the *Kaiserreich*. This antipathy toward eastern European Jews could also be interpreted as a legacy of Salomon Maimon's German-language autobiography (written in the 1790s), in which many of these same Ostjuden tropes appeared, though such language was quite prevalent in other places throughout the Vormärz. Just as reformers sought to define themselves as German, they also created new, exclusionary markers for Jews who did not follow their path.[94] Religious ideology was thus central in the dispute between Fürst and Rehfuß, yet the attainment of Bildung was equally important, especially due to the influence that rabbis, preachers, and teachers had on the current generation.

Zimmern clearly supported the reform position. He claimed that his intercession in the *Mannheimer Morgenblatt* was supported "in the name and at the commission of the great majority of the community members," though as Hans-Martin Mumm noted, Zimmern enjoyed lording over the Heidelberg Jewish community and often acted in an autocratic manner. Nonetheless, Zimmern couched his *Erklärung* (declaration) in terms of continuous progress, where reform always encountered resistance. This allowed Zimmern to draw on the history of changes and reformation in other religions: "as in every movement, the light follows the shadow, and the good is always born out of a storm ... the new is condemned and the old is praised." Zimmern, in these sentiments and in the direct association of Fürst with the "old" sentiments, presented resistance to reform as a normal occurrence that would eventually be overcome.[95] And since Zimmern was wholeheartedly behind the Reform movement's search to create a bourgeois religion, one can only assume that to him Reform Judaism was to Orthodoxy what Protestantism was to Catholicism (and perhaps, since Zimmern was liberal, he would associate the Lichtfreunde/Deutschkatholiken movements both to Catholicism and conservative Protestantism).[96]

Another important implication of this piece by Zimmern was the publicly announced split in the Jewish community. This certainly was the first time in the Badenese press that the head of a major Jewish community (Heidelberg was fifth largest) publicly rebuked the local rabbi.[97] This discussion in Heidelberg revealed that the community's cohesion over fundamental religious ideals no longer existed (although they were all publicly supportive of emancipation).

Fürst responded swiftly to the original April letter, publishing a response in the *Heidelberger Journal* on May 4, 1845, in which he qualified his signature and acceptance of the Orthodox position, saying that he only regarded his signature as a recognition "in which the reform of Judaism should not solely be measured by outward purposes, but rather its authenticity must primarily be found *within itself*."[98] Fürst's hedging is clear; he did not believe the rabbinical conference in Brunswick to be an acceptable institution for internal Jewish change. He did, however, accept that there was a possibility of a higher "institution" which could decide such matters. Fürst's view on Judaism was clearly opposed to Zimmern's belief, and it also differed from the views of the reformers at the rabbinical conferences. Fürst's response was printed in the *AZdJ* two weeks later, on May 19, 1845, but with a biting critique by the editor of the *AZdJ*, Dr. Ludwig Philippson.[99] Philippson challenged Fürst's equivocation and did not believe Fürst's sincerity and explanation for his signature to the protest, asking why he signed the petition *without* being forced to do so. Philippson also criticized the hypocrisy of Fürst, a moderate reformer, and questioned why he aligned himself with so many other archconservatives who opposed *any* religious reforms, even the ones which Fürst supported.

Nonetheless, this appearance in the German Jewish press, as well as the witty rejoinders by Philippson, were ancillary to the local public discussion that took place from May 6 to 16, 1845. Many statements of solidarity from reform-friendly communities appeared in the local press.[100] These statements brought a certain amount of public pressure on Fürst, especially in the face of a political situation where reform was not merely expected but demanded. The critiques of Fürst's positions, much like that from the *AZdJ*, must have been particularly hurtful for someone who had some university education. As a commentator wrote in the *Mannheimer Abendzeitung* on May 10, 1845, Fürst had bound himself to "the Polish-Hungarian coalition against German *Bildung* und *Wissenschaftlichkeit*" (education and scholarliness). The author also wrote that Fürst had "betrayed" and "abandoned" the Heidelberg Jewish community, transgressions that the author claimed had prompted him to qualify his signature to the Orthodox petition. Another critique by "Verus" (Latin for "real/true") in the *Heidelberger Journal* on May 9, 1845, was even more scathing. The author first questioned Fürst's equivocation, contending that the latter's self-proclaimed inability to understand the document did not make sense. The author continued by asserting that "from Mr. Fürst, from whom we are accustomed to hearing modest claims that exhibit his practical and scholarly efficacy, we should at a minimum expect that he would understand what he signed."[101] Verus then detailed Fürst's negative relationship with Rehfuß and the religious changes implemented in the community. Verus continued his attacks on Fürst, tying the local rabbi to the Orthodox petitioners, calling them all "Duodezrabbinerlein" ("small, petty rabbis who overestimate their influence"). He further hoped the Orthodox would "only [be] a corn on the progressive feet of the time" and also prodded Fürst to make his views heard in Frankfurt at the second rabbinical conference, that is, if he was truly dedicated to reform.[102] Clearly, public attacks showed both ideological and personal invective in the place of calm and reason, demonstrating that Jews were very comfortable with confrontation and ridicule—on both sides of the ideological divide.

Fürst reacted quickly and harshly to these characterizations, and agitated against the whole community in his *Heid Jour* response on May 10, 1845. Fürst railed against what he perceived as writers who were "the most dishonorable and characterless, most unrighteous people" (*der ehr- und charakterloseste, verworfenste Mensch*). He responded as a man who was slighted and under attack, despite his active *political* engagement on behalf of Jewish equality over his eighteen years of service. He thus used his political actions to shield himself from *religious* accusations. Shortly thereafter, two articles in the local press challenged Fürst, yet both authors refrained from vituperation and invective. In his second piece in this discussion, Verus claimed that Fürst had vilified (*schmähte*) the community, pointing out that "this is also evident through your protestation" and that "those who have eyes to see would see and judge [Fürst's actions as] romping and squabbling" (*mit wildem Toben und Zanken*) over the past eighteen years of his service. At the end, another response, written by "many Israelite residents" drew attention to Fürst's "characteristic ranting" (*charakterisierende Schimpfen*) and asked him to read Song of Songs 7:10 ("And your mouth like choicest wine. Let it flow to my beloved as new wine; Gliding over the lips of sleepers"). For those who knew the Talmud, as Fürst would have, these local Jewish residents were clearly mocking Fürst's Orthodox position, saying that he was speaking with the dead, with those who believed in the old ways of being Jewish.[103]

Pressure did not just come from the Jewish community. An article in the *Heid Jour* about the counterrabbinical conference in Mannheim referred to Fürst as "one of the 77."[104] Unlike the other Badenese signatories to the Orthodox protest (Jakob Löwenstein from Gailingen and Hirsch Traub from Mannheim), Fürst was the only rabbi publicly confronted by his congregants in 1845. It is clear that reformers sought to belittle Fürst's efforts, and the publication of this piece in the Mannheim press was no surprise, given the liberal proclivities in the city and the sympathies of the editors. Perhaps Fürst was singled out by the sympathizers of reform because of his education. They implied that he was betraying the principles on which he was educated and also, and most importantly, that he was being disloyal to the community in which he lived and the principles that Rehfuß had developed. More importantly, this article was an attempt to cast the entire Badenese "conservative reform" movement in a negative public light. It portrayed the nonprogressive rabbis as the ones responsible for the lack of full equality, despite the numerous petitions submitted by Jewish communities and their rabbis to the Ständeversammlung for equality over the years.[105] In essence, these writers painted the Orthodox rabbis as reactionary and antiliberal, which would have been viewed negatively by the *MAbZ*'s more liberal audience.

One of the most telling subjects throughout all of these discussions was the focus on Bildung. There was a clear dichotomy between German and Eastern (Slavic or Hungarian) perspectives, with the former holding the virtues of "enlightened" and "educated," and the latter being held as the diametrical opposite—something that had been propagated since *Sulamith*. Zimmern put Bildung and modernity at the front of his argument. Although he spared Fürst a direct assault, the consequences of limited Bildung are implied throughout. Verus, however, directly questioned Fürst's attachment to the less "educated" group, as Fürst's intellectual acumen was often seen as one of his strengths. Furthermore, Verus could hardly believe that such a learned man had not thought through the implications of the Orthodox petition. Even the use of Fürst's and Rehfuß's disagreements implicitly portrayed Fürst as moderately anti-Bildung. Such an association is not surprising; if the key to entry to the German *Bürgertum* and the foundation of the quid pro quo was Bildung, and Bildung was also a cornerstone of the liberal movement, then Bildung would be an important topic on which ideological confrontation and the Jewish future would hinge. Furthermore, in terms of Bildung, it was the teachers and not the rabbis who "personified the story of Jewish education and acculturation at the same time"—teachers were educated, took state exams, and were the ones who transmitted the values from German society to new generations.[106]

The role of Bildung within these discussions is not surprising, considering that reformers sought to influence Jewish society in a location out of the reach of traditional and Orthodox rabbis.[107] However, when looking at Jewish actions, the way in which this debate unfolded in the local press is also very telling. The supporters of reform took a very aggressive posture in their reactions to the Orthodox petition; they sought to influence public opinion and to put pressure on Rabbi Fürst before both a more reform-friendly general public in the Mannheim/Heidelberg area *and* the more conservative, anti-Jewish public. The full-page Erklärung by Adolph Zimmern was undoubtedly unique and revealed the aggressiveness of reformers and liberals in their contestation and destabilization of tradition and the status quo. Furthermore, the publication in both pro- and anti-Jewish emancipation papers showed Zimmern's understanding of the political situation of Jews in Baden—he needed the support of not only those already convinced of the merits of Jewish emancipation but also those hesitant to support the cause. The Beamten—conservatives and conservative/moderate liberals—were the ones being courted. Zimmern might have hoped he was appealing to that "genius" who would help Jews achieve full equality where many others had failed, and thus, he purposefully presented a picture of a reforming German Jewry to a conservative public, challenging a priori conceptions about Jews and Judaism.

Fürst's publications in the *Heidelberger Journal* are similarly important, if only for their equivocal nature. One can clearly see that the pressure from the Heidelberg community in the press *forced* Fürst to qualify his support for the

Orthodox petition, especially if he wanted his opinions to be respected and heeded, even those written on behalf of Jewish Gleichstellung. The fact that Fürst was forced to explain his signature indicates the power of the press and Jews' understanding of that dynamic.

CONCLUSION

All of the vignettes in this chapter relate to the importance of internal Jewish religious reform to discussions within the German press. Certainly, in the broad picture, all of these stories contribute to the same central narrative that details the struggles of reform, the continuous progress of the movement, and the vehement disagreements among reformers and the Orthodox. Excavating the intricacies of these local debates adds a more nuanced understanding to the histories of Jewish reform by focusing on how these discussions took place in and affected local communities.

Moreover, it is clear in each of these stories that the German Jewish press played second fiddle to the local press. Jewish actors in Baden and elsewhere chose the non-Jewish papers because they were more important and better suited for achieving their objectives. The local newspapers had more immediacy of printing and a higher rate at which news could be disseminated to the public. The local papers also had a far greater reach than the German Jewish press, since they reprinted other papers' articles at a more frequent rate. Furthermore, they were geared toward non-Jewish audiences, the ones that German Jews in favor of reform wanted to reach. As such, pan-German newspapers provided an even more important avenue for the presentation of Jewish reform. Despite the local nature of most conflicts—like Geiger's appointment in Breslau and the circumcision debate in Frankfurt—the stakes were high for Jews across the German states. In all of these discussions, local and pan-German concerns became locked in a struggle for supremacy, though the stakes for reformers were even higher—as the challengers to the status quo, they needed others (Christian Germans) to validate and support their right to exist in the spectrum of religiosity. Reformers did not need to send their news to other Jews via the German Jewish press; they needed more, and more favorable, coverage in the local press so that Christians could read their voices and hopefully become allies in their struggle for reform and, ultimately, emancipation.

The fact that most of these writings were published locally also showed how important the discussion was to Christians. The editors chose to include recriminations, accusations, and rebuttals as part of a broader public discussion about Jewish lives. Perhaps the editors did so out of a belief in the power of a rational public space wherein the best argument won, but perhaps they also did so because they desired changes to Judaism and saw this discourse as a vehicle to put pressure on key individuals to effect change. Furthermore, editors used this discussion to convince audiences that German Jews had changed and were worthy of emancipation.

Moreover, these discussions incurred some risk. Radical reformers saw only a positive benefit from bringing these internal Jewish discussions before the non-Jewish public, and they pushed forward with a cavalier sense that as society became more liberal, eventually the public (but especially liberal lawmakers) would become converts to their cause—much like what happened as discussions of rights for the Lichtfreunde and Deutschkatholiken evolved in 1845 and 1846. These brazen actions flew in the face of general Jewish traditions by making their religion a public matter. Even though most of these discussions occurred in more liberal papers, and even if the papers themselves were more sympathetic to Jewish reform and emancipation, one cannot assume that most readers shared these political sentiments in full. If we accept that Badenese liberals (who were known as more liberal than most state liberal groups) did not fully embrace Jewish emancipation until 1846, and only as a function of the discussions of Deutschkatholiken rights, then the broader public likely lagged behind. As such, these public discussions carried significant risk. They could be used against Jews in any political discussion about their rights. As seen in the Fauth discussion (chap. 2), the bar for Jews was not *individual* emancipation but *group* (or at least an overwhelming majority) emancipation. These discussions also attracted scrutiny to the Jewish religion, just as the Damascus Affair had done in 1840. Changes in Judaism could be put under the microscope and debated in society in a way that other religions were not. As such, changes in the Jewish religion could potentially be viewed as a proxy for other societal battles going on, including those over the secularization, liberalization, and democratization.

FOUR

THE FIGHT FOR JEWISH ADMISSION TO CONSTANCE IN THE BODENSEE PRESS, 1846

But on our religion, the holy teaching of God, we will never yield and for just that reason we will be faithful, honest, truth-loving, and loyal citizens.

—D., "Gailingen," *Seeblätter*, 102 (August 25, 1846), 429

The debates about Jewish emancipation and Jewish religious reform often manifested themselves in the states and cities where there were both larger Jewish populations and, in most cases, a more liberal political atmosphere. These debates appeared in some of the largest newspapers throughout the German states, all of which promoted liberal ideas to their readership. Even regionally, like in the Mannheim/Heidelberg area, the debates about Jewish emancipation and religious reform had significant reverberations. Yet the larger cities and intellectual and political centers of power were not the only locations where these debates occurred—they also took place on the peripheries. In the case of the Grand Duchy of Baden, few locations were more peripheral and distant from the political and intellectual centers of the state as the Bodensee (Lake Constance).

The city of Constance, which sits directly on the lake and borders Switzerland, was not very large during the 1840s, having a population of about five thousand inhabitants. While it was a regional political center, it was not nearly as important within the grand duchy as the cities in the old Badenese margraviates or even the city of Freiburg am Breisgau—the intellectual center of ultramontane Catholicism in southwest Germany. Constance had, despite its strong Catholic tradition, a more liberal climate than other areas in the former Vorderösterreich, and this development manifested itself in several ways: in the removal of the Catholic Archbishopric during the 1820s (it was moved to Freiburg); in the interest in modernization during the 1830s and 1840s, which brought steamboats to the city; and in the creation and development of a Deutschkatholiken community during the 1840s.

Constance, unlike the major cities of the Protestant north in Baden, had no official Jewish community. In fact, none of the large cities in the former Vorderösterreich—Offenburg, Freiburg, and Constance—did. In the case of Constance, Jews were expelled in 1448—in the wake of the Council of Constance—and they had not been allowed back as permanent residents since that time (though occasionally a Jewish trader could reside there temporarily).[1] Still, there were significant Jewish communities nearby; in fact, the Jewish communities near Constance constituted a significant proportion of the region's towns—in two cases, between 40 and 50 percent of the populace. Furthermore, these Jewish communities were among the largest in the grand duchy.

The Jewish communities near Constance were distinctly different from the urban Jewish communities in Karlsruhe and Mannheim; they were indicative of traditional rural Jewish communities known as *jüdische Landgemeinden* (Jewish rural communities). Despite the assumption that rural communities tended to be more conservative, the history of Jewish reform in the German states and in Baden in particular indicates that reform rabbis represented a diverse array of Jewish communities, with many rabbis serving in small and medium-sized towns, as well as in larger cities—not very different from their Orthodox counterparts.[2] This situation demonstrated that the complex relationship between rabbis, reform, and community was more than just geographically dependent.

The perception of rural communities as traditional, Orthodox, and conservative was not always reality.[3] In the Hegau (near Constance), two prominent towns close to each other, Randegg and Gailingen, had significant Jewish reform leanings, although the rabbis were ideological opposites. The rabbis, Leopold Schott (Randegg) and Jakob Löwenstein (Gailingen), were both active writers, and both were involved in the reform debates gripping German Jewry during the Vormärz (though they were on opposing sides). As Gisela Roming wrote about these two men: "Leopold Schott und Isaac [*sic*] Löwenstein—two rabbis, who were active in the 1830s and 1840s in Gailingen and Randegg: One who was completely receptive to novelties, the other nervously committed to the retention of traditional Judaism. In questions of reform they were bitter opponents."[4] It was unsurprising, then, to observe within local newspapers published around Constance that both of these men participated in this discussion in the Constance press in 1846. Their participation—one as a writer of an article and the other as an object of discussion—helped elucidate the confluence of reform and emancipation in the local newspapers.

The debates in Constance about Aufnahme—the readmittance of Jews into the city—were necessary because emancipation in the Badenese Landtag stalled after passage by the Lower Assembly in late August 1846. However, this local debate took on additional importance for Jews in the Hegau region for two reasons: foremost, state rights and local rights were treated as distinct due to the perseverance of communal structures from early modern "hometown" Germany, which were preserved in the new grand duchy in 1806. For instance, while Jews were citizens of Baden, legislation passed at the state level did not necessarily affect their status at the local level—such a right was left to the municipalities, which could deny them residency and local citizenship despite their physical presence in a town. A second reason for participating in this debate was their continuing status as *Schutzbürger* under the *Gemeindeordnung* of 1831, which had liberated all remaining Badenese Christians from local outsider status. As Robert Heuser points out, Jews were "the only noteworthy underprivileged group left in an emancipated environment," an environment in which they could neither partake in the communal goods (like firewood) nor be elected to public office. In addition, the Gemeindeordung retained legislation prohibiting Badenese Jews from moving to cities that had no Jewish residents. As Rürup details, "the Reform Assembly of 1831 had brought no progress for Jewish emancipation, only steps backward."[5] The consequence of these continuing disabilities prevented the Hegau Jews from moving to Constance and establishing a community there, but as a result of these debates and the support of a few key local and radical politicians, Jewish fortunes in the region soon began to change.

Hegau Jews' participation in the debates about their inclusion to Constance during the mid-1840s in many ways resembled what happened within the emancipation and internal Jewish reform debates elsewhere in the grand duchy (chaps. 2 and 3). However, the dispute in the Constance press differed from the one in northern Baden in that the subjects of emancipation and religious reform were, from the outset, concurrent and intertwined. Nonetheless, Jewish participation in the fight for their rights helped them agitate for residential rights within Constance, and it also undergirded their claims to political equality in Baden. In making these arguments and by writing in a cogent, lucid—and sometimes sardonic—manner, the Jews of the Hegau not only claimed the local Constance newspapers as their own forum for communication, they simultaneously used these papers to demonstrate alternative visions of a future that included them as full and equal German citizens, while also destabilizing and contesting societal views of German Jews.

JEWISH PARTICIPATION IN THE CONSTANCE PRESS IN THE EARLY 1840S

During the mid-1840s, German Jews around larger cities participated in a significant fashion in the local press about issues related to political rights and the Jewish religion. In Constance, Jews' participation in the press was only possible for those who lived in towns distant from the city. The nearest major Jewish community was Wangen, a community that had approximately 224 Jewish residents in 1825 and that was about forty kilometers from the city (map 4.1).[6] Randegg and Gailingen, towns that had larger Jewish populations and were centers of Jewish life—they were each the administrative center of a rabbinical district—were further away and only accessible by roads that were not as well traveled.[7] It would be natural to assume that it was difficult for Jews to participate in the Constance press given the distance necessary for news to travel. Also, remote towns like Gailingen had undergone a complete change in socioeconomic orientation after the Napoleonic period; before its inclusion in Baden in 1806, the town had been more closely associated with Schaffhausen and Diessenhofen in Switzerland than with other cities in Vorderösterreich. In fact, Baden's joining of the Prussian Zollverein (Prussian Customs Union) in 1834 made things worse for Gailingen, and both Jews and Christians opposed the decision.[8]

Despite these structural and geographical impediments for the Jewish residents of the Hegau, there was a remarkable presence of Jewish writings in the local newspapers in Constance. The increasing participation and appearance of German Jewish items in the Constance newspapers throughout the 1840s indicated several things. First of all, Jews were a topic of local interest. Secondly, Jews were not afraid to express their views, either against Christians or other Jews. Thirdly, Jews thought the local papers were necessary to present themselves to the public and to promote a different narrative about themselves. Lastly, Jews understood the power of these papers as they sought *Zulassung* (permission) to live in the city and be accepted as *Bürger* (local citizens).[9] The mid-1840s, when the Constance press increased in importance for German Jewry, were not, however, the first time that a Jew had written a letter in either of the local newspapers.

Rabbi Leopold Schott from Randegg was the first to publish an essay in the Constance press, doing so in October 1840 in the *Konstanzer Zeitung* (*KonZtg*). Schott sent a letter to the paper in response to a letter from *Pfarrer* (pastor) Merk from Hausen an der Aach (near Singen). This discussion was very brief,

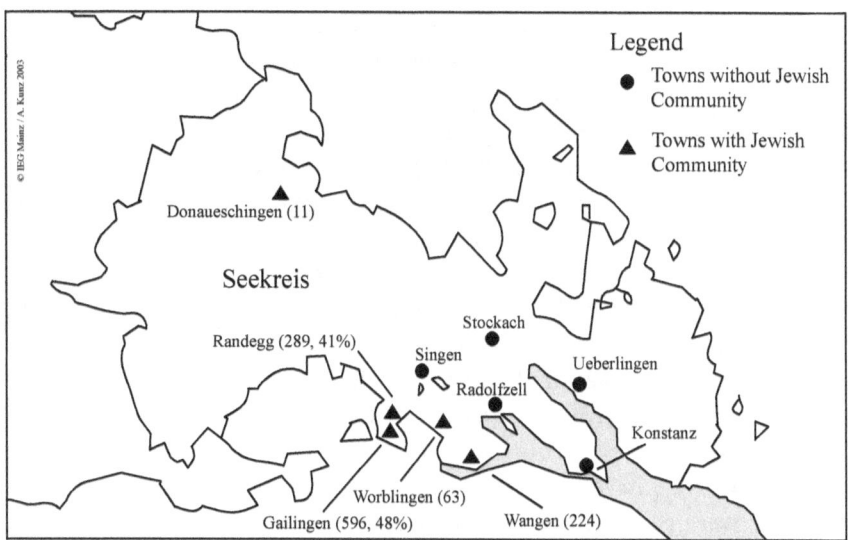

Map 4.1. Map of the Seekreis (Lake District) with Jewish Communities. Base map: © Dr. Andreas Kunz and IEG Maps (http://ieg-maps.uni-mainz.de).

just three letters in total (two of which were from Pfarrer Merk), and pertained to the Teachers' Conference in Bohlingen (near Radolfzell on the Zellersee [Lake Zell]), which took place on September 24, 1840. While the discussion was short, it was an important local example that showed how Jews were viewed by local, small-town preachers, and demonstrated that a rabbi could defend Judaism and Jewish educational practices in the press when needed.

Over the course of the 1840s, Jews increased their presence in both major newspapers—the *KonZtg* and the *Seeblätter*—to promote their own political, religious, and economic interests. This was especially true when the focus centered on those issues related to either general emancipation or to the Zulassung to live in Constance, which took a dramatic turn in a positive direction during 1846. However, not only political events were present as discussions in the Constance press. In 1840, there were also discussions about religion, and this was an element in the 1846 discussion as well. Although the issue of religious reform was included in these discussions, the rabbinical conferences were a popular topic for public consumption; between the *KonZtg* and the *Seeblätter*, the rabbinical conferences were mentioned only once, in a short news article attributed to *Didaskalia* (a journal from Heidelberg/Frankfurt).[10] Although this brief article warmly welcomed the second conference, the lack of other news about it reflected the general lack of impact, despite Schott's own participation and dramatic exit alongside Zacharias Fränkel. Nonetheless, the absence of official press coverage should not lead us to jump to any conclusions, since many of the themes of reform would be present in later arguments.

There were two contributions by Jews in Constance newspapers that were very unique for their form. Both of these writings showed Jews' willingness to use alternative writing forms and their particular effectiveness in broadcasting the message of their long-standing inequality and desire to live in Constance. First, on April 16, 1846, a short *Zwiegespräch* (dialogue) between two Jews from the area was published.[11] The dialogue was about the number of electors (*Wahlmänner*) in the cities of Gailingen and Wangen, which were four and two, respectively. The issue was that Gailingen, if only Christian residents were counted, would qualify for two electors, whereas with the Jews included, it could have four. In Wangen, on the other hand, only Christian residents were counted for the elector determination. This small dialogue was an implicit attack on the inequity of the electoral system in Baden and the continued suppression of the Jewish political voice, even though Jews were counted for representational purposes. The same went for the follow-up article from May 5, 1846, which detailed the Randegg Jewish community's desire to sue the local bureaucratic offices for the lost voting rights that were detailed in the Zwiegespräch. The author characterized the lost voting as a right, that perhaps shows most clearly the intention of the magnanimous (Grand Duke) Karl Friedrich to lead toward the emancipation of the Israelites of Baden; among the rights previously granted to the Israelites of Baden, which says most clearly that in his own fatherland, he is not just a Jew, but also a Badener.[12]

Both of these articles appear to be written by Jewish pens, advocating from the authors' point of view for rights for all Jews. These contributions reflected the beginnings of an agitation for more rights, showing Badenese Jews as objects of a campaign of injustice against of the wishes of the first grand duke, to whom the country owed its formation and to whom Jews throughout the grand duchy looked for inspiration throughout their struggles—similar to the way in which Adolph Zimmern praised the first grand duke in the Mannheim press (chap. 2).

The other article was a petition from the Jüdenschaft from August 21, 1846, in the *KonZtg* (see petition below). Unlike the other petitions that were usually lengthy and written in a very clear German, this petition took the form of a poem, printed on half a page and written in a German dialect from the Lake Constance region. Additionally, this petition was signed by thirty-four members of the Jewish community, all of whose names were printed in the paper. This poem was clearly meant to convey several themes. Writing it in the local vernacular rather than High German was meant to show that Jews were familiar with the dialect. Moreover, since the authors rhymed the poem, we can deduce that they did not just "know" the local language in a marginal way; these Jews wanted to show publicly to the entire region that they were as local as the other residents. It was furthermore a reflection of their real living conditions in which Jewish lives and rites were considered as community events.[13]

Worum,	Whereabouts,
Dorum.	Thereabouts
Aß wer's hawe gehert,	As we have heard, we shall be given
Es soll es werd' beschert,	Emancipation because for a long
Die Emanzipiring,	time the experience has given
Weil längst die Erfahring	lessons that all suppression in faith
Hab gewe Belehring,	would be absurd;
Daß all Uenterdrücking	
Im Glabe sei Unding;	
So hawe mer's Herz g'faßt	So, we have taken heart and have
Un sogleich zum B'schluß paßt	come to the conclusion that our
Es solle unsre Lait,	people, who are educated and
Die grundgelehrt uns g'schait,	smart, should convene to petition
Sich z'sammen separiren	for freedom.
Un Freihait petioniren.	
Zwar wisse mer Alle,	Although we all know no favor
Es g'schiet aim kan G'falle,	is being given to us if Israel's
Wenn Israels Aeste	branches enroll themselves as
Sich melde als Gäste.	guests, and yet we were a chosen
Un doch sin mer g'wesen	people for two thousand years.
Als Volk auserlesen	
Vor zwa tausig Johre	
Die Heere un Store,	The rebellious crowd, they are
Sie dorfen es glawen	permitted to believe this and need
Un Kahn Schreck mehr hawen.	have no fear. That what they fear
Das was se jetzt ferchten	today and what we already noticed
Un was mer schon merchten	is never our power because that
Isch nimme unser Macht,	was laughed at.
Denn *die* wurd' so verlacht,	
Jedoch die Conkerenz	However, the competition is the
Isch dest e Consequenz!	consequence thereof! So that

Damit Sie sich nun könne erhol un fasse,
So wollen mer stelle aus e Schein,
Was mer künftighin als wolle thun un lasse,
Wenn mer erst kommen nach Konstanz nein:
"Mer verspreche kainem zu thun eppes zu weh,
Sondern wolle Jeden lassen mache un geh;
Mer wolle nemme verlieb mit 50 prozentlich
(Für Extra-Newes sin mer b'sonders erkenntlich).
Was mer verzehre holen mer bai unsre Lait,
Des were Se selber finde billig un g'schait;

Am Schawes sitzt mer zum Borich oder Säftel,
Un spricht vom Handel oder sonstige G'schäftel.
Esse dort e Zwiebel- oder Knoblich-Würstel,
Des stillt aim de Hunger un macht aim kan Dürstel;
Denn dorum dar er se doch nit g'holt
Aß mer bloß essen un trinken sollt,
Un um de Schnabel im Wirthshaus z'wetzen,
Der Mauses die Tafeln mit den Gesetzen
unter Dunner un Blitzen
Un mit Aengsten un Schwitzen"
E g'schatter Mann wird's so nit glaben
Un höre aus Schrei'n,

they could recover and hold it, we will issue a certificate of what we will henceforth do or not do if we finally come to Constance:

"We promise to do nothing to harm anybody; rather, we will let everyone do and go. We will accept with 50 percent for special news we are particularly grateful what we consume we pick up from our people they will find it just and fair.

On Shabbat we sit to have Borscht or juice and speak of trade or other business, eat there an onion or garlic sausage that quenches hunger and does not make us thirsty, for Moses did not get the Tablets with the laws that we should simply eat and drink and chatter in the tavern. He fetched them under thunder and lightning and with fear and sweating."

A clever man will not believe it and cease his cries that we want like moths to intrude in the houses.

Aß wollten wir uns wie die
   Schaben
In d' Häuser drängen ein.
Denn höre S'es mit lauttem Schall   Then they hear it with a roaring
Jetzt kommt erst noch der Thales   sound, so here finally comes Thales:
"Mer g'höre wahrhaft selber All   "We truthfully all belong to those
Aach zu den *Lieber-Alles*."   who want 'rather all' [*liberales*]."

Petition from "Der Jüdenschaft," *Konstanzer Zeitung*, August 21, 1846, Nr. 100B, p. 751

Much like the other article, this poem made a clear point about the iniquity of the Jewish existence, even arguing that "the emancipation, because for a long time the experience [in a clearly mocking reference to Jews' current status as second-class citizens] has given lessons that all suppression in faith would be absurd." These phrases reiterated statements on Jewish political disabilities as detailed in the Zwiegespräch and throughout the many different debates in the Badenese Lower Assembly. The authors also played with prevalent anti-Jewish tropes to turn them on their heads, whether it was by mentioning a usurious percentage (*Mer wolle nemme verlieb mit 50 prozentlich*) or satirizing their own "chosenness" as a people (*als Volk auserlesen*), lack of power (*Isch nimme unser Macht, Denn die wurd' so verlacht*), or the belief that Jews were looking to harm non-Jews (in two separate instances). Furthermore, at the end of the poem, the clear connection between Jews and a more radical liberal position was emphasized by playing on the words *Lieber-alles*, which could be literally translated as the "loving of everything" or "rather all" but which most likely was used to sound like the Latin phrase *liberales* (liberals, or in this meaning liberalism). While clamoring for more liberalism, these Jews also tied themselves to the history and philosophical tradition of the West, drawing on the Greek philosopher Thales and proclaiming that they, too, were part of this society, not separate from it, as claimed by Paulus, Merk, and other anti-Jewish liberals. The writers also undercut one of Voltaire's claims that Jews had no philosophy or that Jews, in order to be philosophers, had to do so in a deistic and non-Jewish way. Taken together, these passages in the poem reflect the Jews' ease within society while also functioning as an attempt to laugh together with sympathetic Christians at what they would consider absurd beliefs within a more liberal, enlightened society.[14]

Furthermore, the poem utilized a local dialect from the Lake Constance region as a means of directly mocking the very *public* discussion about Jewish

Aufnahme into the city's social fabric and Jews' historical difference. The application of the local German dialect challenged one of the arguments against Jews' incorporation—namely, that they (modern Jews) only spoke High German and not dialects, meaning that they were like foreigners who were unable to speak the local forms of German. With this vernacular usage, Jews claimed to be as native as all of the Christians who had been there for centuries. That the petition was written in this language is not only significant for these Jews' claim of inclusion in the fabric of the region's populace, but it also staked a claim to the German nation and as part of the multifarious German groups that comprised it. In fact, as Martin Schneble has pointed out, the Jews in the Hegau were well-integrated into their communities, as Christian residents and Jews all spoke the different local languages, including the local Yiddish dialect.[15] The poem is simply another reflection of this tenuous coexistence.

The poem's significance, however, lies not only in its form, but in the context of its publication. The poem appeared as part of a discussion that took place in both the *KonZtg* and the *Seeblätter* between August 9 and September 10, 1846. By expanding the parameters to include contributions in these newspapers through the summer of 1847, when the Jews were, in fact, granted incorporation into Constance, there is a varied public profile for local Jews—participation by Jews on behalf of their own interests, both against arguments from Christians and other Jews, as well as participation seen through the arguments of others in the discussions. These authors intended to prove that German Jews had fulfilled their part of the quid pro quo and that despite the division among Jews in terms of their religiosity, they were worthy not only of being citizens (*Staatsbürger*) but also of being local residents. Throughout this discussion, local Jews publicized their intellectual virtues, which revealed the religious differences among them, all while refuting virulent anti-Jewish attacks from one determined contributor to the *KonZtg*. By writing these articles, German Jews made claims to the local newspapers as their own while also contesting and destabilizing their opponents' preconceived notions about Jews. Throughout this discussion, Jews also presented a different vision of the future—a liberal future that included the Hegau Jews (as well as all other Jews) as equally respected individuals and as Germans who could freely practice Judaism without public degradation.

This discussion in 1846 was an important antecedent to the official, communal debate and vote on Jewish Aufnahme in 1847. Both of these discussions were an important consequence of other developments in Badenese society—namely, the discussions about the rights of the Deutschkatholiken. Similar to the Lichtfreunde's (Friends of Light) challenge to Lutheran orthodoxy, the Deutschkatholiken sought to challenge the rise of religious orthodoxy in the Catholic Church (Ultramontanism). The cardinal question about these dissident groups was the legal status of their followers. Across the German states—as a legacy of the Peace of Westphalia in 1648—only three recognized Christian confessions were officially tolerated and recognized by the state: Catholicism, Lutheran (Evangelical), and Calvinism (Reformed). If members of dissident Christian confessions officially left one of the three state-sanctioned confessions, they would lose their legal status; in other words, dissidents would occupy a similar legal position to Jewish Badeners.

Moreover, the fight against dissenting religious confessions was catalyzed by the threat of secularization. As mentioned before in the discussion about the origins of Jewish reform and the shutting of the Beer Temple in 1823, *any* reform—whether from Jews or Christians—was perceived as a threat to the order and stability of society. When Badenese assemblyman Karl Zittel introduced a motion in the Lower Assembly for "freedom of religion" in December 1845, such a reality was nearing fruition. Zittel's motion "stressed the sacred inviolability of an individual's own understanding of spiritual matters" and took aim at the Catholic Church. The motion did not specify the Deutschkatholiken in its wording, and as a result, it could be interpreted more broadly. Opponents of the motion picked up on Zittel's intention, and directly attacked it and the dissenters by trying to Judaize them, polemicizing this motion as a "second crucifixion of Christ." The opponents, unlike the liberals, had the support of the populace in this regard, and attacking Zittel's motion not only reflected "popular animosity toward Jews but also dignif[ied] it [anti-Judaism] as an article of faith." Despite such vituperative challenges, many liberals became converts to Jewish emancipation, and embraced their new respect for the Jews' situation to press forward for Gleichstellung as well as continuing their fight against the "theocratic and hierarchical state."[16]

As a consequence, and for the first time in the grand duchy, discussions about Jewish rights took on a different tone. The discourse in Constance flowed directly from the most spectacular positive development in German Jewish political life in the state: the commission report in August 1846 from August Brentano (the leader of the radical Liberal faction) *supporting* Jewish emancipation. After Brentano's speech, the Lower Assembly voted for the first time in favor of Jewish Gleichstellung. Thirty-six Abgeordneten voted in favor of Jewish emancipation, whereas only fifteen had voted in favor the year before. The 1846 vote was a clear signal in favor of Jewish rights, which then radiated out to all corners of the state. Despite the failure to pass this legislation through the Upper Assembly or the State Ministry (i.e., the grand duke), Jews were certainly aware of the nature of the political change in Baden. As a result of this change, Jews and their allies sought other avenues of legal inclusion.[17]

In southern Baden, Jews and their allies furthered their quest by seeking admittance to Constance, from which they had been excluded since 1448. The most spectacular personality involved in these discussions was Joseph Fickler, who was Constance's perhaps most prominent political personality during the Vormärz. Since 1837, Fickler had served as editor of the *Seeblätter*, which Elmar Fetscher called Germany's "most progressive and modern" newspaper. In the late 1840s, Fickler was both the head of the *Bürgerausschuß* (civic council) and the leader of the local Deutschkatholiken community.[18] Within these multiple roles, Fickler fought against the Catholic Church and entrenched authority and for freedom of religion—for the Deutschkatholiken and for Jews; he was at the forefront of the fight for Jewish emancipation and Aufnahme. Over the course of the 1840s, Fickler became more radical in his beliefs and actions. In 1842, he split from the mainstream liberals in Baden after coming to the belief that they had only gone "halfway" in their support for liberal ideology (a refrain that would be repeated during by many Badenese democrats during the revolution of 1848). He also believed in a more popular liberalism and disdained mainstream liberals' insistence on the leadership and superiority of the upper bourgeoisie. He desired a more "liberal" Constance with a more robust economy, which he believed Jews could provide. As he wrote, "incidentally, I believe it to be good luck, if many *income-earning* people [the Jews] would come to Constance." Fickler edited the *Seeblätter* as a reflection of his ideological beliefs, and he directly appealed to the petite bourgeoisie. Fickler was sympathetic to those on the margins, especially to those whose rights were threatened by the state; as such, he certainly understood the stakes for Jews seeking admittance to his city.[19]

Gert Zang, in his history of the city of Constance, has argued that the agency and impetus behind the Aufnahme debate belonged to Fickler, given his prominence within the city.[20] However, just as German Jews interceded in the debates about emancipation and reform in Mannheim, Frankfurt, and Berlin, they were also active agents here. And yet, the Jews of the Hegau depended on Fickler and other allies who were committed to their cause and amplified their voices in the press. Fickler's participation as editor was extremely important, and the *Seeblätter* was the most important platform for Jews' contributions to these discussions, though Jewish voices also appeared in the *KonZtg*, the most popular paper in the region. In both of these papers during 1846, multifarious Jewish voices appeared—individuals, communal organizations, and bourgeois associations—and they all argued for Jewish honor, pride, and equality on their own terms.

The first "Jewish" contribution in the discussion during 1846 was the Zwiegespräch described previously. However, this contribution was separate from the debate about Aufnahme, which took place after Josef Fickler introduced legislation to the Bürgerausschuß in June 1846. The first article from this discussion appeared in the *Seeblätter* on August 9, 1846, and came from Gailingen. The author of this article excoriated the local Bezirksrabbiner, Jakob Löwenstein, arguing for the hiring of a religious leader "to lead the people on the path of light and truth, in other words: true religiosity," instead of their current rabbi, who "ogles at darkness instead of going into the light, and who instead of teaching peace, accuses others from the pulpit and showing hostility." The author furthermore wrote that Löwenstein "portrayed the spirit of the time, our time, as a spirit of hell [*Höllengeist*], besmirched excellent men with unabashed suspicion" and also attacked the local Jewish association, *Eintracht* (Unity).[21] Clearly, this contributor believed that Löwenstein was a traditional and Orthodox rabbi of the worst kind; he was so incensed by Löwenstein's refusal to introduce a more modern Jewish religious experience that he recommended relocation for the rabbi.

A response appeared in the *Seeblätter* on August 18, 1846, from the Jewish community leadership. The response was signed by all six members of the Synagogenrat. This contribution was a defense of Rabbi Löwenstein, saying that "the sermons ... were so far very edifying and educative" and that the community was "fortunate" (*beglükt*) to have such "rich" (*gehaltvolle*) sermons.[22] It was clear that the council wished to frame Löwenstein not as a strict traditional rabbi but as one who followed the rules of the Oberrat and, therefore, the quid pro quo. Furthermore, the council members denigrated the statements of the first article writer as exhibiting "personal hatred" (*Privathasses*) rather than a generally accepted opinion from within the community. Since three members of the Synagogenrat were members of Eintracht, this response made it clear that at least some members of the association rejected the first author's categorization of Löwenstein.

The last remarks on the internal Jewish discussion was a small *Gegenerklärung* (counterexplanation) submitted by Eintracht, from September 10, 1846. Thirty members of the association attached their names to the contribution, written in response to the piece from August 18, 1846. The association specifically targeted the three members of the council who were also members of the association, writing that "this association currently has 46 members, and 30 of them, the majority, whose signatures endorsing these lines were given to the editors, are *not* in agreement with the 'Erklärung' of the six Synagogue Council members." In this small counterexplanation, several things stand out.

The Eintracht group was clearly reform-leaning. Since Gailingen was typically considered one of the more "traditional and orthodox" rural Jewish communities, this perspective goes against the typical description of communities like this, though reform often found fertile ground in smaller, rural communities.[23] However, this association might have only reflected the community elite rather than representing the full spectrum of congregants' beliefs. Nonetheless, thirty of the forty-six members of Eintracht signed this Gegenerklärung, which showed that there was a deep split in the community about the direction and definition of reform and progress.

When looking at all three of these texts, we should also consider that Löwenstein was one of the seventy-seven rabbis who signed the Orthodox petition against the Brunswick rabbinical conference in 1845. Until this point, no one in the Gailingen Jewish community had tried to hold Löwenstein accountable in the local press, as Adolph Zimmern and others had done in Heidelberg to Rabbi Fürst. Even though the first article did not mention the petition directly, one can surmise that the writer was a supporter of reform and that he believed Löwenstein to be one of the rabbis who was holding German Jewry back. It should also be noted that Löwenstein did not attend the Mannheim rabbinical conference for Badenese rabbis, and he did not sign the 1845 petition from the other Badenese rabbis in support of Jewish emancipation. While some supporters believed that he gave "fulfilling" sermons (despite being forced by the Oberrat to do so and even resisting this task), Löwenstein was an avid supporter of modern Orthodox religiosity, and his writings in both the *Allgemeine Zeitung des Judenthums* against the Brunswick rabbinical conference and then later in the *Der treue Zions-Wächter* confirmed this.[24]

While it may seem as though this discussion in the Constance press was a religious spat that took place in front of the non-Jewish public, it was much more than that. Given the context of the political scene in Baden and Constance in the summer of 1846, "Jewish" writings were fully political in nature and were intended for a much broader public. The first and last articles were intended to show that Jews from Gailingen, the third-largest Jewish community in Baden (behind Mannheim and Karlsruhe) but proportionally the largest Jewish community in the state (almost 50 percent), were not as backward as commonly assumed. Given that many Germans probably also read the other newspapers from Baden and saw the insertions from other cities about religious reform and the counterprotest against the seventy-seven Orthodox signatories, such an article reinforced the belief that many Badenese Jews followed a modern path. Numerous other local newspaper clippings from this period revealed that most Christians agreed that a substantial number (although not a majority) of Jews were acceptable either as full citizens or as Constancers.²⁵ These public internal Jewish disputes, although intended to show Jews' acceptability as residents and adherence to the quid pro quo, probably also reinforced the belief among those that were already predisposed against Jewish rights that Jews were not acceptable in their entirety. Therefore, since *some* Jews were not ready for emancipation, *all* Jews could and should be withheld from emancipation more broadly and Aufnahme in particular.

These three articles indicate the different available channels through which these discussions could occur. The first text was by an individual who, although he may have expressed a belief shared by many (or at least supported in large part, as the Gegenerklärung would have us believe), still took to the pen and sought to influence the public. In this discussion, there was also a direct response from the community's leadership. The Erklärung might have been an attempt to protect the community from the perception that the council had turned against the rabbi. However, Fickler also made a very important intercession in this discussion. He briefly commented on the six Synagogue Council members, stating that they belonged to "the sinister party of old Jews [Altjuden]"—in other words, the Orthodox.²⁶ At the same time, Fickler commented that the first writer, who had been attacked by the Synagogue Council, was a member of the *lichtfreundlichen Partei* (Party of the Friends of Light). Fickler's role as head of the Deutschkatholiken in Constance and as editor of the *Seeblätter* gave him a bully pulpit to comment on these writings (similar to what Ludwig Philippson had done with Rabbi Löwenstein [see chap. 3]) and to praise those he favored. It would also appear that the first writer and Fickler knew each other, and one could surmise that Fickler could have even solicited the article. The fact that the Jewish community leadership decided to support Löwenstein, however, was not a surprise. In terms of public perception, this would not have helped their cause in a more liberal Constance, especially given the context of the anti-Jewish political pieces that were written throughout this period. Lastly, the appearance of the Gegenerklärung confirmed that a Jewish political association existed, showing Jews' active associational life even in such a rural setting.

These discussions further reflected a very personal aspect. The subject of these articles was Rabbi Jakob Löwenstein, and whether he was an appropriate leader for modern Badenese Jewry. As Gisela Roming has asserted, "many conflicts seem to have been caused more by social tensions and *personal differences* than by fundamental disagreements on issues of Bildung or religious reform."²⁷ However, this analysis has proved that Roming's characterization of this conflict was not necessarily accurate; there was a clear religious division between Löwenstein and his detractors. However, Roming is correct that these disagreements, instead of staying ideological, moved into the personal sphere. Combatants attacked each other and often suggested that a person take a specific action, such as moving away, which then necessitated a defense of the rabbi.

Moreover, this personal attack signaled that living in the communities had become intolerable to some on the periphery of rural and traditional Jewish life. Löwenstein did not contribute to this discussion, yet these writings indicate that the internal Jewish conflict that had hitherto remained outside of public purview was now laid bare for all to see. Levinson has noted that "most of the traditionalists, the 'communal orthodoxy,' found possibilities for compromise which would not destroy the unity of the community." Yet this situation clearly changed after the 1845 Orthodox petition. Cooperation had given way to public confrontation between opposing sides, and they were no longer unified in presenting a public face, thus confirming Brämer's assertion about the dissolution of intra-communal unity.[28]

JEWISH INTERCESSIONS IN THE DEBATE ABOUT JEWISH INCLUSION

As mentioned earlier, this religious discussion was part of the larger societal debate that appeared in both the *KonZtg* and the *Seeblätter*. While all of the entries in the *Seeblätter* were pro-Jewish, the entries in the *KonZtg* had a mixed character. The *KonZtg* of the 1840s is today considered a "liberal" paper, although "liberal" was a catchphrase for an ideology that meant different things to different people. Unlike the *Seeblätter* and the *Tagesherold* (which began publishing in 1847), the *KonZtg* was not necessarily attached to one party, and it was definitely not a paper in the service of a member of the Bürgerausschuß, like Fickler's *Seeblätter*.[29] Nonetheless, in both newspapers there was a vibrant discussion about Jewish inclusion, and the political discussions about Jewish emancipation, as well as those about Zulassung/Aufnahme, were very public. This discussion furthermore revealed that local Jews were keen to represent themselves and were not afraid of debating those who would deny them what they felt were their rights.

The contributors to the *KonZtg*, despite the changing political landscape vis-à-vis the Jews in the grand duchy, argued against Jewish inclusion, drawing on "liberals" who opposed Jewish emancipation, such as the former intellectual leader of Baden's liberals, Karl von Rotteck. The author of the August 26 article mentioned that "not the tossing around of empty phrases, only persuasive [*überzeugende*] words can change their view." In response to this call, an anonymous article appeared in the *Seeblätter* on August 30, 1846, highlighting a contribution from a local Jewish man, "D," on August 25, 1846.[30] Fickler placed this anonymous article just after a contribution from Randegg Rabbi Leopold Schott. This article's reference to D's article and its placement on this particular page could indicate that Fickler purposefully juxtaposed them (just as he perhaps did with two pro-Jewish articles on August 25) to make a statement that Jewish voices should be heard and heeded and were, in fact, "persuasive."

The articles by a contributor from Gailingen and from Rabbi Schott show the combative way they both fought (and needed to fight) the aggressive anti-Jewish polemics in the *KonZtg*. D's piece from August 25, 1846, aggressively attacked the August 17 article from the *KonZtg*. This author mocked the earlier writer's historical bona fides, writing: "That Moses built the Jews into a self-sufficient people ... or a ruling people, in opposition to their earlier servitude, so that the people had to have and at once received political laws: What a novelty! What a discovery! What perspicacity for someone to discover this!" D then sarcastically noted that the other author's "evidence" (*Beweis*) made him "the most sagacious historian of all time." The writer further chided the first author by criticizing Christian actions during the Middle Ages, saying that "the two sons of Jacob were mere amateurs [*Stümper*] in the practice of horror and persecution, murder and revenge" in comparison to the atrocities committed against Jews. This article, however, was not just a pointed response to the selective reading of the Bible and Jewish texts by the first author; in a true liberal and enlightened way, D restated the belief of Jews across the country, and their liberal supporters, that "our cause (the equalization) will prevail because right must triumph, even if it is a long fight." He furthermore laid out, in the strongest terms possible, the condition on which Jews would prevail: "But on our religion, the holy teaching of God, we will never yield, and for just that reason, we will be faithful, honest, truth-loving, and loyal citizens."[31] In other words, Jews would be accepted for who they were and wanted to be, not for what Christians wanted them to become.

Schott's piece began with reference to Fickler's first reply in the *Seeblätter* and to the piece from August 17, 1846, in the *KonZtg*, which he labeled "a second tractate of hate." Schott then appealed to Fickler to help spread "a word of peace and brotherly love." Despite the appeal for brotherly love, Schott mocked his adversary, similar to D's article, bringing up the Talmud as evidence of Jews' loyalty to the lands in which they lived: "The Talmud (you hear, the Talmud!) also teaches us ... [that] the law of the land is the law."[32] That such a criticism came from a rabbi certainly goes to show the frustration that Schott must have felt, especially given his involvement in the petition campaign and the recent passage of Gleichstellung in the Lower Assembly (which he noted by citing Brentano's Commission Report from 1846). But the thrust of Schott's message was the refutation of the falsehoods that had been put forward by his opponents. Schott felt that his opponents did not contextualize their argument, having left out or misread information that did not fit their views of Jews or Judaism. Examples from Schott's contribution include the success of Jews in Alsace, the participation of Jews in the Seekreis (Lake District, or the Hegau) in "social and non-profit organizations" (*gesellige und gemeinnützige Vereine*), and the original author's misreading of the contribution from Gailingen on August 9, 1846, where he falsely interpreted the attack on Löwenstein to be an attack on all rabbis.

Jewish participation in this discussion did not end with these two individuals' pieces; the Eintracht board also published an article on August 31, 1846, in the *KonZtg*. From the beginning, the article declared the opponent from August 17, 1846, to be "a knight, who has ridden here on the old nag of prejudice [*Vorurteil*], armed with the shield of lies and the sword of unkindness ... [and appears here] as a herald of fairy tales from sinister and barbaric times, pronouncing war upon the Jews." The board was clear that their opponent in this discussion was a throwback to the Middle Ages and the horrors inflicted on the Jews, as seen in the *Seeblätter* article from 25 August.[33] They furthermore rejected their opponents' claims against Judaism by providing examples of Jewish laws regarding *Nebenmenschen* (neighboring persons). The board ended its contribution by directly engaging with their opponents' claim that Jews were not Germans. In a show of pride, the Verein rhetorically asked its opponent questions about Jewish participation in political and cultural life. Two questions are noteworthy. The first one draws attention to Jewish contributions in German culture: "And do you not know, Mr. Knight, that among the greatest of our contemporary poets that Jews write for the German *Volk*—write and fight for their rights, their freedom, for their Enlightenment—and are those not Germans?" The second question addressed Jewish donations to the restoration of Hamburg after the great fire of 1842: "And when the beautiful city on the sea, the German Hamburg, suffered such a horrible fire, and the Israelites of Germany, who partook of this German disaster with a full heart and contributed help with full hands—are those not Germans?"[34] These questions, while not directly addressing the contributions of Jews from Baden, pointed to a greater theme to which Eintracht was devoted—a united German state. This organization sought to promote pan-German sentiment, and indeed, the greatest number of German contributions during the 1840s came from Jews. This article, while not mentioning his name, was referring to Berthold Auerbach's achievements as the *Volksdichter* (people's poet), especially after his success as author of the *Schwarzwälder Dorfgeschichten* (Black Forest village tales) and his new *Volkskalender* (*Der Gevattersmann* [The godfather's treasury]), and also to the other Jews who contributed to German cultural life—the composer Giacomo Meyerbeer (Jacob Meyer Beer), the Viennese humorist Moritz Saphir, and the fighter for Jewish emancipation, Gabriel Riesser.[35] Throughout his arguments, the author also defended the honor of German Jews—the knight reference was chosen carefully. Moreover, the author embraced the concept of cultural capital as a commodity to exchange for political rights, just as Salomon Heine had attempted to do in Hamburg by drawing on myriad contributions to society in the cultural and philanthropic realms (chap. 2).

That all of these Jewish contributions from the Randegg and Gailingen area employed similar tactics means they cannot be considered coincidental. Much like the petition campaign for emancipation and Gleichstellung that spread across Jewish communities throughout Germany, these writings were most likely a concerted effort, perhaps stemming from Eintracht. Since the organization was generally reform-leaning—as shown by the Gegenerklärung—its members may have sought out Rabbi Schott's assistance, despite his Austritt from the Frankfurt Conference. These statements by Jews in the Hegau revealed that they were not willing to stand by while others slandered (*verläumdet*) them or their coreligionists and, furthermore, that they would aggressively fight, just like those referred to in the Eintracht article, for the rights and freedoms of all Germans. Thus they were not just the beneficiaries of these efforts, but actively produced and reproduced actions to change public perception. Brentano's pro-Jewish commission report and the Lower Assembly's concurrent passage of Gleichstellung certainly emboldened Jews to take part in these discussions and defend themselves. The resulting discussion was a great reflection of the entire pre-1848 "liberal" ascension in Germany. On the one hand, those whose power was in peril sought to retain their prominence by using hatred, lies, and medieval bigotry. On the other hand, Jews and their allies produced measured, reasoned refutations to parry many claims while promoting a spirit of Menschenliebe similar to that seen in the discussion of Jewish philanthropy and that Schott called "brotherly love."[36]

CONCLUSION

Jewish participation in these debates, whether or not it was influential on the 1847 debates, shows pointedly that German Jews from both very liberal and very conservative areas understood that the fight for their rights was tied to the local press. Jewish reformers and liberals were uninhibited in their participation, attacked their opponents with voracity, and treated local newspapers—both the *KonZtg* and the *Seeblätter*—as the most important venue for their written intercessions. They clearly understood the audiences that they were trying to reach, as seen in their publication choices. The Eintracht association's response to the anti-Jewish pieces in the *KonZtg* indicates that they tried to spread their ideas to the same audience that their opponents were trying to reach. In the case of Rabbi Leopold Schott, he wished to reach the *Seeblätter*'s audience and knew that Fickler was sympathetic to Jews' cause and was aware that his audience was probably quite receptive to his arguments.

These debates also revealed that the local newspaper was a venue in which Jews from the region destabilized and "discursively resisted" prior definitions of Jews through their writings and actions.[37] By participating in the debates described in this chapter, Jews showed not only that they were equals in terms of language but also that they were performing an action equivalent to that of their opponents. Writing in fluent German (and in the case of the poem, in the local dialect) revealed that these Jews had acquired the skills and knowledge that Christians had demanded of them and that integrated them into the broader local culture. Participation of Jews in the local press caused such a stir that people felt compelled to write against them. The words and actions of these Jewish writers generated instability, which was an additional assault on the status quo that had emerged during the ascendancy of liberals during the 1840s. Furthermore, even within German Jewry, local newspapers were locations that helped dispel notions of Judaism as an antiquated religion, thus promoting a redefinition of Judaism and its adherents as the antithesis of those who sought to deny them equality—that is, Jews and their supporters were the ones who were modern, and Judaism was a religion that was fully compatible with the demands of modernity and participation in society as equals.

Many of the contributions that appeared were the result of the ongoing discussions about Jewish life in relation to the German state. As such, these articles were reactions to other contributors. Jews' responses in the local and pan-German papers, such as those regarding the commission report from Assemblyman Fauth in the Mannheim press or the one from Rabbi Schott regarding the article from Pastor Merk, clearly indicate that as early as the beginning of the 1840s, Jews attached their names to writings that counteracted the falsehoods and polemics of anti-Jewish writers. The lucidity with which these respondents presented themselves was something that had become the norm for Jews. The fact that two prominent reform-leaning rabbis were involved in these discussions shows us something else. Both Leopold Schott from Randegg and Hayum Wagner from Mannheim defended Judaism in the press, establishing that the arguments for Jewish emancipation and equality were no longer just the preserve of lay figures in the field of rights and law, like Gabriel Riesser, Leopold Ladenburg, or Heinrich Bernhard Oppenheim. This was further confirmed by the engagement by other Badenese rabbis and their promotion of Jewish Gleichstellung in the press via their printed petitions.

However, the argument meant more than that. Throughout this chapter, the fight for Jewish emancipation and its offshoot, the admittance of Jews to Constance, was not just for the educated, the clerical, or the elite. The fight for Jewish rights became a communal affair, involving more than just the most important figures. Jews in southern Baden were very active in trying to influence public opinion through their writings, and for the most part, they wished to show progress and defend their honor in front of a very discerning public. It was not just individuals who became involved; organizations rallied to produce statements that challenged their opponents. Additionally, Jews engaged in producing works that undercut counterarguments to Jewish inclusion. The petition by "Die Jüdenschaft" in the *KonZtg* is a one-of-a-kind appearance, yet its power was rooted in the language of the local region. The Jews from the Hegau attached their names to a document that reflected their localness, Jewishness, and Germanness at the same time.

However, Jewish expressions in the press were not just created to counter arguments made by Christians or to advocate for political benefits. The local papers were fraught with discussions and disputes about Jewish religious life and especially between reformers and the defenders of traditional and modern Orthodoxy. Indeed, the two spheres of engagement, the political and the religious, were often linked in discussions about Jewish fortunes. The loudest Jewish voices were often those that advocated for religious reform. The writings by liberal and reform-leaning Jews attacked traditionally higher-ranking figures. The lack of deference to authority reflected the increasingly politicized nature of public discussion throughout the later Vormärz in the Badenese press and the changed position of authoritative figures in society. That Jews made these arguments in front of Christians instead of keeping them within the Jewish community also shows that they felt that inter-religious discussions were important topics for public consumption. Perhaps most importantly, liberal and reform Jews crafted their writings to make an impact on Christians and to influence public opinion to support a particular side in a dispute.

Many Jews fully espoused the bourgeois sensibilities of their non-Jewish counterparts and sought areas within which they could demonstrate them.

Jewish writers were engaged in promoting new religious and societal ideas, and they sought, like their Christian counterparts (the political radicals and the religious Lichtfreunde), to upend the status quo. As seen through the publications in the various press organs in Baden, Badenese Jews thought of themselves as more than *just* Jews—they were Constancers, Heidelbergers, Mannheimers, Badeners, and, ultimately, Germans. Acculturation had flourished among Jews, and they clearly felt themselves as part of the local populace. One could alternatively say that the actions of Jews in the papers showed the public a version of what an equal society could look like. Instead of leaving the arguments and business of the country to others, Jews inserted themselves into the society in which they lived and made contributions, one in which internal Jewish matters, like internal Christian matters or secular state matters, were open for public debate. In the end, much like the earlier discussion about emancipation, Jews consciously acted and demonstrated that they were equal to "other Germans."

CONCLUSION

Fighting for Inclusion in Vormärz German Society

DURING THE 1840S, GERMAN JEWS sought legal equalization and respect for themselves, their culture, and their religion. While negotiations and debates in the political arena occurred in the legislative chambers, an equally important discussion took place in the German press and the arena of public opinion. It was in front of the public that Jews, their supporters, and their antagonists sparred about Jews' fitness for equality. Central to all of these political discussions was a debate about Judaism, its compatibility with German society, its modernity, and the nature of internal Jewish religious reform.

Throughout these discussions in the German press, Jews participated at higher rates than ever before. Perhaps the increase in participation was a function of the number of Jews who had achieved Bildung. Maybe Jews participated because they believed they had to personally do more to alter long-held belief systems among the German populace. This increase was perhaps driven by its chronological context; in an era of liberal ascendancy, Jews believed they had to publicly demonstrate that they deserved consideration as Germans and were inherently worthy of emancipation. As an extension of the crisis surrounding the Damascus Affair, Jews became involved in intellectual discussions to defend Judaism in increasing numbers, facilitated in large part by the creation of new German-Jewish journals. Jews increasingly faced off with their antagonists, who had not yet been significantly challenged by Jewish voices in the local press, in the recognition that Jewish emancipation would not be won on a theoretical, abstract basis driven by the *gelehrte Journalen* and academic books, but on the plane of the everyday. It was in the world of the local that Jews needed to indicate that they were just as German as others, and what better place to do so than in the pages of the local newspapers. German Jews' participation on behalf of their own lives within the pages of the local newspapers was also inherently a discussion about German society and the future of German identity and citizenship.

By writing clearly and cogently, German Jews presented their case to the German public. Through regular articles and news reports, German Jews used a method of communication that was familiar to all Germans. However, Jews' contributions did not end with commonplace journalistic articles. Many Jews used a variety of literary genres to show they were comfortable wielding the tools expected of those who had acquired Bildung to directly appeal for emancipation. These intercessions, while distinct in format and message, were all part of the same conversations—whether that was a part of a discourse on emancipation, religious reform, or both.

These discussions accomplished quite a bit, and from the multiplicity of voices in these discussions, it appears that Jews treated local newspapers as if they were their own spaces of communication. In the case of the radical reformers, the local and pan-German papers (which happened to be some of the most popular papers in all the German states) did not just function as if they were their home—these papers *were* their home. Some Jews recognized that relationship at the time, yet histories of the Reform movement have generally focused on the moderate reformers and their creation and promulgation of a distinct and engaged German Jewish press. The reformers, especially lay reformers, were active in making the local and pan-German papers into forums for Jewish issues. Without a doubt, this process was facilitated by sympathetic editors, whose liberal political proclivities aligned with those of Jews who sought to influence the public by presenting themselves as modern, engaged Jewish German citizens.

Within the period of the 1840s, the discussion about Jewish emancipation and religious reform not only showed Jews' direct participation on a substantial level beyond treatises, petitions, and the German Jewish press, it also demonstrated to the general public Jews' capacity on several different fronts. The ability to participate in such a varied manner, based on one's awareness of the evolving bourgeois public sphere, was a prerequisite for journalistic engagement; that is, Jews needed to have attained a sufficient level of Bildung before their voices would be included. Since newspaper editors and their publishers were (along with censors) the gatekeepers to the public broadcasting of information, anything less than proper (*gebildete*) writing abilities could easily have been dismissed or rejected, as could be seen when the *AAZ* printed only two articles deemed worthy to encourage a formal and proper debate. Jews' accumulation of cultural and social capital was also increasingly reflected in public discourse throughout this period. Many of these discussions actively built Jews' case for inclusion and equality, and expressed the hope that more German Christians would become their allies. Whether it was the promotion of Menschenliebe or patriotism, or the recollection of Jewish lives devoted to German ideals, Jews presented a picture to the public of a group that was yearning for formal, lasting equality, not only because they demonstrated the vicissitudes necessary to be equal, they actively believed that they *already were equal*. As Ludwig Philippson wrote in the *AZdJ* in 1850: "It is not you who emancipate the Jews; they have long since emancipated themselves, you are merely completing their outward emancipation. From the moment Jews step out of the ghetto, when they take part in all of the industrial and intellectual aspirations of mankind, when their children attend primary and secondary schools and universities, when their men participate in the sciences, art, industry, and the crafts, when their women pursue a general education—from that moment forward they are emancipated, and have no need to wait for a few words in the constitution."[1] Philippson was wrong that Jews "have no need to wait," however, as legal equality was an important obstacle to be overcome. All of this capital that Jews had accumulated throughout the Vormärz was now waiting to be cashed in to achieve that last remaining, painstaking step in achieving full emancipation.

These discussions about Jewish fitness for inclusion all took place within greater societal debates, especially a Germany-wide debate about the nature of the state and whether or not it should become more secular or remain more religious, as the state was the "protector of religion." Debates on Jewish rights and inclusion, discussions that lasted much longer than those involving the Lichtfreunde and Deutschkatholiken, did not receive favorable evaluation until the rights of these dissident and more liberal Christian groups were under threat. As the two Christian groups' demands sought to upend the balance of the tripartite religious system (Catholic, Lutheran, and Reformed), a space emerged in which Jewish rights could be seen in a similar light. The opening up of this religious space to other groups threatened traditional and orthodox definitions of German society, and threatened the control of society by various governments. As was seen in the hesitancy of the Prussian king in allowing Jewish reform in Berlin during the 1820s, once a modicum of reform and leniency was permitted in society, then the door was opened for further reform and, potentially, revolution.[2] One could make the case that the evolution of the liberal movement in Baden and increased Jewish reform in that state symbolized the Prussian king's worst fears. The liberalization of German society during the Vormärz provided the context for small openings and more permissive attitudes toward various beliefs, including more freedom of the press and the inclusion of Jews as contributing members of society. Once Jews were granted greater rights and inclusion by Christian Germans and not just "toleration," it was not unrealistic for them and their allies to demand that final step to make what they felt de facto exist as a de jure reality. The recognition of Jewish rights was an implicit recognition that society had fundamentally changed and that the forces of authority (princes, monarchs, and priests) that had ruled society were not the sole arbiters and source of societal values. In the context of the Vormärz, it was the liberal bourgeoisie that increasingly became the source of societal mores, and it was this class that German Jews sought to convince of their suitability for full inclusion.

These debates about Jewish emancipation and Jewish religious reform—whether they were separated or intertwined—appeared in diverse locations. They materialized in major and minor newspapers in the most important cities and towns throughout the German states, including the Grand Duchy of Baden. They also assumed a variety of forms: not only did German Jews use traditional means of drawing attention to their ideas and needs, like the newspaper article, they dug deep into German cultural and social practices, even using seldom-used forms like the Nekrolog. All of these intercessions in the debates combatted the prejudices and inaccuracies spilled by anti-Jewish polemicists, while also attempting to present a positive image of German Jews in order to shift the narrative about them. But Jews also took on opponents from within their own communities as they sought to shape the future of Judaism in the German states. Reformers were the most active individuals in bringing their ideas into the public sphere, and they took their ideological opponents to task for their perceived lack of support for modernization and, therefore, emancipation. This can be seen in the writings of those who supported the radical reform societies in both Frankfurt and Berlin, yet there was also vituperation and antagonism expressed by the reformers who wrote against their rabbis throughout the grand duchy—in communities big (Mannheim and Heidelberg) and small (Randegg and Bühl).

All-in-all, the accumulation of cultural and social capital and the demonstration of the vicissitudes (Bildung) necessary for inclusion in German society and the granting of citizenship helped shape and redefine what being Jewish meant; in other words, the process of dissimilation and hybridization had not only taken root but was also an important part of how Jews negotiated with Christian Germans about the terms of their inclusion. Jews were willing to risk public scrutiny of their religion—opening up a potential can of worms—in the hope that their arguments in the newspapers would convert other Germans to believe in emancipation, and by default, a more secular society where religion was not the basis for inclusion or exclusion of them. Certainly, reformers were trying to both shame nonreformers into coming around to their program (if one looks at the Badenese Jews' denigration of Ostjuden and Orthodox supporters of the petition) and to create boundaries in which "Jews' position in society is defined not only by the collectives to which they seek to belong but also by those they do not want to resemble and those they can afford to ignore."[3] Looking at many of these discussions in a different way, the vociferousness of Jews' antagonists in their denial of Gleichstellung and inclusion, as well as the Orthodox attacks against religious reform (whether moderate or radical), shows an implicit recognition that change had happened and was a threat to the status quo and their positions of authority. In response to these changes, Jews' opponents created their own definitions of what Judaism meant (in the case of the Orthodox) and, more generally, what Jewishness and Germanness meant and how these two identities overlapped and coexisted.

The struggles for emancipation and over religious reform did not end during the 1840s. The revolutions of 1848 provided a temporary gain for many Jews across the German states when the Frankfurt Parliament granted Jews emancipation (followed by legislation on the state level), but in the wake of the revolution's ultimate failure, the fight for full equality stalled until the 1860s. Baden was the first in the series of states that granted full emancipation to Jews (1862) over the course of that decade, with the German empire enshrining emancipation into its constitution in 1871. Still, the appearance of gains for Jewish citizens of the German states (and later, of Germany) was never as simple as granting Jews rights as a panacea. Informal exclusion accompanied formal inclusion, and in many states, as analyzed by Peter Pulzer, anti-Jewish animus on the state level became worse after formal equality was granted. Alongside increased demands for emancipation in the post-1848 era, religious animosity among Jews also increased. Reform communities increased membership rapidly in the middle of the nineteenth century, and this led to a formal split in many communities, such as those in Baden (1869) and Prussia (1876).[4]

Moreover, there was continual pressure to conform to perceived norms of Germanness over the second half of the nineteenth century, and conversions to Christianity occurred frequently enough. However, as theories of race became more prevalent over the course of the century, conversion was no longer considered enough to get rid of the taint of Jewishness, though as seen through Georg von Sarachaga-Uria's portrayal of Moritz von Haber in 1843, there were already those who believed that *geborene Israelite[n]* would always be Jews despite conversion. The reactions to the inclusion of Jews and their successes was an assault against Jews' worthiness of citizenship and an argument for a politics of exclusion that reversed Jews' gains during the liberal era.

In the world of newsprint, German Jews built on their increased participation during the Vormärz and became important contributors in the expanding press landscape. Jews gained increasing prominence in the field of journalism since many Jews with university degrees were still excluded from working in governmental jobs, including those in law and education. Two Jewish families, the Mosses and Ullsteins, founded notable publishing enterprises that produced material for the broader public. The German Jewish press kept expanding, including more voices, and intellectual leaders established their own publishing houses and book clubs to make sure there were venues for stories and items of interest on Jewish topics for Jewish audiences. The German Jewish public sphere, and especially the press, became a model for Jews in other countries, and in places like Russia and the Ottoman Empire, Jewish presses blossomed in the second half of the nineteenth century.[5]

Much work still needs to be done in the examination of the German and European press in order to determine more completely how Jews participated therein around specific important post-1848 events. Moreover, there needs to be work done on the individual Jewish communities and the individual town and city presses throughout the other thirty-five German states and the Austrian empire. In each of these communities, the development of Jewish rights and Jewish religious reform were contingent on the conditions of Jewish life there, the development of that specific German state (or in the case of Prussia, the specific region of that state), that state's relationship to reform and secularism in the abstract and Jewish reform in the particular, and the role of liberalism (or the growth of a liberal movement) in those towns and states. In terms of deciphering Jewish participation in the press in those societies, one would also need to know the more specific conditions under which the press developed there, as there was no universal press system, other than censorship as directed by the Carlsbad Decrees and the Deutscher Bund.

Furthermore, scholars need to consider how Jews participated in more general societal events, as many of the Jews involved in the 1848 revolutions and afterward did not "understand themselves as engaged in Jewish politics," but similar to how Auslander draws our attention to evaluating Jews acting in Jewish ways even when they "are not consciously" doing so, Green argues that "by their very presence at the heart of revolutionary politics these [liberal, Jewish] men cemented the synergy between Jewish and liberal causes because they embodied the connection between the two."[6] Clearly, there is room for researching what that meant for Jewish liberals before, during, and after the revolutions, and how they did or did not express their Jewish identity through their public writings and private correspondence.

Further research should also delve into the specific sections of the newspaper in order to discern how Jews appeared in and used the press. Jews had—for decades—participated as economic agents in the pages of the *Anzeiger* (classified section) in terms of promoting their businesses and presenting personal items to the public (such as *Todesanzeigen*). Yet more exploration of the types of items that appeared in that section have not necessarily been incorporated into studies about Jewish communities. For instance, if one were to look at studies of the Jewish communities of Heidelberg or Karlsruhe, the local press may be included but not what was printed at the back of the paper. The classifieds can provide information about the individuals and the types of businesses they ran, but they can also reveal how individuals responded to events in their communities—especially before the news sections were less censored. We can also see, at times, how the Jewish community used this section to fulfill a need, such as reaching out to the broader community to seek a tradesman who could help build or repair a synagogue.[7] In essence, we can make our picture of the social and cultural history of Jewish communities more complete by viewing the back section of the newspaper with more regularity and scrutiny.[8]

While there has been intermittent scholarship on Jews who participated as journal editors during the Enlightenment, there still needs to be more scholarship done on the tools that those individuals used to present ideas to the public. One of those tools that needs more investigation is the feuilleton. Liliane Weissberg published an article (2021) that closely analyzes the development of this convention in the German press and how it became—by the end of the nineteenth century—"the 'Jewish part' of a German press that was also identified as Jewish." But Jews did not just have their ideas and thoughts published "below the line" (the *Feuilletonstrich*, or the line that separated the sections) during the second half of the nineteenth century; there are numerous examples of stories by Jews that were published during the Vormärz, including controversial pieces like "Spielgeschichten" (Gaming stories) by Moritz Cohen, which criticized the elite gambling culture in Baden-Baden. There were also other types of feuilleton items that involved Jews as subjects, like German Jewish poet and scholar Ludwig Wihl's "Des Juden Vaterland" (Fatherland of the Jews), which argued for Germany as Jews' fatherland and expressed longing for the oak tree—a linked symbol of German freedom and nationalism with the Jewish tree of life. Nonetheless, these appearances in the paper have not come under scrutiny, either as individual pieces, as part of an author's oeuvre, as part of a tradition of writing in the feuilleton, or even as part of a broader attempt by

Jews to contribute to and shape Vormärz German liberalism. More work on the feuilleton could also elucidate the ties of the feuilleton to middlebrow Jewish literature and the work of Jonathan Hess.[9] With the creation of the Feuilleton Project (https://www.feuilletonproject.org/), hopefully these items and this section of the paper will receive deserved attention.

Another potential avenue for research is that opened up by Corey Ross and Heidi Tworek. Ross, who wrote *Media and the Making of Modern Germany*, looks at the development of entertainment as an important factor in successful media enterprises, including print media. He evaluates how this media "shap[ed] social, cultural, and political life . . . up to 1945." Within the world of print communication, Ross examines newspapers, *Generalanzeiger* (general advertisers), and illustrated papers in this age of mass media, which demanded a more exciting, impactful, and superficial type of writing than the erudite articles from earlier eras. Tworek, whose recent book, *News from Germany: The Competition to Control World Communications, 1900–1945*, uncovers the development of news wire services (like Reuters) and the role they played in the empire and the development of communication in the early twentieth century. In the middle of the nineteenth century, three individuals of Jewish origin—Paul Julius Reuter (England, original name, Israel Beer Josaphat), Bernhard Wolff (Germany), and Charles Havas (France)—helped develop these kinds of communication channels in their respective countries. In Germany, Wolff eventually succeeded in developing a monopoly for telegraphic services, aided by Bismarck's policies regulating news distribution, which pushed Reuters out of Germany. As a result, the Wolff Telegraphisches Büro ended up becoming the German government's main supplier of news in exchange for a semiofficial status, which meant the government could vet political dispatches and that the service would be available to government agencies. The "Jewishness" of these forms of communication, news services, and entertainment; how they were used by the Jewish and non-Jewish public alike; and how they were perceived by the general public and politicians are topics that still need to be explored. Some studies have already analyzed the different parts of the newspaper during the Nazi period, but the period beforehand offers numerous opportunities for future research.[10] Moreover, the question remains about how Jews across the world interacted with the telegraph and the expansion its use throughout the nineteenth and early twentieth centuries.

All-in-all, the research on Jews' participation in the mainstream (that is, not German Jewish) press and other emerging forms of communication is an area that is ripe for scholars to pursue. The importance of uncovering Jews' engagement in these different genres and methods of communication will allow us to gain a fuller picture of German and German Jewish society from the late Enlightenment through the Second World War and potentially beyond. We will be able to see more clearly the issues surrounding some of the most important events for Jewish Germans in imperial Germany, including the Antisemitism Dispute of 1879 to 1881, in which Heinrich von Treitschke not only demanded that Jews "become German" but also repeated the canard from the 1840s that Jews had control of the press. Treitschke furthermore believed that the "Jewish pens" of the liberal press did not accurately reflect the voice of the people, who—like Treitschke—believed in the efficacy of antisemitism as a descriptor of the problems within German society.[11] Just like the disputes in the 1840s, Jews and their allies (or at least those opposing antisemitic scapegoating) combatted Treitschke, his supporters, and the ideas they peddled.

A significant difference existed between the Antisemitism Dispute and the one that occurred during the 1840s. Foremost, the 1840s was still part of the Enlightenment era—or at least, the Kantian notion of the improvement of man was still operative in this era of liberal ascendancy—though by no means did such enlightening go unchallenged. We see this in the liberal demands for freedom of the press and their evolution on the notion of Jewish rights. In this era, German Christians and German Jews increasingly embraced common causes.

The 1879 to 1881 Antisemitism Dispute occurred during an era in which the opposite was true and in which ideas of racial classification and superiority were prevalent, though as Todd Weir has argued, the rise of antisemitism was directly linked to religion and a renewed defense of the confessional state. Yet we should also be mindful of how antisemitism was central to liberalisms in the European center and periphery.[12] Despite changed circumstances, Jewish Germans continued demonstrating their adherence to cultural norms and building cultural and social capital in Germany, though unfortunately, those standards were from a bygone era. Indeed, as George Mosse mentioned years ago, Jews' adherence to Bildung as the basis for their inclusion and acceptance in society—one of the factors demanded in the quid pro quo—became their "new faith," although it turned into nothing more than a "noble illusion." Treitschke's lecture went further to acknowledge that education, or in this case Bildung, was an ideal that the populace as a whole had rejected and that he believed liberals saw as having an "unfailing moral force." Instead, Treitschke argued that instead of enlightening the public, the overreliance on Bildung had led to "social 'degeneration.'"[13]

Reading from and participating in the press has been an important part of Jewish life since the Enlightenment. And while Jews and Jewish culture have changed and adapted over the past 250 years, the participation in communication has been consistent—even as the world has seen dramatic events (such as revolutions and unifications), as the values in society have shifted dramatically, and as successive waves of antisemites have tried their own "solutions" to Jews' presence in society. Nevertheless, Jews have actively engaged their antagonists, upheld their religion and their existence, and defended their actions by acculturating, by building cultural and social capital, and by fulfilling their part of the quid pro quo. As Ludwig Bamberger, one of the leading liberals and Jewish Germans of the Bismarckian era, wrote as part of the Antisemitism Dispute: "Fortunately, though, culture is just the opposite of the linear propagation of a single national spirit [*Volksgeist*], and German culture stands so high because it managed to assimilate and digest so much."[14] This sentiment was just as true in the 1840s as it was when Bamberger wrote these lines in 1880. And just like those who prevented Jews from full integration during the Vormärz, polemicists in 1880 and beyond kept moving the bar for inclusion higher and demanding more of Jews.

Despite the challenge before them, German Jews continued to participate extensively in local and pan-German newsprint. For many of the participants, their interventions, rejoinders, and publicization of their deeds were existential. While their Christian supporters helped facilitate spaces for self-promotion and contributed to these debates at various spots, it was ultimately up to Jews themselves to "join the debate" and become active agents in the promotion of a modern Jewish culture and religion that conformed to mid-nineteenth German notions of modernity. The result of their efforts bore some fruit—the accumulation of cultural capital and the continual demonstration of middle-class virtues caught the attention of some German liberals and influenced decisions in the Badenese Lower Assembly (1846), in the Constance city council (1847), and, later, the Frankfurt Parliament (1848).

Yet despite these apparent advances in the cause of Jewish emancipation and reforms in Jewish society and practice, as well as the support of growing numbers of non-Jewish Germans advocating on their behalf, the demands of both anti- and philosemitic polemicists sometimes converged. Regardless of how much German Jews resembled Germans at large and became Jewish Germans in their virtues, actions, religious practices, and publishing practices, the solution to the question of Jewish equality could ultimately only be resolved by a decision to walk away from Judaism and convert to Christianity, which ultimately would have resulted in the disappearance of Judaism from German society, a step that most Jews were not willing to take and for which they would never yield.

APPENDIX A

Badenese Synagogue Ordinance (1824)

Note: There are empty rows in the table that follows because I wanted to leave in categories of laws that had been promulgated in other German states. The categories used here are those from Lowenstein's charts.

Table A.1 Badenese Synagogue Ordinance

Category 1: Policing Regulations	
Private services forbidden	X
No children under the age of:	5
Category 2a: Folk Practices Forbidden	
No swaying during prayer	X
No loud praying along with cantor	X
No graggers during Purim (during the reading of the book of Esther)	X
No leaving seat to kiss Torah	X
No disturbances or disturbing singing on Tisha B'Av (9th of Av)	
No disturbances (Unfug) during service	
No gathering before or after service in front of synagogue	
No disturbances (Unfug) on Simchat Torah	X
Where ten persons cannot congregate, all male family heads and sons and Jewish workers and servants obligated to attend services	
No leaving before the end of the service	
No jesters at weddings	X

Table A.1 (*continued*)

Category 2b: Limitation of Participation to Rabbi or Cantor	
Only rabbi can correct mistakes in prayers	
Prayer leading is the responsibility of the cantor	
Category 3: Prohibitions of Public Display of Jewish Ceremonies and Folk Customs	
No wearing of Pantoffeln, wooden shoes, or anything that would harm the dignity (*Würde*) of the synagogue	
Items that do not belong to the service should not be brought to the synagogue	
No wearing of *Kirchenkleider* (prayer shawls?) in the street	X
Category 4: Liturgical Changes	
Category 5: Regulations for Greater Dignity and Formality	
Regulations for precedence in calling to the Torah (Hiuvim)	
Robes for rabbis or cantors	X
Youths not permitted to take Torah from the Ark on Simchat Torah	X
Category 6: Regulations Concerning Music	
No secular melodies allowed	X
No bass and soprano Beisänger	X
Choir instituted	X (boys)
Category 7: Introduction of German	
German sermons	X (weekly)
Prayer for government in German	X
Category 8: Miscellaneous	
Auction of honors and calls to the Torah forbidden	X
Reduction in number of blessings (*mi sheberachs*) on call to the Torah	X
Only six people called to the Torah on Sukkot (*Laubhüttenfest*)	
No additions to the usual seven called to the Torah on the sabbath	X (three are permitted)

Unmarried girls permitted in synagogue	X
Confirmations introduced	X
Limits on Torah reading by bar mitzvah	X (must prove ability)
List of fines can be presented to local governmental authorities in case of nonpayment	
Catechism lessons ordered	X (schoolbooks)

Source: Steven M. Lowenstein, "The 1840s and the Creation of the German-Jewish Reform Movement," in *Revolution and Evolution: 1848 in German-Jewish History*, edited by Werner E. Mosse, Arnold Paucker, and Reinhard Rürup (Tübingen, Germany: J. C. B. Mohr, 1981), 286–97.

APPENDIX B

Published Will and Testament of Salomon Heine

Note: Organizations were only denoted "Christian" or "Jewish" if they specifically named the religious group. However, one could easily make the case (to which I am not opposed) that many, if not most, of the nonreligious or secular organizations should be considered "Christian" as many organizations did not accept Jews as members or provide services for Jews.

Table B.1 Salomon Heine's Published Will and Testament

Organization	Amount (Hamburg Courant, unless otherwise noted)	Type of Organization
Hamburg Christian poor	3,000	Christian
German Jewish poor	3,000	Jewish
Portuguese Jewish poor	400	Jewish
Altona Christian poor	1,500	Christian
Altona German Jewish poor	1,500	Jewish
Altona Portuguese Jewish poor	300	Jewish
Poor in Ottensen	800	Poor
Both Christian advancement societies—jointly	2,000, plus outstanding loans	Christian
Jewish Advancement Society	3,000, plus outstanding loans	Jewish
Jewish hospital	30,000	Jewish
General hospital	10,000	Medical
Deaf-and-Dumb Hospital	3,000	Medical

Table B.1 *(continued)*

Organization	Amount (Hamburg Courant, unless otherwise noted)	Type of Organization
Old Blind Hospital	3,000	Medical
New Blind Hospital	5,000	Medical
Kindergarten	4,000	Education
School for Morally Depraved Children	4,000	Education
Amelie Sieveking Institute for Sick Women	3,000	Medical
Dutch Poor Relief Society	2,000	Poor
Both Freemason hospitals	2,000	Medical
Society for Housing Assistance for Released Prisoners	1,000	Education
New Jewish Temple Society	8,000	Jewish
Jewish Free School	9,000	Jewish
Jewish Women's Society	2,000	Jewish
Talmud Torah School	6,000	Jewish
Society for the Clothing of Poor Boys and Girls	4,000	Poor
Society to Alleviate Poor Widows	3,000	Poor
Clothing Distribution Society	3,000	Poor
Society to Promote Useful Occupation among the Jews	8,000	Jewish
Scholarship Society	3,000	Education
Furnace Distribution Society	2,000	Poor
Bread and Soup Distribution Society	3,000	Poor
Society to Support Postpartum Women	2,000	Poor
Society for the Support of Old Men	2,000	Poor
Sick Visitation Society	2,000	Medical
Society to Support Rent Payments	4,000	Poor
Society for Widows	5,000	Poor
Society for Rooms for Unmarried Women	1,500	Poor

Table B.1 (continued)

Organization	Amount (Hamburg Courant, unless otherwise noted)	Type of Organization
Schoolhouse in Ottensen, which the deceased endowed together with H. Donner in Altona	4,000	Education
Altona Orphanage	2,000	Poor
To the building of the burned-down St. Petri Church	4,000	Christian
To the building of the burned-down Nicholas Church	4,000	Christian
To the building of the burned-down new synagogue, if it takes place within five years	5,000	Jewish
To the building of the burned-down old synagogue	5,000	Jewish
To the Jewish Community of Hannover, his birthplace	5,000	Jewish
The child of the deceased Mr. Maier there (Hannover)	3,000 Mark Banco (MB)	Personal
Hr. M. Leo	40,000 MB	Personal
Business associates	12,000, 10,000, 6,000, and 2,000, per individual, the higher amounts being for those who had worked longer for him	Personal
Karl Heine	Named sole heir (about 11 million MB)	Personal
Heinrich Heine and his brothers	8,000 MB each, and the debts owed to the deceased are canceled	Personal

Source: *Augsburger Allgemeine Zeitung*, 6 (January 6, 1845), 44–45.

NOTES

INTRODUCTION

1. Adolph Zimmern, "Erklärung," *Mannheimer Morgenblatt*, 111B (May 11, 1845), 473. The translation of the term *"Versammlung"* is more directly rendered as "assembly." However, following David Philipson, I will use the term "conference" throughout this book for consistency.

2. *Allgemeine Zeitung des Judenthums*, 27 (July 1, 1844), 372–75.

3. Ismar Schorsch, *From Text to Context: The Turn to History in Modern History* (Waltham, MA: Brandeis University Press, 2003), 125; David Sorkin, *Jewish Emancipation: A History across Five Centuries* (Princeton, NJ: Princeton University Press, 2019), 119–27.

4. Zimmern, "Erklärung."

5. Michael Meyer, *Response to Modernity: A History of the Reform Movement in Judaism* (New York: Oxford University Press, 1988), 134.

6. David Sorkin, *The Transformation of German Jewry, 1780–1840* (New York: Oxford University Press, 1987), 107.

7. Through most of this study, I use the commonly referenced term *German Jews* to refer to the majority of the Jewish population. In some instances, I shift to using *Jewish Germans* to signify those Jewish citizens who saw themselves as part of a greater German brotherhood with Christians.

8. Till van Rahden, *Jews and Other Germans: Civil Society, Religious Diversity and Urban Politics in Breslau, 1860–1925*, trans. Marcus Brainard (Madison: University of Wisconsin Press, 2008). Throughout this text, I will use lowercase "liberals" to speak more generally of those Germans who believed in liberal ideology, whereas I will use uppercase "Liberals" to signify the party of liberals that were elected to the Badenese Lower Assembly.

9. James Sheehan, *German Liberalism in the Nineteenth Century* (Chicago: University of Chicago Press, 1978), and Dieter Langewiesche, *Liberalism in Germany*, trans. Christiane Banerji (Houndmills, UK: Macmillan, 2000). For more on liberals in Baden, see Dagmar Herzog, *Intimacy and Exclusion: Religious Politics in Pre-Revolutionary Baden* (Princeton, NJ: Princeton University Press, 1996).

10. Quotes from Paul Mendes-Flohr, *German Jews: A Dual Identity* (New Haven, CT: Yale University Press, 1999), 26–28. See also Simone Lässig, "Bildung als kulturelles Kapital? Jüdische Schulprojekte in der Frühphase der Emanzipation," in *Juden, Bürger, Deutsche: Zur Geschichte von Vielfalt und Differenz 1800–1933*, ed. Andreas Gotzmann, Rainer Liedtke, and Till van Rahden (Tübingen, Germany: Mohr Siebeck, 2001), 264.

11. Pierre Bourdieu, "The Forms of Capital," in *Handbook of Theory and Research for the Sociology of Education*, ed. J. G. Richardson (New York: Greenwood Press, 1986), 241–58; Lässig, "Bildung als kulturelles Kapital?" 266–72. Free schools were supported by wealthy Jews to help poor Jewish students receive a more secular education (Simone Lässig, *Jüdische Wege ins Bürgertum: Kulturelles Kapital und Sozialer Aufstieg im 19. Jahrhundert* [Göttingen: Vandenhoeck & Ruprecht, 2004]).

12. Bourdieu, "Forms of Capital," 248–49.

13. Lässig, "Bildung als kulturelles Kapital?" 264, 298.

14. These voices were overwhelmingly men's voices, though occasionally a woman's voice did appear (and is noted). This is not to diminish women's role or place in German and German Jewish society; this was, however, a reflection of bourgeois society's organization of gender roles in the public sphere at that time.

15. Yi-Fu Tuan, *Space and Place: The Perspective of Experience*, 6th ed. (Minneapolis: University of Minnesota Press, 2008 [1977]), 73, 179.

16. Van Rahden, *Jews and Other Germans*.

17. Robert Liberles, "Was There a Jewish Movement for Emancipation?" *Leo Baeck Institute Yearbook* (hereafter *LBIYB*) 31 (1986): 40–42. See, for instance, Sam Mustafa's *Germany in the Modern World: A New History* (Plymouth: Rowman & Littlefield, 2011). This is not to minimize the outstanding research that is being done on Jewish life in Germany. The point is more that general studies fail to properly include Jewish life and concerns in more substantial ways other than as recipients of benevolence. More recently, Helmut Walser Smith (*Germany: A Nation in Its Time; Before, during, and after Nationalism, 1500–2000* [New York: Liveright, 2020], chap. 7) includes prominent Jewish converts to Christianity from the Vormärz (Heinrich Heine and Rahel Levin Varnhagen) but does not go into Jewish life other than to mention the violence Jewish people faced. Smith's only reference to Jewish activity in the Vormärz was Jewish philanthropists' inclusion in bourgeois efforts to help the poor (224–25).

18. Sheehan, *German Liberalism*; Langewiesche, *Liberalism in Germany*; recently, a new edited volume (Abigail Green and Simon Levis Sullam, eds., *Jews, Liberalism, Antisemitism: A Global History*, [London: Palgrave Macmillan, 2020]) reconceptualizes the relationship of Jews to liberalism through a transnational lens, including calling for more work to be done on Jews' role in the creation and migration of liberal ideas, especially after the 1848 revolutions. Another important angle of this volume is the relationship of liberalism and antisemitism, and how "liberalisms" were not always proemancipation but could just as easily have antiemancipation and exclusionary tendencies.

19. Herzog, *Intimacy and Exclusion*, 132–39.

20. See especially the works that deal specifically with the fight for Jewish emancipation, such as Mosche Zimmermann, *Hamburgischer Patriotismus und deutscher Nationalismus. Die Emanzipation der Juden in Hamburg 1830–1865* (Hamburg, Germany: Hans Christians, 1979), and Shulamit S. Magnus, *Jewish Emancipation in a German City: Cologne, 1798–1871* (Stanford: Stanford University Press, 1997).

21. Sarah Abrevaya Stein, *Making Jews Modern: The Yiddish and Ladino Press in the Russian and Ottoman Empires* (Bloomington: Indiana University Press, 2004), 4–5.

22. Sorkin, *Transformation*; Lässig, *Jüdische Wege ins Bürgertum*; Benjamin Maria Baader, *Gender, Judaism, and Bourgeois Culture in Germany, 1800–1870* (Bloomington: Indiana University Press, 2006); Andreas Gotzmann, "Der Geiger-Tiktin-Streit—Trennungskrise und Publizität," in *In Breslau zu Hause? Juden in einer mitteleuropäischen Metropole der Neuzeit*, ed. Manfred Heitling, Andreas Reinke, and Norbert Conrads (Hamburg, Germany: Dölling und Gallitz, 2003), 81–98; Johannes Valentin Schwarz, "'Der Gegenstand böte genügend Attraktion'. Ein Forschungsüberblick der jüdischen Presse des 18. bis 20. Jahrhunderts im deutschen Sprach- und Kulturraum," *Jahrbuch für Kommunikationsgeschichte* 9 (2007): 1–75.

23. Jonathan Frankel, *The Damascus Affair: "Ritual Murder," Politics, and the Jews in 1840* (Cambridge: Cambridge University Press, 1997).

24. Magnus, *Jewish Emancipation in a German City*, 130–43; James F. Harris, *The People Speak! Anti-Semitism and Emancipation in Nineteenth-Century Bavaria* (Ann Arbor: University of Michigan Press, 1994). Harris devotes an entire chapter to the Bavarian press and Jewish emancipation during the 1848 revolutions, though it does not investigate Jewish contributions to this discussion or those discussions during the Vormärz.

25. Robert Weltsch, "Redakteur der Jüdischen Rundschau. Ein Kapitel der Geschichte der jüdischen Presse in Deutschland," in *Die deutsche Judenfrage. Ein kritischer Rückblick* (Königstein, 1981), 83–93, as found in Michael Nagel, "Jüdische Presse und jüdische Geschichte: Möglichkeiten und Probleme in

Forschung und Darstellung," in *Die jüdische Presse: Forschungsmethoden—Erfahrungen—Ergebnisse*, ed. Susanne Marten-Finnis, Markus Bauer, and Markus Winkler (Bremen, Germany: edition lumière, 2007), 32; Jonathan M. Hess, "Studying Print Culture in the Digital Age: Some Thoughts on Future Directions in German Jewish Studies," *LBIYB* 54 (2009): 35–36.

26. Eleonore Lappin and Michael Nagel, introduction to *Deutsche-jüdische Presse und jüdische Geschichte: Dokumente, Darstellungen, Wechselbeziehungen*, vol. 1, ed. Eleonore Lappin and Michael Nagel (Bremen, Germany: edition lumière, 2008), 17–18.

27. Jonathan Skolnik, *Jewish Pasts, German Fictions: History, Memory, and Minority Culture in Germany, 1824–1955* (Stanford: Stanford University Press, 2014), 2.

28. Sorkin, *Transformation*.

29. David A. Meola, "Making News: Jewish Germans and the Expansion of Print Culture during the Vormärz," in *Marketing Strategies and German Literature in the Long Nineteenth Century*, ed. Vance Hall and Ervin Malakaj (Berlin: de Gruyter, 2020), 122; Todd Samuel Presner, *Mobile Modernity: German, Jews, Trains* (New York: Columbia University Press, 2007), 3–4. Presner uses the term *German/Jewish* to tease out the complex and tense relationship between Germans and Jews.

30. *Hannoversche Morgenzeitung*, 51 (March 30, 1845), 203.

31. Kurt Koszyk, *Geschichte der deutschen Presse, Teil 2: Deutsche Presse im 19. Jahrhundert* (Berlin: Colloquium, 1966), 90; Johannes Valentin Schwarz, "Redaktion ohne Telefon—ein kurzer Blick hinter die Kulissen eines jüdischen Periodikums in Deutschland vor 1850," in *Die jüdische Presse in europäischen Kontext, 1868–1990*, ed. Susanne Marten-Finnis and Markus Winkler (Bremen, Germany: edition lumière, 2006), 55.

32. Leora Auslander, "The Boundaries of Jewishness, or When Is a Cultural Practice Jewish?," *Journal of Modern Jewish Studies* 8, no. 1 (March 2009): 48.

33. David A. Meola, "Becoming Public: Jews in Baden and Hannover and Their Role in the German Press, 1815–1848" (PhD diss., University of British Columbia, 2012), chap. 3.

34. Rainer Liedtke, *Jewish Welfare in Hamburg and Manchester c. 1850–1914* (Oxford: Clarendon Press, 1998), 2.

35. Throughout this study, the terms *emancipation* and *Gleichstellung* are interchangeably used, just as they were by those who wrote about these topics at that time.

36. In some publications, the Reformfreunde are referred to as the Reformverein. I use the former term except where it appears in a direct quote; the phrase "German-Jewish Church" comes from the title of *Eine deutsch-jüdische Kirche. Die nächste Aufgabe unsrer Zeit. Von einem Candidaten der jüdischen Theologie* (Leipzig, Germany: Otto Wigand, 1845).

1. THE DEVELOPMENT OF JEWISH LIFE AND THE GERMAN NEWSPAPER DURING THE EARLY NINETEENTH CENTURY

1. Statistics for table 1.1 come from Stefi Jersch-Wenzel, "Bevölkerungsentwickeln und Berufsstruktur," in *Deutsch-jüdische Geschichte in der Neuzeit*, Band 2, *Emanzipation und Akkulturation, 1780–1871*, ed. Michael A. Meyer and Michael Brenner (Munich: C. H. Beck, 1996), 59; statistics for Hamburg come from Steven M. Lowenstein, "The Beginning of Integration: 1780–1870," in *Jewish Daily Life in Germany, 1618–1945*, ed. Marion Kaplan (Oxford: Oxford University Press, 2005), 100.

2. Herzog, *Intimacy and Exclusion*, 5–6; Werner E. Mosse, ed., *Das Deutsche Judentum und der Liberalismus: Dokumentation eines internationalen Seminars der Friedrich-Naumann-Stiftung in Zusammenarbeit mit dem Leo Baeck Institute, London* (Sankt Augustin, Germany: Comdok-Verlagsabteilung, 1986).

3. Lothar Gall, *Der Liberalismus als regierende Partei: Das Grossherzogtum Baden zwischen Restauration und Reichsgründung* (Wiesbaden, Germany: Franz Steiner, 1968).

4. For more on Karl Friedrich's changes to Badenese society, see Harald Stockert, "1801–1815: Ein 'goldenes Zeitalter' unterm badischen Greif?" in *Geschichte der Stadt Mannheim*, Band 2, *1801–1914*, ed. Ulrich Nieß and Michael Caroli (Heidelberg, Germany: Regionalkultur, 2007), 13–20.

5. Mack Walker, *German Home Towns: Community, State, and General Estate 1648–1871* (Ithaca, NY: Cornell University Press, 1971); regarding Jewish policies in the German states in the post-Napoleonic era and their ties to the ancien régime, see Sorkin, *Jewish Emancipation*, chap. 12.

6. For more on Jewish life in Karlsruhe, see Ernst Otto Bräunche, "Vom Schutzjuden zum Bürger zweiter Klasse: Die jüdische Gemeinde bis zum Erlass des Judenedikts 1809," in *Juden in Karlsruhe: Beiträge zu ihrer Geschichte bis zur nationalistischen Machtergreifung*, ed. Heinz Schmitt, Ernst Otto Bräunche, and Manfred Koch (Karlsruhe, Germany: Badenia, 1988), 41–80.

7. Sorkin, *Transformation*, 107; Stefi Jersch-Wenzel, "Rechtslage und Emanzipation," in Meyer and Brenner, *Deutsch-jüdische Geschichte*, 2:19–23; Shmuel Feiner, *Moses Mendelssohn: Sage of Modernity*, trans. Anthony Berris (New Haven, CT: Yale University Press, 2010), 135; Shulamit Volkov, *Germans, Jews, and Antisemites: Trials in Emancipation* (Cambridge and New York: Cambridge University Press, 2006), 179. English translations of Dohm's title are not standardized, specifically regarding the term *Verbesserung*. I have used the translation "improvement," while others, including Shmuel Feiner and David Sorkin, use the term *amelioration*. I believe *improvement* allows us to view debates about emancipation in terms of changing Jews' lives and not just the lifting of restrictions, though both concepts went hand-in-hand.

8. Sorkin, *Transformation*, 5; Shulamit Volkov, "The 'Verbürgerlichung' of the Jews as a Paradigm," in *Bourgeois Society in Nineteenth Century Europe*, ed. Jürgen Kocka and Allan Mitchell (Oxford: Berg, 1993), 373; Also see Jürgen Kocka, "The European Pattern and the German Case," in *Bourgeois Society in Nineteenth Century Europe*, ed. Jürgen Kocka and Allan Mitchell, 3–39, for a more general sense of what being bourgeois in the early nineteenth century meant.

9. Adolf Kober, "Emancipation's Impact on the Education and Vocational Training of German Jewry," *Jewish Social Studies* 16, no. 1 (January 1954): 3–32; Adolf Kober, "Emancipation's Impact on the Education and Vocational Training of German Jewry," *Jewish Social Studies* 16, no. 2 (April 1954): 151–76.

10. Johann David Michaelis, "Arguments against Dohm (1782)," in *The Jew in the Modern World: A Documentary History*, 3rd ed., ed. Paul Mendes-Flohr and Jehuda Reinharz (Oxford: Oxford University Press, 2011), 34–36; Immanuel Kant, "The Euthanasia of Judaism (1798)" in Mendes-Flohr and Reinharz, *Jew in the Modern World*, 113–14; Jacob Friedrich Fries, "On the Danger to the Well-Being and Character of the Germans presented by the Jews," in Mendes-Flohr and Reinharz, *Jew in the Modern World*, 285–86; Stefan-Ludwig Hoffmann, "Brothers or Strangers? Jews and Freemasons in Nineteenth-Century Germany," trans. Pamela Selwyn, *German History* 18, no. 2 (April 2000): 149.

11. Berthold Rosenthal, *Heimatgeschichte der badischen Juden seit ihrem geschichtlichen Auftreten bis zur Gegenwart* (Bühl, Germany: Konkordia, 1927), 226, Freimann-Sammlung; Jersch-Wenzel, "Rechtslage und Emanzipation," 23–26.

12. Reinhard Rürup, *Emanzipation und Antisemitismus* (Frankfurt: Fischer Taschenbuch, 1987), 49–50.

13. Bräunche, "Vom Schutzjuden zum Bürger zweiter Klasse," 76. Bräuche used the quote from Generallandesarchiv Karlsruhe (GLAK) 74/3689. It should be noted that Preuschen (the Karlsruhe commissioner) also wrote that Jews "due to their national character were suited to no handicraft or artisanal occupations."

14. Rürup, *Emanzipation und Antisemitismus*, 56. For more on the development of Jews' legal position within Mannheim from 1660 to the first few years after they city's incorporation into the grand duchy, see Sarah Pister, "Stadtfremde in Mannheim: Zur Aufnahme und Integration von In- und Ausländern in eine landesherrliche Stadt des späten 18. und frühen 19. Jahrhunderts" (PhD diss., University of Mannheim, 2021), 116–135; data for map 1.1 comes from Franz Hundsnurscher and Gerhard Taddey, *Die jüdischen Gemeinden in Baden: Denkmale, Geschichte, Schicksale* (Stuttgart, Germany: W. Kohlhammer, 1968). The population statistic for Karlsruhe comes from the *Karlsruhe Zeitung*, 27 (January 27, 1829), 147. The number for the Heidelberg Jewish population is cited for the year 1827, while the base population is from 1830 (Marie-Lise Weber, "Heidelberg in der Umbruchszeit zwischen 1789 und 1819," in *Vom alten zum*

neuen Bürgertum: Die mitteleuropäische Stadt im Umbruch 1780–1820, ed. Lothar Gall [Munich: R. Oldenbourg, 1991], 413). The percentages for Mannheim and Karlsruhe were calculated using city population statistics from the year 1830 (Dieter Hein, "Umbruch und Aufbruch: Bürgertum in Karlsruhe und Mannheim 1780–1820," in Gall, *Vom alten zum neuen Bürgertum*, 455).

15. Bert Wallet, "Napoleon's Legacy—National Government and Jewish Community in Western Europe," *Simon Dubnov Jahrbuch* 6 (2007): 291–309; Deborah Hertz, *How Jews Became Germans: The History of Conversion and Assimilation in Berlin* (New Haven, CT: Yale University Press, 2007), 51. King Frederick William II admitted ten additional families to Berlin, abolished the *Leibzoll* (entrance tax), and stopped forcing Jews to buy excess (and inferior) porcelain when they married.

16. Jael B. Paulus, "Emanzipation und Reaktion 1809–1862," in Schmitt, Bräunche, and Koch, *Juden in Karlsruhe*, 81.

17. Wendy Brown, *Regulating Aversion: Tolerance in the Age of Identity and Empire* (Princeton, NJ: Princeton University Press, 2006), 28.

18. Heinrich Bernhard (H. B.) Oppenheim, "Kritik des Kommissionsberichts der Badischen 2ten Kammer über die bürgerliche Gleichstellung der Juden," *Mannheimer Abendzeitung*, 179 (2 August 1842), 719–20. Oppenheim used the term *rights* to describe the political situation of Jews in Baden in 1842. As he put it, "In Baden the Jews are both voters and electors—so they have the most important political rights; only the people do not have the right to name them [the Jews] as their representatives."

19. Herzog, *Intimacy and Exclusion*, 54; Jürgen Stude, *Geschichte der Juden in Landkreis Karlsruhe* (Karlsruhe, Germany: G. Braun, 1990), 78–79; Doron Avraham, "German Liberalism and the Militarisation of Civil Society, 1813–1848/49," *European Review of History: Revue européenne d'histoire* 17, no. 4 (2010): 613. Stude notes that in the town of Östringen (near Bruchsal), eight Jews were granted local rights, and the local populace tried to take away those rights once they realized they would have to share communal items, such as firewood. The Badenese state denied the request and defended the Jews' rights to residency.

20. Uri R. Kaufmann, *Kleine Geschichte der Juden in Baden* (Karlsruhe, Germany: G. Braun, 2007), 50–51.

21. Andreas Brämer, *Rabbiner und Vorstand: Zur Geschichte der jüdischen Gemeinde in Deutschland und Österreich 1808–1871* (Vienna: Böhlau, 1999), 23–26; Wallet, "National Government," 295.

22. Gisela Roming, "Religiosität und Bildung in Jüdischen Landgemeinden," in *Jüdisches Leben im Bodenseeraum: Zur Geschichte des alemannischen Judentums mit Thesen zum christlich-jüdischen Gespräch*, ed. Abraham P. Kustermann and Dieter R. Bauer (Ostfildern, Germany: Schwabenverlag, 1994), 99–108; Uri R. Kaufmann, "Das jüdische Schulwesen auf dem Lande: Baden und Elsaß im

Vergleich 1770–1848," in *Jüdisches Leben auf dem Lande: Studien zur deutsch-jüdischen Geschichte*, ed. Monika Richarz and Reinhard Rürup (Tübingen, Germany: Mohr Siebeck, 1997); Wallet, "National Government," 295, 303; Kober, "Emancipation," part 1, 25; Andreas Kennecke, "HaMe'assef: Die erste moderne Zeitschrift der Juden in Deutschland," in *Haskalah: Die jüdische Aufklärung in Deutschland 1769–1812*, ed. Christoph Schulte (Wolfenbüttel: Wallstein, 1999), 180; Steven M. Lowenstein, "The 1840s and the Creation of the German-Jewish Religious Reform Movement," in *Revolution and Evolution: 1848 in German-Jewish History*, ed. Werner E. Mosse, Arnold Paucker, and Reinhard Rürup (Tübingen, Germany: J. C. B. Mohr, 1981), 260–61.

23. Meola, "Becoming Public," 178–80, 238–48; *Augsburger Allgemeine Zeitung*, 152 (May 31, 1844), 1215; *Deutscher Allgemeine Zeitung*, 146 (May 25, 1844), 1192; *Vossische Zeitung*, 122B and 127 (May 28, 1844, and June 3, 1844); the advertisement in question: *Karlsruher Zeitung*, 257 (September 25, 1816), 1168 (it also appeared on September 27, 1816, and October 4, 1816); Tilde Bayer, *Minderheit in städtischen Raum: Sozialgeschichte der Juden in Mannheim während der 1.Hälfte des 19. Jahrhunderts* (Stuttgart, Germany: Thorbecke, 2001), 126–29. In 1821, the state granted this new Jewish school official recognition and placed it under the authority of the school commission.

24. Hertz, *How Jews Became Germans*, 106–8 (emphasis in original).

25. Brown, *Regulating Aversion*, 9.

26. Marjoke Rietveld-van Wingerden and Nelleke Bakker, "Education and the Emancipation of Jewish Girls in the Nineteenth Century: The Case of the Netherlands," *History of Education Quarterly* 44, no. 2 (Summer 2004): 208; French National Assembly, "Declaration of the Rights of Man and of Citizen (August 26, 1789)," "Debate on the Eligibility of Jews for Citizenship (December 23, 1789)," "Decree Recognizing the Sephardim as Citizens (January 28, 1790)," "The Constitution of France (September 3, 1791)," and "The Emancipation of the Jews of France (September 28, 1791)" as well as Roman Republic, "First Emancipation in Rome (February 1799)," and Pier Gian Maria de Ferrari, "Tearing Down the Gates of the Venetian Ghetto (July 10, 1797)," in Mendes-Flohr and Reinharz, *Jew in the Modern World*, 123–28 and 145–47.

27. Napoleon Bonaparte, "The Infamous Decree (1808)," in Mendes-Flohr and Reinharz, *Jew in the Modern World*, 161–63. See also Sorkin, *Jewish Emancipation*, chap. 9.

28. Edward Timms, "The Pernicious Rift: Metternich and the Debate about Jewish Emancipation at the Congress of Vienna," *LBIYB* 46 (2001): 15; Brian E. Vick, *The Congress of Vienna: Power and Politics after Napoleon* (Cambridge, MA: Harvard University Press, 2014), 185–87; Vick takes this language from J. L. Klüber, *Acten des Wiener Congresses in den Jahren 1814–1815*, Band 2 (Erlangen, Germany: Palm, 1815–19), 320–21, 456.

29. The seminal study on *Landjuden* (rural Jews) is Utz Jeggle's *Judendörfer in Württemberg* (Tübingen, Germany: Tübinger Vereinigung f. Volkskunde e. V., 1969; new version, 1999). See also the case studies in Richarz and Rürup, *Jüdisches Leben auf dem Lande*; Lowenstein, "Religious Reform Movement," 255–97.

30. Caesar Seligmann, *Geschichte der jüdischen Reformbewegung Von Mendelssohn bis zur Gegenwart* (Frankfurt: J. Kauffmann, 1922), 31; Simone Lässig, *Jüdische Wege ins Bürgertum*, 443.

31. Liliane Weissberg, "Newspaper Feuilletons: Reflections on the Possibilities of German-Jewish Authorship and Literature," in *The Future of the German-Jewish Past: Memory and the Question of Antisemitism*, ed. Gideon Reuveni and Diana Franklin (Lafayette, IN: Purdue University Press, 2021), 150.

32. Hannah Barker and Simon Burrows, introduction to *Press, Politics, and the Public Sphere in Europe and North America, 1760–1820*, ed. Hannah Barker and Simon Burrows (Cambridge: Cambridge University Press, 2002), 14; Heinz-Dietrich Fischer, *Handbuch der politischen Presse in Deutschland 1480–1980: Synopse rechtlicher, struktureller und wirtschaftlicher Grundlagen der Tendenzpublizistik im Kommunikationsfeld* (Düsseldorf, Germany: Droste, 1981), 42; Johannes Weber, "Gründerzeitungen: Die Anfänge der periodischen Nachrichtenpresse im Norden des Reiches," in *Historische Presse und ihre Leser: Studien zu Zeitungen, Zeitschriften, Intelligenzblättern und Kalendern in Nordwestdeutschland*, ed. Peter Albrecht and Holger Böning (Bremen, Germany: edition lumière, 2005), 11; Theodor Stein, "Südwestdeutsche Zeitungsgeschichte: Ein Überblick über die Anfänge bis zum Jahre 1933," in *Von der Preßfreiheit zur Pressefreiheit: Südwestdeutsche Zeitungsgeschichte von den Anfängen bis zur Gegenwart*, ed. Klaus Dreher (Stuttgart, Germany: Konrad Theiss, 1983), 27–35; Günter Stegmaier, "Von der Zensur zur Pressefreiheit," in Dreher, *Von der Preßfreiheit zur Pressefreiheit*; Johannes Weber, "The Early German Newspaper—A Medium of Contemporaneity," in *The Dissemination of News and the Emergence of Contemporaneity in Early Modern Europe*, ed. Brendan Dooley (Surrey: Ashgate, 2010), 75–76. Duke Heinrich Julius of Wolfenbüttel financially supported the *Aviso Relation* in 1609, and Elector (*Kurfürst*) Karl Ludwig von der Pfalz's role was as his region's first journal editor.

33. James Van Horn Melton, *The Rise of the Public in Enlightenment Europe* (Cambridge: Cambridge University Press, 2001), 89–92; J. Weber, "Gründerzeitungen," 39; Amos Bitzan, "The Problem of Pleasure: Disciplining the German Jewish Reading Revolution, 1770–1870" (PhD diss., University of California Berkeley, 2011).

34. Craig Calhoun, introduction to *Habermas and the Public Sphere*, ed. Craig Calhoun, (Cambridge: Massachusetts Institute of Technology Press, 1992), 12–13; Jürgen Habermas, *Structural Transformation of the Public Sphere: An Inquiry into a Category of Bourgeois Society*, trans. Thomas Burger and Frederick

Lawrence (Cambridge: Massachusetts Institute of Technology Press, 1989), 36–37, 53–54; Thomas Habel, "Deutschsprachige Rezensionszeitschriften der Aufklärung: Zur Geschichte und Erschließung," in Albrecht and Böning, *Historische Presse und ihre Leser*, 43. The *gelehrte Zeitungen* have also been known as *Journals* or as *Zeitschriften*. In note 6 of his article, Habel provides a brief history of the terms and when they first appeared.

35. Habel, "Deutschsprachige Rezensionszeitschriften," 58; quote from Kai Lückemeier, *Information als Verblendung: Die Geschichte der Presse und der öffentlichen Meinung im 19. Jahrhundert* (Stuttgart, Germany: Ibidem, 2001), 31–38.

36. Brigitte Tolkemitt, *Der Hamburgische Correspondent: Zur öffentlichen Verbreitung der Aufklärung in Deutschland* (Tübingen, Germany: Max Niemeyer, 1995), 1–10, 26, 43–64, quote from 38.

37. J. Weber, "Gründerzeitungen," 40.

38. Astrid Blome, "Regionale Strukturen und die Entstehung der deutschen Regionalpresse im 18. Jahrhundert," in Albrecht and Böning, *Historische Presse und ihre Leser*, 78.

39. Lückemeier, *Information als Verblendung*, 29, 65; Blome, "Regionale Strukturen," 79, 95; Weissberg, "Newspaper Feuilletons," 147; Ian F. McNeely, *The Emancipation of Writing: German Civil Society in the Making, 1790s–1820s* (Berkeley: University of California Press, 2003), 221, 231. McNeely notes that by 1800, the combined circulation of the 160 gazettes in existence was 100,000 copies, meaning that approximately 1 million people read these papers.

40. Astrid Blome, "Offices of Intelligence and Expanding Social Spaces," in Dooley, *Dissemination of News*, 212; J. Weber, "Early German Newspaper," 76.

41. Fischer, *Handbuch der politischen Presse*, 46.

42. Lückemeier, *Information als Verblendung*, 125, 133, 219. Ironically, the *Rheinische Merkur* had been rumored to be founded in part by the Prussian regime, which shut the paper down in 1816.

43. Lückemeier, *Information als Verblendung*, 63, 69–70; Daniel Moran, "Cotta and Napoleon: The French Pursuit of the *Allgemeine Zeitung*," *Central European History* 14, no. 2 (June 1981): 92. The *Allgemeine Zeitung* was originally called the *Neueste Weltkunde*. Lückemeier also notes that the *AAZ*'s circulation was approximately 1,000 at its low point during the Napoleonic era and then 10,500 in 1847. Horst Heenemann has more complete statistics, as follows: 1789 (year), 1,400 (circulation); 1812, 1,007; 1815, 2,718; 1823, 4,089; 1824, 3,602; 1845, 9,172; 1846, 9,562; 1847, 9,847; 1848, 11,155. The *AAZ*'s two largest competitors were the *Vossische Zeitung* and the *Spenersche Zeitung*, both based in Berlin. The *Vossische Zeitung*'s circulation numbers were: 1840, 9,820; 1845, 7,000; 1847, 19,850; 1848, 24,000. The *Spenersche Zeitung*'s circulation numbers were: 1827, 10,000; 1828, 11,000; 1845, 9,000 ("Die Auflagenhöhe

der deutschen Zeitungen. Ihre Entwicklung und ihre Probleme" [PhD diss., Universität Leipzig, 1930], 33, 36).

44. Jacob Toury, *Die politische Orientierung der Juden in Deutschland: Von Jena bis Weimar* (Tübingen, Germany: J. C. B. Mohr [Paul Siebeck], 1966), 11.

45. Lückemeier, *Information als Verblendung*, 72, 143–45, 188–91; Bernhard Fischer, *Die Augsburger "Allgemeine Zeitung" 1798–1866, Register der Beiträger / Mitteiler*, part 1, 1798–1832 (Munich: K. G. Saur, 2003), 158; Bernhard Fischer, *Die Augsburger "Allgemeine Zeitung" 1798–1866, Register der Beiträger / Mitteiler*, part 2, 1833–1849 (Munich: K. G. Saur, 2004), 165–166; James Retallack, "From Pariah to Professional? The Journalist in German Society and Politics, from the Late Enlightenment to the Rise of Hitler," *German Studies Review* 16, no. 2 (May 1993): 175–223; Daniel Moran, *Toward the Century of Words: Johann Cotta and the Politics of the Public Realm in Germany, 1795–1832* (Berkeley: University of California Press, 1990), 38; Stegmaier, "Von der Zensur," 141–50. Heine's articles were distributed over 133 different days during the period of 1831 to 1849. Moran notes that the *AAZ*'s financial standing was shaky by the end of the 1820s.

46. Elisabeth Hüls, "Die 'Deutsche Tribüne' 1831/32: Ein Oppositionsblatt im Vormärz. Entwicklung des Blattes, äußere Rahmenbedingungen und Zensurkämpfe," in *Deutsche Tribüne (1831–1832): Herausgegeben vom J. G. A. Wirth*, Band 2, *Darstellung, Kommentar, Glossar, Register, Dokumente*, ed. Elisabeth Hüls and Hedwig Herold-Schmidt (Munich: K. G. Saur, 2007), 40–47; quote from: Robin Lenman, "Germany," in *The War for the Public Mind: Political Censorship in Nineteenth-Century Europe*, ed. Robert Justin Goldstein (Westport, CT: Praeger, 2000), 35–36.

47. Robert Darnton, *Censor at Work: How States Shaped Literature* (New York: W. W. Norton, 2014), 29, 44–46.

48. Bärbel Holtz, "Einleitung: Staatlichkeit und Obstruction—Preussens Zensurpraxis als politisches Kulturphänomen," in *Preussens Zensurpraxis von 1819 bis 1849 in Quellen*, ed. Bärbel Holtz (Berlin: de Gruyter Akademie Forschung, 2015), 66–67. Fraternities (*Burschenschaften*) were constructed in response to the French invasion of Germany, and during the post-Napoleonic period, these groups were often antiauthoritarian, masculine, and nationalist. For more, see, Karin Breuer, "Competing Masculinities: Fraternities, Gender and Nationality in the German Confederation, 1815–30," *Gender & History* 20, no. 2 (August 2008): 270–87; James M. Brophy, "'The Modernity of Tradition': Popular Culture and Protest in Nineteenth-Century Germany," in *Protest, Popular Culture and Tradition in Modern and Contemporary Western Europe*, ed. Illaria Favretto and Xabier Itcaina (London: Palgrave Macmillan, 2017), 24; Hildegard Müller, *Liberale Presse im badischen Vormärz: Die Presse der Kammerliberalen und ihre Zentralfigur Karl Mathy 1840–1848* (Heidelberg, Germany: Carl Winter Universitätsverlag, 1986), 38; Frank Thomas Hoefer,

Pressepolitik und Polizeistaat Metternichs: Die Überwachung von Presse und politischer Öffentlichkeit in Deutschland und den Nachbarstaaten durch das Mainzer Informationsbüro (1833–1848) (Munich: K. G. Saur, 1983).

49. Frederik Ohles, *Germany's Rude Awakening: Censorship in the Land of the Brothers Grimm* (Kent, OH: Kent State University Press, 1992), 37–47, 79–87; Konrad Dussel, *Deutsche Tagespresse im 19. und 20. Jahrhundert* (Münster, Germany: LIT, 2004), 31–35; Arthur Hübscher, *Hundertfünfzig Jahre F. A. Brockhaus 1805 bis 1955* (Wiesbaden, Germany: F. A. Brockhaus, 1955), 99–101; Holtz, "Einleitung," 28. Each printed sheet had sixteen pages of printed text; Hüls, "Die 'Deutsche Tribüne,'" 32–33, 39. The Bavarian government asked Moritz Saphir (another German Jewish convert to Christianity) to publish articles against the *DT* in *Der deutsche Horizont*, and it tried to pressure Cotta to close the paper.

50. Dussel, *Deutsche Tagespresse*, 35–38.

51. Lenman, "Germany," 47; T. C. W. Blanning, *The Culture of Power and the Power of Culture* (Oxford: Oxford University Press, 2002), 127; Hüls, "Die 'Deutsche Tribüne,'" 30, 39.

52. Müller, *Liberale Presse*, 76.

53. Ohles, *Germany's Rude Awakening*, 7.

54. Hanno Tauschwitz, *Presse und Revolution 1848/49 in Baden: Ein Beitrag zur Sozialgeschichte der periodischen Literatur und zu ihrem Einfluss auf die Geschichte der badischen Revolution 1848/49* (Heidelberg, Germany: Esprint, 1981), 144.

55. McNeely, *Emancipation of Writing*, chap. 8; Blanning, *Culture of Power*, 113–14; Tauschwitz, *Presse und Revolution*, 148; Nagel, "Jüdische Presse und jüdische Geschichte," 26.

56. Anke Bethmann, *Freiheit und Einheit als Leitmotive der öffentlichen Diskussion um die Neuordnung Deutschlands: Eine Studie zur Geschichte der Revolution von 1848/49 im Königreich Hannover* (Hamburg, Germany: Dr. Kovač, 2000), 59. As Bethmann declares: "No other basic right in the pre-March literature dealing with state laws would be so emphatically demanded as the right of freedom of the press."

57. Stegmaier, "Von der Zensur," 140.

58. Stein, "Südwestdeutsche Zeitungsgeschichte," 70; McNeely, *Emancipation of Writing*, chap. 8; Abigail Green, "Intervening in the Public Sphere: German Governments and the Press, 1815–1870," *Historical Journal* 44, no. 1 (March 2001): 155–75.

59. Stein, "Südwestdeutsche Zeitungsgeschichte," 71; Herzog, *Intimacy & Exclusion*, 11; Stegmaier, "Von der Zensur," 147.

60. The Mathy quote is cited in Müller, *Liberale Presse*, 43–45; Udo Leuschner, *Vom Intelligenzblatt zur demokratischen Kampfpresse: Mannheimer Zeitungen bis 1850*, 2008 (1973), accessed July 28, 2020, www.udo-leuschner.de

/zeitungsgeschichte, 56; Rainer Schimpf, "Der 'Freisinnige' und der Kampf der badischen Liberalen für die Pressefreiheit," in *Die Anfänge des Liberalismus und der Demokratie in Deutschland und Österreich 1830–1848/49*, ed. Helmut Reinhalter (Frankfurt: Lang, 2002), 157. Leuschner notes that *Der Wächter am Rhein* was very antimonarchical, and it called the *Landesvater* (father of the country, or ruling sovereign) a *Zwingherrschaft*, or rule by forceful means.

61. Christine Berger, "Politische Presse im Vormärz," in *Seeblätter: Reprint eine revolutionäre Zeitung*, ed. Christine Berger and Wolfgang Kramer (Constance: Stadler, 1998), 24; Tauschwitz, *Presse und Revolution*, 172, 291–92; Berger, "Politische Presse"; Leuschner, *Mannheimer Zeitungen bis 1850*, 8–12.

62. McNeely, *Emancipation of Writing*, chap. 8; Müller, *Liberale Presse*, 76.

63. Leuschner, *Mannheimer Zeitungen bis 1850*, 8–9.

64. Berger, "Politische Presse in Vormärz," 22–33; Leuschner, *Mannheimer Zeitungen bis 1850*, 75; Müller, *Liberale Presse*, 81. In fact, several former contributors to the *Rheinische Zeitung* came to Baden to work for the *MAbZ* (Dussel, *Deutsche Tagespresse*, 31–38). Included in the Constance opposition press was *Der Leuchtturm* (The lighthouse), a moderate-liberal paper, and the *Deutsche Volkshalle*, a democratic-liberal paper.

65. Müller, *Liberale Presse*, 81–84.

66. Müller, *Liberale Presse*, 154–58, 184, 211. *Die Rundschau* became the focal point for other liberals in Baden.

67. Leuschner, *Mannheimer Zeitungen bis 1850*, 80; Herzog, *Intimacy & Exclusion*, 7, 32–33, 42–47; Müller, *Liberale Presse*, 158. It should be noted that Herzog relates these antiliberal tendencies during the fight over "Bodies and Souls," in which both conservatives and liberals fought over the legality of mixed (interconfessional) marriages, which the Catholic Church strongly opposed.

68. Müller, *Liberale Presse*, part C; Stein, "Südwestdeutsche Zeitungsgeschichte," 75.

69. Shmuel Feiner, *The Jewish Enlightenment*, trans. Chaya Naor (Philadelphia: University of Pennsylvania Press, 2004); Shachar Pinsker, *A Rich Brew: How Cafés Created Modern Jewish Culture* (New York: New York University Press, 2018), 144–46; Feiner, *Moses Mendelssohn*, 40. Feiner examines the public writings of Mendelssohn and other Jewish writers that embraced the Enlightenment and criticized Judaism, including Israel Zamosc, Judah Hurwitz, Baruch Schick, and Napthali Herz Ullman.

70. Alexander Altmann, *Moses Mendelssohn: A Biographical Study* (Tuscaloosa: University of Alabama Press, 1973), 198–99; Feiner, *Jewish Enlightenment*, 221; Feiner, *Moses Mendelssohn*, 9–10. Feiner notes that it was Issak Euchel who was the leader of the "Mendelssohn cult." In chapter 8 of *Transformation*, Sorkin details Mendelssohn's beliefs and how Hirsch argued

against him, and ultimately "held Mendelssohn responsible for the disintegration of Jewish life" (158).

71. David Sorkin, *Moses Mendelssohn and the Religious Enlightenment* (Berkeley: University of California Press, 1996), chaps. 7, "Intercessions," and 8, "Rights." Mendelssohn also published *Phädon, or the Immortality of the Soul* (1767) and was also asked to defend Jews from the hostility of Christians. This volume included the defense of other Jewish communities under siege by German governments, such as his 1769 defense of the Altona Jewish community, whose members were accused of defaming Christianity. Mendelssohn was also involved in a dispute in Mecklenburg-Schwerin about early burial, in which he took a position opposite to that of Rabbi Jacob Emden of Altona. In addition, Mendelssohn also helped Jews in Switzerland avoid a procreation ban, defended the "Aleinu" prayer in Königsberg, and wrote a treatise on Jewish property laws for the Prussian government.

72. Feiner, *Moses Mendelssohn*, 83–106, 153–86. Mendelssohn countered conversion requests by Johann Caspar Lavater—a Swiss theologian—and the satirist August Cranz, who believed that Judaism coerced and compelled its members to join. He also responded directly to Göttingen professor Johann David Michaelis's assertions that Jews would always be a separate nation.

73. Feiner, *Moses Mendelssohn*, 51, 54; Jacob Toury, "Die Anfänge des jüdischen Zeitungswesens in Deutschland," *Bulletin of the Leo Baeck Institute* 38/39 (1967): 93–123; Kennecke, "Erste moderne Zeitschrift," 181. As Kennecke notes, Mendelssohn switched to German as his scholarly language on the advice of Gotthold Lessing.

74. Toury, "Jüdischen Zeitungswesens," 109–19, at 116.

75. Pawel Maciejko, "The Jews' Entry into the Public Sphere—The Emden-Eibeschütz Controversy Reconsidered," *Simon Dubnow Institute Yearbook* 6 (2007): 135–37, 153–54; Gershom Scholem, *Sabbatai Sevi: The Mystical Messiah, 1626–1676* (Princeton, NJ: Princeton University Press, 1976). As Maciejko notes, during the controversy, Emden's printing press published nine books and twenty-four anti-Eibeschütz pamphlets in both Hebrew and German. The Sabbatean movement was very popular but was discredited in 1666 after Zevi was forced by the Ottoman sultan to convert to Islam or face death. Instead of becoming a martyr, Zevi chose conversion.

76. Kennecke, "Erste modern Zeitschrift," 181, 185–6, 193; Andreas Kennecke, "Der 'HaMe'assef' und sein erster Herausgeber Isaac Euchel," in *Zwischen Selbstbehauptung und Verfolgung: Deutsch-jüdische Zeitungen und Zeitschriften von der Aufklärung bis zum Nationalsozialismus*, ed. Michael Nagel (Hildesheim: Olms, 2002), 68; Johannes Valentin Schwarz, "The Origins and the Development of German Jewish Press in Germany till 1850: Reflections on the Transformation of the German Jewish Public Sphere in Bourgeois Society," *International*

Federation of Library Associations and Institutions (IFLA) Conference Paper, Jerusalem, Israel, 2000, accessed November 8, 2007, http://www.ifla.org/IV/ifla66/papers/106-144e.htm; Lässig, *Jüdische Wege ins Bürgertum*, 446. It should be noted that while Euchel was the *Kopf* (head) of the *Me'assef*, it was a collaborative project between many *Maskilim*. Also, look at "Tabelle 2" (table 2) in Schwarz's paper to see the resemblances of the programs of the two journals.

77. Kennecke, "Erste modern Zeitschrift," 180, 187; Sorkin, *Religious Enlightenment*, 81. This integrationist and modernization sentiment is found in the following statement by Kennecke: "It would not be for the readers who already have advanced an opinion on something, but rather for those, who would want to educate themselves and others."

78. Iris Idelson-Shein, "Rabbis of the (Scientific Revolution: Revealing the Hidden Corpus of Early Modern Translations Produced by Jewish Religious Thinkers," *American Historical Review* 126, no. 1 (March 2021): 54–81.

79. Lässig, *Jüdische Wege ins Bürgertum*, 470, 689, appendix 5; *Sulamith* 2 (1817), 354; Siegfried Stein, "Die Zeitschrift Sulamith," *Zeitschrift für die Geschichte der Juden in Deutschland* 7 (1937): 194; Baader, *Bourgeois Culture*, chap. 1. Lässig describes the division of the 1834–35 circulation among *Beamten* and *Fürstenfamilien* (princely families). Although there are no subscribers in this list from Baden, we know from an 1817 edition of *Sulamith* that Grand Duke Ludwig was a reader and subscriber to the periodical and that he allowed a short letter acknowledging his readership to be publicly printed in the journal.

80. Uri R. Kaufmann, "Ein jüdischer Deutscher: Der Kampf des jungen Gabriel Riesser für die Gleichberechtigung der Juden 1830–1848," *Aschkenas* 13, no. 1 (2003): 223–27; Moshe Rinott, "Gabriel Riesser: Fighter for Jewish Emancipation," *LBIYB* 7 (1962): 31–32. Riesser had intended *Der Jude* to have a political and a religious section, but he could not find anyone who would write the latter section.

81. Margaret T. Edelheim-Muehsam, "The Jewish Press in Germany," *LBIYB* 1 (1956): 166. For more on Philippson and his importance to mid-nineteenth century German publishing, see Meola, "Making News."

82. Seligmann, *Geschichte der jüdischen Reformbewegung*, 94; Derek Penslar, "Introduction: The Press and the Jewish Public Sphere," *Jewish History* 14 (2000): 3; *AZdJ* 6, 12 (March 19, 1842), 165; Lässig, *Wege ins Bürgertum*, 449, 479, 491; *Hannoversche Morgenzeitung (HMz)*, 51 (March 30, 1845), 203; Valentin Schwarz, "Redaktion ohne Telefon," 55; Nils Roemer, *Jewish Scholarship and Culture in Nineteenth-Century Germany: Between History and Faith* (Madison: University of Wisconsin Press, 2005), 38; Judith Bleich, "The Emergence of an Orthodox Press in Nineteenth-Century Germany," *Jewish Social Studies* 42, no. 3/4 (Summer–Autumn 1980): 336. For example, here is the list of contributors to Geiger's *Wissenschaftliche Zeitschrift für jüdische Theologie*: Theodor Creizenach,

Mendel Hess (editor of *Der Israelit des neunzehnten Jahrhunderts*), Isaak Markus Jost, Gotthold Salomon, Samuel Hirsch, Samuel Holdheim, Bernhard Wechsler, Leopold Zunz, and Joseph Maierthe. *AZdJ* changed from a thrice-a-week format to a weekly one beginning in July 1839. *Sulamith*'s highest circulation level was 282 (1834–35), and each of the reform-leaning papers in the 1840s had circulations of 500 or greater, with the *AZdJ* peaking around 1,600. The *AZdJ*'s circulation rivaled papers in many German cities, having more or close to the same circulation as papers from Bremen (*Bremer* and *Weser Zeitungen*), Würzburg (*Würzburger Zeitung*), and Munich (*Münchener Zeitung*). There are reasons to believe that readership for some German Jewish publications may have been even higher than the traditional estimate of 10 readers per subscription, as Isaak Markus Jost claimed that 50 individuals would read each printed copy of his *Israelitische Annalen* (*Israelite Annals*, 1839–41).

83. Frankel, *Damascus Affair*, 240–43; Kerstin von der Krone, "Die Berichterstattung zur Damaskus-Affäre in der deutsch-jüdischen Presse," in *Jewish Images in the Media*, Relation, n.s., vol. 2, ed. Martin Liepach, Gabriela Melishek, and Josef Seethaler (Vienna: Austrian Academy of Sciences Press, 2007), 155–56.

84. Arguably, these writings, especially *The Nineteen Letters*, were public sensations and drew intense responses from the reform camp, especially from Abraham Geiger. See his reviews of *The Nineteen Letters* in *Wissenschaftliche Zeitschrift für jüdische Theologie* 2 and 3 (1836): 351–59, 518–48; *Wissenschaftliche Zeitschrift für jüdische Theologie* 1 (1837): 74–91. Hirsch sent an essay to the *AZdJ* in defense of his publication of *Erste Mittheilungen aus Naphtalis Briefwechsel*, published during 1839. The defense ("*Würdigung der Bemerkungen zu den Mittheilungen aus Naphthalis Briefwechsel in No. 1 der isr. Annalen*" [In appreciation of the remarks to the *Disclosures from Naphthali's Letter Exchange in No. 1 of the Israelite Annals*]) was published in the *AZdJ* 3, 23–25 (February 21, 23, and 26, 1839), 90–92, 94–96, & 98–100; *AZdJ* 4, 24 (June 13, 1840), 352. An example here is Hirsch's advertisement for a "teacher, precentor, and butcher" position in the Grand Duchy of Oldenburg.

85. Jakob Löwenstein, *AZdJ* 8, 30 (July 22, 1844): 417; Jakob Löwenstein, "Entgegnung, die Fortbildung des Judenthums betreffend," *AZdJ* 8, 35 (August 26, 1844): 490–94 (the translation of the title is "Rejoinder, dealing with the advancement of Jewry"); Ludwig Philippson, "Ueber die Fortbildung des Judenthums," *AZdJ* 8, 30 (July 22, 1844), 417–20; Ludwig Philippson, "Die Fortbildung des Judenthums und die erste Rabbinerversammlung," *AZdJ* 8, 35 (August 26, 1844), 489–90.

86. Bleich, "Orthodox Press," 329, 336–38.

87. Lässig, *Jüdische Wege ins Bürgertum*, 468; Henry Wassermann, "Preliminary Impressions and Observations concerning 'Jewish' Advertisements

in the *Leipziger Allgemeine Zeitung* in 1840," in *Integration und Ausgrenzung. Studien zur deutsch-jüdischen Literatur- und Kulturgeschichte von der Frühen Neuzeit bis zur Gegenwart*, ed. Mark H. Gelber, Jacob Hessing, and Robert Jütte (Tübingen, Germany: Max Niemeyer, 2009), 83. Wassermann postulates that the reprinting of advertisements from the *Leipziger Allgemeine Zeitung* in the German Jewish press shows that "the German-Jewish press of the mid-19th century should not be discussed without taking into consideration what was being printed in contemporary German dailies"; such was the case in the *AZdJ* from January 28 and February 4, 1843 (Nrs. 4 & 5, pp. 45–46 & 61–63), when a "Hannoverian Christian" wrote about the September 1842 Judengesetz.

88. "*Jüdische Angelegeneheiten*," *MAbZ*, 215 and 216 (September 13 and 14, 1842): 865–66, 869; Edelheim-Muehsam, "Jewish Press in Germany," 163; Johannes Valentin Schwarz, "Öffentlichkeit," in *Makom: Orte und Räume im Judentum. Real. Abstrakt. Imaginär*, ed. Michal Kümper, Barbara Rösch, Ulrike Schneider, and Helen Thein (Hildesheim: Olms, 2007), 191; David A. Meola, "'Revolutionary Behavior'—How German Jews Became Masters of Their Own Domain, 1750–1850," *Eighteenth-Century Thought* 6 (2016): 186. The *AZdJ* gave permission for the reprinting of the letters from Dutch ministers, who all vouched for the patriotism and upstanding nature of Jews in the Kingdom of the Netherlands, and these were presented to the public to help sway public opinion toward Jewish favor, in order to show non-Jewish readers what the results of Gleichstellung could look like. The article from *Hildesheimsche Allgemeine Zeitung & Anzeigen*, 73B (June 20, 1845) was reprinted from the *AZdJ* and details Levi Bodenheimer's arrival as the new rabbi in Krefeld (Prussia). The sentiment described by Edelheim-Muehsam, that the German Jewish press was mainly for Jews, is echoed throughout modern historiography.

2. JEWISH EMANCIPATION IN THE BADENESE AND GERMAN PRESS

1. Abigail Green, "1848 and Beyond: Jews in the National and International Politics of Secularism and Revolution," in Green and Sullam, *Jews, Liberalism, Antisemitism*, 344–45; for more on the debate about secularism in German society during the mid-nineteenth century, see Todd Weir, *Secularism and Religion in Nineteenth-Century Germany: The Rise of the Fourth Confession* (Cambridge: Cambridge University Press, 2014).

2. Weissberg, "Newspaper Feuilleton," 152.

3. *Kölnische Zeitung* (*KölZtg*), 56 (February 25, 1844), Supplement (*Beilage*). More about the Haber Affair can be found in David A. Meola, "Mirror of Competing Claims: Antisemitism, Honor, and Citizenship in Vormärz Germany," *Antisemitism Studies* 4, no. 1 (April 2019): 3–47.

4. "Betrachtung und Aufschlüsse über die Habersche Sache," *Deutsche Monatsschrift für Literatur und öffentliches Leben* 1 (January to June), ed. Karl Biedermann (Leipzig: Mayer und Wigand, 1844), 142.

5. Stephan Rohrbacher, *Gewalt in Biedermeier: Antijüdische Ausschreitungen in Vormärz und Revolution 1815–1848/9* (Frankfurt: Campus, 1993), 111–44, 170–71, 186–201, and 221–22. According to Rohrbacher, during the Hep-Hep riots in 1819, there were seven violent anti-Jewish confrontations, most notably in Karlsruhe, Mannheim, and Heidelberg.

6. Norbert Bachleitner, "The Beginnings of the Feuilleton Novel in France and the German-Speaking Regions," in *Nineteenth-Century Serial Narrative in Transnational Perspective, 1830s–1860s*, ed. Daniel Stein and Lisella Wiele (Cham, Switzerland: Palgrave, 2019), 21. Bachleitner summarizes Niklas Luhmann's model on "the mass media as a system of communication dedicated to the autoreflection of society" (20).

7. Douglas Moggach, "Bruno Bauer," *Stanford Encyclopedia of Philosophy*, accessed July 24, 2020, https://plato.stanford.edu/entries/bauer/. For more on the fight for Jewish emancipation in Rhenish Prussia and how (and why) Rhenish liberals evolved on the issue sooner than Badenese liberals, see Magnus, *Jewish Emancipation in a German City*, chap. 5. Particularly interesting is Magnus's division of emancipation supporters into three camps: pragmatists (in other words, it was "good business, good politics"); rationalists, for whom emancipation fit into a broader philosophical ideology; and true believers, who sympathized with the Jews' cause (135).

8. "Δ Karlsruhe, 26. Dec.," *DAZ*, 274 (December 30, 1843); "Karlsruhe, den 29. Dez. (D.A.Z)," *VZ*, 2 (January 2, 1844); *AZdJ* 8, 3 (January 15, 1844), 28. The *VZ* reprinted the *DAZ* article, although the date provided is incorrect.

9. Reinhard Rürup, "German Liberalism and the Emancipation of the Jews," *LBIYB* 20 (1975): 63. See Karl von Rotteck, Second Chamber Speech, September 27, 1833. The idea that Jews would receive emancipation when the rest of German society was free from the oppression of the elites was echoed by Heinrich Heine in 1854. Rürup took this Heine quote from Arno Herzig, *Judentum und Emanzipation in Westfalen* (Münster: Aschendorff, 1973), 96.

10. Meola, "Revolutionary Behavior," 203.

11. Toury, *Die politische Orientierung*, 11–12. See note 42 in Toury's work for a list of Jews and baptized Jews who participated in the local and provincial presses in the Rhineland, especially the *Rheinische Zeitung*.

12. B. Fischer, *Die Augsburger "Allgemeine Zeitung,"* Part 2, 155. Salomon von Haber, *AAZ*, 283 and 284 (October 10 and 11, 1833), 1437–38 and 1441–43; Samuel Meyer, "Das auserwählte Volk," *AAZ*, 235 (August 23, 1845), 1876–77; *AAZ*, 224 B (August 12, 1845), 1789.

13. Frankel, *Damascus Affair*, 280, 442; Paul Lawrence Rose, *German Question/Jewish Question: Revolutionary Antisemitism from Kant to Wagner* (Princeton, NJ: Princeton University Press, 1990), 258–60; Nathan Rosenstreich, *Jews and German Philosophy: The Polemics of Emancipation* (New York: Schocken, 1984), 92–93. Ghillany published *Das Judenthum und die Kritik: Oder es bleibt bei den Menschenopfern der Hebräer und bei der Nothwendigkeit einer Zeitgemässen Reform des Judenthums* in 1844 (Stuttgart, Germany: Johann Adam Stein [available through Google Books]), and the text was submitted without comment or critique to the Badenese Lower Assembly—a sign of wholesale acceptance.

14. *AAZ*, 123–125 (May 3–5, 1833) in the *Ausserordentliche Beilage zur AAZ*, Nr. 164–167, 653–54, 657–58, and 661–62; *AAZ*, 150B (May 30, 1839), 1157–58, and 161B (June 10, 1839), 1246–47.

15. Meola, "Becoming Public," 89–99.

16. Rohrbacher, *Gewalt in Biedermeier*, see note 5 in this chapter; Martin Krauss, "Zwischen Emanzipation und Antisemitismus (1802 bis 1862)," in *Geschichte der Juden in Heidelberg*, ed. Peter Blum (Heidelberg, Germany: Brigitte Guderjahn, 1996), 189–99. Krauss details the 1848 conflict that occurred (and its ensuing violence) against Leopold Ehrmann, who had successfully petitioned the government to make new clothes. The violence against him is often conflated with more general violence of the era.

17. Rürup, *Emanzipation und Antisemitismus*, 74; Sorkin, *Jewish Emancipation*, 78–79.

18. Herzog, *Intimacy and Exclusion*, 59.

19. Rürup, *Emanzipation und Antisemitismus*, 75–76; Herzog, *Intimacy and Exclusion*, 54–59; Weir, *Secularism and Religion*, 2.

20. Karl Mathy, *Die Verfassungsfeier in Baden am 22. August 1843* (Mannheim, Germany: Fr. Bassermann, 1843), v.

21. Elias Eller, in Mathy, *Die Verfassungsfeier*, 29–31.

22. Franz Burkardt Fauth, "Bericht der Petitions-Commission über mehrer von Israeliten eingereichte Vorstellungen, Gleichstellung ihrer politischen und bürgerlichen Rechte mit jenen der christlichen Staatsbürger betreffend," *Mannheimer Morgenblatt* (*MM*), 48–54 (February 25–28 and March 1–4, 1845; no printing on March 3), 197–98, 203–4, 207–8, 211–12, 219–22, and 225–26.

23. Fauth, "Bericht der Petitions-Commission," 221, 222 (emphasis in original), and 226; Heinrich Eberhard Gottlob Paulus, *Die jüdische Nationalabsonderung nach Ursprung, Folgen und Besserungsmitteln. Oder über Pflichten, Rechte und Verordnungen zur Verbesserung der jüdischen Schutzbürgerschaft in Teutschland* (Heidelberg, Germany: Winter, 1831), Freimann-Sammlung.

24. Weir, *Secularism and Religion*, 60–61.

25. *Heidelberger Journal*, 62, 83, 106, 109, and 121B (March 3 and 26, April 18 and 21, and May 4, 1845), 246–47, 330–31, 427, 439, and 489.

26. The first name is not revealed in the text, but it is probably Marx Eller, the father of Dr. Elias Eller.

27. Leopold Ladenburg, "Der Bericht des Abgeordneten Fauth über die Gleichstellung der Juden," *MAbZ*, 68 Extra-Beilage (hereafter, Ex-B) and 70 Ex-B (March 11 and 13, 1845); Hayum Wagner, "Beleuchtung des Commissionsberichts über mehrere Petitionen der Israeliten um Gleichstellung in ihren politischen und bürgerlichen Rechten mit denen der christlichen Staatsbürgern, erstattet von dem Abgeordneten Fauth in der 2ten badischen Kammer am 18. Februar," *MAbZ*, 73 Ex-B (March 16, 1845). For more on the evolution and structure of Badenese courts, as well as Ladenburg's influential and long-lasting career within Mannheim's legal community—including his appointment as the first Jewish *Obergerichtshofadvokat*, see Karl Otto Scherner, *Advokaten, Revolutionäre, Anwälte: Die Geschichte der Mannheimer Anwaltschaft* (Sigmaringen, Germany: Jan Thorbecke, 1997).

28. Heinrich Bernhard (H. B.) Oppenheim, "Ueber ein neues—altes Projekt zur bürgerlichen Gleichstellung der Juden und über die sogenannte Selbstemanzipation," *MAbZ*, 154 Ex-B (July 5, 1842), 1–3; H. B. Oppenheim, "Kritik des Kommissionsberichts der Badischen 2ten Kammer, über die bürgerliche Gleichstellung der Juden," *MAbZ*, 179 (August 2, 1842), 719–20.

29. Throughout this section, I will be using symbols to identify some authors. I have tried to approximate the symbols used in the original sources; †††, "Merkwürdiger Industrie-Fall einiger Kinder Israels," *MAbZ*, 206 (September 2, 1842), 829; A, "Merkwürdiger Industrie-Fall einiger Kinder Israels," *MAbZ*, 207 (September 3, 1842), 833; "Jüdische Angelegenheiten," *MAbZ*, 215 and 216 (September 13 and 14, 1842), 865–66 and 869. These were originally collected and printed in the *Allgemeine Zeitung des Judenthums*.

30. It should be noted that the *Reformfreunde* published its complete program "Reform in Judenthum" in the *Heid Jour*, 155 (June 7, 1844), 654; 157 (June 9, 1844), 663; and 158 (June 10, 1844), 669. This announcement had only one response to it, *Heid Jour*, 178 (June 27, 1844), 741. As translated in Meyer, *Response to Modernity*, 122.

31. Homo, "Lösung der Kardinalfrage," *Heid Jour*, 83 (March 26, 1845), 331 (emphasis in original).

32. *Heid Jour*, 106 (April 18, 1845), 427.

33. *MM*, 50 (February 27, 1845), 207. The reference was to paragraph 6 of Fauth's report.

34. *MM*, 57 (March 7, 1845), 241; Bayer, *Minderheit im städtischen Raum*, 126–27.

35. *MM*, 61 (March 12, 1845), 259.

36. I will only be citing from the *MAbZ* piece, entitled "Offenes Sendschreiben an den Herrn Berichterstatter der Petitions-Commission der zweiten badischen Kammer, Oberamtmann Fauth, in Schwetzingen," Nr. 67 (March 10, 1845), 267.

37. Fauth, *MM*, 61 (March 12, 1845), 259.

38. Zimmern, "Offenes Sendschreiben."

39. Anonymous, "Erläuterndes Wort," *MM*, 62 (March 13, 1845), 263; indeed, the "quote" from Fauth was actually incorrectly given. It was a paraphrase of the sentiments of Fauth, which were correctly interpreted.

40. Tauschwitz, *Presse und Revolution*, appendix, 21, 28; Berger, "Politische Presse in Vormärz," 25.

41. Gustav Toepke, *Die Matrikel der Universität Heidelberg. 5te & 6te Teile* (Heidelberg, Germany: Carl Winter's Universitätsbuchhandlung, 1904; repr., Nendeln, Liechtenstein: Kraus Reprint, 1976); Volker Keller, *Jüdisches Leben in Mannheim* (Mannheim, Germany: Edition Quadrat, 1995), 91. Dr. Ladenburg came from one of the most important Jewish families in Mannheim. He was the youngest son of Wolf Hayum Ladenburg, who was counted among the wealthiest and most successful businessmen in the city. Leopold attended the University of Heidelberg and matriculated on November 5, 1827, at the age of eighteen. He would later serve as the *Vorsteher* of the Mannheim Jewish community from 1849 to his death in 1881 (Rosenthal, *Heimatgeschichte der badischen Juden*, 267). Ladenburg also participated in early attempts for Gleichstellung by directly appealing to the Landtag in the following two writings: "Die rechtlichen Verhältnisse der Israeliten in Baden" (The legal situation of the Israelites in Baden") and "Die Gleichstellung der Israeliten Badens mit ihren christlichen Mitbürgern" (The equalization of the Israelites of Baden with their Christian fellow citizens). The Mannheim Klaus was a rabbinical seminary and was well-known throughout Germany. Much like the idea of Bildung in nineteenth-century Germany, the Klaus was an institution of higher learning, and as Monika Preuß argues, it was a center that helped promote bourgeois ideas of education and piety (*Frömmigkeit*) among German Jews and rabbis. See Monika Preuß, *Gelehrte Juden: Lernen als Frömmigkeitsideal in der frühen Neuzeit* (Göttingen, Germany: Wallstein, 2007). Wagner attended the University of Heidelberg (matriculating on November 18, 1828, at the age of twenty-two) and was a student there at the same time as Ladenburg. He was the only Mannheim rabbi to attend the rabbinical conferences (1845 and 1846). Along with Abraham Adler, *Prediger* (preacher) from nearby Alzey, they published the journal *Die Reform des Judenthums*, which lasted for nine months.

42. Leopold Ladenburg, "Der Bericht des Abgeordneten Fauth über die Gleichstellung der Juden," *MAbZ*, 68 Ex-B (March 11, 1845); "Dokumente über die Wirkungen der Gleichstellung der Juden in Holland," *MAbZ*, 112 Ex-B (May

11, 1844). Included in these documents were letters on behalf of the Jews from the interior minister, finance minister, justice minister, war minister, president of the Amsterdam Tribunal, and General Chassé. These documents were originally printed in the Badenese press in the *MAbZ*, 215 (September 13, 1842), 865–66, and 216 (September 14, 1842), 869, under the title "Jüdische Angelegenheiten" (Jewish matters). These were reprints of documents shared in the *AZdJ* 6, 35 (August 26, 1842), 517–21, under the rubric "Holland."

43. Ladenburg, "Der Bericht des Abgeordneten Fauth"; Herzog, *Intimacy and Exclusion*, 77–78 and notes 76 and 77; Dieter Hein, "1830–1848: Bürgerlicher Aufbruch," *Geschichte der Stadt Mannheim*, Band 2, *1801–1914*, ed. Ulrich Nieß and Michael Caroli (Heidelberg, Germany: Regionalkultur, 2007), 230. During the 1846 discussion, many Liberals, like Alexander von Soiron, started following the tactics of conservatives and ignoring public opinion, especially when such opinion is "led astray." Ladenburg was in a circle mentored by Adam von Itzstein, which included Friedrich Daniel Bassermann, Lorenz Brentano, Karl Mathy, and Alexander von Soiron—all future members of the Badenese Second Chamber. While some of them were democrats (like Brentano), most—including Ladenburg—followed Karl Mathy's constitutional liberalism and were not as radical as Hein suggests.

44. Hayum Wagner, "Beleuchtung des Commissionsberichts über mehrere Petitionen der Israeliten um Gleichstellung in ihren politischen und bürgerlichen Rechten mit denen der christlichen Staatsbürgern, erstattet von dem Abgeordneten Fauth in der 2ten badischen Kammer am 18. Februar," *MAbZ*, 73 Ex-B (March 16, 1845).

45. C. . . . n, *Karlsruher Zeitung*, 199B (July 20, 1837). See Ladenburg's and Wagner's contributions from the *MAbZ*.

46. Björn Siegel, "Jewish Philanthropy and the Formation of Modernity: Baron de Hirsch and His Vision of Jewish Spaces in European Societies," in *Space and Spatiality in Modern German-Jewish History*, ed. Simone Lässig and Miriam Rürup (London: Berghahn, 2017), 182; Derek Penslar, *Shylock's Children: Economics and Jewish Identity in Modern Europe* (Berkeley: University of California Press, 2001), 91; Maria Benjamin Baader, "Rabbinic Study, Self-Improvement, and Philanthropy: Gender and the Refashioning of Jewish Voluntary Associations in Germany, 1750–1870," in *Philanthropy, Patronage, and Civil Society: Experiences from Germany, Great Britain, and North America*, ed. Thomas Adam (Bloomington: Indiana University Press, 2004), 169; Liedtke, *Jewish Welfare*, 2 and 9.

47. Simone Lässig, "*Bürgerlichkeit*, Patronage, and Communal Liberalism in German, 1871–1914," in Adam, *Philanthropy, Patronage, and Civil Society*, 200; Thomas Adam, introduction to *Philanthropy, Patronage, and Civil Society*, 3; Baader, "Rabbinic Study," 169; Thomas Adam, "Stiften in deutschen

Bürgerstädten vor dem Ersten Weltkrieg: Das Beispiel Leipzig," *Geschichte und Gesellschaft* 33, no. 1 (2007): 72.

48. Abigail Green, "Rethinking Sir Moses Montefiore: Religion, Nationhood, and International Philanthropy in the Nineteenth Century," *American Historical Review* 110, no. 3 (June 2005): 650; Penslar, *Shylock's Children*, 108–9.

49. Baader, "Rabbinic Study," 170; Green, "Rethinking Sir Moses Montefiore," 653–54.

50. Benedict Anderson, *Imagined Communities: Reflections on the Origin and Spread of Nationalism*, rev. ed. (London: Verso, [1983] 2006); Brendan Dooley, introduction to *Dissemination of News*, 2–3.

51. *AAZ*, 137 (May 16, 1844), 1093; *KölZtg*, 220 (August 7, 1844).

52. Zimmermann, *Hamburgischer Patriotismus*, 79.

53. August Lewald, *Hamburg* (Karlsruhe: F. Gutsch & Rupp, 1842), 5, 7–8, 44–45.

54. Müller, *Liberale Presse*, 123–24; *Oberdeutsche Zeitung*, 111–134 (May 12–June 8, 1842); "Eighteenth-Century Currencies and Exchange Rates," Internet Archive Wayback Machine, accessed July 28, 2020, http://web.archive.org/web/20070829061816/http://www.hudsonrivervalley.net/AMERICANBOOK/18.html; Lawrence H. Officer, "Five Ways to Compute the Relative Value of a UK Pound Amount, 1830 to Present," MeasuringWorth, 2011, accessed July 28, 2020, www.measuringworth.com/ukcompare/; Zimmermann, *Hamburgischer Patriotismus*, 83. At least 1,000 florins of these contributions were from "communal" contributions that were only noted with a single entry, so the number of contributors was undoubtedly larger. According to MeasuringWorth, 500 Rhenish florins, the currency of Baden, was the equivalent in 1842 of approximately 52 pounds sterling and 12 shillings (1 pound sterling = 9 florins 30 kreuzer; 1 pound Sterling = 20 Shillings = 240 Pence). In *Hamburgischer Patriotismus*, Zimmermann notes the vast sums that were donated by communities throughout the German states and all of Europe, which totaled over 1 million Mark Banco.

55. *Oberdeutsche Zeitung*, 111–34 (May 12, 1842–June 8, 1842); "Sparbuch," *Oberdeutsche Zeitung*, 120 (May 23, 1842).

56. C.K., *Oberdeutsche Zeitung*, 116 (May 16, 1842), 455 (emphasis in original).

57. Zimmermann, *Hamburgischer Patriotismus*, 87–88; "Gailingen," *Konstanzer Zeitung*, 104 (August 31, 1846), 782. This use of charity for other, more political purposes was expressed by the Hamburg correspondent in *Der Orient* 2, 21 (May 21, 1842), 161.

58. Hundsnurscher and Taddey, *Jüdischen Gemeinden in Baden*. Diersburg was the seventeenth-largest Jewish community in Baden and had approximately 225 Jewish residents (from 1842).

59. G. Meyer, "Bitte," *Seeblätter*, 75 (June 23, 1846), 322.

60. *MAbZ*, 179 (July 4, 1846), 715.

61. J. G. Meyer, "Empfangsbescheinigung," *MAbZ*, 351 (December 24, 1846), 1403; Meyer, "Bitte," 322. This plea was also printed in the *Oberrheinische Zeitung*, 172 (June 21, 1846), 792).

62. Penslar, *Shylock's Children*, 111–12. Supposedly Heine went to the home of someone requesting charity to check and make sure the children were clean and well-kempt.

63. John Efron, Steven Weitzman, and Matthias Lehmann, *The Jews: A History*, 2nd ed. (Upper Saddle River, NJ: Pearson, 2014), 175; Moses Maimonides, *Mishneh Torah: Gifts to the Poor 10:7–14*, Sefaria.org, accessed September 18, 2018, https://www.sefaria.org/Mishneh_Torah%2C_Gifts_to_the_Poor.10.7-14?lang=bi. There are eight levels of charity according to Maimonides (in descending rank): (1) supporting a fellow Jew so that they will not be dependent on others; (2) giving to the poor without knowing to whom you give and without them knowing who gave; (3) knowing to whom one gives, but them not knowing who gave; (4) not knowing to whom one gives, but the recipient knowing the giver; (5) giving directly to a poor person but doing so before being asked; (6) giving to the poor after being asked; (7) giving inadequately but willingly and with a smile; and (8) giving under duress.

64. Arno Herzig, "Salomon Heines Testament und der Jurist Gabriel Riesser," in *Salomon Heine in Hamburg: Geschäft und Gemeinsinn*, ed. Beate Borowka-Clausberg (Göttingen, Germany: Wallstein, 2013), 64.

65. Susanne Wiborg, *Salomon Heine: Hamburgs Rothschild, Heinrichs Onkel* (Hamburg, Germany: Hans Christians, 2004), 61–62; Joseph Mendelssohn, *Salomon Heine: Blätter der Würdigung und Erinnerung für seine Freunde und Verehrer* (Hamburg, Germany: B. S. Berendsohn, 1845), 11; Sylvia Steckmest, "Salomon Heine—Bankier und Philanthrop," in *Stadt und Zivilgesellschaft. 250 Jahre Patriotische Gesellschaft von 1765 für Hamburg: Geschichte—Gegenwart—Perspektiven*, ed. Sigrid Schambach (Göttingen, Germany: Wallstein, 2015), 95. The quote is from Liedtke, *Jewish Welfare*, 127. Wiborg notes that in his philanthropic endeavors, Heine also enticed Christians to give Jews emancipation, offering to extend the credit available in the *Hermann Heine'sche Stiftung* to Christians should the measure pass.

66. *AAZ*, 364 (December 29, 1844); *AAZ*, 2 (January 2, 1845); "Freie Städte. Hamburg 30. Dec.," & "* Hamburg, 30 Dez.," *AAZ*, 6 (January 6, 1845); *DAZ*, 1 (January 1, 1845), 2; *KölZtg*, 362 (December 27, 1844).

67. Mendelssohn, *Salomon Heine*, 13; Green, "Rethinking Sir Moses Montefiore," 649–50; Mordecai Rozin, *The Rich and the Poor: Jewish Philanthropy and Social Control in Nineteenth-Century London* (Brighton, UK: Sussex Academic Press, 1999).

68. Zimmermann, *Hamburgischer Patriotismus*, 129; Steckmest, "Salomon Heine—Bankier und Philanthrop," 94–95; Arno Herzig, "Die Patriotische

Gesellschaft und die Hamburger Juden," in *Stadt und Zivilgesellschaft*, 59–68.

69. Meola, "Revolutionary Behavior," 198–200. Oberlandrabbiner Isaac Beer published a Todes-Anzeige ("death announcement") in May 1817 for his son, Levy, in the *Amtsblatt für die Provinz Ostfries- & Harrlingerland* (p. 455) that demonstrated these tendencies.

70. "Hamburg, 23. Dez.," *AAZ*, 364 (December 29, 1844).

71. *AAZ*, 2 (January 2, 1845), 13–14 (my emphasis); Liedtke, *Jewish Welfare*, 126–27. Between 550 and 1,000 people attended the hospital dedication.

72. "Freie Städte. Hamburg, 30. Dez.," *AAZ*, 6 (January 6, 1845), 44 (emphasis in original, an article reprinted from the *Weser Zeitung*).

73. Beate Borowka-Clausberg, "Salomon Heine im Portrait," in *Salomon Heine in Hamburg*, 27–28; "*Hamburg, 30. Dez.," *AAZ*, 6 (January 6, 1845), 44–45.

74. Wiborg, *Salomon Heine*, 88–89. This stanza was not included in the *AAZ* printing.

75. "Wartung" (attention) was not included in the original printing.

76. *KölZtg*, 362 (December 27, 1844); Moran, *Toward the Century of Words*, 14.

77. *MAbZ*, 10 (January 11, 1844).

78. Wendy Anne Stross, "Magazines of Mortality: A Cultural History of the Obituary in Eighteenth-Century London" (PhD diss., University of Toronto, 2004), 10; Bridget Fowler, *The Obituary as Collective Memory* (Abingdon, UK: Routledge, 2007); Nigel Starck, *Life after Death: The Art of the Obituary* (Melbourne: Melbourne University Press, 2006); Ralf Georg Bogner, *Der Autor im Nachruf: Formen und Funktionen der literarischen Memorialkultur von der Reformation bis zum Vormärz* (Tübingen, Germany: Max Niemeyer, 2006); Thomas Goetz, *Poetik des Nachrufs: Zur Kultur der Nekrologie und zur Nachrufszene auf dem Theater* (Vienna: Böhlau, 2008); Gerhard Hay, ed., *Deutsche Abschiede* (Munich: Winkler, 1984).

79. Bogner, *Der Autor im Nachruf*, 4.

80. Heinrich Heine, "Ludwig Marcus," *AAZ*, 124B (May 3, 1844), 985–86; "Ludwig Marcus," *Der Orient* 5, 24 (June 11, 1844): 192.

81. Roemer, *Jewish Scholarship*, 27; Hanns Günther Reissner, *Edward Gans. Ein Leben im Vormärz* (Tübingen, Germany: Mohr Siebeck, 1965); Heinrich Heine, "Ludwig Marcus," *AAZ*, 123B (May 2, 1844), 979–81.

82. Amos Elon, *The Pity of It All: A Portrait of the German-Jewish Epoch 1743–1933* (New York: Picador, 2002), 126.

83. Heinrich Heine, "Spätere Note (1854) in 'Ludwig Marcus. Denkworte,'" In *Aus Vermischte Schriften*, Volume 1 (Hamburg: Hoffmann and Campe, 1854). Published online by *Heinrich Heine Denkmal*, edited by Wolfgang Fricke. Accessed June 16, 2022. http://www.heinrich-heine-denkmal.de/heine-texte/marcus.shtml.

84. Reinhard Rürup, "German Liberalism," 63; Friedrich Battenberg, *Das Europäische Zeitalter der Juden*, vol. 2, 2nd ed. (Darmstadt: Primus, 2000), 103.

85. W—r, "David Zimmern," *MAbZ*, 172 (27 June 1845). Emphasis in original; *AAZ*, 165B (14 June 1845), 1318.

86. W—r, "David Zimmern," *MAbZ*, 172 (June 27, 1845); Herzog, *Intimacy & Exclusion*, 56. Herzog also uses this quote but only takes it from the official *Verhandlungen* of the Lower Assembly. Zimmern is not mentioned by name; it is only noted that "a member of Baden's Jewish High Council" (Oberrat) spoke this in front of the assembly in 1833.

87. Michael Brocke and Julius Carlebach, ed., *Biographisches Handbuch der Rabbiner, Teil 1: Die Rabbiner der Emanzipationszeit in den deutschen, böhmischen und grosspolnischen Ländern 1781–1871*, Band 2 (Munich: K. G. Saur, 2004), 905–6; Ephraim Willstätter, *Allgemeine Geschichte des Israelitischen Volkes: Von der Entstehung desselben bis auf unsere Zeit* (Karlsruhe: D. R. Marx. 1836), ix–xvii, quote from xvi, Freimann-Sammlung (emphasis in original).

88. Deborah Hertz, "Dueling for Emancipation: Jewish Masculinity in the Era of Napoleon," in *Jüdische Welten: Juden in Deutschland vom 18. Jahrhundert bis in die Gegenwart*, ed. Marion Kaplan and Beate Meyer (Göttingen, Germany: Wallstein, 2005), 69–85. See, for example, the lives of the Itzig family, who were given full Prussian citizenship before the edict of 1812.

3. JEWISH RELIGIOUS REFORM IN THE GERMAN AND BADENESE PRESS

1. "Dokumente über die Wirkungen der Gleichstellung der Juden in Holland," *MAbZ*, 112 Ex-B (May 11, 1844).

2. The exception was Bavaria, where the Catholics dominated. In Baden, despite there being more Catholics than Protestants, Jews continued to acculturate toward Protestantism, which was the religion of the governmental elite.

3. Baader, *Bourgeois Culture*, 10; Michael A. Meyer, "Jewish Self-Understanding," in *German-Jewish History in Modern Times*, ed. Michael A. Meyer (New York: Columbia University Press, 1997), 123–24 and 151–52. For example, even though the Berlin Jewish community numbered over seven thousand persons by the 1840s, few regularly attended the synagogue, which had one thousand seats.

4. Meyer, *Response to Modernity*, 111–12.

5. Mordechai Breuer, *Modernity within Tradition: The Social History of Orthodox Jewry in Imperial Germany*, trans. by Elizabeth Petuchowski (New York: Columbia University Press, 1992), 3; Brämer, *Rabbiner und Vorstand*, 14 and part 2, chap. 3, "*Streitsachen*." Brämer analyzed the Tiktin-Geiger Affair, the

Parteienstreit (parties conflict) in Darmstadt, the introduction of a second, more liberal rabbi (Levi Herzfeld) in Brunswick, and the conflict in Offenbach.

6. Guenther W. Plaut, Solomon Bennett Freehof, and Howard A. Berman, *The Rise of Reform Judaism: A Sourcebook of its European Origins* (50th anniversary ed.) (Philadelphia: Jewish Publication Society, 2015), 23 (emphasis in original). I am following Michael A. Meyer's use of a capital R when speaking specifically about the Reform movement. Otherwise, I will use a lower-case r when writing more generally about internal Jewish religious reform.

7. Philipp Lenhard, *Volk oder Religion? Die Entstehung moderner jüdischer Ethnizität in Frankreich und Deutschland 1782–1848* (Göttingen, Germany: Vandenhoeck & Ruprecht, 2014), 121.

8. Meyer, *Response to Modernity*, 6; Lenhard, *Volk oder Religion*, 170.

9. Plaut, Freehof, and Berman, *Rise of Reform Judaism*, 23.

10. Assembly of Jewish Notables, "Answers to Napoleon," accessed May 20, 2021, https://people.ucalgary.ca/~elsegal/363_Transp/Sanhedrin.html; Paula Hyman, *The Jews of Modern France* (Berkeley: University of California Press, 1998), 44. Hyman notes that the "Assembly of Jewish Notables," which preceded the Sanhedrin during the Napoleonic period, relied on *dina de-malkhuta dina* in justifying their allegiance to Napoleon and the French state, which became the basis for similar arguments by German Jews, who used the French example as evidence on their behalf (*AZdJ* 8, 27 [July 1, 1844], 372–75). This sentiment of obedience to the state as stated by the Sanhedrin was confirmed by the rabbinical conference in Brunswick in 1844; for a more thorough discussion of *dina de-malkhuta dina* throughout the history of Jewish diasporic life, see Gil Graff, *Separation of Church and State: Dina de-Malkhuta Dina in Jewish Law, 1750–1848*. Tuscaloosa: University of Alabama Press, 1985.

11. Schorsch, *From Text to Context*, 125. For more on questions of Christian intermarriage during the early nineteenth century, see Herzog, *Intimacy and Exclusion*.

12. Breuer, *Modernity within Tradition*, 3; Baader, *Bourgeois Culture*, 7.

13. Meyer, "Jewish Self-Understanding," 145; Lenhard, *Volk oder Religion*, 192; Meyer, *Response to Modernity*, 103–4; Andreas Gotzmann, "Zwischen Nation und Religion: Die deutschen Juden auf der Suche nach einer bürgerlichen Konfessionalität," in *Juden, Bürger, Deutsche: Zur Geschichte von Vielfalt und Differenz 1800–1933*, ed. Andreas Gotzmann, Rainer Liedtke, and Till van Rahden (Tübingen, Germany: Mohr Siebeck, 2001), 254–55.

14. Lässig, *Jüdische Wege ins Bürgertum*, 253. A notable exception was in the Duchy of Oldenburg where Chief Rabbi Samson Raphael Hirsch was responsible for school visitation and reporting on local Jewish schools' compliance with state regulations (Lowenstein, "Religious Reform Movement," 259–61; see also Lässig, "Bildung als *kulturelles Kapital*?," 263–98).

15. Rürup, *Emanzipation und Antisemitismus*, 67; Lowenstein, "Religious Reform Movement," 260. As Rürup notes in footnote 109 (p. 190), over half of the Badenese Jewish communities rejected this type of reform. See also Wallet, "National Government"; Esther Ramon, "Geschichte der jüdischen Erziehung in Karlsruhe von 1730–1933," in Schmitt, Bräunche, and Koch, *Juden in Karlsruhe*, 302–6; Kaufmann, *Kleine Geschichte der Juden*, 77; Jael B. Paulus, "Jüdischer Kultus im Widerstreit unterschiedlicher innerjüdischer Gruppierungen," in Schmitt, Bräunche, and Koch, *Juden in Karlsruhe*, 248–52.

16. Deborah Hertz, "The Troubling Dialectic between Reform and Conversion in *Biedermeier* Berlin," in *Towards Normality? Acculturation and Modern German Jewry*, ed. Rainer Liedtke and David Rechter (Tübingen, Germany: Mohr Siebeck, 2003), 104; Deborah Hertz, "The Mendelssohns Leave Judaism, the Beers Reform Judaism," *Shared History Project: 1700 Years of Jewish Life in German-Speaking Lands*, accessed May 26, 2021, https://sharedhistoryproject.org/essay/the-mendelssohns-leave-judaism-the-beers-reform-judaism; Hertz, "Reform and Conversion," 113–14; Steven M. Lowenstein, *The Berlin Jewish Community: Enlightenment, Family, and Crisis, 1770–1830* (New York: Oxford University Press, 1994), 137–39. See also Christopher M. Clark, *The Politics of Conversion: Missionary Protestantism and the Jews in Prussia, 1728–1941* (Oxford: Clarendon Press, 1995), for a look at the development, goals, methods, and results of the societies' endeavors; Andreas Brämer, "A Success Story? Prussia's Jewish Educational Policy in the Aftermath of the Emancipation Edict (1812–1870)," *Jewish Quarterly Review* 106, no. 3 (Summer 2016): 413–14. As Brämer notes, Jewish teachers could easily evade attention, and examinations of teachers could be superficial.

17. Kerstin von der Krone, "The Representation and Creation of Spaces through Print Media. Some Insights from the History of the Jewish Press," in *Space and Spatiality in Modern German-Jewish History*, ed. Simone Lässig and Miriam Rürup (New York: Berghahn, 2017), 131; Gotzmann, "Geiger-Tiktin-Streit," 81–98; Judith Bleich, "Clerical Robes: Distinction or Dishonor?" *Tradition: A Journal of Orthodox Jewish Thought* 50, no. 1 (Spring 2017): 16–17. For an excellent look at how race, emancipation, and fashion intertwined, see Laura Arnold Leibman, "The Material of Race: Carribean Jews, Clothing, and Manhood in the Age of Emancipation and Liberal Revolution," in Green and Sullam, *Jews, Liberalism, Antisemitism*, 97–130; Meyer, "Jewish Self-Understanding," 159–60; "Posen," *DAZ*, 147 (May 26, 1844), 1199; "Von der schlesischen Grenze," *DAZ*, 152 (May 31, 1844), 1237; "Berlin," *DAZ*, 152 (May 31, 1844), 1238; Sorkin, *Jewish Emancipation*, 155. The 1847 law in Prussia demoted Judaism to a "private association," and while Jewish schools in Prussia were elevated to "public institutions," Jews in the Poznan district (almost 38 percent of Prussia's Jews) were held under special legislation. The quote is from Moritz Veit,

Der Entwurf einer Verordnung über die Verhältnisse der Juden und das Edikt vom 11. März 1812 (Leipzig: Brockhaus, 1847), 16. Translation by David Sorkin.

18. Lowenstein, "Religious Reform Movement," 261; J. Paulus, "Emanzipation und Reaktion," 87–89. The societies include the *Verein zur Förderung des Ackerbaus unter dem Israeliten* (Society for the promotion of farming among the Jews, 1822), the *Verein der jüdischen Gewerbetreibenden* (Society of Jewish tradesmen, 1826), the *Verein zur Verbesserung der bürgerlichen Verhältnisse der Juden in Baden* (Society for the improvement of the civic status of the Jews in Baden, 1835), and the *Allgemeine Landesverein in dem Grossherzogthume Baden zur Verbesserung der inneren und äusseren Zustände der Juden* (General society in the Grand Duchy of Baden for the improvement of the inner and outer condition of Jews, 1845); Lowenstein, "Religious Reform Movement," 261; see also Gisela Roming, "Geschichte der jüdischen Gemeinde Gailingen," *Gailingen— Geschichte einer Hochrhein-Gemeinde*, ed. Franz Götz (Gailingen, Germany: Hegau-Bibliothek, 2004), 340–55, for more on educational developments in Gailingen, which was a very traditional and Orthodox community in Baden; for more on both Jewish students attending Christian schools and the funding of Jewish schools, see Oberrath (Naphtali) Epstein, *Die Rechtsverhältnisse der öffentlichen israelitischen Schulen im Grossherzogthum Baden dargestellt in einer Sammlung der darauf bezüglichen Gesetze und Verordnungen* (Carlsruhe: A. Bielefeld, 1843), Freimann-Sammlung. Epstein details the legislation on education from 1835 through 1842.

19. M(ayer) Rosenfeld, *Feierlicher Act der Religionsprüfung der zu entlassenden Schulkinder: Entworfen und abgehalten in der* Synagoge zu Carlsruhe *am Sabbath den 23. April 1836 (6. Ijar 5596)* (Carlsruhe, Germany: D. R. Marx, 1836), Freimann-Sammlung; Rürup, *Emanzipation und Antisemitismus*, 70. In fact, as Rürup details, Assemblyman Fauth (the commission reporter—see chap. 2 of this volume for more on the dispute about this report) in 1845 believed that "die Landjuden sind des Landmanns Unglück" (the rural Jew is the rural man's misfortune). Note how similar this is to Heinrich von Treitschke's formulation from the Antisemitism Dispute (see the conclusion to this volume).

20. Baader, *Bourgeois Culture*, 53–56; Meyer, *Response to Modernity*, 41, 55–56.

21. Quote from Meyer, *Response to Modernity*, 57–58; Lenhard, *Volk oder Religion*, 192 and 195; Lowenstein, "Religious Reform Movement," 259.

22. Throughout this section, I will be using symbols to identify authors. I have tried to approximate the symbols used in the original sources.

23. Robert Liberles, *Religious Conflict in Social Context: The Resurgence of Orthodox Judaism in Frankfurt am Main 1838–1877* (Westport, CT: Greenwood Press, 1985), 28; Baader, *Bourgeois Culture*, 11.

24. See Meyer, *Response to Modernity*; Michael A. Meyer, "Alienated Intellectuals in the Camp of Religious Reform: The Frankfurt Reformfreunde,

1842–1845," *AJS Review* 6 (1981): 61–86; David Philipson, "The Reform Movement in Judaism. IV. The Frankfort Society of the Friends of Reform," *Jewish Quarterly Review* 17, no. 2 (January 1905), 307–53.

25. *Eine deutsch-jüdische Kirche*.

26. Meyer, "Jewish Self-Understanding," 161; Ari Joskowicz, *The Modernity of Others: Jewish Anti-Clericalism in Germany and France* (Palo Alto, CA: Stanford University Press, 2014), 78–81, at 80. Joskowicz looks specifically at *Eine deutsch-jüdische Kirche* that compared the rabbis to the Catholic Church and then called for Jews to follow the *Deutschkatholiken* to "purge [sic] the despotic elements within Judaism, once and for all" (Joskowicz's summary) and to cease being "oriental and rabbinic" (original author's words). See, for instance, commentary in the *Vossische Zeitung*, 44 (February 21, 1845, "Eingesandt"), from someone who questioned the necessity of Jews following the ideas of Johannes Ronge, leader of the Deutschkatholiken, and also from the *DAZ*, 139 (May 19, 1845, "Berlin," 1291), which directly linked the Deutschkatholiken to Jews. Also see the *DAZ* from April 15, 1845, which looks specifically at Jewish reform in comparison to Christian reform.

27. Valentin Schwarz, "Redaktion ohne Telefon," 55.

28. Newspaper circulation numbers come from: *Hannoversche Morgenzeitung*, 51 (March 30, 1845, 203), and Heenemann, "Die Auflagenhöhe," 33, 36, 48, and 56–57.

29. Ludwig Philippson, "Der Frankfurter Verein," *AZdJ* 7, 30 (July 24, 1843): 438; Herzog, *Intimacy and Exclusion*, 67.

30. Liberles, *Orthodox Judaism in Frankfurt*, 50.

31. Robin Judd, *Contested Rituals: Circumcision, Kosher Butchering and Jewish Political Life in Germany, 1843–1933* (Ithaca, NY: Cornell University Press, 2007), 26.

32. Judd, *Contested Rituals*, 4 and 22, quote from 4.

33. Robin Judd, "Samuel Holdheim and the German Circumcision Debates, 1843–1876," in *Redefining Judaism in an Age of Emancipation: Comparative Perspectives on Samuel Holdheim (1806–1860)*, ed. Christian Wiese (London: Brill, 2006), 131; Judd, *Contested Rituals*; Andreas Gotzmann, *Jüdisches Recht in kulturellen Prozess. Die Wahrnehmung der Halacha im Deutschland des 19.Jahrhunderts* (Tübingen, Germany: J. C. B. Mohr, 1997).

34. "Frankfurt, 11 February," *FJ*, 43 (February 12, 1843). The edict was issued on February 8.

35. Liberles, *Orthodox Judaism in Frankfurt*, 55–57, taken from Richard Schwemer, *Geschichte der Freien Stadt Frankfurt a.M.*, vol. 3, part 1 (Frankfurt: J. Baer, 1915), 383–84; "†, Frankfurt a. M., 22 Aug.," *DAZ*, 148 (August 26, 1843), 1435. As seen in this

article, the censor in Frankfurt prevented a counteradvertisement (*Gegenanzeige*) to be printed against the RF, while allowing one for the organization a few days earlier.

36. "Frankfurt, 27. Juni," *FJ*, 177B (June 29, 1843); "Frankfurt, 29. Juni," *FJ*, 183B (July 5, 1843); "Frankfurt, 10. Juli," *FJ*, 188 (July 10, 1843).

37. Arno Herzig, *Gabriel Riesser* (Hamburg, Germany: Ellert & Richter, 2008), 109–13; Meyer, "Alienated Intellectuals," 76–77; "*†, Frankfurt a. M., 3 Jul.," *AAZ*, 188 (July 7, 1843), 1503. Riesser was known for his more radical religious views, including circumcision, but he often did not wade into public disputes about religion, as he tried to keep his focus on Jews' rights and Jewish emancipation. It was widely believed by the public that Moritz Stern, Theodor Creizenach, and Gabriel Riesser were at the head of the RF. Despite disavowals, Riesser's and Stern's names are generally associated with the group.

38. "*, Frankfurt a. M., 27 Jul.," *DAZ*, 122 (July 31, 1843), 1179; "Δ, Frankfurt a. M., 20 October," *AAZ*, 297 (October 24, 1843), 2373; "☿, Frankfurt a. M., 11 Nov.," *AAZ*, 322 (November 18, 1843), 2575–76. This was the son of Karl von Rothschild, who lived in Naples. Both Karl and his son, Anselm, attended the Frankfurt rabbinical conference in 1845 as members of the gallery.

39. "♄, Frankfurt a. M., 2 Dec.," *DAZ*, 250 (December 6, 1843), 2427; "Δ, Frankfurt a. M., 10 Dec.," *AAZ*, 348 (December 14, 1843), 2781.

40. "♄;, Frankfurt a. M., 27 Dec.," *DAZ*, 275 (December 31, 1843), 2670; Leopold Stein, "Der Frankfurter Reform-Verein vom Standpunkte des fortschreitende Rabbinismus," *Literaturblatt des Orients. Berichte, Studien und Kritiken für jüdische Geschichte und Literatur*, 46–48 (November 14, 21, and 28, 1843), 721–27, 741–44, and 762–66; "†, Frankfurt a. M., 3. Jan.," *DAZ*, 7 (January 7, 1844), 59; "†, Frankfurt a. M., 15. Febr.," *DAZ*, 50 (February 19, 1844), 399.

41. "☉, Frankfurt a. M., 1 Febr.," "Die Rabbiner über den jüdischen Reformverein," *AAZ*, 39 (February 8, 1844), 305–6.

42. For the difficulties of Jews marrying non-Jewish spouses, see the newspaper clippings about Ferdinand Falkson, from Königsberg, who married a Christian woman in England and fought unsuccessfully to have his marriage recognized in Prussia. See, in the *DAZ*: "Königsberg," 359 (December 24, 1844), 3186–87; "Aus der Niederlausitz," 4 (January 4, 1845), 27; and "Königsberg," 44 (February 13, 1845), 395.

43. "⊠, Frankfurt a. M., 9. Februar," *AAZ*, 48 (February 17, 1844), 382–83; "☉, Frankfurt a. M. Ende Februars," "Die Judenreform und die Beschneidung," 66B (March 6, 1844), 523–24; "Frankfurt a. M., 22. März," *DAZ*, 86 (March 26, 1844), 689–90; Alexander Behr, *Lehrbuch der mosaischen Religion* (Munich: Carl Wolf, 1826), Freimann-Sammlung.

44. "☉, Frankfurt a. M. Ende Februar," "Die Judenreform und die Beschneidung," 66B (March 6, 1844), 523–24; "♄, Frankfurt a. M., 22. März,"

DAZ, 86 (March 26, 1844), 689–90; Mordechai Breuer, "The Jewish Minority in the Enlightened Absolutist State," in *German-Jewish History in Modern Times*, vol. 1, *Tradition and Enlightenment: 1600–1780*, ed. Michael A. Meyer (New York: Columbia University Press, 1996), 157; Johann Andreas Eisenmenger, *Jewry Revealed*, in *Nathan the Wise by Gotthold Ephraim Lessing with Related Documents*, edited by Ronald Schechter (Boston: Bedford/St. Martin's Press, 2004), 121–27. To see how Eisenmenger's ideas aligned with those of German liberals in the Vormärz, see Brian E. Vick, *Defining Germany: The 1848 Frankfurt Parliamentarians and National Identity* (Cambridge, MA: Harvard University Press, 2002), 85.

45. Joskowicz, *Modernity of Others*, 78–80. See, for instance, commentary in the *Vossische Zeitung* on February 21, 1845 (Nr. 44) from someone who questioned the decision of some Jews to follow the ideas of Johannes Ronge, leader of the Deutschkatholiken, and also from the *Deutsche Allgemeine Zeitung*, 139 (May 19, 1845), 1291, which directly tied the Deutschkatholiken to Jews. Also see the *DAZ*, 105B (April 15, 1845), 1001–2, which looks specifically at Jewish reform in comparison to Christian reform.

46. "*, Frankfurt, 27. Juni," *FJ*, 177B (June 29, 1843); "*, Frankfurt, 27. Juli," *FJ*, 208 (July 29, 1844).

47. Philipson, "Frankfort Society," 337; "*, Königsberg, 1. Oct.," *DAZ*, 192 (October 9, 1843), 1862; Jill Storm, "Culture and Exchange: The Jews of Königsberg, 1700–1820" (PhD diss., Washington University in St. Louis, 2010), 293–96. Freistadt was no stranger to being a part of the German public sphere, as he took part in an exchange in the *AAZ* in 1837 about Jewish education in his native city. Freistadt was a professor at the Albertina.

48. Simone Ladwig-Winter, *Freiheit und Bindung: Zur Geschichte der Jüdischen Reformgemeinde zu Berlin von den Anfängen bis zu ihrem Ende 1939* (Teetz, Germany: Hentrich & Hentrich, 2004), 65, 210. As Ladwig-Winters notes, there were 327 families in Berlin that supported the RG, along with another 426 families in other communities; (+, Berlin), *DAZ*, 41 (February 10, 1846), 371. The correspondent reported the same numbers that Ladwig-Winters provided and enlisted the following cities from where support for the RG came: Altona, Brilon, Breslau, Kosel, Dessau, Düsseldorf, Elsoff, Giessen, Gleiwitz, Hamm, Königsberg, Mannheim, Mühlhausen, Werl, and Neustadt an der Saale; Liberles, *Orthodox Judaism in Frankfurt*, 50; Lowenstein, "Religious Reform Movement," 263–64.

49. As cited in Plaut, Freehof, and Berman, *Rise of Reform Judaism*, 61; Philipson, "Frankfort Society," 322.

50. Meyer, "Jewish Self-Understanding," 161; Meyer, *Response to Modernity*, 123; anonymous, *DAZ*, 138 (August 16, 1843), 1335; "Frankfurt am Main," *DAZ*, 139 (August 17, 1843), 1343; "Darmstadt," *FJ*, 231 (August 22, 1843); Louis Simon,

FJ, 312 (November 12, 1843); Ludwig Philippson, "Leitender Artikel," *AZdJ* 7, 28 (July 10, 1843), 405–7; Ludwig Philippson, "Der Frankfurter Verein," *AZdJ* 7, 30 (July 24, 1843), 438–40; "Frankfurt, 14. August" *FJ*, 224B (August 15, 1843).

51. "☿, Frankfurt a. M., 6. Jan.," *DAZ*, 11 (January 11, 1844), 82; "Frankfurt, den 26sten März," *VZ*, 77 (March 30, 1844); "†, Frankfurt a. M., 24. März," *DAZ*, 88 (March 28, 1844), 706; anonymous, *DAZ*, 137 (May 16, 1844), 1118; "*, Frankfurt, 10. Mai," *FJ*, 131 (May 11, 1844); "*, Frankfurt a. M., 13. Dec.," *DAZ*, 262 (December 18, 1843), 2542.

52. "☉, Frankfurt a. M., 24. April," *AAZ*, 119 (April 28, 1844), 950; "✕, Frankfurt a. M., 8. Mai," *AAZ*, 133 (May 12, 1844) 1060; "Frankfurt a. M., 9. Mai," *AAZ*, 134 (May 13, 1844), 1070; "Frankfurt a. M., 9. Mai," *AAZ*, 139 (May 18, 1844), 1111; "Vom Rhein," *AAZ*, 243 (August 30, 1844), 1940. The report claimed that the middle class paid 3 kr. tax per 1,000 kr. Wealth and was strong-armed into reporting all its income, while the Rothschilds paid only ½ kr. per 1,000 kr. wealth and reported its income as it saw fit.

53. Meyer, *Response to Modernity*, 124; "Berlin, 19. Octbr. – D. Allg. Ztg.," *FJ*, 295B (October 25, 1844); Vanessa Krahl, "Das Selbstverständnis der Reformrabbiner und die Entwicklung der deutsch-jüdischen Reformbewegung bis 1848" (PhD diss., Technische Universität Berlin, 2011), 123. As is well known, Sachs was offered the position after Dr. Zacharias Fränkel, chief rabbi in Dresden and head of the positive-historical school of Jewish reform (now known as Conservative Judaism), turned down the offer because the king would not grant him official status akin to Christian clergy. The article "+, Berlin, 8 Jun." *DAZ*, 162 (June 11, 1845), 1518–19, argues that the RG was created as a reaction to the Orthodox in Berlin, which were labeled as "a Polish Jewry in (the) German Volk."

54. "□, Berlin, 28 Aug." *DAZ*, 243 (August 31, 1845), 2335; Ladwig-Winters, *Freiheit und Bindung*, 57; Schad, "Problems of Moderate Reform," 174–75. As Schad noted, any and all reforms, regardless of the severity of change, were seen as gateways to further changes, and as such, Sachs' call for reforms were met with resistance. Schad also mentions that only eighty-six members of the community protested, though it was a mix of the Orthodox and the reformers who were opposed to Sachs's election for a variety of reasons.

55. Most articles in the *DAZ* were quite negative toward Sachs, including the portrayal of Sachs refusing to eat with a reformer ("Berlin, 13. Aug.," 228, [August 16, 1845], 2179), his antipathy toward the RG (□, Berlin, 17. Aug.," 232 [August 20, 1845], 2214), and his alleged search for a new position in the town of Brody (236 [August 24, 1845], 2259), which proved to be untrue ("*, Berlin, 22 Aug.," 237 [August 25 1845], 2267, and "Berlin, 15 Sept.," 261 [September 18, 1845], 2503. There was one supportive evaluation ("‖, Berlin, 3. Sept.," 249 [September 6, 1845], 2394–95) that indicated Sachs positively influenced synagogue attendance and that a new synagogue might even be necessary for those who want to follow his direction.

56. "†, Berlin, 8. April" *DAZ*, 101 (April 11, 1845), 959; "(+), Berlin, 19. April" *DAZ*, 103 (April 13, 1845), 978; "∇, Berlin, 12. April" *DAZ*, 105B (April 15, 1845), 1001–2; "(+), Berlin, 2. Mai" *DAZ*, 125 (May 5, 1845), 1167. Specifically, the correspondent draws on a text from Dr. Ludwig Wihl, a member of the RF in Frankfurt, who asked his community to join with the Berlin community, and who advocated for a positive religious position and not, as has been mentioned earlier, a strictly negative one.

57. "(+), Berlin, 30. March" *DAZ*, 92 (April 2, 1846), 847; Ladwig-Winters, *Freiheit und Bindung*, 66–67. The location chosen, the Gropius Panorama, cost the community 1,450 gold thalers yearly for the duration of the lease. Due to the community's nonofficial standing, the lease had to be put in the names of three individuals (in this case, Adolph Meyer, Joseph Berend, and Dr. Sigismund Stern), who were personally responsible for the contractual obligations of the lease. "</>, Berlin, 8. Oct.," 284 (October 11, 1845), 2766: This report noted that more than 700 people attended the High Holiday services and that the community raised over 4,000 thalers to cover the cost of the services. "</>, Berlin, 9. Oct." 286 (October 13, 1845), 2790–91: This report, by the same author as the *DAZ* article from Nr. 284, went into much more detail than the previous article, such as that the services were held in the English House (where many RG meetings were held) and that the new liturgy no longer exhibited an "empty generality" and had freed itself from a "national distinctiveness" (*nationalen Besonderheit*) without giving up its "idiosyncratic historical development" (*eigenthümliche geschichtliche Entwickelung*). "(+), Berlin, 18. Jun.," *DAZ*, 171 (June 20, 1846), 1582: This report mentioned that the community was looking to hire either Dr. Gotthold Salomon or Dr. Naphthali Frankfurter, both preachers from Hamburg. Another report ("</> Berlin, 16. Sept.," *DAZ*, 262 [September 19, 1846], 2331) announced that the community finally settled on Dr. Samuel Holdheim, the chief rabbi for Mecklenburg-Schwerin, instead of Rabbi Dr. Mendel Hess, editor of *Der Israelit des neunzehnten Jahrhunderts* and chief rabbi for the Duchy of Saxe-Weimar, or Dr. Samuel Hirsch, chief rabbi of Luxemburg; Ladwig-Winters, *Freiheit und Bindung*, 67. Ladwig-Winters noted that the community's first choice was, in fact, Dr. Abraham Geiger in Breslau. His reasons for declining the job were not listed.

58. Ladwig-Winters, *Freiheit und Bindung*, 60; Krahl, "Selbstverständnis," 125.

59. Ralph Bisschops, "Samuel Holdheim and Sigismund Stern: The Clash between the Dogmatic and Historicist Approach in Classical German Reform Judaism," in Wiese, *Redefining Judaism in an Age of Emancipation*, 243; Lowenstein, *Berlin Jewish Community*, 192.

60. Meyer, *Response to Modernity*, 132–33. This sentiment was expressed most pointedly by the Kingdom of Bavaria, which forbade its rabbis from attending the

conference, since it was believed that religious reform (of any kind) represented a threat to stability.

61. There were also three other conferences that were either planned or took place (Wiesbaden, 1837; Mannheim, 1847 [planned: reformers]; and Dresden, 1847 [planned: positive-historical]).

62. Liberles, *Orthodox Judaism in Frankfurt*, 201. This legislation allowed dissident religious communities to form their own recognized entities. This right was first granted to Christians in 1873.

63. "**, Breslau, 6. Mai," *DAZ*, 131 (May 11, 1845), 1214–1215; Sylvan D. Schwartzman, *Reform Judaism in the Making* (New York: Union of American Hebrew Congregations, 1955), 46; David Philipson, "The Rabbinical Conferences, 1844–6," *Jewish Quarterly Review* 17, no. 4 (July 1905): 657, 662; Meyer, *Response to Modernity*, 134. An instance where the "morally binding" nature of the conferences worked was in Randegg (Baden), where Rabbi Leopold Schott petitioned the Oberrat in Karlsruhe to eliminate the Kol Nidre prayer (see *AZdJ* 9, 17 [April 21, 1845], 255).

64. Meyer, *Response to Modernity*, 134; Schwartzman, *Reform Judaism in the Making*, 67–70; Philipson, "Rabbinical Conferences," 675. Other religious discussions not mentioned previously but that were sent to committee included the proportion of Hebrew and German to be used in a religious service, the idea of the Messiah in Judaism, the problem of Sabbath observance, improvements in Shofar and Lulav rituals (holiday observance), and possible modifications to marriage laws.

65. Meyer, *Response to Modernity*, 134–35. It should be noted that the majority of these rabbis came from Germany and Hungary and not, as claimed by reformers, from Poland and Hungary. For a detailed look at both the reformers and orthodox petitioners, see Lowenstein, "Religious Reform Movement," 276–85, and *Der Israelit des neunzehten Jahrhunderts*, 30 (March 30, 1845), 100–103. This publication of the Orthodox protest is the *only* appearance of the Orthodox perspective in the German Jewish press. Regarding how the petition was seen in the non-Jewish press, see for instance, the *FJ*, Numbers 96 ("Von der Elbe, im März—Hamb. C.," April 7, 1845), 114B ("Der Vorstand der isr. Gemeinde," Offenbach, April 25, 1845), 118B ("**, Frankfurt, 27. April—Einges.," April 29, 1845), 140 ("** Giessen, 20. Mai—Corresp., May 23, 1845), 146 ("Hamburg im Mai 1845–Eingesendet.," May 29, 1845), 152 ("*, Alzey, 25. Mai—Corresp.," June 4, 1845), and 157 Beilage 2 ("Die Reformfreunde in der dortigen israelitischen Religionsgemeinde [Giessen]," June 9, 1845).

66. David Philipson, "The Breslau Rabbinical Conference," *Jewish Quarterly Review* 18, no. 4 (July 1906): 661–62; Meola, "Becoming Public," 176; "Zeit bringt Rosen," *Ostfriesische Zeitung*, 50 (June 23, 1824), 419; Meyer, *Response to*

Modernity, 137; David Philipson, "The Frankfort Rabbinical Conference, 1845," *Jewish Quarterly Review* 18, no. 2 (January 1906): 255–65. Reformers planned a fourth rabbinical conference for Mannheim in 1847, but it was canceled due to the political and societal tumult in the grand duchy. In many Jewish communities, even in more conservative places like the Kingdom of Hannover and the city of Emden (East Frisia), demands for vernacular (German) services dated back to the 1820s.

67. Schwartzman, *Reform Judaism in the Making*, 71–72; Philipson, "Frankfort Rabbinical Conference," 253, 286. See the letters from Fränkel and Schott in the different organs of the German Jewish press: *AZdJ* (31, [July 28, 1845], 474–76), *Der Orient* (Leopold Schott, "Mein Austritt aus der Rabbinerversammlung," 39 [September 24, 1845], 311–12), and *Der Israelit des neunzehnten Jahrhunderts* ("Der Austritt Fränkels und Schotts aus der Rabbinerversammlung," 31 [August 3, 1845], 256–58), as well as the letters and responses to Fränkel in those organs from Jewish communities around Germany, like those from the Hannover Jewish community (*Der Orient*, 33, [August 13, 1845], 258). Very interestingly, Schott had previously written an article in the *AZdJ* giving the reasons why he had chosen to participate in the second conference ("Ueber Theilnahme an der bevorstehenden zweiten Rabbinerversammlung in Frankfurt," 27 [June 30, 1845], 405–7). It should be noted that Fränkel did not attend the Brunswick conference, whereas Schott did. Fränkel was invited to participate and left after he was unable to direct the "spirit" of the conference in his more conservative "positive-historical" direction.

68. *DAZ*, 205 (July 24, 1845), 1950; "Frankfurt, 20. Juli.," *FJ*, 200 (July 22, 1845); *AAZ*, 204 (July 23, 1845), 1630–31 (just a recap of his letter); "(Eingesandt) Frankfurt, den 19ten Juli.," *VZ*, 171 (July 25, 1845); Philipson, "Frankfort Rabbinical Conference," 289–90. See footnote Nr. 5 for Philipson's description of these anti-conference responses in *Der Orient* and the English Jewish publication *The Voice of Jacob*.

69. Philipson, "Breslau," 621.

70. Michael A. Meyer, *Judaism within Modernity: Essays of Jewish History and Religion* (Detroit, MI: Wayne State University Press, 2001), 216. Wagner participated in both the 1845 and 1846 conferences, and he agreed with Philippson on this point; he used this argumentation for his essay on the Gleichstellung debate, described in chapter 2. Wagner was also set to host the 1847 conference in Mannheim before it was canceled. One notable exception to keeping the Sabbath on Saturday came from Samuel Holdheim, who eventually became the preacher for the reform community in Berlin. He was originally the chief rabbi in Mecklenburg-Schwerin and was one of the foremost Talmudic scholars in the German states. See Michael A. Meyer, "'Most of My Brethren Find Me Unacceptable': The Controversial Career of Rabbi Samuel

Holdheim," *Jewish Social Studies* 9, no. 3 (Spring/Summer 2003): 1–19, as well as Wiese, *Redefining Judaism in an Age of Emancipation*, for different views about Holdheim's religious and theological views, especially in comparison to other contemporary German rabbis.

71. Philipson, "Breslau," 658–61; Werner Meiners, "Oldenburg," in *Historisches Handbuch der jüdischen Gemeinden in Niedersachsen und Bremen*, ed. Herbert Obenaus (Göttingen, Germany: Wallstein, 2005), 1172–96. Wechsler took over the position vacated by Samson Raphael Hirsch, who had succeeded Dr. Nathan Marcus Adler in Emden. *Die Reform des Judenthums* was dedicated to the rabbinical conferences, but it lasted for only nine months during 1846. A correspondent in the *MAbZ* ("Vom Rhein," 1 [January 1, 1847]) lamented its demise, believing its short life was due to reform's "victory" over traditionalism and orthodoxy.

72. *Hannoversche Morgenzeitung*, 51 (March 30, 1845), 203.

73. "**, Breslau, 16. Aug.," *DAZ*, 232 (August 20, 1845), 2215; "**, Breslau, 17. Aug.," *DAZ*, 235 (August 23, 1845), 2247–48.

74. "Hannover," *FJ*, 219 (August 10, 1845); "0, Frankfurt a. M., 18. Sept.," *DAZ*, 266 (September 23, 1845), 2558–59. This latter letter was challenged a few days later ("_, Frankfurt a. M., 24. Sept.," 270 [September 27, 1845] 2602) by a correspondent who brought to light a letter signed by the *Aufgeklärten* (enlightened ones) to the conference. This letter clearly followed a common arguing technique used by reformers to question the *gebildet* (educated) nature of those who wrote these protests, thus lumping them together with the Orthodox protestors. The article also criticized Fränkel's behavior, which this writer deemed to be in step with the Orthodox.

75. "∇, Berlin, 12. April," *DAZ*, 105B (April 15, 1845), 1001–2; "∇, Berlin, 25. April," *DAZ*, 118 (April 28, 1845), 1106; (+, Berlin), *DAZ*, 41 (February 10, 1846), 371. The correspondent elucidates the following cities from where support for the RG came: Altona, Brilon, Breslau, Kosel, Dessau, Düsseldorf, Elsoff, Giessen, Gleiwitz, Hamm, Königsberg, Mannheim, Mühlhausen, Werl, and Neustadt an der Saale.

76. "☉, Frankfurt, 16. Juli," *DAZ*, 196 (July 18, 1845); advertisement for the Eintrittskarten and "Berlin, 8. Juli—D. A. Z." from: *FJ*, 190 (July 12, 1845); "*, Frankfurt, 14. Juli.—Eingesandt," 193B (July 15, 1845); "Berlin, 8. Juli—Berl. Ztg." *FJ*, 189 (July 11, 1845). The latter designation refers to the *Vossische Zeitung*, whose official title was *Königlich priviligierte Berlinische Zeitung*.

77. "☿, Frankfurt a. M, 17. Jul.," *DAZ*, 201 (July 20, 1845), 1915; "*, Frankfurt a. M., 23. Jul.," 207 (July 26, 1845), 1970; "☿, Frankfurt a. M., 28. Jul.," *DAZ*, 213 (August 1, 1845), 2022; "B, Frankfurt, 29. Juli," *FJ*, 108–2B (July 30, 1845). See Baader, *Bourgeois Culture*, for more about how women became a focal point for reformers and the Orthodox as Judaism transitioned into a nineteenth-century bourgeois religion.

78. "□, Berlin, 17. Aug.," *DAZ*, 232 (August 20, 1845), 2214; "*, Vom Taunus, 16. Sept.," *DAZ*, 265 (September 22, 1845), 2546.

79. "B, Frankfurt, 29. Juli," *FJ*, 108–2B (July 30, 1845).

80. Orthodox Response: "Frankfurt a. M." *DAZ*, 236 (August 26, 1846), 2138, reprinted from the *FJ*); RF response, "V, Frankfurt, 16. Aug.," *DAZ*, 232 (August 20, 1846), 2089–90, and from another supporter of more radical reform, "□, Frankfurt a. M., 11. Aug.," 227 (August 15, 1845), 2050.

81. Ismar Schorsch, "Emancipation and the Crisis of Religious Authority: The Emergence of the Modern Rabbinate," in Mosse, Paucker, and Rürup, *Revolution and Evolution*, 213–27.

82. Kaufmann, *Kleine Geschichte der Juden*, 77; Paulus, "Jüdischer Kultus im Widerstreit," 248–52. This ordinance, while spreading reform ideas to more rural areas, also shut down the reform synagogue established by the Kusel and Haber families in Karlsruhe.

83. Lowenstein, "Religious Reform Movement," 286–97. For more about the history and contentiousness of clerical robes, see Judith Bleich, "Clerical Robes: Distinction or Dishonor?" *Tradition: A Journal of Orthodox Jewish Thought* 50, no. 1 (Spring 2017): 9–34.

84. Stude, *Juden in Landkreis Karlsruhe*, 92; Brämer, *Rabbiner*, 24; Lowenstein, "Religious Reform Movement," 282; Rosenthal, *Heimatgeschichte der badischen Juden*, 350; Bleich, "Emergence of an Orthodox Press," 330. Of note is the generational differences within rabbinical families. In the Präger family (Bruchsal), the father (Elias Präger) held onto more conservative religiosity while his son, Moses Präger, wrote a popular Badenese reform prayer book (1854) and was reviled by the Orthodox. As Rosenthal has noted, there was a "scharfen Auseinandersetzung" (heated exchange) between Traub and Wagner about the instituting of the practice of confirmation.

85. Rürup, *Emanzipation und Antisemitismus*, 68–69; Roming, "Geschichte der jüdischen Gemeinde Gailingen," 341; Krauss, "Zwischen Emanzipation und Antisemitismus," 201–4; Rosenthal, *Heimatgeschichte der badischen Juden*, 335; Hans-Martin Mumm, "'Denket nicht: Wir wollen's beim Alten lassen.' Die Jahre der Emanzipation 1803 bis 1862," in *Jüdisches Leben in Heidelberg: Studien zu einer unterbrochenen Geschichte*, ed. Norbert Giovannini, Jo-Hannes Bauer, and Hans-Martin Mumm (Heidelberg, Germany: Das Wunderhorn, 1992), 32–33. Rehfuß was the son of a rabbi in Altdorf (Baden); he attended the lyceum (a high-level school) in Rastatt and attended university in Heidelberg.

86. Krauss, "Zwischen Emanzipation und Antisemitismus," 201–2; Jakob Rehfuß, *Der Orient* 6, 2 (January 8, 1845), 12 (the article was originally dated December 29, 1844); Lässig, *Jüdische Wege ins Bürgertum*, 253. This invective was started in *Der Israelit* 5, 36 (September 8, 1844), 290–91. It was so bellicose that the editor—the very liberal Dr. Mendel Heß—felt compelled to note that he

would be providing space for Fürst to write a response. Fürst did respond but did so first in *Der Orient* 4, 47 (November 19, 1844), 363–66. Fürst's reply was likewise published in *Der Israelit* 6, 4 and 6–8 (January 26, 1845, and February 9, 16, and 23, 1845), 32, 40, 46–48, 56, and 62–63.

87. Krauss, "Zwischen Emanzipation und Antisemitismus," 209. Krauss noted that the public spat in the German Jewish press was due to Fürst kicking Rehfuß's widowed wife out of the housing provided for the teacher's family (Salomon Reckendorf, *Der Orient*, 4, 52 (December 24, 1844), 405–6). It should also be noted that while Fürst was being attacked in the press, he continued to publish items which he had written on behalf of Jewish emancipation, including a petition to change the Jewish oath to be equivalent to the Christian one. See *AZdJ*, 9, 3 (January 13, 1845), 33–36, and *Der Orient*, 5, 3 (January 15, 1845), 18–20.

88. *Der Israelit des neunzehnten Jahrhunderts*, 6, 30 (March 30, 1845), 100–103; see, for instance, the chapter "The Rabbinical Elite on the Defensive," in Feiner, *Jewish Enlightenment*, where he details the Wessely Affair, which was a conflict between the lay leaders of the Berlin Jewry, a Christian supporter (August Cranz), and the rabbinical elite in Poland. At issue was Wessely's publication *Divrei shalom ve'emet*, which Feiner described as the first writing in the Jewish *Kulturkampf* (culture war).

89. *MAbZ*, 115 (April 26, 1845); Adolph Zimmern, "Erklärung," *MM*, 111B (May 11, 1845), 473; *AZdJ*, 9, 21 (May 19, 1845), 314.

90. Zimmern, "Erklärung," 473.

91. Frederick Beiser, *Enlightenment, Revolution, and Romanticism: The Genesis of Modern German Political Thought, 1790–1800* (Cambridge, MA: Harvard University Press, 1992), 15–18. Zimmern parroted the same core sentiments as liberal German philosophers during the late Enlightenment, especially in relation to the state's role in protecting individuals' rights.

92. Zimmern, "Erklärung," 473 (emphasis in original).

93. "Bühl," *MAbZ*, 118 (May 3, 1845), 473 (emphasis mine).

94. Rosenthal, *Heimatgeschichte der badischen Juden*, 351; Jack Wertheimer, *Unwelcome Strangers: East European Jews in Imperial Germany* (Oxford: Oxford University Press, 1987); Salomon Maimon, *Salomon Maimon: An Autobiography*, trans. J. Clark Murray (Urbana: University of Illinois Press, 2001); Meola, "Becoming Public," 238–48; Ari Joskowicz, "Jews and Other Others," in Green and Sullam, *Jews, Liberalism, Antisemitism*, 70. Baden also looked unfavorably at all non-Badenese Jewish teachers, even if they were from other German states. The government only wanted to employ foreigners in extreme situations. More specifically, in *Salomon Maimon*, pages 80–81 contain Maimon's criticism of Polish Jews, whom he considered "unenlightened." In Hannover and Hildesheim, and as part of a broader discussion of Jewish rights in Hannover, some Jews used the geographical origins of teachers (often from Posen) as

code for those who lacked Bildung and were, thus, perceived as not educating Hannoverian Jews properly. Joskowicz writes about Jewish liberals and their relationship to "other Others" in the post-1848 era, although these sentiments are clearly rooted in pre-1848 ideas as seen in the discussion in this chapter.

95. Zimmern, "Erklärung," 473; Mumm, "Denket nicht," 49; Liberles, *Orthodox Judaism in Frankfurt*, 201. As the history of German Jewry indicates (look at any general history about the German Jewry during the nineteenth century), Zimmern's prophecy would come to fruition. Likewise, the formation of *Austrittsgemeinden* throughout Germany showed how strong reform sentiment was throughout the country. We can assume this since it was the Orthodox communities that were splitting off from and pulling out of the communities rather than the opposite (the reformers splitting off from the community).

96. This was certainly recognized in the public sphere, as an article in the *MAbZ* points out ("Aus dem Badischen," 280 [October 13, 1845], 1210).

97. Certainly, the historical context of Heidelberg as an economic center and hub of Jewish life in the Kurpfalz (before 1806) is important, as reflected in David Zimmern's participation in the Badenese *Oberrat*.

98. Salomon Fürst, *Heid Jour*, 121 (May 4, 1845), 487 (emphasis in original).

99. *AZdJ*, 21 (May 19, 1845), 314–15.

100. From Heidelberg, *MAbZ*, 115 (April 29, 1845); from Bühl, *MAbZ* 118 (May 3, 1845); from Schwetzingen and Abenheim, *MAbZ*, 122 (May 7, 1845), 487; from Karlsruhe, *MAbZ*, 134 (May 20, 1845); from Nußloch, *MAbZ*, 135 (May 21, 1845), 539. Response by Dr. Löwenthal from Mannheim (reprinted in *Der Israelit* on June 8, 1845) *MAbZ*, 136 (May 26, 1845), and Billigheim near Mosbach, *MAbZ*, 146 (May 26, 1845), 559.

101. *MAbZ*, 125 (May 10, 1845), 499; Verus, "Die Erklärung des Herrn Bezirks-Rabbinen Fürst dahier," *Heid Jour*, 126 (May 9, 1845), 509; Mumm, "Denket nicht," 39. Mumm pointed out that Salomon Friedländer, a university student from Brilon (Westphalia), publicly criticized Fürst about his signature and might have been the author of the *Heid Jour* article, which clearly came from a member of the Jewish community.

102. Gotthold Salomon, *Die Rabbiner-Versammlung und ihre Tendenz. Eine Beleuchtung für ihre Freunde und Feinde* (Hamburg, Germany: B. S. Berendsohn, 1845), 26; Verus, "Die Erklärung," 509. The term *Duodez* is an obscure one that is not found in any standard dictionary. It typically refers to a type of printing format for a book that is one-twelfth the size of a standard printing sheet. However, there are terms like *Duodezfürst* that translate as "petty prince" or "kinglet." The term *Duodezrabbiner* also appears in the following publication that was printed only three months before this discussion took place, wherein Salomon also uses the term pejoratively to accuse traditional rabbis of having prejudged the conference as a "Sitz der Spötter" (seat of mockers/maligners).

One cannot help noticing the similarity in language used by those who sought emancipation and reform. See Heine's comments in his *Nekrolog* for Ludwig Marcus in chapter 2.

103. Salomon Fürst, *Heid Jour*, 127 (May 10, 1845), 513; Feiner, *Jewish Enlightenment*; *Heid Jour*, 130 (May 14, 1845), 525; *Heid Jour*, 132 (May 16, 1845), 535; "Song of Songs," *Tanakh* (Philadelphia: Jewish Publication Society, 1985), 1415. See the Babylonian Talmud, tractates Sanhedrin 90b, Yebamoth 97a, and Bechoroth 31b. I would like to thank Dr. Russell Jay Hendel at Towson University for supplying me with the Talmudic passages and knowledge for this insight. In Feiner, *Jewish Enlightenment*, see especially the end of chapter 3 through chapter 6, where Feiner detailed how the rabbinical elite were on the defensive. Surely, Fürst as a more conservative rabbi (even though he was a "modern" rabbi), felt threatened by a new generation of lay and ecclesiastical figures who looked to usurp his remaining and waning authority.

104. See, for instance, the rubric "Aus dem Oberrheinkreis," *MAbZ*, 173 (June 28, 1845), and the identical piece in the *MM* 152 (June 28, 1845), 635.

105. See for instance, Oberrat Naphtali Epstein's petition *Gehorsamste Vorstellung und die hohe Zweite Kammer der Ständerversammlung des Großherzogthums Baden, betreffend die bürgerlichen und politischen Rechte der Badener, israelitische Religion: Mit einer Beilage, enthaltend der betreffenden Auszug der gr. Bad. Gesetzgebung* (Karlsruhe: D. R. Marx, 1832), Freimann-Sammlung. Also see *Heid Jour*, "Gehorsamste Bitte" 147 and 149 (June 1 and 3, 1846), 633–34 and 642–43; GLAK 231 Nr. 1424 (this file contains the 1835 petition for Gleichstellung from the Karlsruhe Jewish community that had over 50 signatures as well as a petition from around the grand duchy that had 1,848 signatures, or approximately 10 percent of the Jewish population of the country); GLAK 231 Nr. 1425 (this file also contains the 1844 petition from Salomon Fürst, district rabbi from Heidelberg, the 1846 Second Chamber Commission Report from Representative Brentano recommending Gleichstellung, and the 1846 petition from the Synagogenrat in Gailingen, which Rabbi Löwenstein did not sign).

106. Lässig, *Jüdische Wege ins Bürgertum*, 447; Bethmann, *Freiheit und Einheit*, 158–66. The argument about Bildung is included in the following studies: Volkov, *Germans, Jews, and Antisemites*, chap. 9 ("Climbing up the Social Ladder"); George Mosse, *German Jews beyond Judaism* (Bloomington: Indiana University Press, 1985); Sorkin, *Transformation*, 5; Gabriele von Glasenapp, "Zwischen Selbstinszenierung und Publikationsstrategie: Der Lehrer als Autor und Akteur in der deutschsprachigen Ghetto literature," in *Judentum und Aufklärung: Jüdisches Selbstverständnis in der bürgerlichen Öffentlichkeit*, ed. Arno Herzig, Hans Otto Horch, and Robert Jütte (Göttingen, Germany: Vandenhoeck & Ruprecht, 2002), 219.

107. Lowenstein, "Religious Reform Movement," 260–61.

4. THE FIGHT FOR JEWISH ADMISSION TO CONSTANCE IN THE BODENSEE PRESS, 1846

1. Helmut Maurer, *Konstanz im Mittelalter*, Band 2, *Vom Konzil bis zum Beginn des 16. Jahrhunderts* (Konstanz, Germany: Stadler, 1989), 65–66.
2. Roming, "Religiosität und Bildung," 107; Lowenstein, "Religious Reform Movement," 265–66.
3. Roming, "Religiosität und Bildung," 98; Pnina Navé Levinson, "Aus dem religiösen Leben Orthodoxie und Liberalismus," *Juden in Baden 1809–1984: 175 Jahre Oberrat der Israeliten Badens*, ed. Jael B. Paulus (Karlsruhe, Germany: Oberrat der Israeliten Badens, 1984), 92. Roming claims that the reform trend came from the cities and that the rural communities "stuck to" (*verhaftet*; in modern parlance, this translates as "imprisoned" or "arrested") older forms of religiosity (thanks to Dr. Michael Nagel for this insight).
4. Roming, "Religiosität und Bildung," 99. Rabbi Löwenstein's correct first name is Jakob, not Isaac. Roming used "Isaac" in this 1994 essay and then corrected the mistake in the 2004 essay "Geschichte der jüdischen Gemeinde Gailingen," in *Gailingen: Geschichte einer Hochrhein-Gemeinde*, ed. Franz Götz (Gailingen, Germany: Hegau-Bibliothek, 2004), 291–380.
5. Robert Heuser, "Die Bedeutung des Ortsbürgerrechts für die Emanzipation der Juden in Baden 1807–1831" (PhD diss., Universität Heidelberg, 1971), 91–92; Rürup, *Emanzipation und Antisemitismus*, 74.
6. It should be noted that Wangen is not forty kilometers away from Constance by boat. The town is only about twenty kilometers away if one were to cross the Zellersee (Lake Zell). Population statistics (from 1825) regarding the four Jewish communities in the Hegau comes from Hundsnurscher and Taddey, *Die jüdischen Gemeinden in Baden*.
7. Despite the towns being only a few kilometers apart, another important factor in this division was the Randegg community's intention to stay separate from the more conservative rabbinate.
8. Roming, "Zur Rechts-," 107–9, 123. This was especially true for Gailingen, as it was only accessible by two roads: one from Dissenhoffen (Switzerland) and the other from Randegg, which had a 20 percent grade, which made access for vehicles particularly difficult (especially in the winter). It was only in the 1860s that a road with a more manageable 5 percent grade was built.
9. In this chapter, we will generally be using the term *Aufnahme*, instead of *Zulassung*, although both terms accurately reflect the situation involving the debate about Jews' admittance into Constance. The term *Bürger*, in this sense, is used to denote a local citizenship in which Jews can officially vote in local elections and be elected as *Wahlmänner* (electors) and not just reside in the city. Jews could not, even as Bürger, be elected as mayor or as assemblymen due to state law.

10. *Seeblätter*, 86 (July 22, 1845), 458.

11. "Zwiegespräch eines Gailinger und Wangener Israeliten," *Seeblätter*, 46 (April 16, 1846), 194.

12. "Randegg," *Seeblätter*, 54 (May 5, 1846), 231.

13. "Petition der Jüdenschaft um bürgerliche Aufnahme in die Stadt Konstanz," *KonZtg*, 100B (August 21, 1846), 751; Uri Robert Kaufmann, "Die jüdischen Landgemeinden des Bodenseekreises," in Paulus, *Juden in Baden*, 168–69. I would like to thank Drs. Markus Hallensleben and Gaby Pailer at the University of British Columbia, and Rachel Reynolds, my editor, for helping me refine this translation.

14. Patricia F. O'Grady, *Thales of Miletus: The Beginnings of Western Science and Philosophy* (Aldershot, UK: Ashgate, 2002); Francois-Marie Arouet (Voltaire), "Jews (1756)," in Mendes-Flohr and Reinharz, *Jew in the Modern World*, 304; Francois-Marie Arouet (Voltaire), "Reply to de Pinto (c. 1762)," in Mendes-Flohr and Reinharz, *Jew in the Modern World*, 308. Thales of Miletus (approximately 620–546 BCE) was, according to O'Grady, one of the first Greeks to look at nondeistic reasoning for explaining the natural world, one that included scientific and rational means. The ideas discussed by Voltaire, as shown earlier, stem from Eisenmenger's *Entdecktes Judentum* and were reiterated by Jacob Friedrich Fries, Heinrich Eberhard Gottlob Paulus, and others who consistently argued against Jews' emancipation.

15. Jacob Toury, "Die Sprache als Problem der jüdische Einordnung in den deutschen Kulturraum," in *Gegenseitige Einflüsse deutscher und jüdischer Kultur: Von der Epoche der Aufklärung bis zur Weimarer Republik*, Jahrbuch des Instituts für deutsche Geschichte, Beiheft 4, ed. Walter Grab (Tel Aviv: Nateev, 1982), 84; Martin Schneble "Alemannische und jiddische Mundart in Gailingen," in Götz, *Gailingen: Geschichte einer Hochrhein-Gemeinde*, 478.

16. Herzog, *Intimacy and Exclusion*, 64, 67–70, and 77 (see especially note 73).

17. *Seeblätter*, 102 (August 25, 1846), 428; Rürup, *Emanzipation und Antisemitismus*, 74.

18. Elmar B. Fetscher, *Die Konstanzer Seeblätter und die Pressezensur des Vormärz 1840/1841* (Sigmaringen, Germany: Jan Thorbecke, 1981), 46; Gert Zang, *Konstanz in der Großherzoglichen Zeit. Restauration, Revolution, Liberale Ära 1806 bis 1870* (Konstanz, Germany: Stadler, 1989), 153–57.

19. Berger, "Politische Presse in Vormärz," 32–34; Josef Fickler, *Seeblätter*, 97 (August 13, 1846), 409–10 (emphasis in original); Fetscher, *Die Konstanzer Seeblätter*, 42. For more on the split between the "full" (radical) and "half" (moderate) liberals in Baden and the revolutions of 1848, especially the tumult in Mannheim following Fickler's arrest on April 8, 1848 by Karl Mathy in Karlsruhe, see Peter Blastenbrei, *Mannheim in der Revolution 1848/49* (Mannheim, Germany: von Brandt, 1997).

20. Zang, *Konstanz in der Großherzoglichen Zeit*, 153–57.

21. "Gailingen," *Seeblätter*, 95 (August 9, 1846), 400.

22. "Erklärung," *Seeblätter*, 99 (August 18, 1846), 418; Roming, "Geschichte der jüdischen Gemeinde Gailingen," 324. Löwenstein refused to give a weekly sermon, as decreed by the Badenese Oberrat, but instead agreed to give a two- to three-hour sermon twice a year.

23. "Gegenerklärung," *Seeblätter*, 109 (September 10, 1846), 462; see Monika Richarz's essay "Ländliches Judentum als Problem der Forschung," in *Jüdisches Leben auf dem Lande: Studien zur deutsch-jüdischen Geschichte*, ed. Monika Richarz and Reinhard Rürup (Tübingen, Germany: Mohr Siebeck, 1997), 1–8, for a quick discussion about the issue of Landjuden in historical research; Ismar Schorsch, "Emergence of the Modern Rabbinate"; Lowenstein, "Religious Reform Movement."

24. Jakob Löwenstein, "Ueber die Fortbildung des Judenthums," *Allgemeine Zeitung des Judenthums (AZdJ)*, 30 (July 22, 1844), 417; "Entgegnung, die Fortbildung des Judenthum betreffend," *AZdJ*, 35 (August 26, 1844), 490–94. For an earlier publication by Löwenstein that shows his Orthodox position, see *Menorah Tehorah oder Das reine Judenthum als Gegenstück des von Dr. M. Creizenach, unter dem Titel* Thariag *herausgegebenen ersten Theils seines* Schulchan Aruch (Schaffhausen, Switzerland: Hurter'schen Buchhandlung, 1835), Freimann-Sammlung. In the foreword, Löwenstein mentioned that he would build "a dam against the forward push of unmosaic novelties" (*zu einem Damme gegen das Andringen unmosaischer Neuerungen*).

25. "Konstanz," *Seeblätter*, 11 (January 25, 1846), 50–52. In this article, the Jews were divided up into two groups: the unacceptable *schwarzen Saamen* (black seeds), that is, those who followed the old, Talmudic ways, and the acceptable *weißen Saamen* (white seeds), who were those who promulgated reform. The article "Konstanz," *KonZtg*, 95 (August 10, 1846), 709–10, claimed that they (the writer and presumably other Christians) wanted the Jews of the "better sort" (*besseren Sorte*)—i.e., those with money and not those "poor" Jews who were considered to be frugal.

26. Josef Fickler, "Anmerkung der Redaktion," in "Erklärung," *Seeblätter*, 99 (August 18, 1846), 418.

27. Roming, "Religiosität und Bildung," 107.

28. Levinson, "Aus dem Leben," 93; Brämer, *Rabbiner*, 16.

29. Berger, "Politische Presse in Vormärz," 31.

30. *KonZtg*, 102 (August 26, 1846), 766; "Konstanz," *Seeblätter*, 104B (August 30, 1846), 442.

31. D., "Gailingen," *Seeblätter*, 102 (August 25, 1846), 428–29. One of the references is to two of Jacob's sons, Simeon and Levi, who, in Genesis 34:25–31, took revenge on the Canaanites and the Perrizites, who had supposedly defiled

their sister Dinah. Simeon and Levi slaughtered all the males of the Canaanite city and plundered it for the Canaanites' transgressions.

32. Schott, *Seeblätter*, 104B (August 30, 1846), 441. In Hebrew this concept is known as *dina de-malchuta dina*.

33. Although there is no proof to suggest this, the piece from August 25 could have been written by a member of the Eintracht board, if not just a normal community member, who participated in discussions about these articles.

34. "Gailingen," *KonZtg*, 104 (August 31, 1846), 782.

35. Michael A. Meyer, "Deutsch werden, jüdisch bleiben," in *Deutsch-jüdische Geschichte in der Neuzeit*, Band II, *Emanzipation und Akkulturation, 1780–1871*, ed. Michael A. Meyer and Michael Brenner (Munich: C. H. Beck, 1996), 208–59.

36. Schott, *Seeblätter*, 104B (August 30, 1846), 441.

37. Thomas Pegelow, "'German Jews,' 'National Jews,' 'Jewish *Volk*,' or 'Racial Jews'? The Constitution and Contestation of 'Jewishness' in Newspapers of Nazi Germany, 1933–1938," *Central European History* 35, no. 2 (June 2002): 200.

CONCLUSION

1. Ludwig Philippson, "Das Judenthum und die Emanzipation," *AZdJ*, 3 (January 14, 1850), 29–31, as quoted in Reinhard Rürup, "Jewish Emancipation and the Vision of Civil Society in Germany," *LBIYB* 51 (2006): 50.

2. Weir, *Secularism and Religion*, 17, 63.

3. Joskowicz, "Jews and Other Others," 88.

4. Peter Pulzer, "Legal Equality and Public Life," in *German-Jewish History in Modern Times*, vol. 3, *Integration in Dispute, 1871–1918*, ed. Steven M. Lowenstein et al. (New York: Columbia University Press, 1997), 154–62; Liberles, *Orthodox Judaism in Frankfurt*, 201.

5. Pulzer, "Legal Equality and Public Life," 190–93; Meola, "Making News," 128–29; Stein, *Making Jews Modern*.

6. Auslander, "Boundaries of Jewishness," 48; Green, "1848 and Beyond," 345.

7. Meola, *Becoming Public*, 132–49.

8. Meola, "Becoming Public," chap. 4. In this text, I analyze five different purposes for newspaper participation: economic, personal, religious, political, and national. The overwhelming majority (above 90 percent) were of the economic variety, but even the small amount from the other four categories can tell us more about those Jewish communities and the individuals who paid for their insertion. Moreover, even the classifieds can be used to detail the economic life of Jewish communities and the material history of these cities.

9. Moritz Cohen (M Honek), "Spielgeschichten," *KölZtg*, 212 (July 31, 1843); Ludwig Wihl, "Des Juden Vaterland," *KolZtg*, Nr. 223 (August 11, 1843); Weissberg, "Newspaper Feuilleton," 151, 154; Jonathan M. Hess, *Middlebrow*

Literature and the Making of German-Jewish Identity (Stanford, CA: Stanford University Press, 2010). The Moritz Cohen piece, in fact, elicited a response in the *AAZ* (Nr. 237, August 25, 1843, 1892–93) and then a counterresponse by Honek in the *KölZtg* (Nr. 244, September 1, 1843). Supposedly, this story about gaming culture was the official reason the Grand Duchy of Baden in October 1843 revoked the permission it had granted Cohen to live in the state, though others believed that his reporting on the Haber Affair was to blame.

10. Corey Ross, *Media and the Making of Modern Germany: Mass Communication, Society, and Politics from the Empire to the Third Reich* (Oxford: Oxford University Press, 2008), 5 and 18; Heidi J. S. Tworek, *News from Germany: The Competition to Control World Communications, 1900–1945* (Cambridge, MA: Harvard University Press, 2019), 23; Pegelow, "German Jews"; Sarah Wobick-Segev, "'Looking for a Nice Jewish Girl...': Personal Ads and the Creation of Jewish Families in Germany before and after the Holocaust," *Jewish Social Studies* 23, no. 3 (Spring/Summer 2018): 38–66; Karl Christian Führer, "Contradicting Nazi Propaganda: Classified Advertisements as Documents of Jewish Life in Nazi Germany, 1933–1938," *Media History* 18, no. 1 (November 2012): 65–76.

11. Marcel Stoetzler, *The State, the Nation, & the Jews: Liberalism and the Antisemitism Dispute in Bismarck's Germany* (Lincoln: University of Nebraska Press, 2008), 32, 51–52, 65.

12. Weir, *Secularism and Religion*, 219–20; Green and Sullam, *Jews, Liberalism, Antisemitism*. See especially Lisa Moses Leff's chapter "Liberalism and Antisemitism: A Reassessment from the Peripheries," 23–45, in which she details how antisemitism was foundational to liberal movements in both Romania and Algeria.

13. Mosse, *German Jews beyond Judaism*, 6, 12; Stoetzler, *Antisemitism Dispute*, 32–33.

14. Stoetzler, *Antisemitism Dispute*, 66. This is taken from Ludwig Bamberger's "Deutschtum und Judentum," in *Der Berliner Antisemitismusstreit*, ed. Walter Boehlich (Frankfurt: Insel, 1965), 171–72.

BIBLIOGRAPHY

ARCHIVAL SOURCES USED

GLAK 231 Nr. 1424
This file includes petitions and writings given to the Lower Assembly both for and against Jewish emancipation between 1835 and 1842.
GLAK 231 Nr. 1425
This file includes petitions and writings given to the Lower Assembly both for and against Jewish emancipation between 1843 and 1863.

Online Primary Sources

Available through the Freimann-Sammlung at the University of Frankfurt (https://sammlungen.ub.uni-frankfurt.de/freimann/nav/index/all):
Behr, Alexander. *Lehrbuch der mosaischen Religion.* Munich: Carl Wolf, 1826.
Eine deutsch-jüdische Kirche. Die nächste Aufgabe unsrer Zeit. Von einem Candidaten der jüdischen Theologie. Leipzig, Germany: Otto Wigand, 1845.
Epstein, Naphtali. *Die Rechtsverhältnisse der öffentlichen israelitischen Schulen im Grossherzogthum Baden dargestellt in einer Sammlung der darauf bezüglichen Gesetze und Verordnungen.* Carlsruhe, Germany: A. Bielefeld, 1843.
———. *Gehorsamste Vorstellung und die hohe Zweite Kammer der Ständerversammlung des Großherzogthums Baden, betreffend die bürgerlichen und politischen Rechte der Badener, israelitische Religion: Mit einer Beilage, enthaltend der betreffenden Auszug der gr. Bad. Gesetzgebung.* Karlsruhe, Germany: D. R. Marx, 1832.
Fries, Jakob Friedrich. *Ueber die Gefährdung des Wohlstandes und Charakters der Deutschen durch die Juden.* Heidelberg, Germany: Mohr and Winter, 1816.

Löwenstein, Jakob. *Menorah tehorah oder das reine Judenthum als Gegenstück des von Dr. M. Creizenach, unter dem Titel Thariag herausgegebenen ersten Theils seines Schulchan Aruch*. Schaffhausen, Switzerland: Hurter, 1835.

Paulus, Heinrich Eberhard Gottlob. *Die jüdische Nationalabsonderung nach Ursprung, Folgen und Besserungsmitteln: Oder über Pflichten, Rechte und Verordnungen zur Verbesserung der jüdischen Schutzbürgerschaft in Teutschland.* Heidelberg, Germany: Winter, 1831.

Rosenfeld, Mayer. *Feierlicher Act der Religionsprüfung der zu entlassenden Schulkinder: Entworfen und abgehalten in der Synagoge zu Carlsruhe am Sabbath den 23. April 1836 (6. Ijar 5596)*. Carlsruhe, Germany: D. R. Marx, 1836.

Rosenthal, Berthold. *Heimatgeschichte der badischen Juden seit ihrem geschichtlichen Auftreten bis zur Gegenwart*. Bühl, Germany: Konkordia, 1927.

Veit, Moritz. *Der Entwurf einer Verordnung über die Verhältnisse der Juden und das Edikt vom 11. März 1812*. Leipzig, Germany: Brockhaus, 1847.

Willstätter, Ephraim. *Allgemeine Geschichte des Israelitischen Volkes: Von der Entstehung desselben bis auf unsere Zeit*. Karlsruhe, Germany: D. R. Marx, 1836.

Available through Google Books:

"Betrachtung und Aufschlüsse über die Habersche Sache." *Deutsche Monatsschrift für Literatur und öffentliches Leben* 1 (January–June), edited by Karl Biedermann. Leipzig: Mayer und Wigand, 1844: 140–48.

Ghillany, Friedrich. *Das Judenthum und die Kritik: Oder es bleibt bei den Menschenopfern der Hebräer und bei der Nothwendigkeit einer Zeitgemässen Reform des Judenthums*. Stuttgart, Germany: Johann Adam Stein, 1844.

Lewald, August. *Hamburg*. Karlsruhe: F. Gutsch & Rupp, 1842.

Mathy, Karl. *Die Verfassungsfeier in Baden am 22. August 1843*. Mannheim: Fr. Bassermann, 1843.

Mendelssohn, Joseph. *Salomon Heine: Blätter der Würdigung und Erinnerung für seine Freunde und Verehrer*. Hamburg, Germany: B. S. Berendsohn, 1845.

Salomon, Gotthold. *Die Rabbiner-Versammlung und ihre Tendenz: Eine Beleuchtung für ihre Freunde und Feinde*. Hamburg, Germany: B. S. Berendsohn, 1845.

Newspapers Researched for This Project

Note: Not all of the newspapers included here were cited in the notes, yet they were an invaluable and important part of this overall project.

Available online through Compact Memory (https://sammlungen.ub.uni-frankfurt.de/cm/nav/index/title):

Allgemeine Zeitung des Judenthums, 1837–48
Der Israelit des neunzehnten Jahrhunderts, 1840–47
Der Orient, 1840–46
Der treue Zions-Wächter, 1845–48

Israelitischen Annalen, 1839–41
Sulamith, 1806–48
Wissenschaftliche Zeitschrift für Jüdische Theologie, 1835–47

Researched through interlibrary loan (in US and/or Germany):
Augsburger Allgemeine Zeitung, 1830–47 (also available through Bayerische Staatsbibliothek Online, https://digipress.digitale-sammlungen.de/calendar/newspaper/bsbmult00000002)
Bruchsaler Wochenblatt, 1842–46
Deutsche Wochenzeitung für Politik und Literatur, 1843
Die Reform des Judenthums (Mannheim), 1846
Hannoversche Morgenzeitung, 1846–49
Hannoversche Zeitung, 1832–49
Heidelberger Journal, 1842–49
Heidelberger Wochenblatt, 1815–17
Karlsruhe Stadt und Land Bote, 1843–48
Karlsruher Zeitung, 1816–49
Kölnische Zeitung, 1840–48
Konstanzer Zeitung, 1840–48
Mannheimer Abendblatt, 1842
Mannheimer Abendzeitung, 1842–48
Mannheimer Journal, 1844–48
Mannheimer Morgenblatt, 1840, 1845–47
Oberdeutsche Zeitung, 1841–42
Oberrheinische Zeitung, 1843–49

Researched in university libraries or city/state archives in Germany:
Amtsblatt für die Provinz Ostfries- & Harrlingerland, 1817 (Niedersächsisches Landesarchiv Aurich)
Deutsche Allgemeine Zeitung / Leipziger Allgemeine Zeitung (Universitätsbibliothek Leipzig)
Frankfurter Journal, 1843–47 (Hessische Landesbibliothek, Wiesbaden)
Hannoversche Morgenzeitung, 1846–49 (Gottfried Wilhelm Leibniz Bibliothek, Niedersächsische Landesbibliothek)
Hildesheimsche Allgemeine Zeitung und Anzeigen, 1830–48 (Hildesheim City Archives)
Karlsruher Zeitung, 1816–49 (Karlsruhe City Archives)
Königlich priviligierte Berlinische Zeitung (Vossische Zeitung), 1843–47 (Universitätsbibliothek Tübingen)
Kölnische Zeitung, 1840–48 (Universitätsbibliothek Tübingen)
Konstanzer Zeitung, 1840–48 (Universitätsbibliothek Heidelberg)
Mannheimer Journal, 1844–48 (Universitätsbibliothek Heidelberg)

Offenburger Wochenblatt, 1845–46 (Offenburg City Archives)
Ostfriesische Zeitung, 1824, 1830–37, 1839, 1840–42, 1844, 1848 (Johannes a Lasco Bibliothek, Emden)
Seeblätter, 1840–48 (Universitätsbibliothek Heidelberg)

SECONDARY SOURCES

Adam, Thomas. Introduction to *Philanthropy, Patronage, and Civil Society*, edited by Thomas Adam, 1–14. Bloomington: Indiana University Press, 2004.

Adam, Thomas, ed. *Philanthropy, Patronage, and Civil Society*. Bloomington: Indiana University Press, 2004.

Adam, Thomas. "Stiften in deutschen Bürgerstädten vor dem Ersten Weltkrieg: Das Beispiel Leipzig." *Geschichte und Gesellschaft* 33, no. 1 (2007): 46–72.

Albrecht, Peter, and Holger Böning, eds. *Historische Presse und ihre Leser: Studien zu Zeitungen, Zeitschriften, Intelligenzblättern und Kalendern in Nordwestdeutschland*. Bremen: edition lumière, 2005.

Alsing, Hans Frederic. *Medaille anlässlich der Einweihung des Krankenhauses der Deutsch-Israelitischen Gemeinde Hamburg*. Hamburg ca. 1841–1850, Kupferlegierung, patiniert, T = 0,35 Dm = 4,5 cm; Jüdisches Museum Berlin, Inv.-Nr. 2010/238/1. Foto: Roman März.

Altmann, Alexander. *Moses Mendelssohn: A Biographical Study*. Tuscaloosa: University of Alabama Press, 1973.

Anderson, Benedict. *Imagined Communities: Reflections on the Origin and Spread of Nationalism*. 1983. Rev. ed. London: Verso, 2006.

Assembly of Jewish Notables. "Answers to Napoleon." Religious Studies 469.06: Judaism in the Modern Age. Accessed August 1, 2018. https://people.ucalgary.ca/~elsegal/363_Transp/Sanhedrin.html.

Auslander, Leora. "The Boundaries of Jewishness, or When Is a Cultural Practice Jewish?" *Journal of Modern Jewish Studies* 8, no. 1 (March 2009): 47–64.

Avraham, Doron. "German Liberalism and the Militarisation of Civil Society, 1813–1848/49." *European Review of History: Revue européenne d'histoire* 17, no. 4 (2010): 605–28.

Baader, Benjamin Maria. *Gender, Judaism, and Bourgeois Culture in Germany, 1800–1870*. Bloomington: Indiana University Press, 2006.

Baader, Maria Benjamin. "Rabbinic Study, Self-Improvement, and Philanthropy: Gender and the Refashioning of Jewish Voluntary Associations in Germany, 1750–1870." In *Philanthropy, Patronage, and Civil Society*, edited by Thomas Adam, 163–78. Bloomington: Indiana University Press, 2004.

Bachleitner, Norbert. "The Beginnings of the Feuilleton Novel in France and the German-Speaking Regions." In *Nineteenth-Century Serial Narrative in Transnational Perspective, 1830s–1860s*, edited by Daniel Stein and Lisella Wiele, 19–48. Cham, Switzerland: Palgrave, 2019.

Bamberger, Ludwig. "Deutschtum und Judentum." In *Der Berliner Antisemitismusstreit*, edited by Walter Boehlich, 149–79. Frankfurt: Insel, 1965.
Barker, Hannah, and Simon Burrows. Introduction to *Press, Politics, and the Public Sphere in Europe and North America, 1760–1820*, edited by Hannah Barker and Simon Burrows, 1–22. Cambridge: Cambridge University Press, 2002.
———, eds. *Press, Politics, and the Public Sphere in Europe and North America, 1760–1820*. Cambridge: Cambridge University Press, 2002.
Battenberg, Friedrich. *Das Europäische Zeitalter der Juden*. Vol. 2. 2nd ed. Darmstadt: Primus, 2000.
Bayer, Tilde. *Minderheit im städtischen Raum: Sozialgeschichte der Juden in Mannheim während der 1. Hälfte des 19. Jahrhunderts*. Stuttgart, Germany: Thorbecke, 2001.
Beiser, Frederick. *Enlightenment, Revolution, and Romanticism: The Genesis of Modern German Political Thought, 1790–1800*. Cambridge, MA: Harvard University Press, 1992.
Berger, Christine. "Politische Presse im Vormärz." In *Seeblätter: Reprint eine revolutionäre Zeitung*, edited by Christine Berger and Wolfgang Kramer, 22–33. Konstanz: Stadler, 1998.
Berger, Christine, and Wolfgang Kramer, eds. *Seeblätter: Reprint eine revolutionäre Zeitung*. Konstanz: Stadler, 1998.
Bethmann, Anke. *Freiheit und Einheit als Leitmotive der öffentlichen Diskussion um die Neuordnung Deutschlands: Eine Studie zur Geschichte der Revolution von 1848/49 im Königreich Hannover*. Hamburg, Germany: Dr. Kovač, 2000.
Bisschops, Ralph. "Samuel Holdheim and Sigismund Stern: The Clash between the Dogmatic and Historicist Approach in Classical German Reform Judaism." In *Redefining Judaism in an Age of Emancipation: Comparative Perspectives on Samuel Holdheim (1806–1860)*, edited by Christian Wiese, 241–77. London: Brill, 2006.
Bitzan, Amos. "The Problem of Pleasure: Disciplining the German Jewish Reading Revolution, 1770–1870." PhD diss., University of California Berkeley, 2011.
Blanning, T. C. W. *The Culture of Power and the Power of Culture*. Oxford: Oxford University Press, 2002.
Blastenbrei, Peter. *Mannheim in der Revolution 1848/49*. Mannheim, Germany: von Brandt, 1997.
Bleich, Judith. "Clerical Robes: Distinction or Dishonor?" *Tradition: A Journal of Orthodox Jewish Thought* 50, no. 1 (Spring 2017): 9–34.
———. "The Emergence of an Orthodox Press in Nineteenth-Century Germany." *Jewish Social Studies* 42, no. 3/4 (Summer–Autumn 1980): 323–44.
Bloch, Erich. *Geschichte der Juden in Konstanz im 19. und 20. Jahrhundert: Eine Dokumentation*. Konstanz, Germany: Rosgarten, 1973.
Blome, Astrid. "Offices of Intelligence and Expanding Social Spaces." In *The Dissemination of News and the Emergence of Contemporaneity in Early Modern Europe*, edited by Brendan Dooley, 207–22. Surrey, UK: Ashgate, 2010.

———. "Regionale Strukturen und die Entstehung der deutschen Regionalpresse im 18. Jahrhundert." In *Historische Presse und ihre Leser: Studien zu Zeitungen, Zeitschriften, Intelligenzblättern und Kalendern in Nordwestdeutschland*, edited by Peter Albrecht and Holger Böning, 101–20. Bremen: edition lumière, 2005.

Blum, Peter, ed. *Geschichte der Juden in Heidelberg*. Heidelberg: Brigitte Guderjahn, 1996.

Boehlich, Walter, ed. *Der Berliner Antisemitismusstreit*. Frankfurt: Insel, 1965.

Bogner, Ralf Georg. *Der Autor im Nachruf: Formen und Funktionen der literarischen Memorialkultur von der Reformation bis zum Vormärz*. Tübingen, Germany: Max Niemeyer, 2006.

Bonaparte, Napoleon. "The Infamous Decree (1808)." In *The Jew in the Modern World: A Documentary History*, 3rd ed., edited by Paul Mendes-Flohr and Jehuda Reinharz, 161–63. Oxford: Oxford University Press, 2011.

Borowka-Clausberg, Beate. "Salomon Heine im Portrait." In *Salomon Heine in Hamburg. Geschäft und Gemeinsinn*, edited by Beate Borowka-Clausberg, 7–31. Göttingen: Wallstein, 2013.

———, ed. *Salomon Heine in Hamburg. Geschäft und Gemeinsinn*. Göttingen: Wallstein, 2013.

Bösch, Frank. *Mass Media and Historical Change: German in International Perspective, 1400 to the Present*. Translated by Freya Buechter. New York: Berghahn Books, 2015.

Bourdieu, Pierre. "The Forms of Capital." In *Handbook of Theory and Research for the Sociology of Education*, edited by J. G. Richardson, 241–58. New York: Greenwood Press, 1986.

Brämer, Andreas. *Rabbiner und Vorstand: Zur Geschichte der jüdischen Gemeinde in Deutschland und Österreich 1808–1871*. Vienna: Böhlau, 1999.

———. "A Success Story? Prussia's Jewish Educational Policy in the Aftermath of the Emancipation Edict (1812–1870)." *Jewish Quarterly Review* 106, no. 3 (Summer 2016): 412–18.

Bräunche, Ernst Otto. "Vom Schutzjuden zum Bürger zweiter Klasse: Die jüdische Gemeinde bis zum Erlaß des Judenedikts 1809." In *Juden in Karlsruhe: Beiträge zu ihrer Geschichte bis zur nationalsozialistischen Machtergreifung*, edited by Heinz Schmitt, Ernst Otto Bräunche, and Manfred Koch, 41–80. Karlsruhe: Badenia, 1988.

Breuer, Karin. "Competing Masculinities: Fraternities, Gender and Nationality in the German Confederation, 1815–30." *Gender & History* 20, no. 2 (August 2008): 270–87.

Breuer, Mordechai. "The Jewish Minority in the Enlightened Absolutist State." In *German-Jewish History in Modern Times*, vol. 1, *Tradition and*

Enlightenment: 1600–1780, edited by Michael A. Meyer, 144–64. New York: Columbia University Press, 1996.

———. *Modernity within Tradition: The Social History of Orthodox Jewry in Imperial Germany*. Translated by Elizabeth Petuchowski. New York: Columbia University Press, 1992.

Brocke, Michael, and Julius Carlebach, eds. *Biographisches Handbuch der Rabbiner, Teil 1: Die Rabbiner der Emanzipationszeit in den deutschen, böhmischen und grosspolnischen Ländern 1781–1871*. Band 2. Munich: K. G. Saur, 2004.

Brophy, James M. "'The Modernity of Tradition': Popular Culture and Protest in Nineteenth-Century Germany." In *Protest, Popular Culture and Tradition in Modern and Contemporary Western Europe*, edited by Illaria Favretto and Xabier Itcaina, 21–43. London: Palgrave Macmillan, 2017.

Brown, Wendy. *Regulating Aversion: Tolerance in the Age of Identity and Empire*. Princeton, NJ: Princeton University Press, 2006.

Calhoun, Craig, ed. *Habermas and the Public Sphere*. Cambridge: Massachusetts Institute of Technology Press, 1992.

———. Introduction to *Habermas and the Public Sphere*, edited by Craig Calhoun, 1–48. Cambridge: Massachusetts Institute of Technology Press, 1992.

Clark, Christopher. *Iron Kingdom: The Rise and Downfall of Prussia, 1600–1947*. Cambridge, MA: Belknap Press of Harvard University Press, 2006.

Clark, Christopher M. *The Politics of Conversion: Missionary Protestantism and the Jews in Prussia, 1728–1941*. Oxford, UK: Clarendon Press, 1995.

Darnton, Robert. *Censor at Work: How States Shaped Literature*. New York: W. W. Norton, 2014.

De Ferrari, Pier Gian Maria. "Tearing Down the Gates of the Venetian Ghetto (July 10, 1797)." In *The Jew in the Modern World: A Documentary History*, 3rd ed., edited by Paul Mendes-Flohr and Jehuda Reinharz, 146–47. Oxford: Oxford University Press, 2011.

Dooley, Brendan, ed. *The Dissemination of News and the Emergence of Contemporaneity in Early Modern Europe*. Surrey, UK: Ashgate, 2010.

———. Introduction to *The Dissemination of News and the Emergence of Contemporaneity in Early Modern Europe*, edited by Brendan Dooley, 1–19. Surrey, UK: Ashgate, 2010.

Dreher, Klaus, ed. *Von der Preßfreiheit zur Pressefreiheit: Südwestdeutsche Zeitungsgeschichte von den Anfängen bis zur Gegenwart*. Stuttgart, Germany: Konrad Theiss, 1983.

Dussel, Konrad. *Deutsche Tagespresse im 19. und 20. Jahrhundert*. Münster, Germany: LIT, 2004.

Edelheim-Muehsam, Margaret T. "The Jewish Press in Germany." *Leo Baeck Institute Yearbook* 1 (1956): 163–76.

Efron, John, Steven Weitzman, and Matthias Lehmann. *The Jews: A History*. 2nd ed. Upper Saddle River, NJ: Pearson, 2014.

"Eighteenth-Century Currencies and Exchange Rates." Internet Archive Wayback Machine. Accessed July 28, 2020. http://web.archive.org/web/20070829061816/http://www.hudsonrivervalley.net/AMERICANBOOK/18.html.

Eisenmenger, Johann Andrea. *Jewry Revealed*. In *Nathan the Wise by Gotthold Ephraim Lessing with Related Documents*, edited by Ronald Schechter, 121–27. Boston: Bedford/St. Martin's Press, 2004.

Elon, Amos. *The Pity of It All: A Portrait of the German-Jewish Epoch 1743–1933*. New York: Picador, 2002.

Favretto, Illaria, and Xabier Itcaine, eds. *Protest, Popular Culture and Tradition in Modern and Contemporary Western Europe*. London: Palgrave Macmillan, 2017.

Feiner, Shmuel. *The Jewish Enlightenment*. Translated by Chaya Naor. Philadelphia: University of Pennsylvania Press, 2004.

———. *Moses Mendelssohn: Sage of Modernity*. Translated by Anthony Berris. New Haven, CT: Yale University Press, 2010.

Fetscher, Elmar B. *Die Konstanzer Seeblätter und die Pressezensur des Vormärz 1840/1841*. Sigmaringen, Germany: Jan Thorbecke, 1981.

Fischer, Bernhard. *Die Augsburger "Allgemeine Zeitung" 1798–1866, Register der Beiträger / Mitteiler*, part 1, 1798–1832. Munich: K. G. Saur, 2003.

———. *Die Augsburger "Allgemeine Zeitung" 1798–1866, Register der Beiträger / Mitteiler*, part 2, 1833–1849. Munich: K. G. Saur, 2004.

Fischer, Heinz-Dietrich. *Handbuch der politischen Presse in Deutschland 1480–1980: Synopse rechtlicher, struktureller und wirtschaftlicher Grundlagen der Tendenzpublizistik im Kommunikationsfeld*. Düsseldorf, Germany: Droste, 1981.

Fowler, Bridget. *The Obituary as Collective Memory*. Abingdon, UK: Routledge, 2007.

Frankel, Jonathan. *The Damascus Affair: "Ritual Murder," Politics, and the Jews in 1840*. Cambridge: Cambridge University Press, 1997.

French National Assembly. "The Constitution of France (September 3, 1791)." In *The Jew in the Modern World: A Documentary History*, 3rd ed., edited by Paul Mendes-Flohr and Jehuda Reinharz, 127. Oxford: Oxford University Press, 2011.

———. "Debate on the Eligibility of Jews for Citizenship (December 23, 1789)." In *The Jew in the Modern World: A Documentary History*, 3rd ed., edited by Paul Mendes-Flohr and Jehuda Reinharz, 123–25. Oxford: Oxford University Press, 2011.

———. "Declaration of the Rights of Man and of Citizen (August 26, 1789)." In *The Jew in the Modern World: A Documentary History*, 3rd ed., edited by Paul Mendes-Flohr and Jehuda Reinharz, 123. Oxford: Oxford University Press, 2011.

———. "Decree Recognizing the Sephardim as Citizens (January 28, 1790)." In *The Jew in the Modern World: A Documentary History*, 3rd ed., edited by Paul Mendes-Flohr and Jehuda Reinharz, 126. Oxford: Oxford University Press, 2011.

———. "The Emancipation of the Jews of France (September 28, 1791)." In *The Jew in the Modern World: A Documentary History*, 3rd ed., edited by Paul Mendes-Flohr and Jehuda Reinharz, 127–28. Oxford: Oxford University Press, 2011.

Fries, Jacob Friedrich. "On the Danger to the Well-Being and Character of the Germans Presented by the Jews." In *The Jew in the Modern World: A Documentary History*, 3rd ed., edited by Paul Mendes-Flohr and Jehuda Reinharz, 285–86. Oxford: Oxford University Press, 2011.

Führer, Karl Christian. "Contradicting Nazi Propaganda: Classified Advertisements as Documents of Jewish life in Nazi Germany, 1933–1938." *Media History* 18, no. 1 (November 2012): 65–76.

Gall, Lothar. *Der Liberalismus als regierende Partei: Das Grossherzogtum Baden zwischen Restauration und Reichsgründung*. Wiesbaden, Germany: Franz Steiner, 1968.

———, ed. *Vom alten zum neuen Bürgertum: Die mitteleuropäische Stadt im Umbruch 1780–1820*. Munich: R. Oldenbourg, 1991.

Gelber, Mark H., Jakob Hessing, and Robert Jütte, eds. *Integration und Ausgrenzung: Studien zur deutsch-jüdischen Literatur- und Kulturgeschichte von der Frühen Neuzeit bis zur Gegenwart*. Tübingen, Germany: Max Niemeyer, 2009.

Gestrich, Andreas. "The Public Sphere and the Habermas Debate." *German History* 24, no. 3 (2006): 413–30.

Giovannini, Norbert, Jo-Hannes Bauer, and Hans-Martin Mumm, eds. *Jüdisches Leben in Heidelberg: Studien zu einer unterbrochenen Geschichte*. Heidelberg, Germany: Das Wunderhorn, 1992.

Goetz, Thomas. *Poetik des Nachrufs: Zur Kultur der Nekrologie und zur Nachrufszene auf dem Theater*. Vienna: Böhlau, 2008.

Goldstein, Robert Justin, ed. *The War for the Public Mind: Political Censorship in Nineteenth-Century Europe*. Westport, CT: Praeger, 2000.

Götz, Franz, ed. *Gailingen: Geschichte einer Hochrhein-Gemeinde*. Gailingen, Germany: Hegau-Bibliothek, 2004.

Gotzmann, Andreas. "Der Geiger-Tiktin-Streit—Trennungskrise und Publizität." In *In Breslau zu Hause? Juden in einer mitteleuropäischen Metropole der Neuzeit*, edited by Manfred Heitling, Andreas Reinke, and Norbert Conrads, 81–98. Hamburg, Germany: Dölling und Gallitz, 2003.

———. *Jüdisches Recht im kulturellen Prozess: Die Wahrnehmung der Halacha im Deutschland des 19. Jahrhunderts*. Tübingen, Germany: J. C. B. Mohr, 1997.

———. "Zwischen Nation und Religion: Die deutschen Juden auf der Suche nach einer bürgerlichen Konfessionalität." In *Juden, Bürger, Deutsche: Zur Geschichte von Vielfalt und Differenz 1800–1933*, edited by Andreas Gotzmann, Rainer Liedtke, and Till van Rahden, 241–62. Tübingen, Germany: Mohr Siebeck, 2001.

Gotzmann, Andreas, Rainer Liedtke, and Till van Rahden, eds. *Juden, Bürger, Deutsche: Zur Geschichte von Vielfalt und Differenz 1800–1933*. Tübingen, Germany: Mohr Siebeck, 2001.

Grab, Walter, ed. *Gegenseitige Einflüsse deutscher und jüdischer Kultur: Von der Epoche der Aufklärung bis zur Weimarer Republik*. Jahrbuch des Instituts für deutsche Geschichte, Beiheft 4. Tel Aviv: Nateev, 1982.

Graff, Gil. *Separation of Church and State: Dina de-Malkhuta Dina in Jewish Law, 1750–1848*. Tuscaloosa: University of Alabama Press, 1985.

Green, Abigail. "1848 and Beyond: Jews in the National and International Politics of Secularism and Revolution." In *Jews, Liberalism, Antisemitism: A Global History*, edited by Abigail Green and Simon Levis Sullam, 341–64. London: Palgrave Macmillan, 2020.

———. "Intervening in the Public Sphere: German Governments and the Press, 1815–1870." *Historical Journal* 44, no. 1 (March 2001): 155–75.

———. "Rethinking Sir Moses Montefiore: Religion, Nationhood, and International Philanthropy in the Nineteenth Century." *American Historical Review* 110, no. 3 (June 2005): 630–58.

Green, Abigail, and Simon Levis Sullam, eds. *Jews, Liberalism, Antisemitism: A Global History*. London: Palgrave Macmillan, 2020.

Habel, Thomas. "Deutschsprachige Rezensionszeitschriften der Aufklärung: Zur Geschichte und Erschließung." In *Historische Presse und ihre Leser: Studien zu Zeitungen, Zeitschriften, Intelligenzblättern und Kalendern in Nordwestdeutschland*, edited by Peter Albrecht and Holger Böning, 41–76. Bremen, Germany: edition lumière, 2005.

Habermas, Jürgen. "Further Reflections on the Public Sphere." Translated by Thomas Burger. In *Habermas and the Public Sphere*, edited by Craig Calhoun, 422–61. Cambridge: Massachusetts Institute of Technology Press, 1992.

———. *Structural Transformation of the Public Sphere: An Inquiry into a Category of Bourgeois Society*. Translated by Thomas Burger and Frederick Lawrence. Cambridge: Massachusetts Institute of Technology Press, 1989.

Hall, Vance, and Ervin Malakaj, eds. *Writing for the German Literary Market in the Long Nineteenth Century*. Berlin: de Gruyter, 2020.

Harris, James F. *The People Speak! Anti-Semitism and Emancipation in Nineteenth-Century Bavaria*. Ann Arbor: University of Michigan Press, 1994.

Hartmann, Regina. "Leipziger Verleger, Presse und Autoren im Kampf um das 'freie Wort': Zum oppositionellen Kommunikationssystem des Vormärz." *Zeitschrift für Germanistik* 7, no. 1 (February 1986): 15–25.

Hay, Gerhard, ed. *Deutsche Abschiede*. Munich: Winkler, 1984.

Hecht, Louise. "'Geschichte der Grossen Israels': Die historiographische Bedeutung von Biographien in der frühen jüdischen Presse." In *Deutsche-jüdische Presse und jüdische Geschichte: Dokumente, Darstellungen, Wechselbeziehungen*, vol. 1, edited by Eleonore Lappin and Michael Nagel, 85–109. Bremen: edition lumière, 2008.

Heenemann, Horst. "Die Auflagenhöhe der deutschen Zeitungen: Ihre Entwicklung und ihre Probleme." PhD diss., Universität Leipzig, 1930.

Hein, Dieter. "Das Stiftungswesen als Instrument bürgerlichen Handels im 19. Jahrhundert." In *Stadt und Mäzenatentum*, edited by Bernhard von Kirchgässner and Hans-Peter Becht, 75–92. Stuttgart, Germany: Jan Thorbecke, 1997.

———. "1830–1848: Bürgerlicher Aufbruch." In *Geschichte der Stadt Mannheim*, Band 2, *1801–1914*, edited by Ulrich Nieß and Michael Caroli, 140–253. Heidelberg, Germany: Regionalkultur, 2007.

———. "Umbruch und Aufbruch: Bürgertum in Karlsruhe und Mannheim 1780–1820." In *Vom alten zum neuen Bürgertum: Die mitteleuropäische Stadt im Umbruch 1780–1820*, edited by Lothar Gall, 447–515. Munich: R. Oldenbourg, 1991.

Heine, Heinrich. "Spätere Note (1854) in 'Ludwig Marcus. Denkworte.'" In *Aus Vermischte Schriften*, vol. 1. Hamburg: Hoffmann and Campe, 1854. Published online by *Heinrich Heine Denkmal*, edited by Wolfgang Fricke. Accessed June 16, 2022. http://www.heinrich-heine-denkmal.de/heine-texte/marcus.shtml.

Heitling, Manfred, Andreas Reinke, and Norbert Conrads, eds. *In Breslau zu Hause? Juden in einer mitteleuropäischen Metropole der Neuzeit*. Hamburg, Germany: Dölling und Gallitz, 2003.

Hertz, Deborah. "Dueling for Emancipation: Jewish Masculinity in the Era of Napoleon." In *Jüdische Welten: Juden in Deutschland vom 18. Jahrhundert bis in die Gegenwart*, edited by Marion Kaplan and Beate Meyer, 69–85. Göttingen, Germany: Wallstein, 2005.

———. *How Jews Became Germans: The History of Conversion and Assimilation in Berlin*. New Haven, CT: Yale University Press, 2007.

———. "The Mendelssohns Leave Judaism, the Beers Reform Judaism." Shared History Project: 1700 Years of Jewish Life in German-Speaking Lands. Accessed May 26, 2021. https://sharedhistoryproject.org/essay/the-mendelssohns-leave-judaism-the-beers-reform-judaism.

———. "The Troubling Dialectic between Reform and Conversion in Biedermeier Berlin." In *Towards Normality? Acculturation and Modern German Jewry*, edited by Rainer Liedtke and David Rechter, 103–26. Tübingen, Germany: Mohr Siebeck, 2003.

Herzig, Arno. "Die Patriotische Gesellschaft und die Hamburger Juden." In *Stadt und Zivilgesellschaft: 250 Jahre Patriotische Gesellschaft von 1765 für Hamburg*.

Geschichte—Gegenwart—Perspektiven, edited by Sigrid Schambach, 59–68. Göttingen, Germany: Wallstein, 2015.

———. *Gabriel Riesser*. Hamburg, Germany: Ellert & Richter, 2008.

———. *Judentum und Emanzipation in Westfalen*. Münster, Germany: Aschendorff, 1973.

———. "Salomon Heines Testament und der Jurist Gabriel Riesser." In *Salomon Heine in Hamburg: Geschäft und Gemeinsinn*, edited by Beate Borowka-Clausberg, 64–72. Göttingen, Germany: Wallstein, 2013.

Herzig, Arno, Hans Otto Horch, and Robert Jütte, eds. *Judentum und Aufklärung: Jüdisches Selbstverständnis in der bürgerlichen Öffentlichkeit*. Göttingen, Germany: Vandenhoeck & Ruprecht, 2002.

Herzog, Dagmar. *Intimacy and Exclusion: Religious Politics in Pre-Revolutionary Baden*. Princeton, NJ: Princeton University Press, 1996.

Hess, Jonathan M. *Middlebrow Literature and the Making of German-Jewish Identity*. Stanford, CA: Stanford University Press, 2010.

———. "Studying Print Culture in the Digital Age: Some Thoughts on Future Directions in German Jewish Studies." *Leo Baeck Institute Yearbook* 54 (2009): 33–36.

Heuberger, Georg. "Jüdisches Mäzenatentum—von der religiösen Pflicht zum Faktor gesellschaftlicher Anerkennung." In *Stadt und Mäzenatentum*, edited by Bernhard von Kirchgässner and Hans-Peter Becht, 65–74. Stuttgart, Germany: Jan Thorbecke, 1997.

Heuser, Robert. "Die Bedeutung des Ortsbürgerrechts für die Emanzipation der Juden in Baden 1807–1831." PhD diss., Universität Heidelberg, 1971.

Hoefer, Frank Thomas. *Pressepolitik und Polizeistaat Metternichs: Die Überwachung von Presse und politischer Öffentlichkeit in Deutschland und den Nachbarstaaten durch das Mainzer Informationsbüro (1833–1848)*. Munich: K. G. Saur, 1983.

Hoffmann, Stefan-Ludwig. "Brothers or Strangers? Jews and Freemasons in Nineteenth-Century Germany." Translated by Pamela Selwyn. *German History* 18, no. 2 (April 2000): 143–61.

Holtz, Bärbel. "Einleitung: Staatlichkeit und Obstruction—Preussens Zensurpraxis als politisches Kulturphänomen." In *Preussens Zensurpraxis von 1819 bis 1849 in Quellen*, edited by Bärbel Holtz, 2–105. Berlin: de Gruyter Akademie Forschung, 2015.

———. *Preussens Zensurpraxis von 1819 bis 1849 in Quellen*. Berlin: de Gruyter Akademie Forschung, 2015.

Hübscher, Arthur. *Hundertfünfzig Jahre F. A. Brockhaus 1805 bis 1955*. Wiesbaden, Germany: F. A. Brockhaus, 1955.

Hüls, Elisabeth. "Die 'Deutsche Tribüne' 1831/32: Ein Oppositionsblatt im Vormärz. Entwicklung des Blattes, äußere Rahmenbedingungen und Zensurkämpfe." In *Deutsche Tribüne (1831–1832): Herausgegeben vom J.G.A.*

Wirth, Band 2, *Darstellung, Kommentar, Glossar, Register, Dokumente*, edited by Elisabeth Hüls and Hedwig Herold-Schmidt, 13–101. Munich: K. G. Saur, 2007.

Hüls, Elisabeth, and Hedwig Herold-Schmidt, ed. *Deutsche Tribüne (1831–1832): Herausgegeben vom J.G.A. Wirth*, Band 2, *Darstellung, Kommentar, Glossar, Register, Dokumente*. Munich: K. G. Saur, 2007.

Hundsnurscher, Franz, and Gerhard Taddey. *Die jüdischen Gemeinden in Baden: Denkmale, Geschichte, Schicksale*. Stuttgart, Germany: W. Kohlhammer, 1968.

Hyman, Paula. *The Jews of Modern France*. Berkeley: University of California Press, 1998.

Idelson-Shein, Iris. "Rabbis of the (Scientific) Revolution: Revealing the Hidden Corpus of Early Modern Translations Produced by Jewish Religious Thinkers." *American Historical Review* 126, no. 1 (March 2021): 54–81.

Jeggle, Utz. *Judendörfer in Württemberg*. 1969. New version, Tübingen, Germany: Tübinger Vereinigung f. Volkskunde e. V., 1999.

Jersch-Wenzel, Stefi. "Bevölkerungsentwickeln und Berufsstruktur." In *Deutsch-jüdische Geschichte in der Neuzeit*, Band 2, *Emanzipation und Akkulturation, 1780–1871*, edited by Michael A. Meyer and Michael Brenner, 57–95. Munich: C. H. Beck, 1996.

———. "Rechtslage und Emanzipation." In *Deutsch-jüdische Geschichte in der Neuzeit*, Band 2, *Emanzipation und Akkulturation, 1780–1871*, edited by Michael A. Meyer and Michael Brenner, 15–56. Munich: C. H. Beck, 1996.

Joskowicz, Ari. "Jews and Other Others." In *Jews, Liberalism, Antisemitism: A Global History*, edited by Abigail Green and Simon Levis Sullam, 69–93. London: Palgrave Macmillan, 2020.

———. *The Modernity of Others: Jewish Anti-Clericalism in Germany and France*. Palo Alto, CA: Stanford University Press, 2014.

Judd, Robin. *Contested Rituals: Circumcision, Kosher Butchering, and Jewish Political Life in Germany, 1843–1933*. Ithaca, NY: Cornell University Press, 2007.

———. "Samuel Holdheim and the German Circumcision Debates, 1843–1876." In *Redefining Judaism in an Age of Emancipation: Comparative Perspectives on Samuel Holdheim (1806–1860)*, edited by Christian Wiese, 127–42. London: Brill, 2006.

Kant, Immanuel. "An Answer to the Question: What Is Enlightenment?" In *What Is Enlightenment?: Eighteenth-Century Answers and Twentieth-Century Questions*, edited by James Schmidt, 58–64. Berkeley: University of California Press, 1996.

———. "The Euthanasia of Judaism (1798)." In *The Jew in the Modern World: A Documentary History*, 3rd ed., edited by Paul Mendes-Flohr and Jehuda Reinharz, 113–14. Oxford: Oxford University Press, 2011.

Kaplan, Marion, ed. *Jewish Daily Life in Germany, 1618–1945*. Oxford: Oxford University Press, 2005.

Kaplan, Marion, and Beate Meyer, eds. *Jüdische Welten: Juden in Deutschland vom 18.Jahrhundert bis in die Gegenwart*. Göttingen, Germany: Wallstein, 2005.

Karp, Jonathan. *The Politics of Jewish Commerce: Economic Thought and Emancipation in Europe, 1638–1848*. Cambridge: Cambridge University Press, 2008.

Katz, Jacob. *A House Divided: Orthodoxy and Schism in Nineteenth-Century Central European Jewry*. Translated by Ziporah Brody. Waltham, MA: Brandeis University Press, 1998.

———. *Jews and Freemasons in Europe 1723–1939*. Cambridge, MA: Harvard University Press, 1970.

Kaufmann, Uri R. "Das jüdische Schulwesen auf dem Lande: Baden und Elsaß im Vergleich 1770–1848." In *Jüdisches Leben auf dem Lande: Studien zur deutsch-jüdischen Geschichte*, edited by Monika Richarz and Reinhard Rürup, 293–326. Tübingen, Germany: Mohr Siebeck, 1997.

———. "Die jüdischen Landgemeinden des Bodenseekreises." In *Juden in Baden 1809–1984: 175 Jahre Oberrat der Israeliten Badens*, edited by Jael B. Paulus, 165–71. Karlsruhe: Oberrat der Israeliten Badens, 1984.

———. "Ein jüdischer Deutscher: Der Kampf des jungen Gabriel Riesser für die Gleichberechtigung der Juden 1830–1848." *Aschkenas* 13, no. 1 (2003): 211–36.

———. *Kleine Geschichte der Juden in Baden*. Karlsruhe: G. Braun, 2007.

Keller, Volker. *Jüdisches Leben in Mannheim*. Mannheim, Germany: Edition Quadrat, 1995.

Kennecke, Andreas. "Der 'HaMe'assef' und sein erster Herausgeber Isaac Euchel." In *Zwischen Selbstbehauptung und Verfolgung: Deutsch-jüdische Zeitungen und Zeitschriften von der Aufklärung bis zum Nationalsozialismus*, edited by Michael Nagel, 67–81. Hildesheim, Germany: Olms, 2002.

———. "HaMe'assef: Die erste modern Zeitschrift der Juden in Deutschland." In "Haskalah: Die jüdische Aufklärung in Deutschland 1769–1812," edited by Christoph Schulte, special issue, *Das achtzehnte Jahrhundert* 23, no. 2 (1999): 176–99.

Knüpfer, Volker. *Presse und Liberalismus in Sachsen: Positionen der bürgerlichen Presse im frühen 19. Jahrhundert*. Cologne: Böhlau, 1996.

Kober, Adolf. "Emancipation's Impact on the Education and Vocational Training of German Jewry." *Jewish Social Studies* 16, no. 1 (January 1954): 3–32.

———. "Emancipation's Impact on the Education and Vocational Training of German Jewry." *Jewish Social Studies* 16, no. 2 (April 1954): 151–76.

Kocka, Jürgen. "The European Pattern and the German Case." In *Bourgeois Society in Nineteenth Century Europe*, edited by Jürgen Kocka and Allan Mitchell, 3–39. Oxford, UK: Berg, 1993.

Kocka, Jürgen, and Allan Mitchell, eds. *Bourgeois Society in Nineteenth Century Europe*. Oxford, UK: Berg, 1993.

Koszyk, Kurt. *Geschichte der deutschen Presse*, Teil 2, *Deutsche Presse im 19. Jahrhundert*. Berlin: Colloquium, 1966.

Krahl, Vanessa. "Das Selbstverständnis der Reformrabbiner und die Entwicklung der deutsch-jüdischen Reformbewegung bis 1848." PhD diss., Technische Universität Berlin, 2011.

Krauss, Martin. "Zwischen Emanzipation und Antisemitismus (1802 bis 1862)." In *Geschichte der Juden in Heidelberg*, edited by Peter Blum, 154–216. Heidelberg, Germany: Brigitte Guderjahn, 1996.

Kümper, Michael, Barbara Rosch, Ulrike Schnieder, and Helen Thein, eds. *Makom: Orte und Räume im Judentum: Real. Abstrakt. Imaginär*. Hildesheim, Germany: Olms, 2007.

Kustermann, Abraham Peter, and Dieter R. Bauer, eds. *Jüdisches Leben im Bodenseeraum: Zur Geschichte des alemannischen Judentums mit Thesen zum christlich-jüdischen Gespräch*. Ostfildern, Germany: Schwabenverlag, 1994.

———. "Zum Stichwort: Jüdisches Leben im Bodenseeraum." In *Jüdisches Leben im Bodenseeraum: Zur Geschichte des alemannischen Judentums mit Thesen zum christlich-jüdischen Gespräch*, edited by Abraham P. Kustermann and Dieter R. Bauer, 9–16. Ostfildern, Germany: Schwabenverlag, 1994.

Ladwig-Winter, Simone. *Freiheit und Bindung: Zur Geschichte der Jüdischen Reformgemeinde zu Berlin von den Anfängen bis zu ihrem Ende 1939*. Teetz, Germany: Hentrich & Hentrich, 2004.

Langewiesche, Dieter. *Liberalism in Germany*. Translated by Christiane Banerji. Houndmills, UK: Macmillan, 2000.

Lappin, Eleonore, and Michael Nagel, eds. *Deutsche-jüdische Presse und jüdische Geschichte: Dokumente, Darstellungen, Wechselbeziehungen*. Vol. 1. Bremen, Germany: edition lumière, 2008.

———. Introduction to *Deutsche-jüdische Presse und jüdische Geschichte: Dokumente, Darstellungen, Wechselbeziehungen*, vol. 1, edited by Eleonore Lappin and Michael Nagel, 9–22. Bremen, Germany: edition lumière, 2008.

Lässig, Simone. "Bildung als *kulturelles Kapital*? Jüdische Schulprojekte in der Frühphase der Emanzipation." In *Juden, Bürger, Deutsche: Zur Geschichte von Vielfalt und Differenz 1800–1933*, edited by Andreas Gotzmann, Rainer Liedtke, and Till van Rahden, 263–98. Tübingen, Germany: Mohr Siebeck, 2001.

———. "*Bürgerlichkeit*, Patronage, and Communal Liberalism in German, 1871–1914." In *Philanthropy, Patronage, and Civil Society*, edited by Thomas Adam, 198–218. Bloomington: Indiana University Press, 2004.

———. *Jüdische Wege ins Bürgertum: Kulturelles Kapital und Sozialer Aufstieg im 19. Jahrhundert*. Göttingen, Germany: Vandenhoeck & Ruprecht, 2004.

———. "Sprachwandel und Verbürgerlichung: Zur Bedeutung der Sprache im innerjüdischen Modernisierungsprozeß des frühen 19. Jahrhunderts." *Historische Zeitschrift* 270, no. 3 (June 2000): 617–67.

Lässig, Simone, and Miriam Rürup. "Introduction: What Made a Space 'Jewish'? Reconsidering a Category of Modern German History." In *Space & Spatiality in Modern German-Jewish History*, edited by Simone Lässig and Miriam Rürup, 1–20. New York: Berghahn, 2017.

———, ed. *Space and Spatiality in Modern German-Jewish History*. New York: Berghahn, 2017.

Leff, Lisa Moses. "Liberalism and Antisemitism: A Reassessment from the Peripheries." In *Jews, Liberalism, Antisemitism: A Global History*, edited by Abigail Green and Simon Levis Sullam, 23–45. London: Palgrave Macmillan, 2020.

Leibman, Laura Arnold. "The Material of Race: Carribean Jews, Clothing, and Manhood in the Age of Emancipation and Liberal Revolution." In *Jews, Liberalism, Antisemitism: A Global History*, edited by Abigail Green and Simon Levis Sullam, 97–130. London: Palgrave Macmillan, 2020.

Lenhard, Philipp. *Volk oder Religion? Die Entstehung moderner jüdischer Ethnizität in Frankreich und Deutschland 1782–1848*. Göttingen, Germany: Vandenhoeck & Ruprecht, 2014.

Lenman, Robin. "Germany." In *The War for the Public Mind: Political Censorship in Nineteenth-Century Europe*, edited by Robert Justin Goldstein, 35–79. Westport, CT: Praeger, 2000.

Leuschner, Udo. *Vom Intelligenzblatt zur demokratischen Kampfpresse: Mannheimer Zeitungen bis 1850*. (1973) 2008. Accessed July 28, 2020. www.udo-leuschner.de/zeitungsgeschichte.

Levinson, Pnina Navé. "Aus dem religiösen Leben Orthodoxie und Liberalismus." In *Juden in Baden 1809–1984: 175 Jahre Oberrat der Israeliten Badens*, edited by Jael B. Paulus, 91–108. Karlsruhe: Oberrat der Israeliten Badens, 1984.

Liberles, Robert. *Jews Welcome Coffee: Tradition and Innovation in Early Modern Germany*. New Brunswick, NJ: Rutgers University Press, 2012.

———. *Religious Conflict in Social Context: The Resurgence of Orthodox Judaism in Frankfurt am Main 1838–1877*. Westport, CT: Greenwood Press, 1985.

———. "Was There a Jewish Movement for Emancipation?" *Leo Baeck Institute Yearbook* 31 (1986): 35–49.

Liedtke, Rainer. *Jewish Welfare in Hamburg and Manchester c. 1850–1914*. Oxford, UK: Clarendon Press, 1998.

Liedtke, Rainer, and David Rechter, eds. *Towards Normality? Acculturation and Modern German Jewry*. Tübingen, Germany: Mohr Siebeck, 2003.

Liepach, Martin, Gabriela Melishek, and Josef Seethaler, eds. *Jewish Images in the Media*. Relation, n.s. Vol. 2. Vienna: Austrian Academy of Sciences Press, 2007.

Lindemann, Margot. *Deutsche Presse bis 1815*. Berlin: Colloquium, 1969.
Lipphardt, Anna, Julia Brauch, and Alexandra Nocke. "Exploring Jewish Space: An Approach." In *Jewish Topographies: Visions of Space, Traditions of Place*, edited by Anna Lipphardt, Julia Brauch, and Alexandra Nocke, 1–23. Hampshire, UK: Ashgate, 2008.
———, eds. *Jewish Topographies: Visions of Space, Traditions of Place*. Hampshire, UK: Ashgate, 2008.
Lowenstein, Steven M. "The Beginning of Integration: 1780–1870." In *Jewish Daily Life in Germany, 1618–1945*, edited by Marion Kaplan, 93–171. Oxford: Oxford University Press, 2005.
———. *The Berlin Jewish Community: Enlightenment, Family, and Crisis, 1770–1830*. New York: Oxford University Press, 1994.
———. "The 1840s and the Creation of the German-Jewish Religious Reform Movement." In *Revolution and Evolution: 1848 in German-Jewish History*, edited by Werner E. Mosse, Arnold Paucker, and Reinhard Rürup, 255–97. Tübingen, Germany: J. C. B. Mohr, 1981.
Lowenstein, Steven M., Paul Mendes-Flohr, Peter Pulzer, and Monika Richarz, eds. *German-Jewish History in Modern Times*. Vol. 3, *Integration in Dispute, 1871–1918*. New York: Columbia University Press, 1997.
Lückemeier, Kai. *Information als Verblendung: Die Geschichte der Presse und der öffentlichen Meinung im 19. Jahrhundert*. Stuttgart, Germany: Ibidem, 2001.
Maciejko, Pawel. "The Jews' Entry into the Public Sphere—The Emden-Eibeschütz Controversy Reconsidered." *Simon Dubnow Institute Yearbook* 6 (2007): 135–54.
Magnus, Shulamit S. *Jewish Emancipation in a German City: Cologne, 1798–1871*. Stanford, CA: Stanford University Press, 1997.
Maimon, Salomon. *Salomon Maimon: An Autobiography*. Translated by J. Clark Murray. Urbana: University of Illinois Press, 2001.
Maimonides, Moses. *Mishneh Torah: Gifts to the Poor 10:7–14*. Sefaria.org. Accessed September 18, 2020. https://www.sefaria.org/Mishneh_Torah%2C_Gifts_to_the_Poor.10.7-14?lang=bi.
Marten-Finnis, Susanne, Markus Bauer, and Markus Winkler, eds. *Die jüdische Presse: Forschungsmethoden—Erfahrungen—Ergebnisse*. Bremen, Germany: edition lumière, 2007.
———. "Zum Geleit." In *Die jüdische Presse: Forschungsmethoden—Erfahrungen—Ergebnisse*, edited by Susanne Marten-Finnis, Markus Bauer, and Markus Winkler, 7–16. Bremen, Germany: edition lumière, 2007.
Marten-Finnis, Susanne, and Markus Winkler, eds. *Die jüdische Presse in europäischen Kontext, 1868–1990*. Bremen, Germany: edition lumière, 2006.
Maurer, Helmut. *Konstanz im Mittelalter*, Band 2, *Vom Konzil bis zum Beginn des 16. Jahrhunderts*. Konstanz, Germany: Stadler, 1989.

McNeely, Ian F. *The Emancipation of Writing: German Civil Society in the Making, 1790s–1820s*. Berkeley: University of California Press, 2003.

Meiners, Werner. "Oldenburg." In *Historisches Handbuch der jüdischen Gemeinden in Niedersachsen und Bremen*, edited by Herbert Obenaus, 1172–96. Göttingen, Germany: Wallstein, 2005.

Melton, James Van Horn. *The Rise of the Public in Enlightenment Europe*. Cambridge: Cambridge University Press, 2001.

Mendes-Flohr, Paul. *German Jews: A Dual Identity*. New Haven, CT: Yale University Press, 1999.

Mendes-Flohr, Paul, and Jehuda Reinharz, eds. *The Jew in the Modern World: A Documentary History*. New York: Oxford University Press, 1995.

Meola, David A. "Becoming Public: Jews in Baden and Hannover and Their Role in the German Press, 1815–1848." PhD diss., University of British Columbia, 2012.

———. "Making News: Jewish Germans and the Expansion of Print Culture during the Vormärz." In *Writing for the German Literary Market in the Long Nineteenth Century*, edited by Vance Hall and Ervin Malakaj, 121–46. Berlin: de Gruyter, 2020.

———. "Mirror of Competing Claims: Antisemitism, Honor, and Citizenship in Vormärz Germany." *Antisemitism Studies* 4, no. 1 (April 2020): 3–47.

———. "'Revolutionary Behavior'—How German Jews Became Masters of Their Own Domain, 1750–1850." *Eighteenth-Century Thought* 6 (2016): 171–203.

Meyer, Michael A. "Alienated Intellectuals in the Camp of Religious Reform: The Frankfurt Reformfreunde, 1842–1845." *AJS Review* 6 (1981): 61–86.

———. "Deutsch werden, jüdisch bleiben." In *Deutsch-jüdische Geschichte in der Neuzeit*, Band 2, *Emanzipation und Akkulturation, 1780–1871*, edited by Michael A. Meyer and Michael Brenner, 208–59. Munich: C. H. Beck, 1996.

———. ed. *German-Jewish History in Modern Times*. Vol. 1, *Tradition and Enlightenment: 1600–1780*. New York: Columbia University Press, 1996.

———., "Jewish Self-Understanding." In *German-Jewish History in Modern Times*. Vol. 2, *Emancipation and Acculturation, 1780–1871*, edited by Michael A. Meyer. New York: Columbia University Press, 1997.

———. *Judaism within Modernity: Essays of Jewish History and Religion*. Detroit, MI: Wayne State University Press, 2001.

———. "'Most of My Brethren Find Me Unacceptable': The Controversial Career of Rabbi Samuel Holdheim." *Jewish Social Studies* 9, no. 3 (Spring/Summer 2003): 1–19.

———. *Response to Modernity: A History of the Reform Movement in Judaism*. New York: Oxford University Press, 1988.

Meyer, Michael A., and Michael Brenner, eds. *Deutsch-jüdische Geschichte in der Neuzeit*, Band 2, *Emanzipation und Akkulturation, 1780–1871*. Munich: C. H. Beck, 1996.

———, eds. *German-Jewish History in Modern Times*. Vol. 2, *Emancipation and Acculturation, 1780–1871*. New York: Columbia University Press, 1997.

Michaelis, Johann David. "Arguments against Dohm (1782)." In *The Jew in the Modern World: A Documentary History*, 3rd ed., edited by Paul Mendes-Flohr and Jehuda Reinharz, 34–36. Oxford: Oxford University Press, 2011.

Moggach, Douglas. "Bruno Bauer." *Stanford Encyclopedia of Philosophy*, March 7, 2002; rev. February 7, 2022. Accessed July 24, 2020. https://plato.stanford.edu/entries/bauer/.

Moos, Samuel (Semi), ed. *Geschichte der Juden im Hegaudorf Randegg*. Gottmadingen, Germany: Eckerlin, 1986.

Moran, Daniel. "Cotta and Napoleon: The French Pursuit of the *Allgemeine Zeitung*." *Central European History* 14, no. 2 (June 1981): 91–109.

———. *Toward the Century of Words: Johann Cotta and the Politics of the Public Realm in Germany, 1795–1832*. Berkeley: University of California Press, 1990.

Mosse, George. *German Jews beyond Judaism*. Bloomington: Indiana University Press, 1985.

Mosse, Werner E., ed. *Das Deutsche Judentum und der Liberalismus: Dokumentation eines internationalen Seminars der Friedrich-Naumann-Stiftung in Zusammenarbeit mit dem Leo Baeck Institute, London*. Sankt Augustin, Germany: Comdok-Verlagsabteilung, 1986.

Mosse, Werner E., Arnold Paucker, and Reinhard Rürup, eds. *Revolution and Evolution: 1848 in German-Jewish History*. Tübingen, Germany: J. C. B. Mohr, 1981.

Müller, Hildegard. *Liberale Presse im badischen Vormärz: Die Presse der Kammerliberalen und ihre Zentralfigur Karl Mathy 1840–1848*. Heidelberg, Germany: Carl Winter Universitätsverlag, 1986.

Mumm, Hans-Martin. "'Denket nicht: Wir wollen's beim Alten lassen.' Die Jahre der Emanzipation 1803 bis 1862." In *Jüdisches Leben in Heidelberg: Studien zu einer unterbrochenen Geschichte*, edited by Norbert Giovannini, Jo-Hannes Bauer, and Hans-Martin Mumm, 21–60. Heidelberg, Germany: Das Wunderhorn, 1992.

Mustafa, Sam. *Germany in the Modern World: A New History*. Plymouth, UK: Rowman & Littlefield, 2011.

Nagel, Michael. "Jüdische Presse und jüdische Geschichte: Möglichkeiten und Probleme in Forschung und Darstellung." In *Die jüdische Presse: Forschungsmethoden—Erfahrungen—Ergebnisse*, edited by Susanne Marten-Finnis, Markus Bauer, and Markus Winkler, 19–37. Bremen, Germany: edition lumière, 2007.

———, ed. *Zwischen Selbstbehauptung und Verfolgung: Deutsch-jüdische Zeitungen und Zeitschriften von der Aufklärung bis zum Nationalsozialismus*. Hildesheim, Germany: Olms, 2002.

Nieß, Ulrich, and Michael Caroli, eds. *Geschichte der Stadt Mannheim, Band 2, 1801–1914*. Heidelberg, Germany: Regionalkultur, 2007.

Obenaus, Herbert, ed. *Historisches Handbuch der jüdischen Gemeinden in Niedersachsen und Bremen*. 2 vols. Göttingen, Germany: Wallstein, 2005.

Oberrat der Israeliten Badens. *Jüdisches Leben in Baden 1809 bis 2009: 200 Jahre Oberrat der Israeliten Badens. Festschrift*. Ostfildern, Germany: Jan Thorbecke, 2009.

Officer, Lawrence H. "Five Ways to Compute the Relative Value of a UK Pound Amount, 1830 to Present." MeasuringWorth, 2011. Accessed July 28, 2020. http://www.measuringworth.com/ukcompare/.

O'Grady, Patricia F. *Thales of Miletus: The Beginnings of Western Science and Philosophy*. Aldershot, UK: Ashgate, 2002.

Ohles, Frederik. *Germany's Rude Awakening: Censorship in the Land of the Brothers Grimm*. Kent, OH: Kent State University Press, 1992.

Paulus, Jael B. "Emanzipation und Reaktion 1809–1862." In *Juden in Karlsruhe: Beiträge zu ihrer Geschichte bis zur nationalsozialistischen Machtergreifung*, edited by Heinz Schmitt, Ernst Otto Bräunche, and Manfred Koch, 81–94. Karlsruhe, Germany: Badenia, 1988.

———, ed. *Juden in Baden, 1809–1984: 175 Jahre Oberrat der Israeliten Badens*. Karlsruhe, Germany: Oberrat der Israeliten Badens, 1984.

———. "Jüdischer Kultus im Widerstreit unterschiedlicher innerjüdischer Gruppierungen." In *Juden in Karlsruhe: Beiträge zu ihrer Geschichte bis zur nationalsozialistischen Machtergreifung*, edited by Heinz Schmitt, Ernst Otto Bräunche, and Manfred Koch, 247–56. Karlsruhe, Germany: Badenia, 1988.

Pegelow, Thomas. "'German Jews,' 'National Jews,' 'Jewish *Volk*,' or 'Racial Jews'? The Constitution and Contestation of 'Jewishness' in Newspapers of Nazi Germany, 1933–1938." *Central European History* 35, no. 2 (2002): 195–221.

Penslar, Derek. "Introduction: The Press and the Jewish Public Sphere." *Jewish History* 14 (2000): 3–8.

———. *Shylock's Children: Economics and Jewish Identity in Modern Europe*. Berkeley: University of California Press, 2001.

Philipson, David. "The Breslau Rabbinical Conference." *Jewish Quarterly Review* 18, no. 4 (July 1906): 621–33.

———. "The Frankfort Rabbinical Conference, 1845." *Jewish Quarterly Review* 18, no. 2 (January 1906): 251–90.

———. "The Rabbinical Conferences, 1844–6." *Jewish Quarterly Review* 17, no. 4 (July 1905): 656–89.

———. *The Reform Movement in Judaism*. 1907. Reprint, New York: Ktav, 1967.

———. "The Reform Movement in Judaism. IV. The Frankfort Society of the Friends of Reform." *Jewish Quarterly Review* 17, no. 2 (January 1905): 307–53.

Pinsker, Shacher. *A Rich Brew: How Cafés Created Modern Jewish Culture*. New York: New York University Press, 2018.

Pister, Sarah. "Stadtfremde in Mannheim: Zur Aufnahme und Integration von In- und Ausländern in eine landesherrliche Stadt des späten 18. und frühen 19. Jahrhunderts." PhD diss., University of Mannheim, 2021.

Plaut, W. Gunther, Solomon Bennett Freehof, and Howard A. Berman. *The Rise of Reform Judaism: A Sourcebook of Its European Origins*. New York: World Union for Progressive Judaism, 1963.

Presner, Todd Samuel. *Mobile Modernity: German, Jews, Trains*. New York: Columbia University Press, 2007.

Preuß, Monika. *Gelehrte Juden: Lernen als Frömmigkeitsideal in der frühen Neuzeit*. Göttingen, Germany: Wallstein, 2007.

Pulzer, Peter. "Legal Equality and Public Life." In *German-Jewish History in Modern Times*. Vol. 3, *Integration in Dispute, 1871–1918*, edited by Steven M. Lowenstein, Paul Mendes-Flohr, Peter Pulzer, and Monika Richarz, 153–95. New York: Columbia University Press, 1997.

Raab, Heinrich. *Revolutionäre in Baden 1848/49: Biographisches Inventar für die Quellen im Generallandesarchiv Karlsruhe und im Staatsarchiv Freiburg*. Stuttgart, Germany: W. Kohlhammer, 1998.

Ramon, Esther. "Geschichte der jüdischen Erziehung in Karlsruhe von 1730–1933." In *Juden in Karlsruhe: Beiträge zu ihrer Geschichte bis zur nationalsozialistischen Machtergreifung*, edited by Heinz Schmitt, Ernst Otto Bräunche, and Manfred Koch, 301–10. Karlsruhe, Germany: Badenia, 1988.

Reinhalter, Helmut, ed. *Die Anfänge des Liberalismus und der Demokratie in Deutschland und Österreich 1830–1848/49*. Frankfurt: Lang, 2002.

Reissner, Hanns Günther. *Edward Gans. Ein Leben im Vormärz*. Tübingen, Germany: Mohr Siebeck, 1965.

Retallack, James. "From Pariah to Professional? The Journalist in German Society and Politics, from the Late Enlightenment to the Rise of Hitler." *German Studies Review* 16, no. 2 (May 1993): 175–223.

Reuveni, Gideon, and Diana Franklin, eds. *The Future of the German-Jewish Past: Memory and the Question of Antisemitism*. Lafayette, IN: Purdue University Press, 2021.

Richardson, J. G., ed. *Handbook of Theory and Research for the Sociology of Education*. New York: Greenwood Press, 1986.

Richarz, Monika. "Ländliches Judentum als Problem der Forschung." In *Jüdisches Leben auf dem Lande: Studien zur deutsch-jüdischen Geschichte*, edited by Monika Richarz and Reinhard Rürup, 1–8. Tübingen, Germany: Mohr Siebeck, 1997.

Richarz, Monika, and Reinhard Rürup, eds. *Jüdisches Leben auf dem Lande: Studien zur deutsch-jüdischen Geschichte*. Tübingen, Germany: Mohr Siebeck, 1997.

Rietveld-van Wingerden, Marjoke, and Nelleke Bakker. "Education and the Emancipation of Jewish Girls in the Nineteenth Century: The Case of the Netherlands." *History of Education Quarterly* 44, no. 2 (Summer 2004): 202–21.

Rinott, Moshe. "Gabriel Riesser: Fighter for Jewish Emancipation." *Leo Baeck Institute* Yearbook 7 (1962): 11–38.

Roemer, Nils. *Jewish Scholarship and Culture in Nineteenth-Century Germany: Between History and Faith*. Madison: University of Wisconsin Press, 2005.

Rohrbacher, Stephan. *Gewalt in Biedermeier: Antijüdische Ausschreitungen in Vormärz und Revolution (1815–1848/9)*. Frankfurt: Campus, 1993.

Roman Republic. "First Emancipation in Rome (February 1799)." In *The Jew in the Modern World: A Documentary History*, 3rd ed., edited by Paul Mendes-Flohr and Jehuda Reinharz, 145. Oxford: Oxford University Press, 2011.

Roming, Gisela. "Geschichte der jüdischen Gemeinde Gailingen." In *Gailingen: Geschichte einer Hochrhein-Gemeinde*, edited by Franz Götz, 291–380. Gailingen, Germany: Hegau-Bibliothek, 2004.

———. "Religiosität und Bildung in Jüdischen Landgemeinden." In *Jüdisches Leben im Bodenseeraum: Zur Geschichte des alemannischen Judentums mit Thesen zum christlich-jüdischen Gespräch*, edited by Abraham P. Kustermann and Dieter R. Bauer, 91–108. Ostfildern, Germany: Schwabenverlag, 1994.

———. "Zur Rechts-, Wirtschafts- und Sozialgeschichte von Gailingen." In *Gailingen: Geschichte einer Hochrhein-Gemeinde*, edited by Franz Götz, 85–128. Gailingen, Germany: Hegau-Bibliothek, 2004.

Rose, Paul Lawrence. *German Question/Jewish Question: Revolutionary Antisemitism from Kant to Wagner*. Princeton, NJ: Princeton University Press, 1990.

Rosenstreich, Nathan. *Jews and German Philosophy: The Polemics of Emancipation*. New York: Schocken, 1984.

Ross, Corey. *Media and the Making of Modern Germany: Mass Communication, Society, and Politics from the Empire to the Third Reich*. Oxford: Oxford University Press, 2008.

Rozin, Mordecai. *The Rich and the Poor: Jewish Philanthropy and Social Control in Nineteenth-Century London*. Brighton, UK: Sussex Academic Press, 1999.

Rürup, Reinhard. *Emanzipation und Antisemitismus*. Frankfurt: Fischer Taschenbuch, 1987.

———. "German Liberalism and the Emancipation of the Jews." *Leo Baeck Institute Yearbook* 20 (1975): 59–68.

———. "Jewish Emancipation and the Vision of Civil Society in Germany." *Leo Baeck Institute Yearbook* 51 (2006): 43–50.

Salomon, Ludwig. *Geschichte des Deutschen Zeitungswesens: Von den ersten Anfängen bis zur Wiederaufrichtung des Deutschen Reiches*, Dritter Band, *Das Zeitungswesen seit 1814.* Oldenburg, Germany: Schulzesche Hof Buchhandlung und Hofbuchdruckerei, 1906.

Sauer, Paul. "Die Judendörfer im Hegau." In *Geschichte der Juden im Hegaudorf Randegg*, edited by Samuel (Semi) Moos, 19–32. Gottmadingen, Germany: Eckerlin, 1986.

——. "Die Judengemeinden im nördlichen Bodenseeraum." In *Jüdisches Leben im Bodenseeraum: Zur Geschichte des alemannischen Judentums mit Thesen zum christlich-jüdischen Gespräch*, edited by Abraham P. Kustermann and Dieter R. Bauer, 37–58. Ostfildern, Germany: Schwabenverlag, 1994.

Schad, Margit. "The Problems of Moderate Reform: The History of the Berlin Liturgical Reforms, 1844–1862." Translated by Thomas Dunlap. In *Redefining Judaism in an Age of Emancipation: Comparative Perspectives on Samuel Holdheim (1806–1860)*, edited by Christian Wiese, 169–90. London: Brill, 2006.

Schambach, Sigrid, ed. *Stadt und Zivilgesellschaft: 250 Jahre Patriotische Gesellschaft von 1765 für Hamburg; Geschichte—Gegenwart—Perspektiven.* Göttingen, Germany: Wallstein, 2015.

Scherner, Karl Otto. *Advokaten, Revolutionäre, Anwälte: Die Geschichte der Mannheimer Anwaltschaft.* Sigmaringen, Germany: Jan Thorbecke, 1997.

Schimpf, Rainer. "Der 'Freisinnige' und der Kampf der badischen Liberalen für die Pressefreiheit." In *Die Anfänge des Liberalismus und der Demokratie in Deutschland und Österreich 1830–1848/49*, edited by Helmut Reinhalter, 157–90. Frankfurt: Lang, 2002.

Schmidt, James, ed. *What Is Enlightenment?: Eighteenth-Century Answers and Twentieth-Century Questions.* Berkeley: University of California Press, 1996.

Schmitt, Heinz, Ernst Otto Bräunche, and Manfred Koch, eds. *Juden in Karlsruhe: Beiträge zu ihrer Geschichte bis zur nationalsozialistischen Machtergreifung.* Karlsruhe, Germany: Badenia, 1988.

Schneble, Martin. "Alemannische und jiddische Mundart in Gailingen." In *Gailingen: Geschichte einer Hochrhein-Gemeinde*, edited by Franz Götz, 477–89. Gailingen, Germany: Hegau-Bibliothek, 2004.

Scholem, Gershom. *Sabbatai Sevi: The Mystical Messiah, 1626–1676.* Princeton, NJ: Princeton University Press, 1976.

Schorsch, Ismar. "Emancipation and the Crisis of Religious Authority: The Emergence of the Modern Rabbinate." In *Revolution and Evolution: 1848 in German-Jewish History*, edited by Werner E. Mosse, Arnold Paucker, and Reinhard Rürup, 205–48. Tübingen, Germany: J. C. B. Mohr, 1981.

——. *From Text to Context: The Turn to History in Modern History.* Waltham, MA: Brandeis University Press, 2003.

Schwartzman, Sylvan D. *Reform Judaism in the Making.* New York: Union of American Hebrew Congregations, 1955.

Schwemer, Richard. *Geschichte der Freien Stadt Frankfurt a.M., Band 3.* Frankfurt, Germany: J. Baer, 1915.

Seligmann, Caesar. *Geschichte der jüdischen Reformbewegung: Von Mendelssohn bis zur Gegenwart.* Frankfurt: J. Kauffmann, 1922.

Sheehan, James. *German Liberalism in the Nineteenth Century.* Chicago: University of Chicago Press, 1978.

Siegel, Björn. "Jewish Philanthropy and the Formation of Modernity: Baron de Hirsch and His Vision of Jewish Spaces in European Societies." In *Space and Spatiality in Modern German-Jewish History,* edited by Simone Lässig and Miriam Rürup, 179–96. London: Berghahn, 2017.

Skolnik, Jonathan. *Jewish Pasts, German Fictions: History, Memory, and Minority Culture in Germany, 1824–1955.* Stanford, CA: Stanford University Press, 2014.

Smith, Helmut Walser. *Germany: A Nation in Its Time: Before, during, and after Nationalism, 1500–2000.* New York: Liveright, 2020.

Sorkin, David. *Jewish Emancipation: A History across Five Centuries.* Princeton, NJ: Princeton University Press, 2019.

———. *Moses Mendelssohn and the Religious Enlightenment.* Berkeley: University of California Press, 1996.

———. *The Transformation of German Jewry, 1780–1840.* New York: Oxford University Press, 1987.

Sperber, Haim. "Philanthropy and Social Control in the Anglo-Jewish Community during the Mid-Nineteenth Century (1850–1880)." *Journal of Modern Jewish Studies* 11, no. 1 (March 2012): 85–101.

Starck, Nigel. *Life after Death: The Art of the Obituary.* Melbourne: Melbourne University Press, 2006.

Steckmest, Sylvia. "Salomon Heine—Bankier und Philanthrop." In *Stadt und Zivilgesellschaft: 250 Jahre Patriotische Gesellschaft von 1765 für Hamburg; Geschichte—Gegenwart—Perspektiven,* edited by Sigrid Schambach, 94–95. Göttingen, Germany: Wallstein, 2015.

Stegmaier, Günter. "Von der Zensur zur Pressefreiheit." In *Von der Preßfreiheit zur Pressefreiheit: Südwestdeutsche Zeitungsgeschichte von den Anfängen bis zur Gegenwart,* edited by Klaus Dreher, 129–53. Stuttgart, Germany: Konrad Theiss, 1983.

Stein, Sarah Abrevaya. *Making Jews Modern: The Yiddish and Ladino Press in the Russian and Ottoman Empires.* Bloomington: Indiana University Press, 2004.

Stein, Siegfried. "Die Zeitschrift Sulamith." *Zeitschrift für die Geschichte der Juden in Deutschland* 7 (1937): 193–226.

Stein, Theodor. "Südwestdeutsche Zeitungsgeschichte: Ein Überblick über die Anfänge bis zum Jahre 1933." In *Von der Preßfreiheit zur Pressefreiheit: Südwestdeutsche Zeitungsgeschichte von den Anfängen bis zur Gegenwart,* edited by Klaus Dreher, 21–100. Stuttgart: Konrad Theiss, 1983.

Stockert, Harald. "1801–1815: Ein 'goldenes Zeitalter' unterm badischen Greif?" In *Geschichte der Stadt Mannheim. Band II 1801–1914*, edited by Ulrich Nieß and Michael Caroli, 1–57. Heidelberg: Regionalkultur, 2007.

Stoetzler, Marcel. *The State, the Nation, & the Jews: Liberalism and the Antisemitism Dispute in Bismarck's Germany*. Lincoln: University of Nebraska Press, 2008.

Storm, Jill. "Culture and Exchange: The Jews of Königsberg, 1700–1820." PhD diss., Washington University in St. Louis, 2010.

Stross, Wendy Anne. "Magazines of Mortality: A Cultural History of the Obituary in Eighteenth-Century London." PhD diss., University of Toronto, 2004.

Stude, Jürgen. *Geschichte der Juden in Landkreis Karlsruhe*. Karlsruhe, Germany: G. Braun, 1990.

Tanakh. Philadelphia: Jewish Publication Society, 1985.

Tauschwitz, Hanno. *Presse und Revolution 1848/49 in Baden: Ein Beitrag zur Sozialgeschichte der periodischen Literatur und zu ihrem Einfluss auf die Geschichte der badischen Revolution 1848/49*. Heidelberg, Germany: Esprint, 1981.

Timms, Edward. "The Pernicious Rift: Metternich and the Debate about Jewish Emancipation at the Congress of Vienna." *Leo Baeck Institute Yearbook* 46 (2001): 3–18.

Toepke, Gustav. *Die Matrikel der Universität Heidelberg. 5te & 6te Teile*. Heidelberg, Germany: Carl Winter's Universitätsbuchhandlung. 1904. Reprint, Nendeln, Liechtenstein: Kraus Reprint, 1976.

Tolkemitt, Brigitte. *Der Hamburgische Correspondent: Zur öffentlichen Verbreitung der Aufklärung in Deutschland*. Tübingen, Germany: Max Niemeyer, 1995.

Toury, Jacob. "Die Anfänge des jüdischen Zeitungswesens in Deutschland." *Bulletin of the Leo Baeck Institute* 38/39 (1967): 93–123.

———. *Die politische Orientierung der Juden in Deutschland: Von Jena bis Weimar*. Tübingen, Germany: J. C. B. Mohr (Paul Siebeck), 1966.

———. "Die Sprache als Problem der jüdische Einordnung in den deutschen Kulturraum." *Gegenseitige Einflüsse deutscher und jüdischer Kultur: Von der Epoche der Aufklärung bis zur Weimarer Republik*, edited by Walter Grab, 75–94. Tel Aviv: Nateev, 1982.

———. "Types of Municipal Rights in German Townships: The Problem of Local Emancipation." *Leo Baeck Institute Yearbook* 22 (1977): 55–80.

Tuan, Yi-Fu. *Space and Place: The Perspective of Experience*. 6th ed. Minneapolis: University of Minnesota Press, (1977) 2008.

Tworek, Heidi J. S. *News from Germany: The Competition to Control World Communications, 1900–1945*. Cambridge, MA: Harvard University Press, 2019.

Valentin Schwarz, Johannes. "'Der Gegenstand böte genügend Attraktion': Ein Forschungsüberblick der jüdischen Presse des 18. Bis 20. Jahrhunderts im deutschen Sprach- und Kulturraum." *Jahrbuch für Kommunikationsgeschichte* 9 (2007): 1–75.

———. "'Ew. Exzellenz ich [...] unterthänig vorzulegen.' Zur Konzessionierung und Zensur deutsch-jüdischer Periodika in den Königreich Preußen und Sachsen bis 1850." In *Zwischen Selbstbehauptung und Verfolgung: Deutsch-jüdische Zeitungen und Zeitschriften von der Aufklärung bis zum Nationalsozialismus*, edited by Michael Nagel, 101–38. Hildesheim, Germany: Olms, 2002.

———. "Öffentlichkeit." In *Makom: Orte und Räume im Judentum. Real Abstrakt. Imaginär*, edited by Michal Kümper, Barbara Rösch, Ulrike Schneider, and Helen Thein, 181–92. Hildesheim, Germany: Olms, 2007.

———. "Redaktion ohne Telefon—ein kurzer Blick hinter die Kulissen eines jüdischen Periodikums in Deutschland vor 1850." In *Die jüdische Presse in europäischen Kontext, 1868–1990*, edited by Susanne Marten-Finnis and Markus Winkler, 43–71. Bremen, Germany: edition lumière, 2006.

———. "The Origins and the Development of German Jewish Press in Germany till 1850: Reflections on the Transformation of the German Jewish Public Sphere in Bourgeois Society." International Federation of Library Associations and Institutions (IFLA) Conference Paper. Jerusalem, August 13–18, 2000. Accessed November 8, 2007. http://www.ifla.org/IV/ifla66/papers/106-144e.htm.

Van Rahden, Till. *Jews and Other German: Civil Society, Religious Diversity and Urban Politics in Breslau, 1860–1925*. Translated by Marcus Brainard. Madison: University of Wisconsin Press, 2008.

Vick, Brian E. *The Congress of Vienna: Power and Politics after Napoleon*. Cambridge, MA: Harvard University Press, 2014.

———. *Defining Germany: The 1848 Frankfurt Parliamentarians and National Identity*. Cambridge, MA: Harvard University Press, 2002.

Volkov, Shulamit. *Germans, Jews, and Antisemites: Trials in Emancipation*. Cambridge: Cambridge University Press, 2006.

———. "The 'Verbürgerlichung' of the Jews as a Paradigm." In *Bourgeois Society in Nineteenth Century Europe*, edited by Jürgen Kocka and Allan Mitchell, 367–91. Oxford: Berg, 1993.

Von der Krone, Kerstin. "Die Berichterstattung zur Damaskus-Affäre in der deutsch-jüdischen Presse." In *Jewish Images in the Media*. Relation, n.s., vol. 2, edited by Martin Liepach, Gabriela Melishek, and Josef Seethaler, 153–76. Vienna: Austrian Academy of Sciences Press, 2007.

———. "The Representation and Creation of Spaces through Print Media. Some Insights from the History of the Jewish Press." In *Space and Spatiality in Modern German-Jewish History*, edited by Simone Lässig and Miriam Rürup, 125–39. New York: Berghahn, 2017.

Von Glasenapp, Gabriele. "Zwischen Selbstinszenierung und Publikationsstrategie: Der Lehrer als Autor und Akteur in der deutschsprachigen Ghetto literature." In *Judentum und Aufklärung: Jüdisches Selbstverständnis in der bürgerlichen Öffentlichkeit*, edited by Arno Herzig, Hans

Otto Horch, and Robert Jütte, 216–40. Göttingen, Germany: Vandenhoeck & Ruprecht, 2002.

Von Kirchgässner, Bernhard, and Hans-Peter Becht, eds. *Stadt und Mäzenatentum*. Stuttgart, Germany: Jan Thorbecke, 1997.

Walker, Mack. *German Home Towns: Community, State, and General Estate, 1648–1871*. Ithaca, NY: Cornell University Press, 1971.

Wallet, Bert. "Napoleon's Legacy—National Government and Jewish Community in Western Europe." *Simon Dubnov Jahrbuch* 6 (2007): 291–309.

Wassermann, Henry. "Preliminary Impressions and Observations Concerning 'Jewish' Advertisements in the *Leipziger Allgemeine Zeitung* in 1840." In *Integration und Ausgrenzung: Studien zur deutsch-jüdischen Literatur- und Kulturgeschichte von der Frühen Neuzeit bis zur Gegenwart*, edited by Mark H. Gelber, Jacob Hessing, and Robert Jütte, 73–85. Tübingen, Germany: Max Niemeyer, 2009.

Weber, Johannes. "The Early German Newspaper—A Medium of Contemporaneity." In *The Dissemination of News and the Emergence of Contemporaneity in Early Modern Europe*, edited by Brendan Dooley, 69–114. Surrey, UK: Ashgate, 2010.

———. "Gründerzeitungen: Die Anfänge der periodischen Nachrichtenpresse im Norden des Reiches." In *Historische Presse und ihre Leser: Studien zu Zeitungen, Zeitschriften, Intelligenzblättern und Kalendern in Nordwestdeutschland*, edited by Peter Albrecht and Holger Böning, 9–40. Bremen, Germany: edition lumière, 2005.

Weber, Marie-Lise. "Heidelberg in der Umbruchszeit zwischen 1789 und 1819." In *Vom alten zum neuen Bürgertum: Die mitteleuropäische Stadt im Umbruch 1780–1820*, edited by Lothar Gall, 409–46. Munich: R. Oldenbourg, 1991.

Weir, Todd. *Secularism and Religion in Nineteenth-Century Germany: The Rise of the Fourth Confession*. Cambridge: Cambridge University Press, 2014.

Weissberg, Liliane. "Newspaper Feuilletons: Reflections on the Possibilities of German-Jewish Authorship and Literature." In *The Future of the German-Jewish Past: Memory and the Question of Antisemitism*, edited by Gideon Reuveni and Diana Franklin, 147–60. Lafayette, IN: Purdue University Press, 2021.

Weltsch, Robert. *Die deutsche Judenfrage. Ein kritischer Rückblick*. Königstein: Jüdischer, 1981.

Wertheimer, Jack. *Unwelcome Strangers: East European Jews in Imperial Germany*. Oxford: Oxford University Press, 1987.

Wiborg, Susanne. *Salomon Heine: Hamburgs Rothschild, Heinrichs Onkel*. Hamburg, Germany: Hans Christians, 2004.

Wiese, Christian, ed. *Redefining Judaism in an Age of Emancipation: Comparative Perspectives on Samuel Holdheim (1806–1860)*. Leiden, Netherlands: Brill, 2007.

Wobick-Segev, Sarah E. "'Looking for a Nice Jewish Girl . . .': Personal Ads and the Creation of Jewish Families in Germany before and after the Holocaust." *Jewish Social Studies* 23, no. 3 (Spring/Summer 2018): 38–66.

Wolff, Eberhard. "Medizinische Kompetenz und talmudische Autorität: Jüdische Ärzte und Rabbiner als ungleich Partner in der Debatte um die Beschneidungsreform zwischen 1830 und 1850." In *Judentum und Aufklärung: Jüdisches Selbstverständnis in der bürgerlichen Öffentlichkeit*, edited by Arno Herzig, Hans Otto Horch, and Robert Jütte, 119–49. Göttingen, Germany: Vandenhoeck & Ruprecht, 2002.

Zang, Gert. *Konstanz in der Großherzoglichen Zeit: Restauration, Revolution, Liberale Ära 1806 bis 1870*. Konstanz, Germany: Stadler, 1989.

Zimmermann, Mosche. *Hamburgischer Patriotismus und deutscher Nationalismus. Die Emanzipation der Juden in Hamburg 1830–1865*. Hamburg, Germany: Hans Christians, 1979.

Zürn, Gabriele. "Die jüdische Gemeinde Altona zwischen Tradition und Moderne: Aufklärung und der Umgang mit dem Tod." In *Judentum und Aufklärung: Jüdisches Selbstverständnis in der bürgerlichen Öffentlichkeit*, edited by Arno Herzig, Hans Otto Horch, and Robert Jütte, 91–118. Göttingen, Germany: Vandenhoeck & Ruprecht, 2002.

INDEX

The letter t. following a page number denotes a table, fig. denotes a figure, and map denotes a map.

AAZ (*Augsburger Allgemeine Zeitung*): charitable donations advertised in, 70t.2.2, 72–74; circulation, 9, 27, 29, 94, 95t.3.1, 176n43; on circumcision, 47, 99–100; *DAZ* responses to articles, 100; on education, 198n47; on emancipation, 47, 74, 76, 150; Heinrich Heine associated with, 29, 47, 73–74, 76–77; on Jewish religion, 95t.3.1, 99, 100–102, 103, 105–6; obituaries in, 47, 48, 71–75, 78; on the Rothschild family, 100, 105–6, 114, 197n38, 199n52; state support of, 29–30; success of, 27, 29–30, 177n44

Adler, Nathan Marcus, 101, 110

advertisements, 21, 27–28, 35, 67–69, 70t.2.2, 75, 182n87

Allgemeine Geschichte des Israelitischen Volkes (Willstätter), 79

Allgemeine Zeitung des Judenthums (*AZdJ*). See *AZdJ* (*Allgemeine Zeitung des Judenthums*)

alternate writing styles in newspapers, 132–33, 133–35, 136, 139, 155

Altona Jewish community, 163, 180n71

anonymous correspondents, 54, 56–57, 101–2, 122–24, 143–44

antisemitism: claims of Jewish difference, 47, 51, 53–54, 133, 135; Damascus Affair (1840), 40, 47, 126, 149, 182n83; Haber Affair, 12, 44–46, 51, 52, 54, 56, 62; Jewish responses to, 7, 54–59, 146–47, 158; violence, 12, 40, 44–45, 47, 49, 51–52, 54, 56, 62, 126, 149, 182n83, 184n5, 185n16

Antisemitism Dispute (1879–1881), 157, 158

Anzeiger (classified) sections, 9, 27–28, 30, 48, 75, 155

Assembly of Jewish Notables, 87, 193n10

Association of the Friends of Reform. See RF (Reformfreunde)

Auerbach, Berthold, 145

Aufnahme (admittance of Jews), 129, 136, 138–39, 141

"Aufruf" letter (RG), 106, 107

Auslander, Leora, 9–10, 154

Austritt (exit) Law, 108

AZdJ (*Allgemeine Zeitung des Judenthums*): circulation of, 39–40, 181n82; Jewish allegiance to the state, 193n10; non-Jewish writers in, 182n88; Orthodox Jewish voices in, 40, 140, 182n84; on rabbinical conferences, 2, 40, 41, 111, 121–22, 140; rabbis' letters in, 40, 111, 121–22, 151; RF (Reformfreunde) discussed in, 104–5

241

Baader, Benjamin, 61, 92–93
Baden, Grand Duchy of. *See* Constance city of; Heidelberg; Karlsruhe; Landtag, Badenese; Lower Assembly, Baden; Mannheim
Baden Jewish community, 15t.1.1, 19map1.1; announced split in, 120–21; citizenship of, 14, 18, 20, 129, 132; civil rights of, 13, 18, 20, 24, 49, 108, 129, 173n18; education, 5, 21, 32, 92; Haber Affair, 10, 12, 44–46, 51, 52, 54, 56, 62; Jewish population of, 14, 15t.1.1, 18; petition for Jewish emancipation (1845), 3, 12–13, 34, 49–51, 54, 59, 82, 137–38, 153; in public life, 20, 51–52. *See also* Haber Affair; Löwenstein, Jakob; Oberrat der Israeliten Badens (Consistory of the Israelites of Baden)
Bamberger, Ludwig, 158
Bauer, Bruno, 46, 47
Bavaria, Kingdom of, 15t.1.1, 29, 30, 31
Beer Jewish community (Berlin), 88, 92, 137
Behr, Alexander, 101, 102
Berlin: appointment of Rabbi Michael Sachs, 105–7, 199n53, 199n54, 199n55; Beer Jewish community, 88, 92, 137; control of newspapers, 27; Orthodox Judaism in, 105–7; rabbis in, 105–7; religious reform in, 22, 90, 92–93, 104, 198n48. *See also* Mendelssohn, Moses; RG (Reformgenossenschaft)
Berman, Howard A., 85, 86
Bildung (formation): in characterizations of the deceased, 78–79; cultural capital, 5, 11, 60–61, 150, 157; Dohmian paradigms of, 17; education, 20–21, 24, 87–91, 187n41, 205n94; family names, 22; Feierlicher Act der Religionsprüfung (Celebration of religious examination, 1836), 90–91; "Fortbildung des Judenthums," 40; Jewish voices in the press, 6, 34, 37–38, 47, 54, 57, 93–94, 131, 138, 140, 143, 146, 182n84; and the liberal movement, 124, 157; literacy, 17, 27, 32, 132–33; Mannheim Klaus (rabbinical seminary), 187n41; occupations, 5, 17, 22, 55, 58, 172n13; Polish Jews and, 120, 122, 123–24, 205n94. *See also* education; emancipation; philanthropy

Bildungsbürgertum (educated middle class), 24
Bildungsfreiheit (freedom of education), 18
Bing, Abraham, 101
Bleich, Judith, 40
blood libels, 40, 47, 126, 149, 182n83
Bodenheimer, Levi, 182n88
Bogner, Ralf Georg, 76
Bourdieu, Pierre, 5, 11
Brämer, Andreas, 84, 142, 194n16
Brentano, August, 137–38, 144, 145
Breslau Jewish community: Abraham Geiger as rabbi of, 89, 111, 112; support for Fränkel and Schott, 113
Breslau rabbinical conference (1846), 108, 110, 111–13, 115
Brit Milah. *See* circumcision
Brunswick rabbinical conference (1844): Adolph Zimmern's endorsement of, 1–2, 118–19; changes proposed by, 40, 109; Fürst opposition to, 118–20; newspaper reports of, 41, 141; obedience to the state, 193n10; Orthodox petition against, 40, 109–10, 113, 118, 120, 123, 140

Carlsbad Decrees, 30
censorship, 25–26, 28, 29–31, 33–34, 154
charity: bequests, 70t.2.2, 72, 74; charitable organizations, 11, 60–61; Harmonie (Jewish society), 65, 66fig.2.1; for a Jew and his family (Leopold Stein), 66–67, 101, 103, 105; Jewish donations, 62, 63, 65, 66fig.2.1, 144; *Menschenliebe*, 61; messages accompanying, 66, 67; newspaper reports of, 22, 48, 53, 62–63; non-Jewish donations, 62, 64t.2.1, 163, 165; published donor lists, 34–35, 65–66, 67, 68–70, 189n54
choirs, 90, 91, 116, 160
Christian reform movements, 8, 93, 102–3, 115, 121, 126, 136–37, 141, 196n26, 198n45
circulation, 9, 25, 27, 29, 35, 39–40, 94, 95t.3.1, 112, 176n39, 176n43, 181n82
circumcision, 98fig.3.1; biblical sources on, 97, 99; Jewish identity, 13, 84, 98–99, 101, 102; as personal choice, 97, 98, 100; in the press, 9, 47, 99–102, 196n26; public

debates on, 97, 98, 100, 102–3; *Rabbinische Gutachen* (rabbinical testaments), 100–101, 102

citizenship: Aufnahme (admittance of Jews), 129, 136, 138–39, 141; Baden Jewish community, 14, 18, 129, 132; Christians on Jews' acceptability as residents, 140, 141, 210n25; civic engagement, 20, 51–52; hereditary citizenship (*erbfreie Staatsbürgerschaft*), 18; mobility, 20, 49–50, 108, 129; obedience to the state, 86–87, 143, 193n10; *Orts/Gemeindebürger* (local citizen), 49; *Schutzbürger* (protected residents), 3, 16, 20, 24, 129; terms of, 3, 20–21, 49–50, 53, 173n15, 173n19, 208n9; voting rights, 49–50, 132

classified advertisements, 9, 27–28, 30, 48, 75, 155

clothing, 89, 116, 160, 204n83

Cohen, Moritz, 155, 211n9

confirmation ceremony, 116, 117, 161, 204n84

Congress of Vienna, 22, 23

Constance, city of: Aufnahme (admittance of Jews), 129, 136, 138–39, 141; *Bürgerausschuß* (civic council), 138, 139, 142; Council of Constance, 13, 127; Jewish population of, 13, 19map1.1, 20; Jews' inclusion in, 13, 20, 127, 129, 132, 136, 138–39, 141, 147; *Zulassung* (permission) to live in, 130, 131, 142, 208n9. See also *KonZtg* (*Konstanzer Zeitung*); *Seeblätter*

conversion to Christianity, 22, 29, 53, 62, 77, 88–89, 109, 153, 168n17, 180n72

correspondents, 29, 47, 54, 56–57, 99–102, 107, 113–15, 122–24, 143–44

Cotta, Georg, 29, 47, 74

Cotta, Johann Friedrich, 29

Council of Constance, 13, 127

Cranz, August, 180n72

Creiznach, Theodor, 105

Croneburg, Benjamin, 37

D (contributor to *Seeblätter*), 127, 142–43

Damascus Affair (1840), 40, 47, 126, 149, 182n83

Darnton, Robert, 30

Das Judenthum und die Kritik (Ghillany), 47, 53

DAZ (*Deutsche Allgemeine Zeitung*): articles on Jewish religion, 95t.3.1; circulation, 9, 95t.3.1; on circumcision, 9, 99, 100–102, 196n26; coverage of rabbinical conferences in, 112, 113–14; on death of Salomon Heine, 74; on Jewish religion, 93, 95t.3.1, 102; Reform movement in, 104, 105, 107, 113–14, 115, 200n57; on Sachs' appointment, 106, 199n55; state government and, 30, 103

death notices: Kirchenbücherauszüge, 74; *Nekrologe* (obituaries), 11, 48, 59, 76, 77–79, 152; *Todes-Anzeigen* (death announcements), 48, 75

decorum, 89, 116, 159, 204n83

Der Chamäleon, 36

Der Freisinnige, 29, 33

Der Grosse Schauplatz, 37

Der Israelit des Neunzehnten Jahrhunderts, 11, 40, 41, 200n57, 202n67

Der Jude, 39

Der jüdische Presse, 41

Der Orient, 11, 40, 100, 118

Der treue Zions-Wächter (TZW), 41, 110, 115, 117, 140

Der Wächter am Rhein, 29, 33

Deutsche Tribüne (*DT*), 29, 30, 31, 33

Deutsche Zeitung, 35

Deutsche Zuschauer, 36

Deutschkatholiken (German Catholics), 93, 102–3, 119, 121, 126, 136–38, 196n26, 198n45

"Die Judenfrage" (Bauer), 46

Die Reform des Judenthums, 112, 117, 187n41

Die Rundschau, 35, 36

dietary laws (kashrut), 83, 104

dina de-malkhuta dina (law of the state is the law), 87, 143, 193n10

Dohm, Christian Wilhelm von, 17, 36–37

Dresden, 39, 110, 199n53

DT (*Deutsche Tribüne*), 29, 30, 31, 33

Dutch Jews, 58, 82, 183n88

eastern European Jews, 119, 120, 122–24, 153, 205n94

Edelheim-Muehsam, Margaret T., 183n88

education: catechism, 161; confirmation ceremony, 116, 117, 161, 204n84; curriculum, 21, 55; donations to, 164–65; freedom of education (*Bildungsfreiheit*), 18; *gebildete* (educated) networks, 5, 37; German as language of, 90; government educational policy, 20–21, 88–89, 193n14, 194n17; of Jewish children, 20–21, 55, 88, 90; Karl Rehfuß, 117, 118, 205n87; press as tool of, 21, 26, 33, 38, 181n77; teachers, 21, 124, 205n94; university education, 5, 18, 29, 39, 54, 76, 96, 102, 115, 117, 122, 154, 187n41

Education Ministerial decree (Kingdom of Prussia, May 1824), 89

Ehrmann, Leopold, 185n16

Eibeschütz, Jonathan, 37

Einkommende Zeitung (Leipzig), 26, 28

Eintracht (Jewish association), 139–40, 141, 144, 146

Eisenmenger, Johann Andreas, 58, 102

Eller, Elias, 51–52, 54

emancipation: Baden petition for (1845), 3, 12–13, 34, 49–51, 54, 59, 82, 137–38, 153; Christian reform movements, 93, 102–3, 121, 126, 136–37, 141, 196n26, 198n45; Christian views of, 8, 47, 53–58, 82, 119, 137–39, 141; dissimilation and Jewish identity, 8; Dohm on, 17, 18; German Confederation (*Deutscher Bund*), 23–24; *Gleichstellung* (equalization), 11, 34, 39, 41–42, 50–51, 117–18, 125, 137–38, 144–45, 182n88, 202n70, 207n105; Jewish participation in debates on, 6–8, 54–59, 82–83, 133–34, 144; Jewish separateness, 47, 53, 59, 81, 96, 134–35, 180n72; Landtag debates on, 49, 50–51, 53, 54, 59, 82; obituaries as commentary on, 48, 76. See also antisemitism; *Bildung* (formation); citizenship; education; Oberrat der Israeliten Badens (Consistory of the Israelites of Baden); philanthropy; religious observance, Jewish

Emden, Jacob, 37, 180n71, 180n75

Emden-Eibeschütz controversy, 37–38, 46, 96

Emmerling, Adolph, 35

Engelsing, Rolf, 26

Enoch, Samuel, 41, 110

Epstein, Naphtali, 116

Ettlinger, Jacob, 41, 110, 115, 117

Ettlinger, Leib, 117

Euchel, Issak, 37, 38, 179n70, 180n76, 182n82

Fauth, Franz Burkardt, 52–59, 82, 119–20, 121, 146

Feierlicher Act der Religionsprüfung (Celebration of religious examination, 1836), 90–91

Feiner, Shmuel, 179n70, 207n103

Fetscher, Elmar, 138

Feuilleton, 27, 44, 155–56

Fickler, Joseph, 138–39, 141, 143. See also *Seeblätter*

Final Act of Vienna (1820), 30

Fischer, Heinz-Dietrich, 28

FJ (*Frankfurter Journal*): circulation, 9, 94, 95t.3.1; on emancipation, 43; on Jewish religion, 95t.3.1, 103–5; personal letters in, 43, 104–5; on rabbinical conferences, 111–12, 114–15; Reform movement in, 104–5; on religious reform, 104; state government influence on, 98, 103

France. See French Jewry; Napoleon

Fränkel, David, 38. See also *Sulamith*

Frankel, Jonathan, 7–8

Fränkel, Zacharias: exit from Frankfurt rabbinical conference, 110–13, 117, 132; rabbinic appointments of, 199n53; *Zeitschrift für religiöse Interessen des Judenthums* (Journal for the religious interests of Jewry), 39

Frankfurter, Naphthali, 200n57

Frankfurter Journal (*FJ*). See *FJ* (*Frankfurter Journal*)

Frankfurt Jewish community: community schism, 105–6; debates on circumcision, 97; Jewish emancipation, 153; *Ober-Post-Amts-Zeitung*, 110–11; rabbis of, 105–7, 114, 199nn53–55. See also RF (Reformfreunde)

Frankfurt rabbinical conference (1845): Fränkel's and Schott's exit from, 110–13, 117, 132; Hebrew as language in prayer, 110–11; press coverage of, 113–15, 203n74; women at, 114

Frederick William III, King (Prussia), 88–89
Frederick William IV, King (Prussia), 89
Freehof, Solomon Bennett, 85, 86
freemasonry, 26
Free Religion movement, 51. See also *Deutschkatholiken* (German Catholics); Lichtfreunde (Friends of Light)
Freiburg, 19map1.1, 29–30, 32–35, 67
Freistadt, Moritz, 103–4, 107, 198n47
French Jewry, 1–2, 16, 23–24, 28, 30, 32, 86–87, 193n10
Fries, Jacob Friedrich, 17, 82
funeral of Salomon Heine, 72–74
Fürst, Salomon, 117, 119–23, 140, 207n103
Fürst-Rehfuß conflict, 118, 120–24, 205n87
FZ (*Freiburger Zeitung*), 29–30, 32, 33, 35

Gailingen, 40, 110, 117, 123, 128, 130, 132, 139, 195n18
gaming culture, 155, 211n9
Gans, Edward, 77
gebildete (educated) networks, 5, 37
Geiger, Abraham, 8, 39, 89, 110–12, 181n82, 182n84, 200n57
Gemeindeordnung (communal ordinance), 20, 129
German Catholics (*Deutschkatholiken*), 93, 102–3, 119, 121, 126, 136–38, 196n26, 198n45
German Confederation (*Deutscher Bund*), 23–24, 30, 33
German Jewish press: circulation of, 38–40, 181n79, 181n82; Damascus Affair (1840), 40, 47, 126, 149, 182n83; government intervention in education, 21; Orthodox Judaism in, 40, 41, 89, 109–10, 118, 120; readership, 38–40, 181n77; relations with German press, 41–42, 182n87; *Sulamith*, 38–39, 40, 124, 181n79; TZW (*Der treue Zions-Wächter*), 41, 110, 115, 117, 140. See also *AZdJ* (*Allgemeine Zeitung des Judenthums*); *Der Israelit des Neunzehnten Jahrhunderts*; *Der Orient*
German language: in German Jewish newspapers, 38–39; as language of prayer, 91, 110, 160, 201n64, 201n66, 202n67; as official language, 22; in religious education, 90; sermons in, 90, 91, 117, 139, 159; vernacular of, 133–35, 146

Gewerbefreiheit (freedom of occupation), 18
Ghillany, Friedrich, 47, 53, 82
Gleichstellung (equalization), 11, 34, 39, 41–42, 50–51, 117–18, 125, 137–38, 144–45, 182n88, 202n70, 207n105
Goldschmidt, Therese, 75
Göler, Julius von, 44, 45
Görres, Joseph, 28
Göttingische Zeitung von gelehrten Sachen (*Gottingische Gelehrte Anzeigen*), 37
Gotzmann, Andreas, 87
Grand Duchy of Baden. See Constance, city of; Heidelberg; Karlsruhe; Mannheim
Green, Abigail, 32, 61, 152
Gropius Panorama, 107, 108, 200n57

Haber, Moritz von, 44–45, 62, 63, 153
Haber, Salomon von, 47
Haber Affair, 10, 12, 44–45, 51, 52, 54, 56, 62
Habermas, Jürgen, 26
Hähner, Friedrich Moriz, 57
halakha, 84, 86–87, 93, 193n10
Hambach Festival, 33
Hamburg fire (1842), 10, 62, 63–66, 64t.2.1, 67, 68, 144
Hamburgische unpartheyische Correspondent (*HC*), 27, 28
Hamburg Israelite Temple Society, 88, 91–92, 102
Hamburg Jewish community: Germanness displayed by, 65–66, 144–45; Jewish population of, 14; Jungfernstieg, 68, 69fig.2.2; philanthropy, 63, 64t.2.1, 65–66, 68; split in, 92; Temple Association (Hamburg), 92
Hamburg Patriotic Society (*Patriotische Gesellschaft*), 70
Hamburg Recuperation Efforts, 63, 64t.2.1, 65, fig.2.1
Ha-Me'assef (*The Gatherer*), 20–21, 38, 180n76
Hannover, 15t.1.1, 21, 205n94
Hannover Jewish community, 21, 113, 165, 202n67, 203n74
Hannoversche Zeitung, 88
Harmonie (Jewish society), 65, 66fig.2.1
Havas, Charles, 156

Hebrew language, 36, 37, 41, 90, 91, 110, 201n64
Hegau Jewish community, 129
Heidelberg: debates on Jewish emancipation, 48, 51, 118; Jewish population in, 18, 49; Karl Rehfuß, 117, 118; *Orts/Gemeindebürger* (local citizen), 49; rebuke of rabbi, 121; *Rundschau*, 35, 36; *Synagogenrat* (synagogue council), 54, 55–56. *See also* Zimmern, Adolph
Heidelberger Journal, 9, 52–53, 54, 55, 82, 121, 124–25
Heine, Heinrich: as *AAZ* correspondent, 29, 47, 73–74, 76–77; beneficiary of Salomon Heine, 165; on Edward Gans's conversion, 77; Ludwig Marcus obituary, 75, 76, 77; relations with Judaism, 74, 76, 77, 81
Heine, Karl, 165
Heine, Salomon, 69fig.2.2; generosity of, 67–74, 70t.2.2, 81, 145, 163, 165; Heinrich Heine, relations with, 72–74; obituaries for, 71–74; tributes to, 71–74; Will and Testament of, 70t.2.2, 72, 163–65
Hep-Hep riots, 45, 184n5
Hertz, Deborah, 22
Herxheimer, Salomon, 110
Herzog, Dagmar, 7
Hess, Jonathan, 8
Hess, Mendel, 200n57
Hesse-Darmstadt, 15t.1.1
Heuser, Robert, 129
Hirsch, Samson Raphael, 40, 109, 110, 179n70, 182n84, 193n14
Hirsch, Samuel, 200n57
Hoffmann, Stefan-Ludwig, 17
Hohenemser, Joseph, 54
Holdheim, Samuel, 107, 200n57, 202n70
Holsteinischen Correspondenten, 27
Horeb (Hirsch), 40
hospitals, 68, 71fig.2.3, 72, 163, 164
Hyman, Paula, 193n10

Infamous Decree [1808], 23
infamous preposition (article 16, Bund Constitution), 24
Insertionsprivileg (insertion privilege), 30, 33

Intelligenzblättern (Intelligencers), 25, 27–28, 32
Israelitische Annalen, 40
Israelitische Volksschule (Israelite elementary school), 55

Jacobson, Israel, 91
Jerusalem, or on Religious Power and Judaism (Mendelssohn), 37
Jeschurun, 41
Joskowicz, Ari, 103
Jost, Isaak Markus, 181n82
Judd, Robin, 97

Kant, Immanuel, 17
Karl Friedrich, Margrave (Baden-Baden, Baden-Durlach) and Grand Duke (Baden), 16, 18, 56, 116, 132
Karlsruhe: contribution of Germans to Hamburg recuperation efforts, 63; Feierlicher Act der Religionsprüfung (Celebration of religious examination, 1836), 90–91; Haber Affair, 12, 44–45, 51, 52, 54, 56, 62; *Oberdeutsche Zeitung*, 63; pogrom in, 45, 46
Karlsruhe Jewish community, 12, 16, 19map1.1, 20, 44–45, 51–52, 54, 56, 62–63, 82, 90–92, 172n13. *See also* Haber Affair; Oberrat der Israeliten Badens (Consistory of the Israelites of Baden)
Karlsruher Zeitung, 21, 62
kashrut (dietary laws), 83, 104
Kennecke, Andreas, 180n73, 181n77
Kirchenbücherauszüge, 74
Kohelet Mussar (Mendelssohn), 36, 37
Kol Nidre prayers, 109
Kölnische Zeitung (*KölZtg*), 9, 21, 32, 74; Haber Affair, 44–45
Königlich priviligierte Berlinische Zeitung. *See VZ* (*Vossische Zeitung*)
KonZtg (*Konstanzer Zeitung*): anti-Jewish polemics in, 143–44; on Aufnahme (admittance of Jews), 136, 142–43; circulation of, 9; dialect used in, 133–35; Eintracht article in support of Jewish rights, 144; Jewish presence in, 130–31, 136–45, 138, 142–43; petition from the

Jüdenschaft, 132–35, 147; political outlook of, 32, 142, 143
Kotzebue, August von, 30
Krauss, Martin, 185n16, 205n87
Kuriöser Antiquarius, 37
Kusel, Jakob, 63, 65, 88, 91

Ladenburg, Leopold, 54, 57–58, 82, 147, 186n27, 187n41, 187n42
Ladwig-Winters, Simone, 198n48, 200n57
Landtag, Badenese, 47; anti-Jewish rhetoric, 50–51, 52–54, 55, 56–59, 119–20, 121; election of liberals to, 14, 46, 50, 56; freedom of the press (*Pressefreiheit*), 33, 34; on Jewish emancipation, 49, 50–51, 53, 54, 59, 82
Lappin, Eleanor, 8
Lässig, Simone, 5–6, 38
Lavater, Johann Caspar, 180n72
Leipziger Allgemeine Zeitung. See *DAZ (Deutsche Allgemeine Zeitung)*
leitende Artikeln (leading articles), 28, 35, 37, 39
Lenhard, Philipp, 85, 92
Lenman, Robin, 30
Leopold, Grand Duke (Baden), 32–33
Lessing, Gotthold, 114
Levinson, Penina Navé, 142
Lewald, August, 62–63
liberalism: election of liberals in Baden, 14, 46, 50, 56, 119; on emancipation, 33–34, 49, 51, 136–38; Haber Affair, 44–46; ideology of, 17, 20; on Jewish equality, 50–51; on Jewish issues, 14, 24, 49, 50–51; language of, 135; in publishing industry, 29, 34; on religious reform, 93–94; tropes in poem in *Konstanzer Zeitung (KonZtg)*, 133–35
Liberles, Robert, 7, 96, 97–98
Lichtfreunde (Friends of Light), 93, 103, 121, 126, 136–37, 141
Liedtke, Rainer, 68
literacy, 26–27, 32
literary genres, 133–35
liturgy, 91, 109, 110, 200n57
Locke, John, 17
Löwenstein, Jakob: Badenese Rabbinical Ordinance (1824), 159–61; decorum during prayer services, 159–60; on Jewish emancipation, 140; opposition to Brunswick rabbinical conference, 40, 110, 123, 140; Orthodox position of, 128, 139, 210n24; personal attacks on, 141–42; Synagogue Council support of, 141–42
Lower Assembly, Baden: discussion of Jewish rights, 49, 119; emancipation petitions in, 12–13, 46, 50, 137–38; motion for freedom of religion, 137. See also Fauth, Franz Burkardt
LTZ (Landtagszeitung), 34, 35

MAbZ (Mannheimer Abendzeitung): criticism of Fürst, 118–21, 122; death notices, 47, 48, 75, 78–79; 1845 Badenese emancipation debate, 82; on emancipation, 54, 57; on the Fauth report, 54, 57–58; Jewish voices in, 54, 56–59; on Orthodox Judaism, 118–21, 123, 203n71; requests for charitable contributions, 67
Magnus, Shulamit, 8, 184n7
Maimon, Salomon, 120, 205n94
Mannheim: debates on Jewish emancipation, 48, 51, 118; Hayum Wagner, 54, 57–59, 82, 112, 117, 147, 187n41, 202n70; Jewish population in, 49; Orthodox-reform conflict in, 117; *Orts/Gemeindebürger* (local citizen), 49–50; religious orthodoxy in, 24, 117; schools in, 21, 55; *Verfassungsfeier* (constitutional celebration), 51–52
Mannheimer Nachrichten, 32
Mannheim Jewish community: civic engagement of, 51–52; on emancipation, 49, 51–53; philanthropy, 67; population, 18, 49; rabbinic leadership, 54, 57, 58–59, 82, 112, 117, 147, 187n41, 202n70; responses to Fauth, 56–59; schools, 55, 187n41
Mannheim Klaus (rabbinical seminary), 187n41
Mannheim rabbinical conference, 140
Marcus, Ludwig, 47, 48, 75, 76, 77–78
marriage, 86, 87, 101, 197n42
Marx, Karl, 34
Maskilim, 37, 85, 179n70
Mathy, Karl, 33, 34, 51

Mayer, Ludwig, 47
Mäzen (patron), 68
McNeely, Ian, 28
Mecklenburgische Gelehrte Nachrichten, 37
Mendelssohn, Moses: defense of Judaism, 180n71, 180n72; on early burial, 180n71; Maskilim, 37, 85, 179n70; popularity of, 36–37, 179n70; relations with Lessing, 114, 180n73; works of, 36, 37, 180n71
Menschenliebe, 61, 68, 70, 81, 151
Messiah, 37, 55, 85, 98, 104, 110, 201n64
Metternich, Clemens von, 23, 29, 31, 33
Meyer, Michael, 103, 109
Meyer, Samuel, 47
Michaelis, Johann David, 17, 180n72
military service, 20, 22, 58
MM (*Mannheimer Morgenblatt*): Fauth report, 52–54, 56–59, 119–20, 121; government support of, 35; on Jewish emancipation, 52–57, 82; Zimmern's criticism of Fürst, 119–20, 121
mobility, 20, 49–50, 108, 129
Montefiore, Moses, 80
Mosse, George, 157
Mosse family, 154
Müller, Hildegard, 35
Mumm, Hans-Martin, 117, 121

Nachrufe (obituaries), 75–76
Nagel, Michael, 8
Napoleon, 1–2, 16, 23–24, 28, 32, 86–87, 193n10
Nathan the Wise (Lessing), 114
Nekrologe (obituaries), 11, 48, 59, 76, 77–79, 152
newspapers: advertisements, 21, 27–28, 35, 67–69, 70t.2.2, 75, 182n87; anonymous correspondents, 54, 56–57, 101–2, 122–24, 143–44; censorship, 25–26, 28, 29–31, 33–34, 154; circulation, 9, 25, 27, 29, 34–35, 39–40, 94, 95t.3.1, 176n39, 176n43, 181n82; education, 20–21, 32, 55, 88, 90; on emancipation, 33–34, 36, 49, 54, 57, 137–38; exposés, 155; *Feuilleton*, 27, 44, 155–56; *gelehrter Artikel* (learned article), 27; government monitoring of, 25–26, 27, 28, 29–31, 33–35; Haber Affair in, 10, 12, 44, 51, 52, 54, 56, 62; as informational medium, 31–32; Intelligenzblätter, 25, 27, 28; Jewish disunity exhibited in, 24; Jewish voices in, 6, 34, 37–38, 47, 54, 57, 93–94, 131–33, 138, 140, 143, 146, 155, 182n84; opinion pieces in, 28, 35–36; postal networks, 31; *Pressefreiheit*, 32, 33; rabbinical conference coverage, 1–3, 40, 110–15, 117, 131–32, 143–44, 203n74; wire services, 156; writing styles in, 132–36, 139. *See also* individual newspapers—e.g., DAZ (*Deutsche Allgemeine Zeitung*); obituaries; philanthropy
Nineteen Letters, The (Hirsch), 40, 182n84

oaths for legal proceedings, 109, 205n87
Oberdeutsche Zeitung, 63–67
Ober-Post-Amts-Zeitung, 110–12
Oberrat der Israeliten Badens (Consistory of the Israelites of Baden): children's education, 20, 21; government relations, 116–18; membership of, 20, 48, 75, 78–79, 81, 116, 119, 206n97; rabbis appointed by, 20, 21; Synagogenordnung, 88, 116, 117, 204n82
obituaries, 11, 48, 59, 69, 71–72, 74–79, 152
ObRhZtg (*Oberrheinische Zeitung*), 34–35, 63, 64t2.1, 65–66, 67, 68–70, 189n54
Ohles, Frederik, 31
opinion articles, emergence of, 28
Oppenheim, Heinrich Bernhard, 54, 147, 173n18
Orthodox Judaism: in Berlin, 105–7; defense of, 105, 110, 117, 119–20, 121–22; Hirsch, Samson Raphael, 40, 109, 110, 179n70, 193n14; need for coexistence, 108–9; opposition to appointment of Rabbi Michael Sachs, 105–7, 199n53, 199n54, 199n55; protest of, 123, 207n105; publications of, 40–41, 110, 115, 117, 140, 182n84; rabbinical conferences opposed by, 40, 109–10, 112–14, 117, 118, 120, 142; relations with state government, 89; on religious reform, 2, 85–86, 89–90, 92, 109
Orts/Gemeindebürger (local citizen), 49–50
Östringen, 173n19

Paulus, Heinrich Eberhard Gottlob, 53
Peace of Westphalia (1648), 17, 137
petition against Brunswick rabbinical conference (1844), 40, 109–10, 113, 118, 120, 123, 140
Phädon, or the Immortality of the Soul (Mendelssohn), 180n71
philanthropy: bequests, 70t.2.2, 72, 74; charitable organizations, 11, 60–61; for a Jew and his family (Leopold Stein), 66–67, 101, 103, 105; Jewish donations, 48, 62, 63, 65, 66fig.2.1, 144; *Menschenliebe*, 61; messages accompanying, 66, 67; newspaper reports of, 22, 48, 53, 62–63; non-Jewish donations, 62, 64t.2.1, 163, 165; published donor lists, 34–35, 65–66, 67, 68–70, 189n54. *See also* Heine, Salomon
Philippson, Ludwig, Rabbi, 2, 39, 94, 103, 111, 121–22, 141, 151, 202n70. *See also AZdJ* (*Allgemeine Zeitung des Judenthums*)
Philipson, David, 111
Plaut, Gunther W., 85, 86
poetry, 133–35, 136, 155
pogroms, 45
Polish Jews, 119, 205n94
postal networks, 31
Präger family, 204n84
prayer, 88–91, 109–10, 116, 159–60, 180n71, 201n63, 201n66, 204n84
Pressefreiheit (freedom of the press), 32–34
Preuß, Monika, 187n41
Prussian Jewish community, 14, 15t.1.1, 18, 21–22, 88–89, 108, 194n16, 194n17
Pulzer, Peter, 153

rabbinical conferences: attendance at, 108, 200n60; Austritt (exit) Law, 108; dissent in, 110–13, 117, 132; holiday observances discussed at, 201n64; on Jewish allegiance to Germany, 2; morally binding changes made at, 109, 201n63; Orthodox opposition to, 40, 109–10, 112, 113, 118, 120–23, 140; press coverage of, 1–3, 40, 110–15, 117, 131–32, 143–44, 203n74
rabbis: appointment of, 105–7, 199nn53–55; authority of, 20–21, 86, 87, 89, 96, 105, 119, 130, 193n14, 199n53; charitable donations by, 65fig.2.1, 66; on circumcision, 97, 100; criticism of, 105, 121, 139; education of, 117, 187n41; German language sermons, 90, 91, 117, 139, 159; *Rabbinische Gutachen* (rabbinical testaments), 100–101, 102; responses to Fauth report, 56, 57, 58–59. *See also* individual headings (e.g., Philippson, Ludwig, Rabbi)
RamBaM (Moses Maimonides), charity according to, 68, 190n63
Randegg, 24, 128, 130, 131map4.1, 132, 201n63, 208n7. *See also* Schott, Leopold
readership: advertisements, 21, 27, 28, 67, 75, 182n87; circulation, 25, 27, 35, 176n39, 176n43; development, 31; German Jewish periodicals, 38–39, 181n77, 181n79; for Intelligenzblätter, 27; of Jewish newspapers, 40, 181n79, 181n82; for scholarly journals (*gelehrte Zeitungen*), 26–27; social class, 26–27, 32, 37–38
reform, Jewish: acculturation of Jews, 83; Christian reform movements, 93, 196n26; demand for a German-Jewish Church, 93; generational differences, 204n84; lay leadership, 92; Orthodox challenges to, 109–10, 113, 115–16, 118, 182n84; representation of, 94; terminology of, 92. *See also* RF (Reformfreunde)
Reformfreunde (RF). *See* RF (Reformfreunde)
Rehfuß, Jakob, 117, 118, 120–21, 122, 205n87
Rehfuß, Karl, 117, 118, 205n87
reine Mosaismus (pure Mosaism), 93
Reiss, Moses, 110
religious observance, Jewish: circumcision, 84, 97–99, 98fig.3.1, 100–103, 105; death customs, 111, 180n71; decorum, 89, 116, 160, 204n83; halakha, 83, 86–87, 93, 193n10; kashrut (dietary laws), 83, 104; language of, 90, 91, 110, 117, 139, 159; marriage, 86, 87, 101, 197n42; Messiah, 37, 55, 85, 98, 104, 110, 201n64; prayer, 88–91, 109, 110, 116, 159–60, 180n71, 201n63, 201n66, 204n84; Rosh Hashanah, 111; Sabbath, 53, 57, 59, 87, 111, 115, 201n64, 202n70; sermons, 90, 91, 117, 139, 159; Torah reading, 91, 116, 159, 160, 161; Yom Kippur prayers, 109, 201n63

religious reform: Christian reform movements, 8, 93, 102–3, 115, 121, 126, 136–37, 141, 196n26, 198n45; circumcision, 84, 97–99, 98fig.3.1, 100–103, 105; halakha, 83, 86–87, 93, 193n10; Jewish support for, 24; lay leadership, 92; prayer, 87–91, 109, 110, 116, 159–60, 201n63, 201n66, 204n84; sermons in German, 90, 91, 117, 139, 159; societal conformity, 21; synagogue attendance, 83, 87, 91, 107, 108, 161, 199n55, 200n57; Torah reading, 91, 116, 159, 160, 161. *See also* education; rabbinical conference headings (e.g., Frankfurt rabbinical conference); RF (Reformfreunde)

religious services, 88–89, 90–91, 107, 108, 116, 159–60, 200n57

residency, rights of, 20, 173n15, 173n19

Reuter, Paul Julius, 156

RF (Reformfreunde): agenda of, 54–55, 98–99, 101, 104, 200n56; Christian respondents on, 54–55; on circumcision, 104; establishment of, 103, 106–8; at Frankfurt rabbinical conference, 114; on kashrut (dietary laws), 104; leadership of, 39, 70, 101, 104–5, 107–8, 197n37; newspaper coverage of, 94, 98, 104–5; success of, 103–5, 107–8, 113. *See also* Stern, Moritz Abraham

RG (Reformgenossenschaft): "Aufruf an die deutschen Glaubenbrüder," 107; in Berlin, 93, 108; founding of, 106–7; leadership of, 107, 108, 200n57; newspaper coverage of, 103–4, 106, 107, 114–15; religious services of, 107, 108, 200n57; support for, 106–7, 108, 113, 198n48, 200n57

Rheinische Merkur, 28, 29

Rheinische Zeitung, 34, 179n64

Riesser, Gabriel, 39, 70, 101, 104–5, 107–8, 145, 197n37

robes, clerical, 89, 116, 160, 204n83

Roming, Gisela, 128, 141–42

Ronge, Johannes, 93, 198n45

Rosh Hashanah, 111

Ross, Corey, 156

Rothschild family, 100, 105–6, 114, 197n38, 199n52

Rotteck, Karl von, 50, 142–43

Rüge, Arnold, 34

rural Jewish communities, 24, 28, 128, 141, 204n82

Rürup, Reinhard, 90, 129, 194n15

Sabbateanism, 37, 85

Sabbath observance, 53, 57, 59, 87, 111, 115, 201n64, 202n70

Sachs, Michael, 105–7, 114, 199nn53–55

Salomon, Gotthold, 200n57, 206n102

Sander, Adolf, 51, 55

Sander, August, 45

Sanhedrin (Paris), 193n10

Saturday as Sabbath, 111, 202n70

Saxony, 15t.1.1, 22

Schad, Margit, 199n54

Schatz, Jacob, 21

Schimpf, Rainer, 33

Schneble, Martin, 136

Schorsch, Ismar, 87

Schott, Leopold: on anti-Jewish rhetoric, 143–44, 146; departure from Frankfurt rabbinical conference, 110–13, 117, 132, 202n67; on Jewish citizenship, 143–44; on Kol Nidre prayer, 201n63; response to Christian minister, 130–31, 146

Schutzbürger (protected residents), 3, 16, 20, 24, 129

Schwartzman, Sylvan, 109

science of Judaism (*Wissenschaft des Judentums*), 39, 48

Seeblätter: articles on Rabbi Jakob Löwenstein, 139, 141; Aufnahme debate, 139; *Bürgerausschuß* (civic council), 138, 139, 142; Jewish contributions to, 34, 131, 138, 143, 146; political outlook of, 34, 142, 143–44; requests for charitable contributions, 67

Seekreis, 131map4.1

Seesen, temple in, 91

sermons in German, 90, 91, 117, 139, 159

shiva observance, 111

Shomer Tsion ha-Ne'eman, 41. *See also Der treue Zions-Wächter* (TZW)

Simon, Louis, 105

Skolnik, Jonathan, 8

INDEX

Smith, Helmut Walser, 168n17
Soiron, Alexander von, 188n43
Sorkin, David, 2, 17, 179n70
splits in Jewish communities, 91–92, 105–6, 120–21, 140, 153, 206n95
Stahl, Friedrich Julius, 53
state government: censorship, 25–26, 28, 29–31, 32, 33–34, 154; on circumcision, 97–98; *Insertionsprivileg* (insertion privilege), 30, 33; intervention in newspapers, 25–26, 27, 28, 29–32, 33–35; Jewish allegiance to, 22–23, 52, 82, 86–87, 193n10; religious reform, 87, 88–90, 117, 193n10; support for conversionary work, 88–89
Stegmaier, Günter, 32
Stein, Leopold, 66–67, 100, 101, 103, 105, 114
Stein, Sarah Abrevaya, 7
Stern, Moritz Abraham, 104–5, 108
Stern, Sigismund, 107
Stolz, Alban, 94
Stross, Wendy Anne, 75–76
Struve, Gustav, 31
Süddeutsches Zeitung für Kirche und Staat (Süddeutsches katholisches Kirchenblatt), 35
Sulamith, 38–39, 40, 124, 181n79
Synagogenordnung (synagogue ordinance, 1824), 88, 116, 117, 159–61, 204n82
Synagogenrat (synagogue council), 54, 55–56
synagogue attendance, 83, 87, 91, 107, 108, 161, 199n55, 200n57
Synagogue Council of Gailingen, 139–40, 141

Tagesherold, 142
Talmud study, 54, 55, 82, 104, 143–44
Tauschwitz, Hanno, 33
teachers, 21, 124, 205n94
Tiktin, Salomon, 89
Todes-Anzeigen (death announcements), 48, 75
Tolerenzpatenten (Patents of toleration), 17–18, 116
Torah reading, 91, 116, 159, 160, 161
Toury, Jacob, 29, 37
Traub, Hirsch, 117, 123
Treitschke, Heinreich, 157

Trier, Salomon, 97, 98, 101, 102, 105
Tworek, Heidi, 156

Über die bürgerliche Verbesserung der Juden (Dohm), 37
Ullstein family, 154
university education, 5, 18, 29, 39, 54, 76, 96, 102, 115, 117, 122, 154

Veit, Moritz, 89
Verein für Cultur und Wissenschaft des Judenthums, 76, 77
Verfassungsfeier (Baden, constitutional celebration), 51–52
Verus (pseudonym), 122, 123, 124
Vick, Brian, 24
Vorderösterreich (Anterior Austria), 16
voting rights, 49–50, 132
VZ (*Vossische Zeitung*; formerly *Königlich priviligierte Berlinische Zeitung*), 9, 74, 95t.3.1, 103, 176n43, 196n26

Wagner, Hayum, 54, 57–59, 82, 112, 117, 147, 187n41, 202n70
Walker, Mack, 16
Wangen, 130, 131map4.1, 208n6
Wasserman, Henry, 182n87
Wechsler, Bernhard, 112
Weil, Gustav, 47
Weissberg, Liliane, 155
Weltsch, Robert, 8
Weser Zeitung, 74
Wessely Affair, 205n88
Westphalia, Kingdom of, 22, 91
Wihl, Ludwig, 155, 200n56
Willstätter, Elias, 90
Willstätter, Ephraim, 75, 79
wire services, 156
Wirth, Johann Georg August, 29
Wirtschaftsbürgertum (economic middle class), 24
Wissenschaft des Judentums, 39, 48
wissenschaftliche Orthodoxie (scientific orthodoxy), 106
Wissenschaftliche Zeitschrift für jüdische Theologie, 39, 181n82
Wolf, Joseph, 38

Wolff, Bernhard, 156
women: business interests of, 75; charitable donations, 64, 66, 164; education of, 151; at Frankfurt rabbinical conference, 114; gender equality, 111; in German Jewish press, 39; Jewish communal roles, 89; matrilineal descent, 99; RG (Reformgenossenschaft), 104; synagogue attendance, 91, 161
Württemberg, Kingdom of, 15t.1.1, 32, 33, 47

Yiddish language, 17, 41
Yom Kippur prayers, 109, 201n63

Zang, Gert, 138
Zeitschrift für die Wissenschaft des Judentums, 39
Zeitschrift für religiöse Interessen des Judenthums (Journal for the religious interests of Jewry), 39

Zimmermann, Moshe, 8, 66
Zimmern, Adolph: on Brunswick conference, 1–2, 118–19; *Erklärung* in *Mannheimer Morgenblatt* (MM), 121, 124; on Jewish acculturation, 118–19; Orthodox Judaism challenged by, 119; on religious reform in German Judaism, 2; response to Fauth, 54, 56; Salomon Fürst, 110, 117, 119–20, 121–22, 140; support of reform position, 121, 296n95
Zimmern, David, 48, 75, 78–79, 81, 119, 206n97
Zittel, Karl, 137
Zugang (admittance) to state universities, 18
Zulassung (permission) to live in Constance, 130, 131, 142, 208n9. *See also* Aufnahme
Zunz, Leopold, 39, 77

DAVID A. MEOLA is Bert & Fanny Meisler Associate Professor of History and Jewish Studies at the University of South Alabama. He received his doctorate in history and master's in European studies from the University of British Columbia in Vancouver. He has published articles in *Antisemitism Studies* and the *Leo Baeck Institute Yearbook* as well as several book chapters. He also served as editor for *A Cultural History of Genocide in the Long Nineteenth Century*.

www.ingramcontent.com/pod-product-compliance
Lightning Source LLC
Chambersburg PA
CBHW030615230426
43661CB00053B/2002